A Mirror Is for Reflection

A Mirror Is for Reflection

Understanding Buddhist Ethics

Edited by

JAKE H. DAVIS

OXFORD
UNIVERSITY PRESS

Oxford University Press is a department of the University of Oxford. It furthers
the University's objective of excellence in research, scholarship, and education
by publishing worldwide. Oxford is a registered trade mark of Oxford University
Press in the UK and certain other countries.

Published in the United States of America by Oxford University Press
198 Madison Avenue, New York, NY 10016, United States of America.

© Oxford University Press 2017

CIP data is on file at the Library of Congress
ISBN 978–0–19–049977–8 (hardcover)
ISBN 978–0–19–049976–1 (paperback)

9 8 7 6 5 4 3 2 1

Paperback printed by Webcom, Inc., Canada
Hardback printed by Bridgeport National Bindery, Inc., United States of America

To all my teachers

Imāya Pariyattiyā Ācariye Pūjemi

Contents

PART THREE: *Karma and Rebirth*

PART FOUR: *Mindfulness, Memory, and Virtue*

PART FIVE: *Intention and Action*

PART SIX: *Politics, Anger, and Equanimity*

Foreword

Owen Flanagan

THIS SPLENDID VOLUME responds to two pressing concerns. The first, which is mainly of concern to Anglophone philosophers, especially those interested in comparative philosophy, is *What exactly is the nature of Buddhist ethics?* What kind of ethics is it? Is it a purely religious theory, where the real reward for goodness is otherworldly, better rebirths, eventually nirvana? Or is it a perfect instance of or model for a secular ethics, a practical way of being in this world for everyone, as the 14th Dalai Lama says it is? If Buddhism is a kind of secular ethics, is it a virtue theory, or an ethics of duty, or some kind of consequentialism? Or is it something entirely new and different on the face of the earth?

The second pressing concern is *What sort of resources for living good human lives does Buddhism provide to the denizens of WEIRD cultures, for Western, educated, industrialized, rich, and democratic peoples?* Sometimes ethical traditions possess internal resources to improve or fix themselves; at other times a tradition will benefit from looking outside itself to get good new ideas or rediscover insights it has lost. Can Buddhism play that role for Abrahamic peoples or for their secular children of the Enlightenment? I'll say a few brief words about each topic.

1.

What kind of ethical theory does Buddhism provide? Buddhism presents a paradox. On the one hand, Buddhism is attractive because Buddhists are seen in the popular imagination as good, better than average in the morality department, practicing what they preach and having high standards of moral excellence. On the other hand, Buddhism doesn't theorize ethics in anything like the systematic way that it is theorized in multiple Western traditions, both sacred and secular—in Judaism, Christianity, and Islam, in Aristotle and Stoicism, and in the modern consequentialist and deontological traditions. It isn't that Buddhism isn't excellent at providing pictures of exemplars, like the Buddha and bodhisattvas on the path, and saying that they exemplify the four unsurpassable virtues of compassion, loving-kindness, sympathetic joy, and equanimity. It is. And it isn't as if Buddhism isn't forthcoming with ethical advice. There are precepts (Don't gossip, take intoxicants, make weapons); there is the noble eightfold path; and there are amazing taxonomies of wholesome and unwholesome states of the heart-mind. What is said to be lacking is a detailed philosophical map that explains how exactly a metaphysic which teaches that impermanence and suffering are basic and ubiquitous, that I am not what I think I am, not a permanent or semipermanent self (*anātman*), and that emphasizes the dangers of false belief and a grasping ego, as well as practice in mindfulness and meditation, connects these insights and practices to an ethical vision of maximal compassion and loving-kindness. How exactly, if it does, does Buddhist metaphysics provide a ground for morality? Does Buddhism, which is atheistic by Abrahamic standards, provide a satisfactory answer to the question *Why be moral?* If I really am no-self (and empty), why care about anything? Who is there to care? What would it even mean for a no-self to care? What sorts of reasons does Buddhism give for awakening *bodhicitta*, the wellspring of compassion, and for taking the bodhisattva's vows? Is it because developing compassion might alleviate my own suffering, if anything will? Or is it that becoming maximally compassionate is good in itself? Or it is for some other set of reasons altogether?

If Buddhist ethics is grounded in Buddhist metaphysics, and not in the utterly contingent features of the way of life of early Buddhists, or in the commands of the God of the Abrahamic traditions, or in heaven's mandate (*tianming*), as is Confucian ethics, or in principles of pure reason, then a different kind of worry arises.[1] Suppose one doesn't accept a metaphysic of no-self (*anātman*), but instead thinks there is a self—a person, *ātman*, a Cartesian soul, a transcendental ego—and that its fate is really important, so important that any ethics worth considering ought to make it possible for the maximum number of selves to flourish. Is such a person, a philosophically different kind of person, for example, a child of the European Enlightenment, ineligible to be a Buddhist, ethically speaking? Or is there a way for such a person to be a Buddhist since Buddhists sometimes say there are no selves but there are persons. And what does this even mean?

This much is clear insofar as the tradition says it again and again: A person who understands or grasps the Buddhist metaphysics of no-self will want to be, or have reason to be, less selfish. Indeed if the individual really understands or grasps no-self, they will want to be a bodhisattva, to be maximally compassionate and loving-kind.

On the surface Buddhism looks as if its no-self metaphysics logically or practically entails moral unselfishness, some kind of other-directed, altruistic morality. If so, there would be a structural isomorphism with Aristotle's virtue theory, Christian ethics, consequentialism, and deontology, each of which finds a warrant for the ethical life in features of persons, human social life, human reason, or God's nature, reason, and will. The difference is that the latter traditions work out the details of the connection between the metaphysics of morals and the demands of morality in elaborate detail, and each extant theory has taken it upon itself to develop a brand name that its fans proudly recite. "I am a consequentialist." "I am a Kantian." "I am a virtue theorist." Pretty much every side would like to claim that Buddhism is a variety or version of their favored theory. But Buddhism doesn't easily fit into any mold.

There is another aspect to the perplexity that is Buddhism. Each brand of modern moral theory has taken it upon itself to explain how a person who abides the relevant theory would perceive, feel, think, and act by developing a distinctive moral psychology. Virtue theorists provide elaborate taxonomies of the psychological dispositions, courage, honesty, kindness, forgiveness, and the like, which taken together constitute character. Some virtue theorists say virtues are necessary for goodness; a few—perhaps only the Stoics—that they are sufficient. Others, some virtue theorists and members of other teams, worry that virtues are too much like habits, too conventional, prone to getting stale, and reflecting whatever moral order is in place to be up to the task of morality, and thus that humans will need to consciously govern themselves, at least some of the time, by reflective principles, such as the principle of utility or the categorical imperative. Again the question arises: What is the Buddhist stance on whether the right equipment is a constellation of virtues, or a general principle—End suffering whenever and wherever one can—or a set of metaphysical beliefs (impermanence, no-self, dependent origination, and emptiness), or trance-like, hallucinatory states that might motivate human kindness? Where in Buddhist moral psychology is reason, what Aristotle called *phronesis*, Confucians call *zhi*, and psychologists call System 2?

Ironically the theorizing in ethics that is commonplace in the Anglophone academy has become so elaborate that ethics as practiced and taught at the highest precincts in analytic philosophy is often mostly meta-ethics, not normative ethics, which the parents were hoping their kids were getting a dose of. The emphasis is not on being good but on what various traditions have thought being good involved, or what terms like *good, bad, right*, and *wrong* mean as ordinary people, philosophers, and theologians use them. When philosophers say they are utilitarian or Kantian or a virtue theorist (or say they "work on" any one of them), it is 100 percent indeterminate whether they abide, or even try to abide, the relevant moral theory. Nothing is even implied about whether they care about being good. All that can be surmised is that they think that *if* there is something like a single rational moral conception, this, their favored theory—or something in its vicinity—would be it.

So another way to put the paradox is that Buddhism is terrific at presenting something like a first-order normative theory, depicting what a morally excellent life is or would be like, and even sometimes sketching or providing a sense of how its metaphysics connects with its ethics but it fails to provide a meta-ethics. Buddhists don't declare whether they are moral realists or fictionalists. Which is it? And outsiders might say, and have said, that doctrines such as no-self and emptiness could as easily be taken to ground nihilism and hedonism about moral value as the moral seriousness of the bodhisattva. So which is it? There is also this concern: Any morality worth taking seriously better provide a robust analysis of free will if it is going to make sense of practices of holding people responsible, punishing people, and so on. But Buddhism is silent on the topic of free will. There is at present a lively debate about whether this lack of theorizing about free will is in fact a good or bad feature of Buddhism, about whether Buddhists missed something about free will or whether we made a really big two-centuries-long mistake in thinking there is or needs to be such a thing as free will.

The paradox of Buddhism seeming to be ethically admirable but not forthcoming on the nature and structure of its ethical theory cannot be explained by the fact that Buddhism is generally atheoretical. It isn't. In fact Buddhist metaphysics is of great interest to mainstream contemporary analytic philosophers precisely because it contains virtuoso theorizing about the nature of reality, truth, knowledge, and the self.

Overall the demand to speak up and declare what kind of theory Buddhist ethics is, what kind of meta-ethics Buddhist meta-ethics is or would be, are demands made outside the Buddhist tradition in terms set by dominant traditions in Western academic ethics. That is not a problem in itself so long as

Buddhism, really the Buddhisms, can speak in their own terms, and so long as the possibility that Buddhism is a sui generis theory, or perhaps no kind of theory at all—just a beautiful and worthy way of living—remains open.

2.

I now turn briefly to the second issue: Can we learn anything practically from Buddhism, even if we accept that it is not theorized in familiar ways, and possibly even if we make a considered judgment that its metaphysics is alien and unacceptable to us? Can Buddhism, or any other deeply philosophical form of life that is not ours, provide practical resources for criticizing and improving our ethics, for finding ways to be better than we are in our own moral project?

Imagine for a moment that we agree Buddhism has elements that look like elements of familiar virtue theories. It does. The fact remains that the virtues are not the same as one sees on other lists of virtues. *Karuṇā* (compassion) is not the same as Aristotle's generosity, or Confucian *ren*, or Christian *agape* or *caritas*, or Hume's fellow-feeling or benevolence, each of which is different from the others. Among other things the scope of *karuṇā* differs. It is compassion for all sentient beings.

Second, most moral forms of life address the question of how to deal with conflicts. Confucius says that a son covers for his father when the father has done wrong. So filial piety trumps the demands of law in extremis. But benevolence trumps propriety for Confucians. What do Buddhists say when there is a conflict between compassion and justice? Some will say that compassion is always the trump for Buddhists. Others will complain that justice as fairness is undertheorized in Buddhism. To which still others reply that justice as fairness is overtheorized by us, and that if compassion were highly developed, there would be much less need for what Hume called "the cautious jealous virtue of justice." This, I claim, is a really worthwhile conversation to have because it encourages reflection on one's own economy of virtues and its strengths and weaknesses. Is it better than merely internal reflection? Sometimes, possibly often, yes.

Buddhists emphasize as ground-level values both compassion for all sentient beings and nonviolence. Are these morally attractive? Do Buddhists give good reasons for anyone to practice these virtues? If the answer is yes, then we have reason to teach our children these values. Buddhists also say, as did the Stoics in our own tradition, that anger is the most dangerous emotion. Like the Stoics, and unlike Aristotelians, Buddhists are skeptical that either personal or political anger can be contained, and they offer practices to mitigate, possibly eliminate it, without at the same time giving up on the projects of demanding economic and social justice. Could this be for us? Would we be better, by our own lights, if we worked on personal and political anger in ways Buddhists recommend?

The point is that as soon as we charitably enter into this space of considering other forms of moral life, we are immediately confronted with things to think about, challenges to our normal ways of thinking about the content, scope, order, and sufficiency of our moral beliefs, virtues, and principles. If upon critical examination our own values and practices look better than the alternatives, then they gain a modest amount of moral confirmation. If they look weaker than we originally thought, we have reason to make adjustments.

In a volume celebrating his life and work on the occasion of his eightieth birthday, Alasdair MacIntyre offers this assessment of the overall state of moral philosophy in the twentieth century:

> On the view that I have found myself compelled to take, contemporary academic moral philosophy turns out to be seriously defective as a form of rational inquiry. How so? First, the study of moral philosophy has become divorced from the study of morality or rather of moralities and by so doing has distanced itself from practice. We do not expect serious work in the philosophy of physics from students who have never studied physics or on the philosophy of law from students who have never studied law. But there is not even a hint of a suggestion that courses in social and cultural anthropology and in certain areas of sociology and psychology should be a prerequisite for graduate work in moral philosophy . . . Yet without such courses no adequate sense of the varieties of moral possibility can be acquired. One remains imprisoned by one's upbringing. (MacIntyre, 2013, p. 31)

I write in hope that the 21st century will be an age in which we take for granted a certain kind of openness to the varieties of moral possibility, which will involve engaging in more cross-cultural philosophy in order not only to understand others but also to actively learn from others. We need not worry that such openness will result in complete loss of moral confidence. There is much agreement among the great world philosophies about what makes for moral excellence. So exposure to a greater variety of moral possibility need not be viewed as an exercise designed to have us completely change our identity or distinctive form of life. It does invite us to yield our unwarranted, cocky confidence that we have discovered the right way of living and being good. We haven't. Other traditions, Buddhism in the present case, have a great deal to contribute to the moral project even as non-Buddhists conceive it.

Note

1. I take it more or less for granted here that Buddhist ethics is grounded in Buddhist metaphysics. But I am aware of another possibility: that Buddhist metaphysics is, as it were, an ex post facto attempt to find a deep justification for the Buddhist form of life. I always ask lay Buddhists in East and Southeast Asia when I visit what no-self (*anātman*) means to them. They almost all—like 90%—say it means: Don't be selfish! I take up this topic in Flanagan (2016).

References

Flanagan, O. (2016). *The geography of morals: Varieties of moral possibility.* New York: Oxford University Press.

MacIntyre, A. C. (2013). On having survived the academic moral philosophy of the twentieth century. In Fran O'Rourke (Ed.), *What happened in and to moral philosophy in the twentieth century? Philosophical essays in honor of Alasdair MacIntyre* (pp. 17–34). Notre Dame, IN: University of Notre Dame Press.

Acknowledgments

THE EDITOR GRATEFULLY acknowledges the following: Christopher Kelley for his ongoing support and collaboration, as well as for his work leading the organization of the conference at Columbia University that served as a seed for this volume; the John Templeton Foundation and the Columbia University Religion Department for their generous support of that conference; Routledge Press and the *Thai Journal of Buddhist Studies* for permission to use previously published material; and Katie Murphy for crafting the index.

Contributors

Amber Carpenter is an associate professor at Yale-NUS. Her primary background is in ancient Greek philosophy, where her published work focuses on the ethics, epistemology, and metaphysics of Plato. An Einstein Fellowship at the Einstein Forum (Berlin) enabled her to pursue work in Indian Buddhist philosophy, and her book on the subject appeared in 2014. She coordinates, with Rachael Wiseman, the Integrity Project (integrityproject.org).

Christian Coseru is an associate professor in the Department of Philosophy at the College of Charleston. He works in the fields of philosophy of mind, phenomenology, and cross-cultural philosophy, especially Indian and Buddhist philosophy in dialogue with Western philosophy and cognitive science. He is the author of numerous articles and of the book *Perceiving Reality: Consciousness, Intentionality, and Cognition in Buddhist Philosophy* (Oxford University Press, 2012). He is currently completing a book on the intersections between perceptual and affective consciousness, tentatively entitled *Sense, Self-Awareness, and Sensibility.*

Jake H. Davis is a postdoctoral associate with the Virtues of Attention project at New York University. He has taught at Brown University and at the City College of New York, and holds a PhD in philosophy from CUNY Graduate Center, with an interdisciplinary concentration in cognitive science, as well as an MA in philosophy from the University of Hawai`i. He has authored and coauthored articles at the intersection of Buddhist philosophy, moral philosophy, and cognitive science, drawing on his textual, meditative, and monastic training in the Theravāda Buddhist tradition of Burma (Myanmar), including work as an interpreter and teacher at meditation retreats.

Bronwyn Finnigan is a continuing lecturer and deputy head of the School of Philosophy at the Australian National University. Her research interest focuses on philosophy of action, mind, and epistemology as they bear on ethics and ethical agency in both Western and Asian philosophical traditions (particularly Buddhist philosophy). She has published several articles in prominent journals and is a coauthor of *Moonshadows: Conventional Truth in Buddhist Philosophy* (Oxford University Press, 2011).

Jay L. Garfield is the Doris Silbert Professor in the Humanities and a professor of philosophy at Smith College, a visiting professor of Buddhist philosophy at the Harvard Divinity School, a professor of philosophy at the University of Melbourne, and an adjunct professor of philosophy at Central University of Tibetan Studies. He has written and edited a number of books in philosophy in Buddhist studies. His most recent are *Moonpaths: Ethics and Emptiness* (with the Cowherds; Oxford University Press, 2015) and *Engaging Buddhism: Why It Matters to Philosophy* (Oxford University Press, 2014).

Charles Goodman is an associate professor in the Philosophy Department and the Department of Asian and Asian-American Studies at Binghamton University. He is the author of several published articles on Buddhist philosophy, ethics, and applied ethics, and of *Consequences of Compassion: An Interpretation and Defense of Buddhist Ethics* (Oxford University Press, 2009). His second book, *The Training Anthology of Śāntideva: A Translation of the Śikṣā-samuccaya*, is forthcoming from Oxford University Press.

Christopher W. Gowans is a professor of philosophy and the chair of the Philosophy Department at Fordham University. He is the author of numerous articles in moral philosophy as well as *Innocence Lost: An Examination of Inescapable Moral Wrongdoing* (Oxford University Press, 1994), *Philosophy of the Buddha* (Routledge, 2003), and *Buddhist Moral Philosophy: An Introduction* (Routledge, forthcoming).

Christopher Kelley holds a PhD from Columbia University. He has taught at Columbia, the New School, and Brooklyn College. He is a cofounder of the Columbia Society for Comparative Philosophy and served as the lead organizer for two conferences on Buddhist philosophy, Mind and Reality (Columbia University, 2006) and Contemporary Perspectives on Buddhist Ethics (Columbia University, 2011).

Damien Keown is Emeritus Professor of Buddhist Ethics at University of London, Goldsmiths. His interests include both theoretical and applied aspects of Buddhist ethics, with an emphasis on contemporary moral problems. He has authored and edited numerous publications, including *The Nature of Buddhist Ethics* (Palgrave, 1992), *Buddhism and Bioethics* (Palgrave, 1995), *Contemporary Buddhist Ethics* (Routledge, 2000), *Buddhism: A Very Short Introduction* (Oxford University Press, 2013), and *Buddhist Ethics: A Very Short*

Introduction (Oxford University Press, 2005). He is also a founding coeditor of the *Journal of Buddhist Ethics.*

Sallie B. King is Professor Emerita of Philosophy and Religion at James Madison University. She is the author of *Buddha Nature* (SUNY Press, 1991), *Journey in Search of the Way: The Spiritual Autobiography of Satomi Myodo* (SUNY Press, 1993), *Being Benevolence: The Social Ethics of Engaged Buddhism* (University of Hawai`i Press, 2005), and *Socially Engaged Buddhism* (University of Hawai`i Press, 2009). She is a coeditor (with Christopher S. Queen) of *Engaged Buddhism: Buddhist Liberation Movements in Asia* (SUNY Press, 1996) and (with Paul O. Ingram) of *The Sound of Liberating Truth: Buddhist-Christian Dialogues in Honor of Frederick J. Streng* (Curzon Press, 1999).

Sara McClintock is an associate professor of religion at Emory University, where she teaches courses in Indian and Tibetan Buddhism, Buddhist narrative traditions, interpretation theory, and Indian philosophy. She is the author of *Omniscience and the Rhetoric of Reason: Śāntarakṣita and Kamalaśīla on Rationality, Argumentation, and Religious Authority* (Wisdom Publications, 2010), an exploration at the intersection of religion, philosophy, and rhetoric in the writings of two eighth-century Indian Buddhist philosophers. She is currently at work on a book on Indian Buddhist epistemological theories of the production of truth and reality through the interaction of conceptual, discursive, and material processes.

Emily McRae is an assistant professor of philosophy at the University of New Mexico. She specializes in Tibetan Buddhist philosophy, ethics, and feminism. Much of her work is devoted to exploring the relationship between the emotions, morality, and contemplative practices such as meditation. She has published articles on emotions and ethics in Asian philosophies, particularly Buddhism, in *American Philosophical Quarterly, History of Philosophy Quarterly, Philosophy East and West, Journal of Buddhist Ethics, Journal of Religious Ethics,* and *Sophia.* Her current projects include papers on the role of empathy in Tibetan Buddhism, the moral psychology of Indo-Tibetan Buddhist ethics, and the Buddhist resources for understanding and responding to the psychology of oppression.

Karin L. Meyers is an assistant professor and the director of the MA program in Buddhist studies at Kathmandu University's Centre for Buddhist Studies at Rangjung Yeshe Institute in Nepal, where she teaches courses in Pali, Indian, and Tibetan Buddhist philosophy, Buddhist history, and religious studies. Her research interests include free will and intention in Buddhism, Buddhist theories of path and mind, and the relationship between contemplative practice and philosophical reasoning.

Jin Y. Park is an associate professor of philosophy and religion and the director of the Asian Studies Program at American University. Park specializes in East Asian Zen and Huayan Buddhism, Buddhist ethics, East-West comparative philosophy, and Buddhist encounters with modernity in East Asia. She is the author of *Buddhism and Postmodernity: Zen, Huayan and the Possibility of Buddhist Postmodern Ethics* (Lexington Books, 2008); the translator of *Reflections of a Zen Buddhist Nun* (University of Hawai`i Press, 2014); the editor of *Buddhisms and Deconstructions* (Rowman & Littlefield Publishers, 2006) and *Makers of Modern Korean Buddhism* (SUNY Press, 2010); and a co-editor of *Merleau-Ponty and Buddhism* (Lexington Books, 2009).

Graham Priest is a distinguished professor of philosophy at the Graduate Center, City University of New York. He is also Boyce Gibson Professor Emeritus at the University of Melbourne and Arché Professorial Fellow at the University of St. Andrews. He works in many areas, including metaphysics, the history of philosophy, and Asian philosophy, but is best known for his work on philosophical logic, especially paraconsistent logic. He is the author of over 200 papers and books, including *In Contradiction* (2nd edition, Oxford University Press, 2006), *Beyond the Limits of Thought* (2nd edition, Oxford University Press, 2002), *Towards Non-Being* (Oxford University Press, 2005), *Doubt Truth to Be a Liar* (Oxford University Press, 2006), *Introduction to Non-Classical Logic* (2nd edition, Cambridge University Press, 2008), and *One* (Oxford University Press, 2014).

Riccardo Repetti is an associate professor of philosophy at Kingsborough Community College, CUNY. His publications focus on free will in analytic philosophy and in Buddhism. He is interested in meditation, consciousness, self, agency, and responsibility. Author of *The Counterfactual Theory of Free Will: A Genuinely Deterministic Form of Soft Determinism* (LAP Lambert, 2010), he has published articles on the ethics of teaching philosophy, contemplative pedagogy, and Buddhism and free will, and is currently writing a monograph and editing an anthology, both on Buddhist perspectives on free will. Rick is also a multiple-decades practitioner and teacher of yoga and meditation.

Mark Siderits recently retired from the Philosophy Department of Seoul National University, where he taught Asian and comparative philosophy. His research interests lie in the intersection between classical Indian philosophy on the one hand, and analytic metaphysics and philosophy of language on the other. Among his more recent publications are *Buddhism as Philosophy*

(Ashgate/Hackett, 2007), *Personal Identity and Buddhist Philosophy: Empty Persons* (Ashgate, 2003), and, together with Shōryū Katsura, *Nāgārjuna's Middle Way: Mūlamadhyamakakārikā* (Wisdom Publications, 2013). He has also edited several collections of work on Indian and analytic philosophy.

Jan Westerhoff is an associate professor of religious ethics at the University of Oxford; a fellow and tutor in theology and religion at Lady Margaret Hall, University of Oxford; and a research associate at the School of Oriental and African Studies, University of London. His publications include *Nagarjuna's Madhyamaka* (Oxford University Press, 2009), *The Dispeller of Disputes: Nagarjuna's Vigrahavyavartani* (Oxford University Press, 2010), and *Reality: A Very Short Introduction* (Oxford University Press, 2011). His research concentrates on systematic aspects of ancient Indian philosophy, especially Madhyamaka.

A Mirror Is for Reflection

Introduction

Jake H. Davis

I.1. For the Purpose of Reflection

Once, the story goes, the Buddha asked his son, "What do you think, Rāhula? What is a mirror for?" And Rāhula answered, "A mirror is for reflection, sir" (MN.i.415).[1]

The term used in the Pāli Buddhist text here, *paccavekkhana*, like the English *reflection*, has two meanings, one referring to an image being thrown back from a surface such as water or glass, and the other referring to the process of careful consideration. These two different sets of connotations make some sense given the literal meaning of *paccavekkhana*, to "look back," "look again," or "re-view." The Buddha plays on these dual meanings of the term to suggest that one should review carefully one's bodily actions, one's speech, and even one's thoughts and mental states, before they occur, during, and also afterward. Those actions of body, speech, and mind that one knows on reflection do not lead to one's own affliction, nor to the affliction of others, nor to the affliction of both, those are wholesome, leading to well-being; those sorts of actions should be done. On the other hand, those actions of body, speech, and mind that one knows on reflection do lead to one's own affliction, to the affliction of others, or to the affliction of both, those are unwholesome, leading to unease; regarding those sorts of actions one should confess any that have been done to one's teacher or fellow practitioners and one should guard oneself from doing such actions again in the future.

The practical advice given here is thus to carefully consider the consequences of one's actions. Notice that not only bodily actions and speech but also the occurrence of thoughts and emotions are classified as actions, *karma* in Sanskrit, *kamma* in the closely related language of the Pāli Buddhist texts preserved in the Theravāda tradition (for the sake of consistency, the terms given in this Introduction are from the Pāli except where otherwise noted). This central focus in Buddhist thought and practice, on the ethical choice to cultivate certain wholesome mental and emotional habits and to weaken other, unwholesome ones, opens up an area of ethical investigation that is underexplored in Western theoretical systems. Yet from the perspective of philosophy as it has been practiced in the West, the Buddha's advice to Rahula also leaves important questions unanswered. Is the discourse suggesting that we are to evaluate whether a state such as anger is wholesome (*kusala*) or un-wholesome (*akusala*) based on its future consequences? Or is the idea that those "mental actions" that are considered unwholesome, such as anger, have bad karmic effects because they are unwholesome, independently of those consequences? Questions such as these have been the subject of a lively de-bate over the past few decades.

In the service of understanding Buddhist ethics, scholars in these debates have often appealed to similarities and differences with Western ethical theo-ries such as Mill's consequentialism or Aristotle's virtue-theoretic approach. This brings out a different aspect of the analogy to reflection: looking into a mirror, we see an image of ourselves. There is a downside to this; if those of us raised in a context dominated by the history of European thought see in Buddhist ethics only reflections of our own philosophical heritage, we may miss new perspectives to be found in Buddhist traditions and also impose on them ideas that are not their own. For instance, some scholars have suggested that while deliberation about action is central to Western conceptions of moral choice, the Buddha's advice to Rahula is something of an exception, and that Buddhist ethics focuses not on this kind of deliberation but instead on train-ing habits of mind to the point that the thought of doing unwholesome actions simply would not arise to be deliberated about (see, e.g., Heim, 2014).

In recent years the academic study of Buddhist ethics has been moving beyond the project of comparison and categorization, renewing the aim to achieve a genuinely cross-cultural, cosmopolitan dialogue on matters that are important to us all. Engaging with perspectives different enough from our own can challenge us to see our assumptions and unquestioned starting points; it can help to point out our cultural blind spots as well as our individual ones. As Owen Flanagan notes in his foreword to this volume, from the perspective of a Westerner considering whether we ought to adopt Buddhist attitudes to-ward anger, or whether Buddhists ought to adopt our attitudes toward politics, in the process of considering whether other forms of moral life could be live possibilities for us we encounter "challenges to our normal ways of thinking about the content, scope, order, and sufficiency of our moral beliefs, virtues, and principles." In this sense too the project of understanding Buddhist ethics can serve the purpose of reflection. This last sense involves both of the meanings of reflection/*paccavekkhana*, for it involves carefully reviewing and considering the image of ourselves, warts and all, that we see reflected back when we engage with a different perspective. By engaging in such critical cross-cultural reflection, Buddhists as well as Western thinkers may find that refinement and adaptation of their views is needed. Indeed such a process of transformation in the course of transmission to new human contexts is as old as the Buddhist teachings themselves.

I.2. The Roots of Buddhist Ethics

The exact dates of the individual venerated as the Awakened One, the Buddha, are a matter of some controversy, and even the existence of such an individual is not immune to skeptical doubt. Yet we can say with considerable confidence that roughly five hundred years before the Christian era certain central doctrines and meditative techniques were promulgated, and a monastic community of monks and nuns was formed, with a gradually expanding list of explicit rules to live by. This "Doctrine and Discipline" is referred to as *dhamma-vinaya* in the language of the Pāli texts preserved by the modern Theravāda Buddhist traditions. These sets of texts were transmitted in a northern Indian dialect to Sri Lanka and later to the peoples of Southeast Asia. Other sets of teachings were transmitted in a variety of dialects, including Sanskrit, in which the Buddha's teachings are referred to as the *dharma* (cognate with Pāli *dhamma*). Texts preserved and innovated in these later lines of transmission were subsequently translated into the languages of Central Asia, the Tibetan plateau, and East Asia. Each of these transmissions to new cultural contexts has involved adaptation and innovation. For this reason the range of modern traditions that are identified as Buddhist display a diversity of ethical, metaphysical, and epistemological claims. In cases such as the modern Theravāda, there have been periods of relative isolation from competing worldviews. In other cases, Buddhist philosophers were continually engaged in lively debates with non-Buddhist Indian or Chinese thinkers. (For an excellent introduction to Buddhist doctrine and its development, see Gethin, 1998).

Despite the diversity of Buddhist thought, certain central doctrinal features are found across most Buddhist philosophical traditions and are a useful starting point for scholars and students unfamiliar with these traditions. The Four Noble Truths are a leading example. The first of these is the Noble Truth of *dukkha*. *Dukkha* is to be contrasted with *sukha*, which connotes pleasure and ease. The first noble truth thus points both to the grosser forms of suffering due to aging, disease, and death as well as to more subtle and pervasive aspects of unease, unsatisfactoriness, and troublesomeness that are inherent in being a conscious being. The second Noble Truth is that the arising of *dukkha* is due to *taṇhā* (Sanskrit: *tṛṣṇā*), a term literally meaning "thirst" and referring to the insatiable force of craving. The third Noble Truth, of cessation of *dukkha*, *dukkha-nirodha-sacca*, points to the possibility of freedom from *dukkha* by removing its cause. To realize the cessation of *dukkha* is to taste for oneself the peace of *nibbāna*. The fourth Noble Truth is the path of practice leading to cessation of *dukkha*, that is *dukkha-nirodha-gāminī-paṭipadā*. This path of practice is broken into eight factors: right view and right aim; right speech, right action, and right livelihood; right effort, right mindfulness, and right concentration. Together these are referred to as the Eightfold Noble Path. Buddhist ethical proposals for how we ought to live and practice can thus be seen as structured by the two opposing poles pointed to by the first Noble Truth, *dukkha*, and by the third Noble Truth, liberation from *dukkha*. The aim of Buddhist practices is to remove the causes of *dukkha* and to replace them with other, better habits of mind, speech, and action.

To go beyond this simple characterization of Buddhist ethics, however, would require us to carefully examine a host of philosophical debates that have occupied ancient Buddhist philosophers as well as modern interpreters, as the chapters of this volume illustrate. For instance, the issue of how to prioritize the goal of eliminating *dukkha* for all sentient beings rather than eliminating the causes of *dukkha* first in oneself has divided Mahayāna Buddhist traditions of Central Asia and East Asia from other schools, such as the Theravāda tradition that is dominant in Sri Lanka and Southeast Asia. In part these differences in ethical advice may turn on ontological questions about the three characteristics of existence: the characteristic of *anicca* or impermanence, the characteristic of *dukkha* or suffering, and especially the characteristic of *anattā* or nonself. Some Abhidharma schools adopt a reductionist or eliminative stance toward the concept of persons, claiming that individuals are nothing more than (a causal process of) mental and physical elements. If nonself is to be understood along these lines, as implying that there are no ultimately real differences between your suffering and mine, this might lead to the ethical conclusion that one should strive equally to reduce all suffering, without prioritizing one's own. While this line of thinking is influential, not all Buddhist philosophers, ancient or modern, would agree with it. For instance, some understand the doctrine of nonself instead as a claim about how we should each relate to our own experience—for instance, by not taking it personally—rather than a claim about what ultimately exists or not. Moreover while all schools have pointed to the unwholesome psychological roots of craving, aversion, and delusion—*lobha, dosa,* and *moha*—some have held that the concepts we use to draw distinctions not only between individual people but also between objects in the world necessarily involve some level of delusion. In contrast, others seem to suggest that use of concepts is both possible and also unproblematic for a being who is fully liberated from the causes of *dukkha*.

To explore these fascinating debates would take us beyond the scope of this introduction. Focusing more narrowly within the realm of Buddhist ethics, while there are differences between the traditions on the specifics of monastic discipline, *Vinaya*, there is general (though not universal) convergence on the claim that lay Buddhists should maintain precepts of refraining from killing, stealing, sexual misconduct, and lying, for instance. Yet in applying and extending such a list to the vast range of situations encountered in human contexts one is tempted to look for a theoretical structure that underlies and justifies these basic Buddhist ethical claims. Modern interpreters have debated what this structure might be, and indeed whether there is such a theoretical structure to be found in Buddhist ethics. In his landmark 1992 monograph, *The Nature of Buddhist Ethics*, Damien Keown pointed out extensive parallels between the suggestions for living found in Buddhist texts, with their focus on *nibbāna*, and the teleological conception of virtue found in the works of Aristotle in particular, with their focus on *eudaemonia*. A rival interpretation of Buddhist ethics along the lines of Western consequentialist theories, which Keown argued against, has found able defenders in the work of Mark Siderits (2003) and Charles Goodman (2009). By approaching the study of Buddhist ethics as a comparison between theoretical systems, the work of these and other scholars gave rise to a lively and fertile philosophical debate. Over the past decade, however, many have come to think that the project of fitting Buddhist ethical thought into Western philosophical categories may be of very limited utility, and the focus of investigations has shifted considerably.

I.3. An Overview of the Chapters

This volume offers a snapshot of the present state of investigation into the nature of Buddhist ethics. Keown's contribution to part I departs substantially from his earlier project of comparing Buddhist with Aristotelian ethics. Indeed he suggests here that Buddhist thought lacks the sort of moral theorizing that could be compared directly to Western meta-ethical systems, and he considers in detail a number of reasons for this "curious absence." Bronwyn Finnigan offers a rigorous demonstration of the philosophical complexities that prevent an easy solution to the question of how to fit Buddhist ethics into Western philosophical categories. She identifies the most salient

philosophical features of virtue-theoretic and consequentialist interpretations in particular, demonstrating the difficulties of deciding between these
two interpretative approaches and arguing that both may be plausible as rational reconstructions of the available textual evidence. Christopher Gowans
also reviews some difficulties with these two interpretative approaches. He
suggests that Indian Buddhist thinkers are best understood as holding moral
theorizing to be mainly unimportant to the practical goals of Buddhist traditions, including living ethically and achieving enlightenment.

If the chapters of part I move us away from the project of comparing and
contrasting with Western ethical theories in order to identify the theoretical
superstructure underlying Buddhist ethical thought, one alternative approach
is to construct ethical theories that speak to contemporary concerns yet are inspired by and derived from Buddhist principles, to greater and lesser degrees.
In her contribution to part II, Jin Park develops an approach rooted in the
nonduality of the Zen and Huayan traditions of Buddhist thought prominent
in East Asia. She examines a number of problems that these nondual perspectives pose for formulating an ethical framework, in particular the tension between an ultimate perspective on emptiness and the phenomenal level
of difference and distinction. Yet Park proposes that an awareness of these
tensions can open a fertile space for ethical reflection and moral cultivation.
Graham Priest also develops an approach that draws out the ethical implications of nonself and emptiness. Priest puts particular emphasis on the value
of equanimity, by which he means a tranquil state of mind something like
ataraxia in the Hellenistic context and *upekṣā/upekkhā* in the Buddhist one.
Whereas Park and Priest develop their own constructive proposals, Christian
Coseru offers a critique of the modern program of Buddhist neuroethics, with
its emphasis on both compassion and empirical paradigms of knowledge.
Coseru investigates a number of ways this empirically oriented program
might advance philosophical understanding of Buddhist ethics: he investigates whether affective neuroscience supplies enough evidence for a naturalized account of Buddhist compassion, whether such a naturalized account of
compassion can advance the philosophical debate concerning freedom and
determinism (for which see also part III), and how recent empirical work
might bear on a consequentialist interpretation of Buddhist ethics.

One downside of constructive approaches is their narrow focus on certain
aspects of Buddhist ethical thought, to the exclusion of complex relationships
with other aspects of doctrine that might be given equal or greater emphasis
in traditional contexts. Particularly noteworthy is the relative lack of emphasis
on the doctrines of karma and rebirth among approaches to Buddhist ethics developed for our contemporary cultural context. In developing one such

constructive approach, for instance, Priest's chapter is explicit about dispensing with aspects of traditional Buddhist frameworks such as rebirth. Part III turns to focus on this issue. Charles Goodman's contribution to the section on karma and rebirth sets out from the premise that in the context of modern scientific worldviews, traditional Buddhist conceptions of karma are giving way to new conceptions that focus not on consequences in future lives but rather on psychological consequences in a single life. Interestingly Goodman not only locates resources for such a psychological understanding of karma in classical descriptions by Buddhist philosophers such as Śāntideva; he also applies this to the question of the nature of Buddhist ethics as a whole, arguing that understanding karma psychologically in fact considerably strengthens the consequentialist interpretation against the virtue-theoretic one. Jan Westerhoff's chapter raises a powerful objection to such naturalistic approaches to Buddhist ethics: if there is no continuity of mind after the decay of the body, then the most effective way to put an end to one's suffering would be suicide rather than the development of ethical behavior, concentration, and wisdom advocated in Buddhist texts. Westerhoff takes as his primary target the general approach to naturalizing Buddhist ethics articulated by philosophers such as by Owen Flanagan, and the suicide objection has particular force within the sort of consequentialist framework advocated by Goodman. Whereas Goodman and Westerhoff focus on theoretical considerations, Sallie King offers a more practical take on the question of karma in the modern social context. Surveying the uses and abuses of the notion of karma from the perspective of the movement toward a Buddhism engaged with social and political issues, King focuses in particular on how the notion of suffering as karmic desert can be used to rationalize unjust institutions, and she draws on Buddhist philosophical resources to offer three pithy rebuttals to such rationalizations.

Taking a similarly practical approach to traditional notions of karma and rebirth, but on a more individual level of ethical transformation, Sara McClintock's contribution to part IV takes up the issue of karmic opacity, how living with the assumed reality of an infinite number of forgotten past lives might lead to ethical transformation in one's present life. McClintock's rich account focuses on how an "ethical reading" can impact a listener's remembrance—perhaps a type of "mindfulness," she suggests—of the fact that one has forgotten most of the formative actions that have brought one to one's current situation. Indeed, as Jay Garfield remarks, cultivating clear awareness is taken in many Buddhist texts to be the foundation of all moral development. Garfield focuses on training in mindfulness as a central contribution that Buddhist traditions can make to contemporary investigations of moral psychology, and to the field of cognitive science more generally. Surveying texts from the classical discourses of the Pāli Buddhist texts and from the Mahayāna philosopher Śāntideva, among others, Garfield argues that mindfulness is practiced for the sake of being able to embody ethical action with an effortless virtuosity, in the way that a masterful jazz artist spontaneously manifests the fruits of his own dedicated and careful practice. Drawing on similar sources from the Pāli texts as well as recent empirical studies, my chapter brings together two themes in Buddhist ethics: the emphasis on mindfulness as foundational to wisdom and the ethical focus on emotional motivations such as hatred and love that give rise to an intention to act. I argue that, taken together, these can in fact offer a foundation for universal ethical values of the sort Western philosophical systems have aimed at, but one founded in shared human experience of various emotional motivations rather than in abstract theoretical reasoning.

A number of modern and ancient interpreters have placed a great deal of emphasis on the role of intention in Buddhist ethics, sometimes overlooking less psychological, more objective factors. Indeed, as noted earlier, one drawback of constructivist approaches such as mine and others surveyed above is that an excessive focus on any one such principle can obscure the context in which it is placed in traditional theories. Karin Meyers's rich exegetical work on Vasubandhu's analysis of intention, in part V, provides one corrective example. Meyers demonstrates how Vasubandhu rejects in his own historical context both the overpsychologization of intention that is characteristic of many modern interpretations of Buddhist theory and also the opposite objective extreme, represented by a Buddhist school that attributed ethical qualities to physical entities. Meyers concludes by noting also that because the freedom Vasubandhu values is not the freedom to do what one desires but rather liberation from suffering, he is not particularly concerned about whether karma might be compelled or free. A number of recent theorists have suggested that the Buddhist understanding of nonself is orthogonal to, or even diametrically opposed to the Western notion of free will. Riccardo Repetti's critical review of this literature argues that Buddhist traditions nonetheless do contain the philosophical resources to enrich the philosophical discussion of free will, and indeed that Buddhist sources pose a serious challenge to the strongest forms of free will skepticism. In a similar vein, Mark Siderits aims to show how Buddhist analyses of action without an agent might prove a resource for contemporary philosophical theories of action. His chapter draws on recent work by E. J. Lowe to help articulate a Buddhist action theory and an approach to free will that features both a conventional, personal level of description and an ultimate, causal level.

In his contribution to part VI, Christopher Kelley engages Buddhist philosophical approaches to the self with a practical, pressing political issue. Kelley
focuses on the apparent contradiction between the Dalai Lama's philosophical
views on selflessness and emptiness, and his endorsement of human rights
law, with its basis in essentialist notions of inherent dignity and inalienable
rights of persons derived from the Western Enlightenment. Kelley resolves
this tension by suggesting that the doctrine of emptiness, as it is employed in
the Madhyamaka philosophy of the Dalai Lama's Tibetan Buddhist tradition,
can offer a better philosophical basis for conceptions of human rights, one
that counteracts essentialism in its many pernicious forms. Amber Carpenter
takes up the relationship of nonself to the political—and emotional—issue of
justice. Carpenter investigates Śāntideva's claim that the roots of anger should
be eliminated, and with it the metaphysical picture of distinct individuals,
some who act and others who are acted upon, that is necessary for resentment
of injustice to arise. Carpenter uses this example to suggest that the domain of
the ethical in Buddhist thought is not centered on issues of justice but on an
ethics of care (*karuṇā*) grounded in dependent arising. Emily McRae's contribution also notes how the forces of aversion as well as attachment cause us to
solidify perceptions of identity. Her discussion focuses on the context of intimate relationships, suggesting that the spaciousness of equanimity (*upekkhā*)
allows us to witness and respond appropriately to controlling behavior or to
laziness, for instance, without seeing it as evidence of our loved one's being
a controlling or lazy person. McRae's chapter closes the volume with a very
practical analysis of equanimity's role and value in manifesting the attitudes
of friendliness, compassion, and sympathetic joy that are central Buddhist
values.

I.4. The Ethical Imperatives of Studying Buddhist Philosophy

The chapters collected in this volume are each focused on one or another particular problem in understanding Buddhist ethics and are focused on these issues
in the narrow way necessary for rigorous examination. Nonetheless they can be
seen as part of a much larger project, one whose time has come. I write these
words on a journey back to the United States from the funeral and cremation of
my teacher, the eminent meditation master Sayadaw U Pandita of Burma. Over
a lifetime of ninety-five years, Sayadaw lived through great political changes,
from British colonial rule of Burma, through the resultant Burmese nationalist independence movement, followed by half a century of a repressive and

isolationist military dictatorship, and—only a few weeks before his death—a democratically elected government, headed by his student Daw Aung San Suu Kyi. Sayadaw's life offers an interesting window into the forces that have shaped how Buddhist thought and practice from South and Southeast Asia, from the Tibetan plateau, and from East Asia are understood today: forces of tradition and of modernity, of European colonialism and of indigenous Asian nationalism, among others. Understanding these forces enables us to better see the promise of and the obstacles to understanding Buddhist ethics.

First, though the British Raj is no more, the colonial divide between ruler and ruled continues to be replicated in the Western academy. The study of European thinkers (those with theological leanings, such as Aristotle and Kant, as well as those without) is given pride of place in the course offerings and hiring practices of Anglophone philosophy departments, while the study of Indian, Chinese, African, and Native American traditions of philosophical thought (which mainly operate without the distinction we draw between religious and secular) is largely relegated to departments of religious studies. It is a sign of progress that many philosophy departments now see the need to have at least one faculty member trained in some area of "non-Western philosophy." Yet this terminology itself reveals also a way of thinking that replicates the political lines drawn by European colonialism; compare the number of positions explicitly advertised as covering non-Indian, non-Chinese, or non-African philosophy. This is not to suggest that Asian colonialism has been any better than European colonialism, much less to deny the fact of Chinese or Burmese Buddhist political domination and intellectual marginalization of less powerful ethnic groups. The point is instead to be aware of how philosophy as studied in the modern academy has been impacted by political history and how far there is to go to achieve a truly global philosophical conversation, one that would assess in an even-handed way different individual thinkers' and different traditions' investigations into various aspects of wisdom and draw the best of each into a cosmopolitan philosophical conversation. This volume aims to take Buddhist (and other) philosophers seriously as conversation partners, in the sense of questioning and debating Buddhist doctrines rather than documenting these as historical curiosities. Because to do so is to overturn the intellectual legacy of European colonialism, this intellectual project is unavoidably a political one as well.

Nonetheless, colonialism has played multiple roles in fostering interest in Buddhist thought and practice today. One direct impact was that political, economic, and religious agents of European colonial regimes traveled to Asia, learned local languages, translated texts, and cataloged and appropriated ideas as well as objects held sacred in local traditions. This occurred even in cultures that were not under European colonial rule, such as in Tibet and Thailand. On the other hand, recent scholarship has shown how local movements developed in Asia in reaction to the imposition of colonial worldviews, attempting to demonstrate the value and contemporary relevance of indigenous traditions. Attempts to show Buddhism to be more "scientific" than the Christian religion of the European colonizers can be seen as an instance of this movement (Sharf, 1995; McMahan, 2008; Braun, 2013). In the case of Burma, these nationalist political forces were directly responsible for popularizing Buddhist meditation and doctrine both nationally and internationally. Shortly after gaining independence from the British, the government of Burma established the Mahasi meditation center in Rangoon, at which Sayadaw U Pandita was trained. And this lineage of teachers and students led directly from the Mahasi Sayadaw, to U Pandita, to the small group of young Westerners who, along with students of theirs, have made mindfulness meditation a rapidly growing phenomenon in the West.

The extent and range of our exposure to differing metaphysical, ethical, and epistemological perspectives in this global information age offers both a challenge and also an opportunity for Buddhist thought and practice to grow in new directions. It presents new opportunities to offer Buddhist proposals for human development to those who might not have considered them before, and new opportunities for Buddhist traditions to engage in critical self-reflection and refinement. Indeed the global interconnections that have allowed the spread of Buddhist ideas and practices to the West also bring into sharp relief the value and necessity of philosophical conversation and reflection. Sayadaw U Pandita commented to me on occasion that from what he could see Western philosophical investigations simply went round and round in intellectual proliferation without arriving at the wisdom promised by the name of the discipline. He had a point. Practitioners of Buddhist meditation sometimes emphasize the nondiscursive or nonconceptual nature of the wisdom gained from meditation practice. And it may well be that one contribution Buddhist philosophy can make to a global philosophical conversation is to help us see our way to an epistemology that balances the value of personal experience with that of rational reflection. However, many traditional Buddhists justify Buddhist metaphysical and ethical claims by appeal to the judgments of those wiser than us, those who see more clearly, the Buddha first and foremost. If this is right, one might think that all that is needed to settle cross-cultural ethical disagreements is to know and to appeal to the authority of the Buddhist teachings as they have been handed down to us. However, one problem with this move is that this same kind of appeal to authority is also employed by other traditions, both religious and scientific, to justify claims that conflict with Buddhist views. In the context of competing worldviews, the appeal to any particular source of authority itself is in need of justification, and to critique another's justification for their views is at least implicitly to suggest that one's own justificatory story is similarly required to be responsive to critical consideration from other perspectives.

The principal aim of this volume is to lay the groundwork for that sort of critical, cosmopolitan philosophical conversation by bringing Buddhist approaches into that exchange in an integral way. In these regards, however, there is much more to be done. For one, the range of Buddhist textual traditions represented here is but a subset of those that should be discussed. The bulk of recent philosophical research has focused on Mahāyāna sources in Indo-Tibetan traditions; more research is needed on sources from the Theravāda, Vajrayāna, and East Asian Buddhist philosophy. Second, the scholars whose work is represented here are for the most part members of the Western academy who were not raised in Buddhist cultures; much more needs to be done to bring thinkers embedded in Buddhist cultures into this conversation, such as Buddhist meditation masters and traditional scholars of Tibet, Japan, and Burma, among others. From this a third direction would follow naturally, of applying the fruits of cross-cultural philosophical investigations to issues faced by Buddhist cultures today. In the years leading up to Sayadaw U Pandita's passing, for instance, the Burmese government, now headed by the Nobel laureate Daw Aung San Suu Kyi, has been faced with the politically fraught, but also ethically fraught, question of how to balance the concerns of the ethnic Burmese majority to preserve the vitality of their Buddhist culture with the preservation of the rights of Muslim and other minority groups. One urgent project would be to demonstrate ways in which contemporary Buddhist approaches to such political problems, as well as contemporary Buddhist approaches to more individual aspects of thought and practice, could be refined and improved by engagement with other philosophical and scientific perspectives. In this way the continuing project should be to benefit global conversations through the contribution of Buddhist approaches and to benefit Buddhist thought through the contribution of other perspectives. My hope for this volume is that it will help to lay the groundwork for future generations to continue to develop such a truly cosmopolitan exchange about issues that matter deeply to us all.

Abbreviation

MN   *Majjhima Nikāya*, volume and page in the Pali Text Society edition. Translations are my own.

Note

1. This is the *Ambalaṭṭhikarāhulovāda Sutta* (MN 61, at MN.i.414ff), my translation. In this discourse Buddha starts up a conversation with Rāhula on the subject of telling lies in jest; according to multiple commentarial traditions, it seems that Rāhula was prone to just this vice (Anālayo, 2011, p. 342).

References

Anālayo. (2011). *A comparative study of the* Majjhima Nikāya. Taiwan: Dharma Drum.

Braun, E. (2013). *The birth of insight: Meditation, modern Buddhism, and the Burmese monk Ledi Sayadaw.* Chicago: Chicago University Press.

Gethin, R. (1998). *The foundations of Buddhism.* Oxford: Oxford University Press.

Goodman, C. (2009). *Consequences of compassion: An interpretation and defense of Buddhist ethics.* New York: Oxford University Press.

Heim, M. (2014). *The forerunner of all things: Buddhaghosa on mind, intention, and agency.* New York: Oxford University Press.

Keown, D. (1992). *The nature of Buddhist ethics.* New York: Palgrave Macmillan.

McMahan, D. (2008). *The making of Buddhist modernism.* New York: Oxford University Press.

Sharf, R. H. (1995). Buddhist Modernism and the Rhetoric of Meditative Experience. *Numen, 42*(3), 228–283.

Siderits, M. (2003). *Personal identity and Buddhist philosophy: Empty persons.* Burlington, VT: Ashgate.

PART ONE

Buddhist Ethics and Western Categories

Chapter 1

"It's Ethics, Jim, but Not as We Know It"

REFLECTIONS ON THE ABSENCE OF MORAL
PHILOSOPHY IN BUDDHISM

*Damien Keown**

1.1. Introduction

What I want to say here falls into two parts. First I comment on some differences between Buddhist and Western ethics, and in particular the paradox of how a religion as ethical as Buddhism appears to have no ethics. I apologize if this formulation of the problem sounds like a Japanese kōan, and by way of orientation I should say that my background is not in East Asian but in Theravāda Buddhism and my comments relate mainly to the southern schools. I think they also apply to Mahāyāna Buddhism in India and perhaps also farther afield, although I hesitate to generalize about East Asian Buddhism, where the picture may be more complicated.

In the second part I offer some speculations as to the reasons for the curious absence of ethics in Buddhism. I am sure it will strike many people as odd that such a claim is even being made—odd, perhaps, in the manner reminiscent of the fairy tale of the emperor's new clothes, and odder still that such a "black hole" has not received much comment before. Perhaps this is because some things about Buddhist ethics seem very familiar on the surface, and this superficial resemblance has masked important underlying differences with Western ethics.

---

*This is an expanded version of my chapter "Buddhism: Morality without Ethics" in Keown (2010, pp. 40–48).

1.2. Buddhist and Western Ethics

There has certainly been a good deal of confusion and uncertainty on the part of Western scholars about the nature and place of ethics in the tradi tion. Opinions have varied considerably from the early pioneers onward. Max Weber famously said, "Ancient Buddhism was merely a religious technology of wandering ... monks" to which there was later tacked on what he called "an insufficiency ethic for the weak" (as cited in Cooper & James, 2005, p. 50). A contrasting perspective was presented by Weber's contemporary Albert Schweitzer (1967, p. 117), who described the Buddha as "one of the greatest men of ethical genius" who "advanced the ethics ... of humanity." Nietzsche described Buddhists as "passive nihilists" and saw their religion as concerned only peripherally with the wider world of human affairs (as cited in Cooper & James, 2005, p. 51). Variants of these views have persisted down to modern times. As late as 1964, Winston L. King, a Christian minister and one of the earliest scholars to take an interest in Buddhist ethics, wrote, "Buddhism deals not with man in society, or among his fellows, but with the individual man facing his eternal destiny. ... The Buddha had little either of concern for society as such or of firm conviction in its possible improvability" (as cited in Cooper & James, 2005, p. 54). Of course not everyone saw things this way. In his early study *The Ethics of Buddhism*, published in 1926, the Japanese scholar Unro Tachibana wrote that Buddhism "esteems ... morality ... above anything else," while the venerable Saddhatissa, a Sri Lankan scholar, sub-titled his classic volume *Buddhist Ethics* (1997) *"The Essence of Buddhism"*. In more recent times, as Buddhist ethics has begun to crystallize as an autono-mous branch of Buddhist studies, scholars have attempted to refine our un-derstanding of Buddhist ethics using the lens of Western typologies, such as consequentialism, deontology, virtue ethics, and particularism.

In considering the numerous contrasting takes on the subject, I can't help being reminded of the parable of the blind men and the elephant in the *Udāna* (69f.). Perhaps, as in the case of the blind men, none of the interpretations is totally wrong, and it may simply depend on which particular part of the beast you have latched onto, but the many distinctive and contrasting interpreta-tions do make us wonder what it is about Buddhist ethics that gives rise to such diversity of opinion.

Certainly, limited or misguided perceptions have played a part, as when scholars had access only to limited segments of the vast scriptural sources now available. There is also some semantic confusion around the term *ethics* itself, which can refer to both moral teachings and moral philosophy. Making use of this distinction, my central point is that while we find plenty of interest in ethics in the sense of moral teachings in Buddhism, the subject of moral philosophy—by which I mean the systematic and critical analysis of moral values and principles—does not appear to exist as an autonomous branch of inquiry in the Buddhist philosophical canon. Buddhist moral *teachings* can be seen in the many precepts, virtues, moral narratives, and stories found in Buddhist sources. These inculcate moral conduct of a high order and are rightly admired and respected.

To take a brief tour through the main divisions of the Pāli canon, in the Buddha's sermons in the *Sutta Piṭaka* there is abundant material relating to moral conduct. He teaches that morality is part of the Eightfold Path that leads to nirvana; sets out codes of conduct such as the Five Precepts; defends the belief in karma against those who reject it; encourages the practice of virtues such as generosity, nonviolence, and compassion; and gives specific guidance to the laity in over 330 discourses, such as in the *Sigālovāda Sutta* (Kelly, 2011).[1] Occasionally rules of thumb are offered to guide ethical decision-making, such as the Buddhist formulation of the Golden Rule, or the advice given to the Kālāmas to consider the likely consequences of their actions as well as the opinions of the wise before taking any action (AN.i.88ff). However, the Buddha rarely explores ethical conundrums, such as whether it is ever right to tell a lie, and if not, how one should respond to the mad axeman who knocks on the door asking about the whereabouts of his victim. And in his discourses very few thorny questions arise such as the kind put to Jesus by rabbis concerning whether it was right to pay taxes to the Romans (Rom. 13:6) and such like.

One early text, however, does remind us of the kind of Socratic debate we are familiar with in Western ethical literature. This is *Milinda's Questions*, a third-century BCE work which purportedly records a debate between the Buddhist monk Nāgasena, who may have been an Indo-Greek monk of Gandhāra, and the Bactrian king Milinda, or Menander (Halkios, 2014, p. 91). One cannot but help contrast the quizzical adversarial style of this text, in which Milinda plays the role of Socratic gadfly, with the general avoidance of controversy in the Buddha's own discourses, which tend to follow the standard Indian pattern of expositions that proceed without challenge or interruption to a foregone conclusion. It is difficult to resist the impression that the format of *Milinda's Questions* owes a good deal to Greek influence on the Bactrian region of Northwest India colonized by Alexander the Great; I will return to consider the place of ethics in Greek thought below.

Turning to the *Vinaya Piṭaka*, tricky questions do sometimes arise in the code of monastic law and are discussed in Vinaya commentaries. Here the circumstances of the case are briefly presented, and then a decision is recorded as to whether a rule has been infringed. An example comes to mind under the third precept, which prohibits the taking of human life (the third *pārājika*), where a monk throws himself off a high place intending to commit suicide but instead lands on top of an unfortunate basketmaker who is killed as a result (Vin. III, 81). The juridical question raised by this rather unlikely scenario is whether an incomplete suicide in which a third party is killed unintentionally constitutes a breach of the precept. Considerable Jesuitical skills were exercised in resolving such cases. This kind of casuistry, however, is limited to the specific needs of the monastic community, and in the West such matters would probably be dealt with under the rubric of law or jurisprudence rather than ethics.

Certain Abhidharma texts also have a bearing on ethical matters. The first book of the *Abhidhamma Piṭaka*, the *Dhammasaṅgaṇī*, contains lists of moral and immoral states of consciousness, but its aim is psychological classification rather than ethical analysis. Later treatises follow the same kind of scholastic exegesis adopted throughout the Abhidharma. For example, Buddhaghosa's fifth-century discussion of *sīla*, or moral conduct, in the first part of the *Visuddhimagga* simply lists the various forms and classifications of monastic deportment and etiquette without ever attempting to explore or question basic ethical presuppositions. Much the same could be said of the *Abhidharmakośa* and other such scholastic compendia. It is also interesting to note in passing that the psychological taxonomy of the Abhidharma does not identify a faculty corresponding to what the Greeks called *phronesis*, or practical wisdom. Indeed it seems that Indian philosophy in general esteems theoretical knowledge above practical wisdom and regards *theoria* as not just a necessary but also a sufficient condition for liberation. For this reason moral conduct is sometimes portrayed simply as a stepping stone to wisdom or relegated to a preparatory stage of the path. Perhaps, then, we are dealing with different cultural conceptions of human flourishing: in the Indian view, *gnosis* alone is enough, whereas in the Western tradition *phronesis* or *prudentia*—that is to say the exercise of skill and judgment in practical affairs—is also thought to be an important virtue.

We do find a good deal of head-scratching in certain genres of Buddhist literature, such as historical chronicles, folk tales, and moral fables, where dilemmas and conflicts inevitably arise, but the analysis of these problematic situations is not pursued systematically and never develops into an autonomous branch of learning. Thus, to conclude this brief survey, I think we can say that while we find the raw data of moral philosophy scattered throughout the Buddhist literary corpus, we do not find any attempt to raise the subject to an analytical level or enshrine it formally in the traditional academic curriculum.

Let me illustrate the contrast with the West through a little autobiographical detail. As a postgraduate in Oxford my researches often took me to the old part of the Bodleian Library, which is reached by passing through the courtyard known as the Schools Quad. Those familiar with this distinguished building will recall that over the various entrances are written in Latin the names of the different branches of learning studied in the lecture rooms within. The dozen or so subjects mentioned, in no particular order, are grammar and history, metaphysics, moral philosophy, logic, music, natural philosophy, law, languages (Hebrew and Greek), arithmetic and geometry, astronomy, rhetoric, and anatomy and medicine. Construction of the Schools Quad was completed in 1624, so we may regard this list as summarizing in a rough and ready way the main branches of Western learning at the start of the early modern period. I wish here to simply note the inclusion of ethics, or moral philosophy, as one of the subjects in the curriculum, clearly identified as an independent subject alongside metaphysics.

As we know, Buddhism too values learning, and a multidisciplinary and comprehensive education has always been prized. The *Jātakas* speak of the Buddha as a bodhisattva mastering all branches of learning, including medicine, in the famous university of Taxila, and the *Lalitavistara* praises Gautama for his proficiency in eighty-six disciplines of the humanities and sciences. Ancient India had many great monastic universities, among them Nālandā, Somapuri, and Valabhī, and there were others elsewhere, like the Mahāvihāra and Abhayagiri monasteries in Sri Lanka. What subjects would have been written over the entrances to the classrooms at, say, Nālandā, where the 10,000 students and 1,500 tutors reputedly assembled for their 100 lectures per day? I think it likely the core syllabus would have featured the *pañca-vidyā* or "five sciences," namely grammar (*śabda*), logic (*hetu*), Buddhist philosophy consisting of subjects such as Abhidharma, Prajñāpāramitā, and Mādhyamika (*adhyātma-cikitsā*), Vinaya, and secular arts and crafts such as medicine (*śilpakarmasthāna-vidyā*). These five subjects came to form the basis of the standard curriculum in Mahāyāna institutions, and while we find plenty of metaphysics in the curriculum, in the form of theories about the nature of reality, in contrast to the Western university curriculum there appears to be nothing corresponding to moral philosophy.

This apparent lack of interest puzzled me as a postgraduate, and when searching for primary sources on Buddhist ethics I often felt I had made some kind of category mistake. I had somewhat naively assumed that there would be treatises on ethics by Buddhist authors, just as there were by Western authors, but I soon realized this was not the case. More than once I felt like crying out in the silence of the library in the manner of Dr. McCoy, "Dammit, Jim! Where have these Buddhists hidden their texts on ethics?"

In contrast to India, ethics has been a central branch of philosophical inquiry in the West since ancient times. Its evolution can be traced from the Greek and Roman authors to the Christian Church fathers, medieval scholastics, and Enlightenment thinkers, down to today's multiplicity of works in applied fields such as bioethics and business ethics. Enter any Western library, and in the philosophy section alongside headings like "Logic," "Metaphysics," and "Epistemology" you will find one labeled "Ethics," containing hundreds if not thousands of works on what is a clearly demarcated and central branch of philosophical analysis. However, no such classification seems to exist in any Buddhist library.

Convenient examples of the kind of problem I would designate as ethical are provided by the so-called Socratic paradoxes in Plato's dialogues. In the *Euthyphro*, Socrates asks whether certain things are good because the gods approve of them, or whether the gods approve of them because they are good. This problem could easily be rephrased in Buddhist terminology by inquiring whether certain acts are bad because they produce bad karma, or whether they produce bad karma because they are bad. Although clearly an important ethical question, I have never seen the problem posed in these terms by Buddhist thinkers. Other dilemmas raised by Socrates include whether virtue is a form of knowledge, whether all of the virtues are one, whether wrongdoing is always the result of ignorance, and whether a virtuous person can be harmed.

Perhaps the most poignant of the dilemmas faced is that in the *Crito*, when Socrates himself considers whether he should attempt to escape from his confinement while awaiting execution. This dilemma, like the others, provides the starting point for reflection that seeks to uncover general action-guiding rules or principles that can ultimately be grounded in a comprehensive ethical theory. Socrates, for example, gives a threefold argument why he should not break the law by escaping: first, we should never harm anyone, and escaping would harm the state by violating its laws; second, by living in a state one tacitly agrees to its laws, and to violate the law is to break an agreement, which is wrong; and third, since the state is like a parent and teacher there is a duty to obey it, just as there is to obey parents and teachers. Each of these arguments appeals to a general rule or principle, namely (1) it is always wrong to harm anyone; (2) we should always keep our promises; (3) we ought to obey and respect parents and teachers. Based on this, Socrates draws a conclusion about what he should do in his particular situation. Analogous dilemmas are thrown up in Buddhist literature, but there seems little interest in pursuing the problems they raise in an attempt to deduce general principles of right conduct. Perhaps, as has been suggested, this is because Buddhist ethics is particularist and has an aversion to moral theories. Perhaps so, but particularism itself is an ethical theory and could have been "owned" as such by Buddhist writers if they had wished to identify with it.

Let me conclude this first part of my essay with a couple of objections to the line of argument I am developing. The first may be made by those suspicious of Western ideological imperialism and "the Western gaze," and who suggest that comparisons of this kind are methodologically flawed by virtue of being Orientalist, ethnocentric, and ahistorical. Surely, it might be said, the West should not be taken as the yardstick by which other cultures are measured. The suggestion has been made, for example, by the late Ninian Smart that if we turned the tables and set up an ethics based on the primacy of *dharma, karma, svadharma, karuṇā,* and *nyāya* and then proceeded to look for this in analytical Western ethics there would not be much left of Western ethics, especially in its modern form (as cited in Bilimoria, Prabu, & Sharma, 2007, p. 20).

This is a fair point, and I agree it would be foolish to reduce ethics to certain specific concepts, whether Western or Eastern, and expect to find them reproduced universally. For this reason I have tried to think of ethics more broadly as a scholarly discourse or branch of learning rather than a particular constellation of concepts and theories. What one should look for as evidence of an interest in moral philosophy, I believe, are not so much particular Western formulations like Kant's categorical imperative as indigenous solutions to the problem this concept was invented to solve, namely how to ground our moral obligations to others, a problem as real for Buddhists as for anyone else. We can see that Buddhism is concerned about others from its moral teachings, but what remains obscure is the philosophical foundation and justification for those concerns. This may take the form of theories of the kind found in the West or indigenous conceptual paradigms, but either way there is a substantive issue here for the ethicist or moral philosopher to grapple with. I think Charles Goodman (2009, p. 72) makes a helpful suggestion, which is that rather than conceiving our project in terms of the imposition of theories by Westerners, we should think of it as drawing up a chair at the table for Śāntideva and inviting learned Buddhist doctors like him to give us, through the rich legacy of their writings, their views on Western theories so that we can find a better way forward together. Similarly there seems no reason why discussions of Buddhist logic cannot be furthered by reference to Western and even Vulcan logic, so we may want to make a space at the table for Mr. Spock as well!

The second objection sounds a note of caution. I'm sure one of the first things that those of us who teach tell our students is that it's dangerous to generalize about Buddhism because you can find counterexamples to almost any statement, and no doubt some colleagues will already have thought of Buddhist thinkers or texts that can be considered as addressing issues falling under the rubric of moral philosophy. Śāntideva, whom I just referred to, is one likely candidate, and no doubt there are others dotted around the broad landscape of Buddhist history, particularly outside India. Here I would say only that while such examples may be found, I doubt they ever came to constitute a school, lineage, tradition, or body of thought within which individuals understood themselves as standing collectively as moral philosophers in the manner of other specialists in their respective domains, such as *vinayadharas* or specialists in monastic law.

1.3. Reasons for the Absence of Ethics

If what I have suggested so far is correct, and the subject of moral philosophy is not found in Buddhism, what might be the explanation? I am not entirely sure where the answer lies, but I will sketch out some possible lines of inquiry.

Perhaps the simplest explanation for this apparent lacuna in Buddhist intellectual life is to suggest that it is not a genuine gap, merely a temporary one waiting to be filled by the discovery of the relevant manuscripts that have so far been lost to history. This suggestion derives its plausibility from the voluminous nature of Buddhist texts in various languages and the fact that only a small percentage has as yet been translated. Perhaps, then, extended discussions of topics like virtue and justice do exist and are simply awaiting discovery. This hypothesis is an attractive one but is unlikely to be correct since manuscripts on all matter of other topics have come to light and it would be curious if only treatises on moral philosophy had selectively been lost. Given the absence of moral philosophy from the Buddhist curriculum, I think it is more likely that the material was never composed in the first place.

A second explanation for the different configuration of knowledge, not unrelated to the first, might also seek to play down the scale of the differences. It might be suggested that knowledge is distributed in different ways in different cultures and that while we may not find ethics represented as an independent discipline, ethical concerns will nevertheless be addressed elsewhere in different categories or under different rubrics. We simply have to look for them. There is some truth in this, and the voluminous moral fables and stories provide a locus or matrix that may embody ethical reflection to some degree. But this similarity cannot be pressed too far. The Greeks also had a rich literature of myths and stories, but in Greece philosophers used them as a starting point for the discussion of ethical conundrums and ultimately the development of comprehensive theories about the nature of the good life. The story of the ring of Gyges and the myth of Er in *The Republic* are examples of such points of departure. Again there are many distinct categories of knowledge that *are* common to East and West—such as epistemology, logic, metaphysics, psychology, grammar, and medicine—so even if Buddhism bakes its philosophical cake differently there are many common ingredients in the recipe.

While on the subject of the Greeks, a point to add here is that although I am concerned mainly with ethics, I think the hiatus in the Buddhist curriculum also extends to what Aristotle calls "the philosophy of human affairs," or political science, that is to say the whole field of human conduct or practical activity that is not directed merely to knowledge or truth. In his ethical writings Aristotle tried to bring out what goodness or virtue consists of and how it is reached at an individual level. At the same time he also believed that the opportunities to become good, and to help others become good, were located predominantly in the wider political community or state. For Aristotle, as for Plato, the state is above all a large and powerful educative agency that gives the individual increased opportunities for self-development and greater capacities for the enjoyment of life. Hence there was a need to explore questions concerning the organization of social and political forces and the laws and institutions that would secure and facilitate the development of good character. Aristotle understood ethics as a branch or subdivision of politics. For this reason in Greek literature of roughly the same period as the Pāli canon we find authors like Plato and Aristotle composing major treatises in which three interwoven themes—politics, justice, and ethics—are repeatedly taken up and explored. As Jay Garfield has noted, "It is a striking feature of Buddhist literature ... that despite the tremendous importance of the structure of a society and its institutions, including predominantly its political structures, in determining the conditions of human life and the possibilities for the attainment of both temporal and spiritual goods, there is very little—really nothing—in the Buddhist philosophical tradition by way of social or political theory. This must be regarded as a serious lacuna in a philosophical system that aims at characterizing the nature of suffering and of its elimination for a being who is eliminably social" (as cited in Bilimoria et al., 2007, p. 279). Mention must also be made here of the influence of Christianity in taking the Greek interest in justice in a social direction in defense of the poor and oppressed. "'Because of the oppression of the weak and the groaning of the needy, I will now arise,' says the Lord. 'I will protect them from those who malign them'" (Ps. 12:5). The Jewish and Christian god is a god of justice. As the Psalms say, "For the Lord is righteous; he loves righteous deeds; the upright shall behold his face" (Ps. 11:7). This Western concept of justice, so pivotal in ethics and politics, barely figures in Buddhist thinking beyond the recognition that sooner or later one gets what one deserves due to the action of karma. At some level, of course, justice is implicit in the underlying concept of dharma, but it was never raised from this diffuse background to the level of a distinct and autonomous concept,

Moving on to more practical ground, a third suggestion is that in the context of a system of religious (as opposed to secular) ethics, the need is for implementation rather than critique. The truth has been revealed by the Buddha, so now there is no longer any need to spend time in speculation. Furthermore would it not be a kind of disrespect or lack of faith in the enlightened teacher to question the moral guidelines he laid down? Given the Buddhist emphasis on pragmatism, moreover, and since human life is short and the path is clear, our energy is most profitably spent in proceeding along it as quickly as possible rather than questioning it. The Buddha's focus was ever on the practical and empirical, particularly the problem of human suffering and its resolution. In the famous simile of the man wounded by an arrow (MN.i.429) he makes the point that the urgent need is to remove the arrow and heal the wound rather than pursue a speculative inquiry into matters such as where the arrow came from, how far away the archer was standing, the trajectory of the shot, and such like. The Eightfold Path has been taught; what matters now is to follow it. In modern times this feature of Buddhist teachings has been echoed by the Thai scholar monk Phra Payutto, who has said, "In teaching the truth, only the things that can be put to use in this life are of value; the things that do not lead to beneficial results in this life, even if they may be true, are not taught" (as cited in in King, 2009, p. 197).

However, similar points could be made about other religions in which we *do* find a well-developed tradition of moral philosophy. The fact that moral teachings have been revealed by a divine teacher in a tradition that stresses the transitory nature of human existence and the urgent need to seek salvation has never been a bar to the development of a critical discipline of Christian ethics. Ethics has always been a central part of the Christian curriculum, and the Church Fathers and great medieval scholars were deeply interested in such matters. There have been countless university chairs in Christian ethics from the sixteenth century onward, but curiously there has never been a chair in Buddhist ethics in any university either in the East or the West. Indeed I think I am the only scholar in the world who has the dubious distinction of having the words "Buddhist ethics" in his job title, a fact that I am all too aware has done little to further my prospects of employment!

Furthermore, the argument concerning the essentially practical nature of Buddhist thought should not be pressed too far. Buddhism is an intellectually dynamic tradition, and from the earliest times there has been philosophical speculation on all kinds of matters, many of which have little direct connection with the practice of the Eightfold Path. Ironically, in view of the Buddha's injunction to focus on practical matters, it was metaphysical speculation concerning the ontological nature of dharmas that came to dominate the landscape of Buddhist philosophy from the early centuries onward.

A fourth suggestion is that certain key Buddhist metaphysical teachings may have hindered or undermined the development of ethics. Two teachings in particular are associated with this claim: the doctrines of no-self (*anattā*) and emptiness (*śūnyatā*). Thus it is sometimes said, with reference to the doctrine of no-self, that the absence of a self entails the absence of moral agency, thereby undermining the basis for ethics. In other words, how can there be morality without a moral agent? And with respect to emptiness it is often claimed in a reductionist way that since all phenomena are empty of self-essence, in the last analysis good and evil are not found, so there can be no foundation for moral values. These notions link up with a third interpretation of Buddhist doctrine, to the effect that enlightened persons, such as buddhas, transcend moral values, and in the last analysis the enlightened sage passes "beyond good and evil," so short-circuiting any need for the development of moral character. This reading, popular with early commentators like Schopenhauer and Nietzsche, has resurfaced as the epistemological problem of whether Buddhas deliberate or make moral choices. If they do not, as some commentators suggest, then there is a sense in which they might be said to have "transcended" ethical deliberation and judgment and in so doing rendered ethics redundant. Intriguing though such speculations are, I do not believe the answer to our question lies in this direction and think the lack of interest in moral philosophy has little to do with an internal conflict between Buddhist doctrines. Indeed such questions would themselves simply have provided more grist for the ethical mill, if one existed in the first place.

A fifth line of inquiry echoes Weber's view that Buddhism began as a renouncer tradition, so questions about the regulation of social life were never part of its agenda. The Buddha's early followers abandoned what the texts call "the cramped and dusty life of the householder" for the freedom to live outside the restrictive norms of ordinary society. In particular, Buddhism rejected the caste system and the tradition of religious law taught in Hindu *Dharmaśāstras*. Perhaps distaste for the complexity and rigidity of this system of social organization steered Buddhism away from a concern with issues concerning the rights and duties of individuals in society. Buddhism never sought to compete with Hinduism in this area and perhaps was content simply to leave the field to its rival. When rules became necessary for the conduct of monastic life it evolved its own regulations in the *Vinaya*. Monks are also often reminded to keep their eye on the ball, so to speak, and not allow themselves to be distracted from their religious practice. *Milinda's Questions*, for example, speaks of the training and duties of princes in some twelve specialist areas, and also of the business of merchants and workers. Monks, by contrast, are reminded that their focus should be on meditation and moral purity.

I find this line of explanation only partially persuasive, since Buddhism was never a movement consisting solely of renouncers and ascetics and soon became woven into the social fabric of the community. Nor do I accept the idea of an unbridgeable gap between the so-called kammatic and nibbanic forms of Buddhism in terms of which laity and monastics have antithetical soteriological goals. At the same time I think there is a sense in which the sociological separation between monk and layman has opened up a gap in ethical aspirations. Thus the high moral standards of the monk were seen as an ideal a layman might aspire to but not realistically expect to attain. My sense is that many lay Buddhists see even the Five Precepts as aspirational rather than normative, and I think the observation of some anthropologists that the Buddhist laity is more concerned with merit making than the observance of the precepts is not altogether incorrect. As S. J. Tambiah put it in his study of Thai spirit cults, "On the whole, ... we must conclude that merit-making through gift-giving is more valued than merit-making through the observance of Buddhist precepts and the pursuit of Buddhist ethical aims." "Strict observance of the precepts," he notes, has "little positive interest for the villager ... not because he devalues them but because they are not normally open to him." Such concerns, he concluded, "are thought to have pertinence primarily for the monk and secondarily for the aged approaching death" (1975, p. 148). Elsewhere in the same study he draws a contrast between the Islamic *mallam* as an interpreter of law and a judge and counselor of men in everyday affairs, while noting, "The Pali doctrinal texts of Buddhism have no implication for the laws and customs of everyday life of the laity" (p. 138). Given a social context in which moral ideals and the demands of daily life are seen as separate, there is clearly less opportunity for moral dilemmas to arise. I think this is one reason for the relative silence of Buddhism on a whole range of social and political issues, unlike, for example, Christianity and Islam, where canon or religious law is understood as having a direct bearing on social life. To take an example, the precept against taking life found in many religions is in clear conflict with the waging of war, but whereas Christianity and Islam, conscious of the dilemma, have developed theories of just war in an attempt to reconcile theory and practice, Buddhism has not. Perhaps the lay-monastic social division has tended to blunt the perception of ethical conflicts to the point where they do not generate sufficient dissonance to call for intellectual resolution. The laity do not feel the force of the discrepancy because they assume that high moral ideals are not applicable to them, and monks are not exposed to the kinds of situations where such conflicts typically arise. The ideals live in one world and the realities in another, and since the rubber never meets the road, so to speak, no ethical traction is generated.

To broaden the context beyond Buddhism and introduce a sixth and final reason, it is noteworthy that Indian philosophy as a whole has shown little interest in ethical theory. Pick up any introduction to the subject and this will be clear. Sue Hamilton's *Very Short Introduction to Indian Philosophy*, published in 2001, for instance, like many other such works, does a fine job of explaining the six *darśanas*, or traditional philosophical schools, but has not a single entry for "ethics" in the index. Other excellent treatments of Indian philosophy barely mention the subject at all. In this connection the late Bimal Matilal wrote, "Certainly, there exists a lacuna in the tradition of Indian philosophy. Professional philosophers of India over the last two thousand years have been consistently concerned with the problems of logic and epistemology, metaphysics and soteriology, and sometimes they have made very important contributions to the global heritage of philosophy. But except [for] some cursory comments, and some insightful observations, the professional philosophers of India very seldom discussed what we call moral philosophy today" (as cited in Bilimoria et al., 2007, p. 16). And in a recent major work on Indian ethics one of the editors, Joseph Prabu, writes, "It is obvious from what I have written that I agree with Matilal and others that there is indeed a lacuna in the tradition of Indian philosophy with respect to moral philosophy. That lacuna is precisely what motivated the present two volumes" (as cited in Bilimoria et al., 2007, p. 33). It seems clear that the Indian philosophical tradition established no precedent for Buddhism to follow in the field of moral philosophy. But why would this be? Philosophers from Hegel onward have suggested that the explanation lies in the supposedly different mentalities or modes of thought characteristic of East and West, describing Eastern thought as mythic or mystical in contrast to Western rationalism. Oswald Spengler (1918/1991, p. 176) attributed it to the imperative nature of ethics in the West:

> We say "thou shalt" in the conviction that so-and-so in fact will, can and must be changed or fashioned or arranged conformably to the order, and our belief both in the efficacy of, and in our title to give, such orders is unshakable. That, and nothing short of it, is, for us, morale.

In the ethics of the West everything is direction, claim to power, will to affect the distant. . . . You "shall," the State "shall," society "shall"—this form of morale is to us self-evident; it represents the only real meaning that we can attach to the word. But it was not so either in the Classical, or in India, or in China. Buddha, for instance, gives a pattern to take or to leave, and Epicurus offers counsel. Both undeniably are forms of high morale, and neither contains the will-element.

To these perhaps there will soon be added a genetic or neuroscientific explanation as to why problems in moral philosophy exercise the minds of some people but not others. However, I doubt anyone needs their neural pathways reconfigured in order to study ethics, and I am skeptical about general theories of diverging mentalities in different parts of the globe. I do not think there is any intellectual impasse that prevents Indians or Buddhists from doing moral philosophy. The reason they never got around to it is more likely because they never saw any need for it.

1.4. Conclusion

To sum up, and to restate the arguments just presented in order of importance, I think there are three main reasons we do not find ethics in the canons of Buddhist thought. The first is the absence of a precedent in Indian philosophy, where intellectual interest was channeled predominantly in the direction of metaphysics. This does not, of course, preclude the development of the subject at a later date, particularly since Buddhism was never afraid to break with tradition, and we still have to explain the absence of a Buddhist Aristotle who could have composed the root text that put the subject in the curriculum. The second reason is that in the West ethics was linked to political science and the development of democracy, while in India political authority remained predominantly in the hands of kings. Reflection on the form of life most conducive to human flourishing is pointless if there is no freedom to choose it. The third, sociological, point is that in Buddhism intellectual interest was focused on the needs of an elite community with a tightly controlled lifestyle, which, while perhaps not as otherworldly as sometimes painted, initially at least had little interest in social or political affairs and did not see the resolution of ethicopolitical dilemmas as part of its job description.

Given these different cultural histories it is hardly surprising that philosophical interest evolved along different lines in India and the West. After the Greek and Hellenistic period in the West, the involvement of Christianity in politics continued to fuel debates over ethical questions such as whether Christians should serve as soldiers in the Roman Army, and in what circumstances the use of force is justified. It is true that in Buddhism the concept of the *cakravartin*, or righteous ruler, provides a kind of placeholder for political theory, but this notion was not developed very far, at least in the classical period. Even the reign of the great Aśoka did surprisingly little to stimulate interest in the subject among Buddhist intellectuals. Perhaps the precedent for this was set by the Buddha himself in a well-known incident near the end of his life reported in the *Mahāparinibbāna Sutta* (DN.ii.72ff). King Ajātasattu, noting that "tathāgatas never lie" (*na hi tathāgatā vitathaṃ bhaṇanti*), sent his chief minister to seek the Buddha's opinion on his plan to attack the Vajjians. Rather than seizing the opportunity to deliver a clear condemnation of violence at the highest level, the Buddha sent back only a cryptic, noncommittal reply (see Ven. Pandita, 2011). This response was quite in keeping with his general strategy of avoiding conflict with the political authorities.

Whatever the merits of these various suggestions, it seems clear that it is only since Buddhism arrived in the West that a nascent discipline of Buddhist ethics has been established and we have also seen the appearance of "engaged Buddhism." Clearly there is some connection or overlap between them, and it can hardly be a coincidence that both these disciplines have arisen at roughly the same time. Without wishing to downplay the enormous contribution of Asian engaged Buddhist leaders, I tend to see engaged Buddhism and Buddhist ethics as corresponding broadly to two major branches of Western learning—politics and ethics—which in the past never developed in Buddhism to the same degree but are now surfacing as central concerns.

As we look to the future it is clear that adaptation is occurring. Buddhist leaders frequently have recourse to Western concepts such as human rights to express their concerns about global issues. Deciding how well this vocabulary expresses Buddhist ideals and values is the kind of task that will face students of Buddhist ethics in the coming decades. In connection with Buddhism and political science, Garfield has written, "The Mahayana canon prides itself on its perpetual openness to new texts. Perhaps it is time to make space in canonical collections of such mahapanditas as Locke, Rousseau, Mill, Jefferson, Dewy, Rawls and Habermas" (as cited in Bilimoria et al., 2007, p. 280).

I think we could do the same in the field of ethics and include *mahāpaṇḍitas* like Aristotle, Kant, and Mill. Perhaps then, as the discipline advances and begins to boldly go where no one has gone before, future generations of scholars in Buddhist studies will be able to say, "It's ethics, Jim, and just as we know it."

Abbreviations

AN   *Aṅguttara Nikāya*, volume and page in the Pali Text Society edition.

DN   *Dīgha Nikāya*, volume and page in the Pali Text Society edition.

MN   *Majjhima Nikāya*, volume and page in the Pali Text Society edition.

Ud.   *Udāna*, page in the Pali Text Society edition.

Vin.   *Vinaya*, volume and page in the Pali Text Society edition.

Note

1. Kelly (2011, p. 10) counts 337 *suttas* directed to lay people in his survey.

References

Bilimoria, P., Prabu, J., & Sharma, R. (2007). *Indian ethics*. Aldershot, UK: Ashgate.

Cooper, D. E., & James, S. P. (2005). *Buddhism, virtue and environment*. Aldershot, UK: Ashgate.

Goodman, C. (2009). *Consequences of compassion: An interpretation and defense of Buddhist ethics*. New York, NY: Oxford University Press.

Halkios, G. T. (2014). When the Greeks converted the Buddha: Asymmetrical transfers of knowledge in Indo-Greek cultures. In P. Wick and V. Rabans (Eds.), *Religions and trade: Religious formation, transformation and cross-cultural exchange between East and West* (pp. 65–115). Leiden and Boston: Brill.

Kelly, J. (2011). The Buddha's teaching to lay people. *Buddhist Studies Review* *28*(1), 3–78.

Keown, D. (Ed.). (2010). *Buddhist studies from India to America: Essays in honor of Charles S. Prebish*. London: Routledge.

King, S. B. (2009). Elements of engaged Buddhist ethical theory. In J. Powers & C. S. Prebish (Eds.), *Destroying Māra forever: Buddhist ethics essays in honour of Damien Keown* (pp. 187–206). Ithaca, NY: Snow Lion.

Pandita, Ven. (2011). The Buddha and the Māgadha-Vajjī War. *Journal of Buddhist Ethics, 18*, 124–144.

Saddhatissa, H. (1997). *Buddhist ethics*. Somerville, MA: Wisdom.

Schweitzer, A. (1967). *Indian thought and its development*. London: A. & C. Black.

Spengler, O. (1918/1991). *The decline of the West*. (C. F. Atkinson, Trans.). Abridged edition. New York: Oxford University Press.

Tambiah, S. J. (1975). *Buddhism and the spirit cults in north-east Thailand*. Cambridge, UK: Cambridge University Press.

Chapter 2

The Nature of a Buddhist Path

Bronwyn Finnigan[*]

2.1. Introduction

Is there a "common element" in Buddhist ethical thought from which one might rationally reconstruct a Buddhist normative ethical theory?

Each Buddhist philosophical tradition and each Buddhist practitioner seeks to be consistent with the Buddha's teachings. Central to the Buddha's teachings were the Four Noble Truths. They are the truths of or about suffering (*duḥkha*), the causes of suffering, the cessation of suffering, and the pathway to the cessation of suffering, namely the Eightfold Path. The Eightfold Path consists of right view, right intention, right speech, right action, right livelihood, right effort, right mindfulness, and right concentration. This might naturally suggest a common element from which one might rationally reconstruct a Buddhist normative ethical theory. There is much disagreement, however, about what this common starting point entails. Some emphasize the relation between the first and third Noble Truths and argue that Buddhist ethics is best construed in consequentialist terms (see Goodman, 2008; Siderits, 2003, 2007; Williams, 1998). On this view, an application, violation, or revision of moral rules of conduct is ethically adjudicated relative to whether it (directly or indirectly) causes the cessation of suffering. Others emphasize those elements of the Eightfold Path that call for the cultivation and expression of various attitudes and states of mind and argue that Buddhist ethics is better theorized as a form of virtue ethics (see Keown, 2001; Cooper & James, 2005). On this view, an application, violation, or revision of moral rules of

[*] Many thanks to Koji Tanaka for substantive input on an earlier draft of this paper.

conduct is ethically adjudicated relative to the attitude, quality, or state of mind thereby expressed. Some insist that no version of virtue ethics can provide a viable reconstruction of Buddhist ethics (see Kalupahana, 1976, p. 60; Goodman 2009; Siderits 2015). Others insist that Buddhist ethics cannot be consequentialist—or at least cannot be utilitarian (see Keown, 2001, p. 177). And yet others argue for integrating these theories into some form of virtue consequentialism (see Clayton, 2006).

I will argue that underlying these positions are at least two distinct ways of thinking about the nature of a path relative to a goal and thus two ways of conceiving the relation between the Eightfold Path and the goal of the Four Noble Truths. The first is what I call an instrumental analysis and the second a constitutive analysis. The terms *instrumental* and *constitutive* are not new to Buddhist ethics literature, although they are typically unanalyzed. They also tend to be associated with utilitarianism and virtue ethics, respectively.[1] I will closely analyze these notions and demonstrate how they provide for two distinct meta-ethical accounts of the normative grounds of Buddhist ethics. I will then raise some difficulties for linking these evaluative relations with particular normative theories and will propose instead to set aside the normative labels and focus on the evaluative relations themselves.

I will then turn to the question of whether one or other meta-ethical analysis better captures the spirit underlying Buddhist ethical thought. I will suggest that three criteria would need to be satisfied by a plausible reconstruction of Buddhist thought as an ethical theory, and I will give reasons to think that at least the first and third of these criteria might be satisfied by both the instrumental and constitutive analyses of the Buddhist path.[2] While I will not go so far as to establish that both analyses are equally legitimate, I will demonstrate that the tensions between these competing rational reconstructions are sufficiently complex to resist an easy resolution into a singular and homogeneous position on the nature of Buddhist ethics.

2.2. An Instrumental Analysis of the Buddhist Path

Defenders of consequentialist reconstructions of Buddhist ethics typically emphasize the cessation of suffering as the central and ultimate goal of Buddhist practice. While Buddhist texts may enjoin various actions, qualities, and practices, their evaluative status is thought to be ultimately justified in terms of their function in generating (producing, causing) the cessation of suffering. A traditional way of reconstructing this justificatory ground in normative ethical terms is as a (negative) form of utilitarianism.[3] This reconstruction presupposes an *instrumental* analysis of evaluative status that is broadly supervenient on causation. That is to say, the normative properties of actions, attitudes, and qualities of agents are conceived as depending only on whether they are means to some valued end and do not count as means to that end unless they are causally relevant to its production. This need not imply that x must be causally sufficient for y. It need merely imply that, for x to count as a means to y, x must (at the very least) be able to make a difference to whether y occurs. This is one way to articulate the utilitarian assumption that the value of the relevant x (action, motive, attitude) depends on the value of the end it generates or contributes to producing.[4]

At this point, however, utilitarian theories diverge. There is disagreement about the nature and class of relevant means (whether actions, motives, attitudes) as well as relevant ends (whether hedonic states or some other goods). There is also disagreement about whether the end must be actually or merely potentially generated for the evaluation of relevant means. The latter allows for the kind of hypothetical reasoning involved in decision making (which requires the ability to determine what *would be* the right thing to do prior to action and thus prior to actual outcomes). The former is beholden to actual outcomes, and thus evaluative status is only genuinely determined post fact. Utilitarians also disagree about how outcomes are evaluated, whether they need to be assessed in terms of some comparative and/or aggregative relation. For some, the value of the relevant x is judged on a case-by-case basis (as in act utilitarianism). For others, x has value only if it (actually or potentially) contributes to generating the best aggregation of valued outcomes. On traditional accounts, the best aggregation is equated with a maximal set. Thus x will have value only if it causes *more* of the valued outcomes than any (possible agent-relative) alternative. In such a case, evaluative status will not be determined simply by the nature of actual outcomes but in hypothetical relationship to alternative possibilities.[5] Despite these variations, most utilitarians accept an instrumental analysis of evaluative status whereby the value of x is determined solely by its (actual or potential) relation to some valued y. While the ethical evaluation of x depends on the *instrumental* aspect of this relation (which is essentially normative and travels in the reverse direction to causation, from end to means rather than cause to effect), the fact of this instrumental relation obtaining is supervenient on an underlying causal relation (the fact that x can at least make a difference to the occurrence of y). Independent of this instrumental-causal relation, x is devoid of value.

This much, I hope, is uncontroversial. Understood in these terms, it is easy to see how instrumental forms of consequentialism can be used to model the relation between the Eightfold Path and the Four Noble Truths. If we extend the class of relevant means to range over the various elements that compose the Eightfold Path, each can be justified as "right" and thus proper aspects of the path in relation to some end toward which they function as means. Extending the class of relevant means in this way can accommodate Buddhist talk about virtues and the cultivation of various qualities. They would each count as good and right to the extent that they count as means to the relevant end and thus are causally relevant to its production. It might also seem that the metaphor of a path naturally suggests this instrumental reading; that is, one follows a path because one is trying to get somewhere. To where is one trying to get? One natural answer is: to *nirvāṇa*. What is *nirvāṇa*? On a straightforward reading, it is the state of complete cessation of suffering as articulated in the third Noble Truth. One might further argue that the relevant end is not agent-relative (viz., cessation of suffering *for me*) but rather universal and agent-neutral (viz., cessation of suffering, in general and as such, for all sentient beings). How might this be justified? In relation to the Buddha's doctrine of no-self (*anātman*) and dependent origination (*pratītyasamutpāda*).

This instrumental analysis of the Four Noble Truths has several implications. First, as mentioned, the instrumental analysis supervenes on causation. When generalized as an analysis of a Buddhist path, it follows that a proper aspect of the path is one that is causally related to the cessation of suffering, and its value (as means) transfers from the value of this effect (as end). Suffering has negative value within a Buddhist framework; the cessation of suffering has positive value. On the assumption that the cessation of suffering is the goal of the Buddhist path, this instrumental analysis implies that wisdom (right view, right intention), modes of conduct (right speech, right action, right livelihood), and modes of mental discipline (right effort, right mindfulness, right concentration) have positive value (are "right" or "good") just in case and to the extent that they are causally related to this positive state of affairs. Independent of their causal contribution to the cessation of suffering, they are devoid of value.

Second, if we emphasize the causal underpinning of the instrumental relation, it might seem that once the end or goal is achieved, it no longer needs a cause, at which point the various aspects of the path will lose their purpose and value *qua means* and thus contributing causes. If this is right, it might then follow that once one achieves *nirvāṇa* (and thus the cessation of suffering) the relevant aspects of the path lose their point and value. Like a ladder no longer required once one has successfully climbed to one's destination, the Eightfold Path is neither required nor of value once the goal has been achieved.[6] This analysis might support certain transcendental accounts of *nirvāṇa* and Buddhahood. According to such accounts, the achievement of *nirvāṇa* is coextensive with a complete escape from *saṃsāra*, the cycle of karmic rebirth that is causally driven by actions and their effects. For some, when one achieves transcendent *nirvāṇa* one entirely transcends the realm of causally efficacious action (*karman*). It would seem to follow, however, that a transcendent Buddha is not an agent, and it thus makes no sense to speak of a Buddha's *good* (compassionate, virtuous) actions.[7] Those who wish to defend this view might find some meta-ethical support in the instrumental analysis of the Buddhist path. Realizing the right view, engaging in good modes of living and mindfulness might thus be understood as necessary means for ordinary human beings to achieve transcendent *nirvāṇa* but lose their point once this goal has been achieved. Once one achieves the goal of the Eightfold Path, once one has climbed to the top of the ladder, the ladder itself can be pushed away.

2.3. A Constitutive Analysis of the Buddhist Path

Those who defend a virtue-ethical reconstruction of Buddhism emphasize the development of certain attitudes, capacities, or mental states, the perfection of which is unified in a certain way of living as exemplified by a Buddha or a bodhisattva. While the Buddhist canon offers several competing lists of the relevantly perfected attitudes (*pāramitās*), most Buddhist traditions and schools consider the following four "immeasurables" (*apramāṇa*) to be characteristic of a Buddha's mode of living. They are loving-kindness (*maitrī*), compassion (*karuṇā*), empathetic joy (*mudita*), and equanimity (*upekṣā*).

How are we to understand these attitudes, their cultivation and perfection, in relation to the goal of a Buddhist path? The instrumental analysis might seem to provide the most straightforward answer. They have value to the extent that they are means to generating the various aspects of the Eightfold Path, which, in turn, have value as means to the cessation of suffering, which is the goal of the path. It is only insofar as loving-kindness, compassion, empathetic joy, and equanimity instrumentally cause us to (e.g.) engage in right actions, right speech, and right modes of livelihood that they have positive value, where the "rightness" of these modes of living is determined in instrumental-causal relation to the cessation of suffering.

This is not the only way to analyze the relevance of these attitudes, however. They might alternatively be analyzed in *constitutive* relation to the Buddhist path. There are several ways to analyze a constitutive relation. The sense relevant to this paper is not a mere mereological sum. Rather, like the instrumental relation, it has a goal or object that is the basis for determining value.

The crucial difference between these two kinds of relation, however, concerns whether the basis for determining value is an *external effect* or an *internal objective* of that which is evaluated.[8]

According to my analysis, the instrumental relation broadly supervenes on an underlying causal relation. If interpreted in efficient causal terms, it implies that the path and goal are separate and distinct, and thus the basis of evaluation is external to the evaluated act. This is standardly assumed by classical hedonic utilitarians, for instance, who take it to be uncontroversial that there is an ontological distinction between actions and the hedonic states produced as a result. If extended to the Buddhist context, it follows that engaged aspects of the Buddhist path are separate and distinct contributing causes of *nirvāṇa*, relative to the production of which they obtain positive evaluative status. In this way, the basis of evaluation (*nirvāṇa*) is external to the evaluated objects (the various aspects of the Eightfold Path).

According to a constitutive analysis, however, the goal of the Buddhist path is not a separate and distinct event that is caused by acquiring and engaging various modes of wisdom, living, and mental discipline. Rather it marks their point of perfection or completion (the *telos*) and thus is actualized in their very engagement. It is an objective that is internal to a way of living rather than an effect that is external to and caused by the living of such a life.

To grasp the difference, consider dancing and the goal of becoming a graceful dancer. This goal is *teleological* and *internal* to the relevant activity to the extent that it is actualized in the dancing rather than being an ontologically separate and distinct effect that is produced by dancing. Of course one might seek to bring about certain effects as a result of being able to dance gracefully (such as entertaining an audience or winning a prize). However, this is merely to say that an action can have multiple goals, some internal and some external. Where the instrumental analysis views the Eightfold Path as a road map to some destination that is separate and distinct from one's present location, the constitutive analysis views it as circumscribing a certain *way* of living, namely one that consists of mutually reinforcing modes of understanding, conduct, and mindful attention. The perfection of these distinct modes of living is analyzed in relation to the cultivation of the four immeasurable attitudes (loving-kindness, compassion, empathetic joy, and equanimity).

The four immeasurable attitudes themselves can be seen to provide a (partial) model for the constitutive analysis of a Buddhist "way" of living. In contemporary discussions, these attitudes are often characterized as emotions. The nature of emotions is a matter of contemporary dispute. Some characterize emotions as simple and basic sensations akin to the phenomenal experience of bodily, physical pain. This characterization is arguably equivalent to the Buddhist notion of *vedanā*. The four immeasurables are more complex. Each is an intentional attitude that is (a) about or directed toward certain kinds of objects construed in certain kinds of ways, and (b) made manifest in certain kinds of bodily and behavioral responses, where (a) and (b) are constitutive of the relevant attitude rather than related to it either as cause or effect. While the four immeasurable attitudes may involve phenomenally simple sensory elements, they are not reductively defined in terms of them. Arguably much the same can be said for many varieties of emotion.

To illustrate this point, consider fear. While the nature of fear is itself subject to much debate, it is arguably not (or not simply) a bare, simple sensation like bodily, physical pain. Rather there is reason to think that it is an intentional attitude that is about or directed toward some object. While the objects of fear differ between subjects, it is nevertheless the case that insofar as one experiences fear one is afraid *of* something. Moreover the object of fear is not necessarily identical with its originating or triggering cause. Consider, for instance, a subject who was once attacked by a dog and subsequently feels fear whenever they pass the building where the event occurred. It seems mistaken to say that they are afraid of the building. It seems more correct to say that they are afraid of dogs (or, perhaps, being harmed by dogs, which is an unwanted possibility about which the subject experiences some agential uncertainty or lack of control), where this fear is occasioned or triggered by the perception of the building (in causal association with the memory of being attacked, which may have been the originating cause of the attitude). Both the originating and triggering cause of the subject's fear of dogs are external to and, in principle, dissociable from this attitude. The object of the subject's fear, by contrast, that of which the subject is afraid (i.e., dogs) is internal and constitutive of the attitude itself.

Of course the relevant attitude would not be that of fear if it did not manifest in certain kinds of bodily and behavioral responses. Physiologically the manifestation of fear may involve a rush of adrenaline, phenomenologically apparent in the form of bodily trembling or increased heart rate or sweating. Behaviorally fear may manifest in variations of "freeze, flight, fight" responses as subtle as an almost indiscernible increase in walking pace or as obvious as crossing to the far side of the street. These bodily, behavioral manifestations are not separate and distinct causal effects of fear, understood as a simple and discrete bodily feeling. Rather the attitude of fear is a bodily, behavioral *orientation* toward (or mode of recoiling from) certain objects.[9]

The four immeasurables can be subjected to a similar analysis. Compassion is canonically characterized as an attitude of aspiring for the diminishment of suffering (in oneself or another). Loving-kindness is characterized as an attitude of aspiring for well-being and happiness (for oneself or another). Empathic joy is an attitude of rejoicing in the happiness of others, and the relevant sense of equanimity is a clear-minded, tranquil mode of responding to the vicissitudes of life. Each is an intentional attitude oriented to certain kinds of objects construed in certain kinds of ways. Each, once sufficiently cultivated, is robustly dispositional in the sense that they reliably manifest in relevant kinds of bodily, behavioral response in relevant kinds of circumstances. The ethical conduct (*śīla*) component of the Eightfold Path (i.e., right speech, action, livelihood) might be understood as three primary ways of manifesting these attitudes, and it is relative to the expression of these attitudes that they are justified as constituents of the path.[10]

2.4. A Qualification and Refinement of the Framing Question

I have claimed that a nominal distinction between instrumentality and constitution is widely used in Buddhist ethics literature and is broadly associated with utilitarianism and some form of virtue ethics. I have demonstrated how these evaluative relations, once analyzed, provide for two distinct meta-ethical accounts of the normative grounds of Buddhist ethics. There are complications, however, in associating these analyses with current work in normative ethical theory.

Contemporary consequentialists, for instance, do not limit themselves to instrumentalism about evaluative status but rather allow themselves a much broader range of evaluative relations. Indeed, some consequentialists include as consequentialist all evaluative relations that can be logically construed as consequential (i.e., all claims of conditional form). Take, for instance, ordered list theory and welfarist consequentialism. Unlike classical utilitarianism, these forms of consequentialism do not consider hedonic states of pleasure and pain to be the only intrinsic goods. Welfarist consequentialism, in particular, includes anything that is thought to have genuine and nonderivative significance for well-being. According to this view, some quality or character trait is considered good to the extent that it contributes to, and thus is properly constitutive of, well-being. Charles Goodman defends welfarist consequentialism as the best reconstruction of Buddhist ethics (see Goodman, 2009, 2015). It would seem, however, that the metaphysical foundation for this particular form of consequentialism better fits the constitutive analysis that we have attributed to virtue ethics than the instrumental analysis that underlies traditional forms of utilitarianism.

Consider also recent criticisms of virtue ethical reconstructions of Buddhism. While at one time quite popular, these reconstructions are now often strongly rejected as incompatible with the metaphysical underpinnings of Buddhist thought.[11] The reason typically offered is that Aristotelian forms of virtue ethics are person-centered in a sense that assumes some essential property of self as evaluative grounds of the various attitudes and character traits that are expressed in action, where this assumed essential self is taken to be incompatible with the Buddhist doctrine of no-self (*anātman*) (see Goodman, 2015; Siderits, 2015; Garfield & Priest, 2015). However, as with contemporary consequentialism, there is much diversity in contemporary virtue-ethical views. Not all contemporary forms of virtue ethics are Aristotelian, neo-Aristotelian, and/or person-centered.[12] And even those that are need not presuppose a permanent, unchanging, essential self (*ātman*) as the metaphysical foundation for evaluating character traits. Similar to welfarist consequentialism, it is open to defenders of, say, a neo-Aristotelian approach to ethics to insist that virtues are character traits that, when perfected or made excellent, mutually constitute and sustain well-being or a good way of living (*eudaemonia*). If plausible, a virtue-ethical reconstruction of Buddhist ethics on a constitutive metaphysical foundation need not be inconsistent with Buddhist views on the self.

Given these considerations, it might seem that there is no settled answer to the question of which contemporary normative ethical theory (consequentialism or virtue ethics) Buddhist thought best approximates. The comparative task cuts both ways; a proper answer is beholden to Western philosophy to provide a clearly demarcated basis for comparison. And Western philosophers disagree about how to distinguish these theories. This is not to deny the potential fruitfulness of comparative analysis in terms of *some* theory as defended by *some* Western philosopher. The above considerations nevertheless reveal the limitations of this approach.

An alternative approach to the framing question is to set aside the normative labels (consequentialism and virtue ethics) and focus instead on the instrumental and constitutive analyses that some versions of these normative theories metaphysically presuppose. While it is arguable that the difference between (e.g.) welfarist consequentialism and well-being-based virtue-ethical theory might, in the end, be merely verbal, the relational structures analyzed above are substantively distinct, diverging over whether the basis for evaluation is internal or external to what is evaluated and potentially requiring distinct arguments to justify.

If we take this alternative approach, however, we still face the question of whether one of these two analyses is more correct, is fundamental, or better represents the spirit of Buddhist ethical thought compared to the other.

Is there a singular best meta-ethical analysis of Buddhist thought, or are both analyses equally legitimate? How might we settle this issue?

One possibility is to assess whether either of these analyses is systematically consistent with Buddhist thought in various respects. There seem to be at least three respects in which such consistency could be tested

1. Consistency with the Buddha's teaching on the Four Noble Truths.
2. Consistency with at least some established Buddhist metaphysical and epistemological theory.
3. A plausible reconstruction of at least some canonical Buddhist text.

Why these three criteria? I take (1) to be obvious insofar as the Four Noble Truths comes closest to being a central tenet of Buddhism and thus a common element underlying the diversity of philosophical views. What about (2)? Since these meta-ethical analyses are contemporary philosophical *reconstructions* of the Buddhist path, their legitimacy will, in part, depend on whether they can be systematically related to more established philosophical views within the Buddhist canon. Historical Buddhist thinkers provided highly sophisticated metaphysical and epistemological analyses of the Buddha's teachings on non-self and dependent origination. It is reasonable to suppose that a plausible reconstruction of Buddhist ethics should be consistent with some such analysis. Indeed, as noted, we already see some rational reconstructions being dismissed precisely because they are taken to be inconsistent with these metaphysical commitments (on some understanding). Finally, it is reasonable to consider whether there is any textual evidence to support either analysis in canonical Buddhist texts that are explicitly concerned with ethical conduct. Hence (3).

Establishing whether and to what extent the instrumental and constitutive analyses of the Buddhist path are consistent with Buddhist thought in *all* three respects is a considerable task beyond the scope of what can be achieved here. Showing that they both satisfy (2), in particular, would require considering how these analyses might systematically relate to the complexities of some Buddhist philosophical system (Vaibhāṣika, Sautrāntika, Yogācāra, Madhyamaka).[13] The remainder of this essay will instead focus on providing some reasons to think that both of these analyses might satisfy (1) and (3).

2.5. Comparative Assessment: Consistency with the Four Noble Truths

The instrumental analysis seems to provide a relatively straightforward reading of the relation between the Eightfold Path and the Four Noble Truths.

On this view, each of the various elements that compose the Eightfold path is justified as "right" and thus a proper aspect of the path to the extent that they contribute to generating the end of *nirvāṇa*, where this is understood as the cessation of suffering.

By contrast, one might worry that the constitutive analysis of the Buddhist path either misconstrues or does not take seriously enough the centrality of suffering to the Four Noble Truths. Traditional metaphors of these truths conceive of the Eightfold Path as a remedy for the disease of suffering that is discovered by the first truth, the causes of which are diagnosed by the second and the possibility of a cure promised by the third. It could be objected that the constitutive analysis has little bearing on the actual cessation of suffering aside from an aspiration for its diminishment. That is, while the cessation of suffering might be an internal *objective* of various attitudes, it does not seem to be a state of affairs that is actually generated as a result of following the Buddhist path. If this is right, the constitutive analysis might seem to be disconnected from, and thus inconsistent with, this central Buddhist idea, the fact of which may give reason to prefer the instrumental analysis.

There are at least two approaches available to the defender of the constitutive analysis of the Buddhist path in response to this challenge. First, compatible with this analysis is the idea that increased perfection in attitudes is coextensive with an actual decrease in suffering. The cessation of suffering need not be conceived as a separate and distinct product of the modes of behavior constitutive of these attitudes but might be itself constitutive of a life oriented by these attitudes. It is arguable, for instance, that a life lived in ways that are compassionate, loving, empathetic, and equanimous is *pleasurable* in a distinct sense that is incompatible with suffering.

Even if this is granted, one might still worry that this response applies only to the agent who is living such a life without any direct implications for the cessation of the suffering of others. Given the Buddha's emphasis on dependent origination and nonself in his discussion of the second Noble Truth, it might be argued that an analysis of the third Noble Truth that did not extend the range of diminished suffering beyond the scope of an individual agent is problematic. The only way for this to be achieved, it could be argued, would be if the constitutive analysis were embedded within the instrumental analysis. That is, one might concede that the personal cessation of suffering might be constitutive of a certain perfected way of living but nevertheless insist that this way of living must be instrumentally related to the global cessation of suffering that is the proper scope of Buddhist concern. Moreover if utilitarianism is rightly associated with the instrumental analysis and virtue ethics with the constitutive, the above could be used as an argument to support an analysis of Buddhist virtue ethics as ultimately embedded within a utilitarian framework.

This is a difficult argument to rebut. However, while not decisive, it might be countered by arguing that the relevant kind of pleasure can transfer to the objects of these attitudes if one conceives of the modes of behavior that are constituents of these attitudes as purposive events with their own constitutive objectives. Consider, for instance, the simple act of smiling. A smile may result in making someone else smile, where this is a separate and distinct effect. However, the act of smiling also brings about a material change in the world, namely a particular change in facial expression (i.e., mouth curved upward, eyes shining, eyelids slightly narrowed). This material change is not a separate and distinct effect of smiling but is internal to it to the extent that the act of smiling would not count as the act of smiling unless this particular change in facial expression occurred.[14] The external effect of causing someone else to smile is dissociable from the act of smiling, but the particular change in facial expression is not. Now consider a more complex action that one might categorize as manifesting compassion, such as comforting a crying friend with a warm embrace. Some would argue that the compassionate action consists in the *attempt* to alleviate suffering; that is, what one is trying to achieve, irrespective of whether one succeeds. On this analysis, one counts as comforting one's friend irrespective of whether one's friend is actually comforted. It might alternatively be argued, however, that the friend *being comforted* and thus no longer suffering in the relevant respect marks the point of completion of the action of "comforting one's friend." As such, the friend being comforted is constitutive of or internal to the action itself. If this is plausible, then bringing about a material change in the object of one's compassion may be constitutive of a behavioral manifestation of this attitude rather than a separate and distinct effect of having acted compassionately. And if this is plausible, then bringing about the cessation of suffering in the objects of one's immeasurable attitudes might be considered constitutive of the behavioral expression of those attitudes rather than a separate and distinct causal effect.

This solution has some rather strong implications. In particular, it would seem that the nature of an action might be indeterminate until it reaches its point of completion. This may be neither apparent nor an issue for actions that have a short temporal duration, such as smiling and comforting friends. In such cases, the material change in the world occurs at the time of, or shortly after, the initiation of the action, and thus the action is complete almost as soon as it is begun.[15] If the object of compassion is the alleviation of suffering of *all* sentient beings, however, it would seem to follow that an action aimed at this objective would not reach its point of completion and thus not come to be until all suffering has been alleviated. This seems unintuitive. The concern might be alleviated, however, if this complex action is identified as a temporally extended *mode of living* analyzable into more discrete action parts with their own constitutive objectives. Hence, while the mode of living that manifests *mahākaruṇā* (i.e., great compassion oriented toward the alleviation of suffering of all sentient beings) may not be properly instantiated until the point at which all suffering is alleviated, this temporally extended mode of living might nevertheless be analyzed into more discrete and relatively more quickly completable action parts, one of which may consist in comforting a crying friend with a warm embrace.

Clearly the story of how the constitutive analysis is consistent with the Four Noble Truths is more complicated than the story that provided for the instrumental analysis. But complicated does not mean false or unjustified. If coherent, then there is reason to think that the constitutive analysis can satisfy (1) for counting as a plausible analysis of Buddhist ethical thought.

2.6. Comparative Assessment: Textual Analysis

I shall close by briefly considering whether our two meta-ethical analyses might be consistent with *some* canonical Buddhist texts concerned with ethical conduct and thus whether they can satisfy (3).

Śāntideva's *Bodhicaryāvatāra* (BCA) is a touchstone for recent reconstructions of Buddhist ethical thought as a normative theory. Śāntideva is a Madhyamaka Buddhist thinker in the Mahāyāna tradition, and this text is thought to best exemplify Mahāyāna values. Central to this tradition is the notion of a bodhisattva and an interpretation of the Eightfold Path as a *bodhisattva* path. A bodhisattva, according to this tradition, is one who has resolved to remain in the realm of suffering (*saṃsāra*) to help liberate all sentient beings from suffering.

It might seem that certain passages in BCA are best read as suggesting a constitutive analysis of the bodhisattva path. A central theme of this text is the cultivation of an Awakened Mind (*bodhicitta*), which is achieved by completing two stages in mental development. The first stage is called "aspirational *bodhicitta*" (*praṇidhicitta*, BCA 1.15), which consists of the resolution to become a bodhisattva for the sake of releasing all sentient beings from suffering. Śāntideva describes the person with this attitude as being like one who "desires to go" (1.16) but is not yet going, like one who has resolved to live compassionately but does not yet express compassion in their conduct. By contrast, the person "who is going" and thus actually expresses compassion in their conduct is identified as "engaging *bodhicitta*" (*prasthānacitta*, 1.15). Śāntideva characterizes this second stage of *bodhicitta* as a superior level of moral development (1.17). While not entirely clear in the text, the transition from aspirational to engaging *bodhicitta* arguably involves transforming the initial resolution (*to be* compassionate, *to live* compassionately) into the intentional (dispositional and thus behavioral) attitude of compassion (*karuṇā*) and eventually great compassion (*mahākaruṇā*) supported by one's gradual attainment of right understanding and reinforced by ever-deepening meditative practices. The goal of the bodhisattva path may thus seem to be internal to the practices and attitudes that constitute such a way of living in the sense that it seems to mark their point of perfection.

Further support for this constitutive analysis of BCA might be found in Śāntideva's response to the question "If the perfection of generosity consists in making the universe free from poverty, how can previous Protectors have acquired it, when the world is still poor, even today?" (5.9). Answer: "The perfection is the mental attitude itself" (5.10). It is also reinforced by Śāntideva's reflections on the limitations of individual agency. "Where is there hide to cover the whole world? The wide world can be covered with hide enough for a pair of shoes alone" (5.13); "Since I cannot control external events, I will control my mind" (5.14). *Bodhicitta*, on this analysis, does not cause one to become a bodhisattva. *Perfected bodhicitta* (i.e., the fully Awakened Mind) is characteristic of the perfected mode of living that is conveniently designated as that of a bodhisattva.

Despite this textual evidence for a constitutive analysis of the bodhisattva path, BCA also provides textual support for the view that the evaluative status of the "bodhisattva way" is ultimately justified in instrumental relation to the cessation of suffering thereby caused. This is implied by Śāntideva's remark "The greatness of the intent comes not from itself but rather from its effect, and so the greatness is equal" (5.14). Śāntideva also suggests that we can overlook a moral code at the time of giving (5.42), where this seems to imply that the grounds for evaluative status might be *external* to (rather than constitutive of) the perfection of generosity, which better fits an instrumental analysis. Finally, his argument for altruism in chapter 8, based on the nonexistence of a permanent self, is perhaps most intuitively read in instrumental terms. He writes, "The continuum of consciousness, like a queue, and the combination of constituents, like an army, are not real. The person who experiences suffering does not exist. To whom will the suffering belong? Without exception, no sufferings belong to anyone. They must be warded off simply because they are suffering. Why is any limitation put on this? If one asks why suffering should be prevented, no one disputes that! If it must be prevented, then all of it must be. If not, then this goes for oneself as for everyone" (8.101–103).[16]

Much contemporary discussion about the nature of Buddhist ethics focuses on negotiating and attempting to systematize Śāntideva's various remarks. Some of these tensions might be construed as orienting around the issue of whether Śāntideva's *Bodhicaryāvatāra* presupposes an instrumental or constitutive analysis of the bodhisattva path. However these particular interpretive issues are resolved, they need not be taken to decisively settle which analysis of the nature of a Buddhist path is the best reconstruction of *Buddhist* thought on ethical matters. Matters appear quite different if we take a different Buddhist text as our point of departure.

Consider, for instance, the less studied and much more esoteric writings of the Japanese Zen Buddhist Dōgen.[17] When training as a Tendai monk, Dōgen became puzzled about the doctrine of original enlightenment (本覚 *hongaku*). According to this Tendai doctrine, all sentient beings have buddha-nature, where this is understood as the view that all sentient beings are already and primordially enlightened. This idea is derived from the *Tathāgatagarbha* tradition of Buddhist thought rather than the *Prajñāpāramitā* tradition that informs the Madhyamaka of Śāntideva. If one were to accept this Tendai idea of buddha-nature, Dōgen puzzled, what is the point of following a Buddhist path aimed at achieving enlightenment given that the relevant causal effect appears to have been already achieved?[18] Indeed the very attempt to achieve that which is already possessed would seem to be counterproductive given that it may actually diminish or lead us away from our primordial buddha-nature. These reflections did not lead Dōgen to reject Buddhist practice, however. Rather they inspired the idea that enlightenment is *not* a transcendental state that lies beyond ordinary life and is caused by following a Buddhist path. Rather it manifests *in* everyday living. "When you find your place where you are, practice occurs, actualizing the fundamental point. When you find your way at this moment, practice occurs, actualizing the fundamental point" (in Tanahashi, 1985, p. 72). Dōgen might be reasonably understood as rejecting the instrumental analysis of the Buddhist path in favor of a constitutive analysis. He does not deny that enlightenment is something to be achieved. Rather this achievement is conceived as an actualization that occurs in one's ordinary mode of living and not as a causal effect of having lived a certain kind of life. "In your study of flowing, if you imagine the objective to be outside yourself and that you flow and move through hundreds and thousands of worlds, for hundreds, thousands, and myriads of eons, you have not devotedly studied the buddha way" (p. 80).

Clearly much more would need to be said to *establish* that Śāntideva and Dōgen actually presupposed one or other of the above analyses of the Buddhist path. Nevertheless, from this brief reflection it seems clear that the instrumental and constitutive analyses of the Buddhist path could each be rendered systematically consistent with some canonical Buddhist texts concerned with ethical conduct. This is not to say that both *are* equally legitimate. Nor is it to pass judgment on the respective legitimacy of a Madhyamaka Buddhist conception of ethical matters, inspired by the *Prajñāpāramitā* tradition, over Zen Buddhist conceptions, inspired by the *Tathāgatagarbha*. It does suggest, however, that adjudicating between these two analyses by reference to Buddhist canonical texts may well depend on how one negotiates the philosophical and cultural issues that differentiate Buddhist traditions. It also shows the dangers of unduly focusing on a limited set of examples. Even if compelling arguments could be provided to show that (e.g.) Śāntideva's *Bodhicaryāvatāra* is most compellingly read in terms of one or the other of the above analyses of the Buddhist path, further argument is required to justify why one should prefer Śāntideva's analysis over that of (e.g.) Dōgen. These issues cannot be readily resolved by the simple assumption of the Buddha's teachings of the Four Noble Truths and Eightfold Path.

2.7. Conclusion

Contemporary philosophers engaged in the project of explaining the nature of Buddhist ethics as a normative ethical theory often assume that there is a "common element" underlying Buddhist thought that ultimately determines what matters with respect to the application, flexibility, and potential revision of rules of ethical conduct. This core element of Buddhist ethics is assumed to be grounded in the relation between ethical conduct and the goal of the Eightfold Path as characterized by the Four Noble Truths.

In this paper I have demonstrated that there are (at least) two distinct ways of analyzing the nature of a path relative to a goal, where these analyses afford two distinct ways of understanding the nature of a Buddhist path. I have also provided reasons for thinking that both can be rendered plausible in terms that are systematically consistent with the Buddha's teaching of the Four Noble Truths and canonical Buddhist texts concerned with ethical practice. This is not to say that, in the final analysis, both analyses of the nature of a Buddhist path and thus all rational reconstructions grounded on their bases are equally legitimate. There may well be a correct position on these issues. Nevertheless I have established that the tensions between these competing rational reconstructions are sufficiently complex to resist an easy resolution into a singular and homogeneous position on the nature of Buddhist ethics.

Abbreviation

BCA Śāntideva, *Bodhicaryāvatāra*. Translations from K. Crosby & A. Skilton in Śāntideva (1998).

Notes

1. The most focused discussion of this distinction can be found in Dreyfus (1995), who employs it to articulate a virtue-ethical analysis of Buddhist thought. The distinction can also be found in Keown (2001) and Clayton (2006).
2. I also believe that the second can be satisfied by both analyses but shall not argue the point in this paper.
3. For a recent defense of this view, see Siderits (2015).
4. Although I will use the language of consequents or ends being "generated" or caused, it is important to recognize that a causal effect is not identical to a consequent or end. A consequent is a component of a conditional and thus irreducibly related to an antecedent. As such it marks a logical relation rather than a causal relation. Nevertheless talk of "actual" or "potential" consequents or ends tends to be framed as a concern with actual or probable products or outcomes. I shall simply note this ambiguity without attempting to resolve it.
5. Some utilize this structure to advance forms of rule utilitarianism, according to which an act is right if it follows a rule that *would* bring about better outcomes *if* everyone followed it than otherwise.
6. This is aside from the value and purpose that the Buddhist path may have *for someone else* who has yet to achieve the goal of the path. However, nuance is still perhaps needed here. It is arguable, for instance, that purpose and value can come apart. A constituent of the Eightfold Path might still have value even if it no longer has a purpose in achieving the goal relative to which it is evaluated. However, this may depend on whether one thinks a causal relation ceases once its effect is fully actualized and how this bears on the status of some x as means. For instance, if some x must be *able* to make an *actual* causal difference to y's occurring in order to count as a means to y, this condition cannot be satisfied in the case of y's being fully actualized. As a result there is no basis for the transference of value from end to means and hence that x loses value once y occurs. If, however, it is sufficient that x must have been able to make such a difference (or *did* make such a difference) to count as a means to that end, then this problem can be averted.
7. For a discussion of some problems that arise for this view, see Finnigan (2010–2011, 2011a, 2011b).

8. Although I am stipulating the terms *constitutive* and *instrumental* to the analyses provided in this paper, I recognize that these terms are not always used in these stipulated senses. For instance, *instrumental* is sometimes used to characterize all conditional relations and thus could be used to describe *both* analyses of goal-directed activities. *Constitutive* can also be used to cover both (e.g., "*x constitutes* the path because it is internally/externally related to *y*").

9. This is not to deny that the ways in which fear manifests may differ between subjects and may be complicated in various ways when other attitudes are simultaneously triggered.

10. How might the remaining aspects of the Eightfold Path fit with this analysis? The wisdom components (*prajñā*) might be justified in relation to the intentional object of these attitudes. The notion of intention (*saṃkalpa*) has a broad interpretive range. *Right* intention might be plausibly construed as correctness in the intentional object toward which one's attitudes are oriented, where the obtaining of such correctness is influenced by obtaining the right view (*dṛṣṭi*). While the *value* of right view and intention are justified relative to *truth*, one might argue that they are *relevant* constituents of the Eightfold Path insofar as they help shape the attitudes that are expressed in our modes of living. The concentration components (*samādhi*) might be similarly justified by their role in facilitating the cultivation of wisdom and thus correction of the intentional objects of the attitudes expressed by modes of ethical conduct.

11. According to Goodman (2009), for instance, no version of virtue ethics can provide a viable model of Buddhist ethics. A similar view is advanced by Siderits (2015).

12. While some Buddhist scholars note this point, few go on to actually engage the relevant differences in contemporary virtue-ethical theory. Examples of non-Aristotelian approaches to virtue ethics can be found in Phillipa Foot (2001), Christine Swanton (2003), Lisa Tessman (2005).

13. It may also require considering the viability of these respective analyses. For instance, Madhyamaka thinkers strongly critique Vaibhāṣika and Sautrāntika. If one or other of our analyses can be justified as consistent only with Sautrāntika, for instance, the question will remain as to whether that is sufficient justification in view of these Madhyamaka critiques. These issues become very complicated very quickly.

14. Similarly, dancing would not count as dancing unless there was some kind of movement in a body, which is a material change in the world.

15. The idea of an action reaching its point of completion by achieving its objective need not be identified with a stopping point. The act of leisurely strolling might be said to achieve its objective at the very point at which it is begun, where this fact does not mark its stopping point. Similarly with the act of smiling; one does not necessarily cease smiling at the point at which one's face changes its demeanor in the relevant way.

16. There is much controversy about how these verses are best analyzed. For a detailed discussion of the relevant issues, see Cowherds (2015) and Finnigan (in press).

17. I owe the following analysis of Dōgen to Koji Tanaka.

18. "Both exoteric and esoteric teachings explain that a person in essence has true dharma nature and is originally a body of 'Buddha nature.' If so, why do all buddhas in the past, present, and future arouse the wish for and seek enlightenment?" (translated and quoted in Tanahashi, 1985, p. 4).

References

Clayton, B. (2006). *Moral theory in Śāntideva's Śikṣāsamuccaya: Cultivating the fruits of virtue*. New York: Routledge.

Cooper, D. E., & James, S. P. (2005). *Buddhism, virtue and environment*. Hants Burlington, UK: Ashgate.

The Cowherds. (2015). *Moonpaths: Ethics and emptiness*. Oxford: Oxford University Press.

Dreyfus, G. (1995). Meditation as ethical activity. *Journal of Buddhist Ethics, 2*, 28–54.

Finnigan, B. (2010–2011). Buddhist meta-ethics. *Journal of the International Association of Buddhist Studies, 33*(1–2), 267–297.

Finnigan, B. (2011a). A Buddhist account of ethical agency revisited: Reply to Garfield and Hansen. *Philosophy East and West, 61*(1), 183–194.

Finnigan, B. (2011b). How can a Buddha come to act? The possibility of a Buddhist account of ethical agency. *Philosophy East and West, 61*(1), 134–160.

Finnigan, B. (in press). Madhyamaka ethics. In D. Cozort & J. M Shields (Eds.), *Oxford handbook of Buddhist ethics*. Oxford: Oxford University Press.

Foot, P. (2001). *Natural goodness*. Oxford: Clarendon Press.

Garfield, J., & Priest, G. (2015). Why ask about Madhyamaka and ethics? In Cowherds, *Moonpaths: Ethics and emptiness* (pp. 1–6). New York: Oxford University Press.

Goodman, C. (2008). Consequentialism, agent-neutrality, and Mahāyāna ethics. *Philosophy East and West, 58*(1), 17–35.

Goodman, C. (2009). *Consequences of compassion: An interpretation and defence of Buddhist ethics*. New York: Oxford University Press.

Goodman, C. (2015). From Madhyamaka to consequentialism: A road map. In Cowherds, *Moonpaths: Ethics and emptiness* (pp. 141–158). Oxford: Oxford University Press.

Kalupahana, D. (1976). *Buddhist philosophy: A historical analysis*. Honolulu: University of Hawai'i Press.

Keown, D. (2001). *The nature of Buddhist ethics*. Hampshire, UK: Palgrave Macmillan.

Śāntideva. (1998). *Bodhicaryāvatāra*. (K. Crosby & A. Skilton, Trans.). Oxford: Oxford University Press.

Siderits, M. (2003). *Empty persons: Personal identity and Buddhist philosophy.* Aldershot, Burlington, UK: Ashgate.

Siderits, M. (2007). *Buddhism as philosophy.* Aldershot, Burlington, UK: Ashgate.

Siderits, M. (2015). Does Buddhist ethics exist? In Cowherds, *Moonpaths: Ethics and emptiness* (pp. 119–140). Oxford: Oxford University Press.

Swanton, C. (2003). *Virtue ethics.* New York: Oxford University Press.

Tanahashi, K. (Ed.). (1985). *Moon in a dewdrop.* New York: North Point Press.

Tessman, L. (2005). *Burdened virtues: Virtue ethics for liberatory struggles.* New York: Oxford University Press.

Williams, P. (1998). *Altruism and reality: Studies in the philosophy of the Bodhicaryāvatāra.* London: Curzon.

Chapter 3

Buddhist Moral Thought and Western Moral Philosophy

Christopher W. Gowans

3.1. Introduction

It is commonly observed, often with perplexity, that there is no obvious and explicit moral philosophy in Indian Buddhism, such as is commonly found in Western philosophy, despite the fact that a moral outlook is at the heart of Indian Buddhism and there are considerable and sophisticated discussions of metaphysical and epistemological issues in this tradition.[1] Broadly speaking, there are two kinds of response to this observation in contemporary philosophical discussions of Buddhist moral thought. First, some persons argue that an analysis of texts from this tradition shows that at least some Buddhists were implicitly committed to some moral philosophy. Important instances of this response are those who have argued that these Buddhists were committed to a theory of what makes an action morally right—usually some form of consequentialism or virtue ethics (or a combination of the two). Second, other persons argue that an analysis of these texts shows that Buddhists were not committed to any such moral philosophy and in fact were opposed to the development of a moral philosophy of this kind in favor of a different approach. According to this response, Buddhists were not even implicitly committed to consequentialism, virtue ethics, or any other Western moral theory. Though there is considerable diversity across the many schools, figures, and texts of Buddhism, I will argue that overall the second of these two lines of interpretation is closer to the truth than the first.

The paper has three parts. First, I will raise objections to both consequentialist and virtue ethics interpretations of Buddhism. Second, I will explain what may be called the nontheoretical stance of Buddhism with respect to moral thought.[2] Third, I will argue that we should be less perplexed about the absence of moral philosophy in Buddhism than some people are.

3.2. Virtue Ethics and Consequentialist Interpretations of Buddhist Ethics

In the Western tradition, moral philosophy is commonly taken to be an analysis of the meaning, structure, and/or justification of some aspects of moral or ethical life, an analysis that aspires to be general, abstract, systematic, and coherent—what is often called a moral (or ethical) theory. Such theories emphasize the intellectual values of consistency and overall coherence, carefully drawn distinctions, rigorously and explicitly formulated arguments, and responses to objections. Consequentialism and (some forms of) virtue ethics are examples of moral theories in this sense. The development and defense of moral theories have been central features of Western moral philosophy since the time of Socrates.

In contemporary discussions of normative ethics, moral theories about moral rightness are classified in different ways. A common classification that is often presupposed in interpretations of Buddhist moral thought is the threefold division of consequentialist, deontological, and virtue theories. These theories are sometimes introduced in this way: consequentialism focuses on the value of consequences of actions; deontology stresses moral duties; and virtue ethics emphasizes moral virtues. However, by itself this brief statement is not a very useful characterization. Sidgwick, Kant, and Aristotle are widely thought to be paradigmatic proponents of consequentialism, deontology, and virtue ethics, respectively. But each of them thinks that consequences, duties, and virtues all have some ethical importance in some contexts. The same may be said of most classical exponents of Indian Buddhist moral thought.

For the purpose of this discussion, a more adequate characterization would need to depict the three theories in terms of what has primary importance and what has secondary importance. A natural and common form of such a characterization presupposes:

> *Ethical Foundationalism.* Ethics has a structure such that some ethical principle or concept is fundamental in the sense that it is not derived from any other ethical principles or concepts, and all other ethical principles or concepts are derived from it.

According to ethical foundationalism, the fundamental ethical principle or concept need not be self-evident. It could be derived from something else. But it cannot be derived from any other ethical principles or concepts.

If ethical foundationalism were correct, then the three ethical theories might be understood as theories of morally right action in the following way (adapting a formulation of Rosalind Hursthouse):

- *Consequentialism* is the view that an action is morally right if and only if, and because, it has appropriately valuable consequences.
- *Deontology* is the view that an action is morally right if and only if, and because, it is done out of respect for or in accord with our moral duties.
- *Virtue ethics* is the view that an action is morally right if and only if, and because, it is what a virtuous agent would characteristically do.[3]

So understood, a consequentialist could maintain that duties and virtues are important, but their importance is entirely derived from their relationship to the value of consequences of actions. And similarly for the other theories. On this characterization, it is at least prima facie plausible to suppose that Sidgwick, Kant, and Aristotle accepted something close to consequentialism, deontology, and virtue ethics, respectively (leaving complications aside). All three speak of one another's concepts, but they disagree about the proper ordering of these concepts.

When we turn to the classical Indian Buddhist sources in both the Theravāda and Mahāyāna traditions, though ethics and reflection on ethics have obvious and central importance, it is not evident that moral philosophy, understood as centered on the development of moral theories, has much, if any, importance. Some particular ideas and passages may seem to pertain to moral theory, but it is difficult to see that they clearly presuppose or are manifestations of consequentialism, deontology, or virtue ethics as just defined. Those who have questioned the attribution of such theories to the classical Buddhist authors were right to do so. I will first argue for this position by reviewing and commenting on the dialectical structure of the debate about these interpretations.

There are several reasons why it might be thought that Buddhists have been committed to a form of virtue ethics. The most important is that most Buddhist texts pertaining to morality are obviously and overwhelmingly about the cultivation and perfection of moral character. In particular they are concerned with the development of moral virtues such as compassion, loving-kindness, generosity, and patience. One of the central reasons virtue ethics has gained such prominence in recent years is the perceived value of its emphasis on moral character, understood as a multifaceted concept involving dispositions, thoughts, attitudes, motives, intentions, feelings, and desires as well as actions. Buddhist ethical texts also stress the importance of properly developing at least many of these features. These texts are as much concerned with the development of moral character, understood in terms of these features, as they are with outward actions and their consequences.

Many interpretations of Buddhist ethics as a form of virtue ethics also stress similarities with Aristotle's eudaemonistic form of virtue ethics.[4] Many obvious differences from Aristotle are not denied, but the formal structure of seeing human life as oriented toward a final end, understood as eudaemonia and constituted by a life of virtue, has been interpreted as having affinities with the pursuit of the ideals of the arahant and the bodhisattva. In all these cases, moral development involves achieving wisdom, virtue, and a positive state of mind.

This is not an implausible suggestion as long as it is realized that Aristotle's eudaemonism does not imply the view that the virtuous agent is basically self-interested, committed to virtue only insofar as it promotes his, and only his, happiness or perfection. This would be seriously at odds with Buddhist ideals. However, this is not Aristotle's ideal either. For example, his virtuous agent cares about the well-being of his friends for their own sake and is prepared to give his life in defense of his city. This is not the universal compassion of the bodhisattva, but neither is it the pursuit of mere self-interest as ordinarily understood. So there is a good deal to be said for the virtue ethics interpretation.

There are also several reasons why it might be supposed that Buddhists have been committed to a form of consequentialist ethics.[5] The most important is that virtually everywhere in Buddhist ethical texts the elimination of suffering is obviously and overwhelmingly the dominant value and concern. Moreover, at least sometimes, promoting happiness is also important. In addition, it is clear that these concerns extend equally to all sentient beings. This would seem to imply that the basic structure of Buddhist moral thought is consequentialist: morally right actions are those that minimize suffering and (perhaps) maximize happiness. There are passages that appear to confirm this interpretation. For example, we are told that it would be justified to cause some suffering in order to prevent greater suffering and that a moral prohibition may sometimes be broken if doing so will have beneficial effects. Such thoughts are precisely those that would be expected of someone committed to consequentialism. Hence, there is a great deal to be said in favor of a consequentialist interpretation.

A deontological interpretation of Buddhist ethics has attracted little support. In one way this is surprising in view of the importance assigned to following moral rules in Buddhism, both rather general rules such as the Five Precepts and the many, more specific ones such as those that govern the monastic communities. These rules would seem to have at least sufficient kinship to moral duties as to invite a deontological interpretation. However, because of the significant role of virtues and consequences highlighted in the first two interpretations, it has evidently not been deemed plausible to suppose that the whole of Buddhist ethics could be fundamentally a matter of respecting the rules it puts forth. Moreover Kant is most closely associated with deontological theories, and Kant's autonomous agent, acting on the basis of pure practical reason, appears to be deeply at odds with the Buddhist understanding of human beings.

In any case, the main debate about which normative theory Buddhists were committed to has been between the virtue ethics interpretation and the consequentialist interpretation, both of which would need to account for the role of rules in Buddhism. Hence, my focus is primarily on this debate.

Such in brief are the central rationales for the main interpretations of Indian Buddhists as implicitly accepting some Western normative moral theory. But do we have reason to think that these Buddhists were concerned with "the foundations and conceptual structure" of ethics (Keown, 1992, p. 196)? Did they think that ethics has a "theoretical unity" (Goodman, 2009, p. 59)? In particular, did they accept, or were they committed to accepting a moral theory with a foundationalist structure such as virtue ethics or consequentialism? If they did, they certainly did not explicitly defend this position. The ethical texts we have from Indian Buddhism are not philosophical treatises that systematically defend moral theories. To my knowledge there are no texts in Indian Buddhism that look much like the well-known ethical treatises of Aristotle, Sidgwick, or Kant. Śāntideva's works perhaps come closest, but this is still not very close.[6] For whatever reason, the Buddhist writers in this tradition apparently did not think it was important to develop and defend a systematic moral theory. The absence of any explicit defense of a moral theory is by itself a reason to doubt that there must be some sense in which they accepted one.

It might be said that they tacitly accepted such a theory even if they did not consciously realize it. After all, as already seen, it is obvious that they put forward positions that clearly seem to raise the question whether virtues or consequences (or perhaps rules) are fundamental. But these positions are likely to raise this question only in the minds of persons who already think in terms of ethical foundationalism or something similar. From the standpoint of contemporary philosophy, it may seem obvious to many persons that there must be some philosophical principle or concept that is fundamental. But it is hard to see that the classical Indian Buddhist thinkers shared this standpoint. Without attributing to them a presupposition such as ethical foundationalism, there is little reason to think these figures must have assumed that one or the other of these ethical theories is correct. Though many of them had the philosophical sophistication to develop such a theory, they evidently lacked an interest in doing so.

In the contemporary debate about these interpretations, various philosophical moves have been or might be proposed to defend one or another of them. To some extent the moves themselves might be challenged for their philosophical cogency. However, aside from this issue, from the point of view of interpretation there needs to be some reason to attribute the tacit acceptance of such moves to these Buddhist thinkers.

In opposition to the consequentialist interpretation, it may be objected that the great emphasis on moral character, and in particular on the importance of mental states such as intentions and motives, and whether or not they are wholesome or skillful (*kusala*), shows that Buddhist ethics is concerned with more than the best consequences of actions. It often seems to matter, not merely what the consequences of an action were, but what the person performing the action intended or whether the person thought the action was good or bad. It may also be said that what often appears to be a principled opposition to responses rooted in such states as anger cannot be explained in purely consequentialist terms. In many circumstances an angry reaction might well result in better consequences than some nonangry reaction.

In response to objections of these kinds, proponents of consequentialist interpretations can point to more complex forms of consequentialism (than act consequentialism) that maintain, for example, that there are consequentialist reasons for people to have certain character traits, where these traits are meant to include various mental states such as intentions and motives. For instance, the character trait of patience (*kṣānti*), one of the Six Perfections, precludes anger, but better results might come about from having this character trait rather than any alternative character trait, even if on occasion an angry reaction would produce better consequences.

Arguments along this line are common features of contemporary discussions of consequentialism. Against this, proponents of virtue ethics do not think that the importance of the virtues can be fully explained in consequentialist terms: they are not valuable solely on account of the consequences they produce. Whatever may be said about this debate on philosophical grounds, the interpretive question is whether there is good reason to suppose that the classical Indian Buddhist writers on ethics were in some way committed to a particular resolution of this debate. In the absence of evidence that they actually engaged in the debate, it is hard to see that they were.

In opposition to the Aristotelian version of the virtue ethics interpretation, it may be objected that it is incompatible with the Buddhist no-self teaching. Aristotle thought a life of virtue fulfilled our natural capacities as human beings. However, if there is no self that could have such a nature, the virtues cannot be understood in this way.

In response to this objection, proponents of the Aristotelian interpretation would no doubt acknowledge that, for Buddhism, in ultimate truth there is no self, but in conventional truth, the form of truth typically presupposed in Buddhist moral discourse, there are many references to selves, and it appears to be regularly assumed that each human being has a capacity for enlightenment—a capacity that, in time, was expressed in the language of *Tathāgata-garbha*. Perhaps this can be understood only at the level of conventional rather than ultimate truth, or perhaps it should be taken as a pragmatic more than a metaphysical point. Either way some kinship with Aristotle might be preserved.

No doubt there are responses to this point. Aristotle's metaphysical framework is deeply at odds with virtually any Buddhist metaphysical position. However, as before, it is not clear that the Indian Buddhist writers on ethics were in some way committed to resolving a debate about virtue ethics in these terms.

Of course, specific Buddhist texts might be cited in support of one of the interpretations, but such citations are not likely to be conclusive. For example, Śāntideva says that what is most important in the Perfections are our mental attitudes. Writing about the Perfection of generosity, he says, "the perfection is the mental attitude itself" (BCA 5:10 in Śāntideva, 1995). Similar points are made about the Perfections of morality and patience (5.11–5.12). These passages might be taken to support a virtue ethics interpretation, according to which, for Śāntideva, mental states (as well as consequences) are crucial for moral rightness. However, there are consequentialist responses to this interpretation (along the lines noted earlier), and the passages themselves are unlikely to settle this debate.

Again, Śāntideva says, "Realizing this, one should always be striving for others' well-being. Even what is proscribed is permitted for a compassionate person who sees it will be of benefit" (BCA 5.84). This might be taken to mean that beneficial consequences are what really matter. However, there is a virtue ethics response to this interpretation: Only a compassionate person may do what is proscribed, and even then this is only permitted, not required (as might be thought from a consequentialist standpoint). Once again the passage is not decisive.

A natural response to this dialectic might be to propose that the proper interpretation is that the Indian Buddhists accepted some hybrid position in which virtues and consequences are in some fashion equally fundamental.[7] However, if this interpretation is to go beyond making the obvious point that they emphasized both virtues and consequences, it will need to attribute to them a more complex theoretical position than either of the original two interpretations do. In the absence of any evident endorsement and argument in its favor, this is no more plausible an interpretation than those it is meant to surpass.

3.3. The Nontheoretical Stance of Buddhism with Respect to Moral Thought

In my view, the best interpretation of the standpoint of Indian Buddhists with respect to moral philosophy overall is not that they accepted normative theories of moral rightness such as virtue ethics or consequentialism. Rather, they implicitly supposed that moral theory in this sense is neither necessary nor even important to living morally and attaining enlightenment, and so they saw no reason to develop such a moral theory. Since they did not think a moral theory should be developed, they did not do so, and this is why there is no explicit manifestation of any moral theory in the texts of these Buddhists.

It is helpful to relate this interpretation to the famous poison arrow simile. In a well-known *sutta* in the Pāli canon, Mālunkyāputta demands that the Buddha take a position on a number of "speculative views" before he will follow him (these concern the eternity and infinity of the world, the relationship of soul and body, and the existence of the Tathāgata after death; MN.i.426–432, in Ñāṇamoli & Bodhi, 1995, pp. 533–536). The Buddha responds with the story of the man wounded by a poison arrow who refuses medical treatment until he is told the answer to various questions, such as the name of the man who wounded him. But surely for the purpose of treating the wound, the Buddha says, he has no need to know the answers to these questions. Likewise, the Buddha declares, taking a position on the speculative views is not beneficial and does not lead to enlightenment. Hence, he does not take a position on these views. Instead, he teaches the Four Noble Truths, which are beneficial because they do lead to enlightenment. In my interpretation, the attitude of the Buddha—and the subsequent tradition of Indian Buddhism—to moral theory is basically the same as the Buddha's attitude toward these speculative views: Determination of the correct moral theory is not beneficial because it does not lead to enlightenment. In short, though some understanding of the ethical aspects of the Eightfold Path is obviously beneficial and productive of enlightenment, understanding moral theory is not (and likewise, *mutatis mutandis*, for the Six Perfections in Mahāyāna Buddhism).

The fact that the Buddha took no position on Mālunkyāputta's speculative views does not mean that he took no position on any philosophical questions. It is evident that he proposed proto-philosophical views pertaining to impermanence, dependent arising, the aggregates, and no-self, and he offered at least the rudiments of philosophical arguments for these ideas. This is the historical basis of the Abhidhamma tradition that developed the Buddha's outlook in systematic philosophical ways and of subsequent Mahāyāna traditions that further expanded and modified this outlook. Wisdom is a crucial part of the path to enlightenment in all Indian Buddhist schools, and wisdom surely involves some philosophical understanding of these metaphysical ideas. But it does not involve moral theory. What the Buddha and Indian Buddhists supposed was that wisdom in this specific sense, together with the meditative disciplines and a commitment to and nontheoretical grasp of the basic Buddhist moral values, is generally sufficient for living morally and pursuing enlightenment. The implicit assumption was that, when questions about the implications of these moral values arise, they should be dealt with on a case-by-case basis without any appeal to moral theory. For example, if a particular situation occurs in which two moral precepts seem to conflict, there should be a determination of what to do in that particular situation. But in making that determination there need not and should not be any determination of what to do in all possible situations in which these precepts might conflict (as commitment to the value of moral theory might imply). By a nontheoretical understanding of basic Buddhist values I mean understanding by and large what commitment to those values ordinarily requires. Such understanding does not necessitate knowing in advance what such commitment requires in every conceivable circumstance. It was supposed that someone who possesses Buddhist wisdom would have sufficient resources to deal with whatever cases might arise.

It may be objected that there is a sense in which we cannot do without moral theory. For example, it might be claimed that, if in a particular circumstance two moral values A and B conflict—for instance, when the best way to enable a person to overcome suffering involves lying or stealing—and a determination is made that A should take precedence over B in this circumstance, then there must be features of this circumstance, let's say X and Y, that justify this. Otherwise, the determination is arbitrary and irrational. Moreover, if this is the case, then in this determination there is a commitment to the principle "If A and B conflict, then A should take precedence over B whenever X and Y are present." Hence, from the standpoint of rationality, there is no avoiding commitment to principles. According to this objection, following such universal principles is the essence of rationality. Since virtuous action must be rational action, and since moral theory is precisely the articulation of such principles, virtuous action requires moral theory.

The position that I am arguing was implicitly accepted by Indian Buddhists is not the position that there are no such principles. It is the position that it is not necessary or important for living morally and pursuing enlightenment to articulate and act on the basis of such principles. In more positive terms, the implicit supposition was that, insofar as a person had overcome the roots of unwholesome (akusala) actions (greed, hatred, and delusion) and had replaced them with the roots of wholesome (kusala) actions (generosity, loving-kindness or compassion, and wisdom), and had grasped the complexity of a specific situation in all its morally relevant particularity, he or she would see what the morally correct course of action would be and would act accordingly. The Indian Buddhists tacitly supposed that there was no need to articulate universal moral principles for this process to work properly. Developing a moral theory that aspires to be the complete set of correct moral principles is thus a needless activity that will divert us from the pursuit of enlightenment.

This approach to morality has affinities with what came to be called the Buddha's (and later Buddhists') use of "skillful means" (upāya-kauśalya) in teaching. The common understanding of skillful means is that the Buddha's teaching was typically addressed to a particular person in a particular context for a particular purpose. Hence, a proper understanding of his teaching on each occasion may require reference to these particularities, and so we should not assume that what was emphasized as important on one occasion would be emphasized as important on all other occasions or was intended as the final and complete statement of some doctrine or principle. Of course, *skillful means* has been interpreted in different ways. The affinity with moral reflection that I am drawing attention to here is in part the need in such reflection to focus on the particularities of each situation. Moral reflection itself requires the employment of a kind of skillful means on this account. Moreover, the common understanding of skillful means is also important for interpreting Buddhist texts that express moral teachings. Those who attribute a moral theory to Buddhists often read passages in these texts as indentations in the ground that are best explained as the tracks of an unseen animal—an implicit moral theory—that must be responsible for them. However, if we see these passages in light of the notion of skillful means, we will be cautious about reading the passages in this way. The context of the passage might well suggest a different reading. It is a common feature of any practical teaching, moral or otherwise, to make statements that should not be taken literally as universal rules but need to be understood as emphasizing something that is appropriate for the occasion. For example, a hitting coach might say to a baseball player, "Stop swinging at the first pitch." This is not intended to be a universal principle that is part of the theory of playing baseball well. It is a temporary bit of advice to a specific player who tends to swing at the first pitch way too often. The rhetorical intent of the statement is not to express a bit of theory to be followed by all but to bring about a certain result in a particular player on a particular occasion.

In the objection above, it was assumed that a moral theory consists of or includes a set of principles stating necessary and sufficient conditions for performing a morally correct action. However, in contemporary Western philosophy, there are several "antitheoretical" understandings of moral philosophy, and some interpreters have suggested that Buddhist moral philosophy is better analyzed as having kinship with one or more of these understandings. The most prominent of these are a nontheoretical conception of virtue ethics, moral particularism, moral phenomenology, and moral pluralism. I believe that each of these interpretations has some merit, but we should also be cautious in making these comparisons in light of the specific implications of these contemporary outlooks.

First, Aristotle (2002, 1094b20–23) claimed that a moral theory requires practical principles that are true only "for the most part." Moreover, he is often read by contemporary virtue ethicists as offering an alternative to a moral theory of what makes an action morally right, an alternative that proposes "true for the most part" guidelines to being and becoming a morally virtuous person (see Pincoffs, 1986). It could be argued that Buddhist moral texts contain some statements that are most reasonably understood as being put forward as "true for the most part" and that these texts are very much concerned with becoming a morally virtuous person. In light of this, it might be claimed that such texts could be interpreted as implicitly committed to virtue ethics in this modified sense (see Whitehill, 1994). There is some merit to this suggestion. However, Aristotle's *Nicomachean Ethics* is nonetheless intended to be an account of the moral life that is general, rather abstract, systematic, unified, and coherent. We do not find a moral theory in this sense explicitly presented in Indian Buddhism. In the absence of this, we should not assume that Indian Buddhists implicitly accepted such a theory. This does not mean that there are no general statements or no analyses of concepts in connection with morality. There are, but they are ordinarily put forward in rather piecemeal fashion, offered for particular purposes as a form of skillful means, and not as parts of an overall systematic moral philosophy.

Second, it has been proposed that Buddhists accepted something close to what philosophers today call moral particularism (see Barnhart, 2012). Since the stance I am attributing to Buddhists stresses the importance of particulars in moral reflection, it might seem that particularism is an apt term for describing this stance. However, we should be careful about the use of this term in philosophical interpretations of Buddhist moral thought. In moral philosophy, Jonathan Dancy (2004) has defended the most prominent form of moral particularism. According to Dancy, particularism says that moral thought does not require moral principles. However, he takes this to be based on holism, the position that something that is a reason in one situation may not be a reason, or may be a reason with the opposite polarity (for example, supporting something rather than opposing it), in another situation. Holism is a controversial philosophical thesis, and I am not suggesting that Buddhists accepted holism, even implicitly. Nor am I suggesting that they rejected it. Holism, we might say, is a second-order theory (that there cannot be a certain kind of first-order theory consisting of moral principles), and Buddhists did not take a position about such second-order theories any more than they took a position about first-order theories. Though they affirmed a number of moral precepts (for example, about not stealing, killing, etc.) that should at least ordinarily be followed, they did not engage in a debate about whether, in general, the fact that an action violates a precept always counts as a reason against it.[8]

Third, it has also been suggested that Buddhism, or at least Śāntideva in the *Bodhicaryāvatāra*, presents not a moral theory such as virtue ethics or consequentialism but a moral phenomenology, specifically an account of the distinction between unenlightened and enlightened moral consciousness (see Garfield, 2010). However, caution is required here as well. In philosophy today, there are two primary ways in which the term *moral phenomenology* (or *phenomenology* in some moral contexts) is understood. On the one hand, it may refer to moral inquiries that draw on the work of Husserl and subsequent traditions that grow out of his work. But it is not plausible to suppose that in his moral thought Śāntideva was implicitly employing a Husserlian analysis of appearances. On the other hand, in recent work by some analytic moral philosophers, moral phenomenology is taken to involve an account of various moral experiences as they are undergone by a person (the first-person point of view), experiences such as indignation, gratitude, and remorse. The assumption of those who appeal to moral phenomenology so understood is that how such moral phenomena appear or feel to a person should play a significant role in the development of normative or meta-ethical theories. It is no doubt true that Śāntideva (and other Buddhists) were centrally concerned with moral experiences, and to that extent they may be said to offer a moral phenomenology in this second sense. However, this concern is part of the larger soteriological program of overcoming suffering, and this program has many elements that cannot reasonably be considered phenomenology. These include the Madhyamaka metaphysics of dependent arising and emptiness discussed in detail in the chapter on wisdom. This metaphysics is fundamental for Śāntideva's moral outlook, and so this outlook takes us well beyond the purview of moral phenomenology in the second sense.[9]

Finally, it has been proposed that early Buddhist ethics exemplifies a form of value pluralism (see Velez de Cea, 2010).[10] This is true to an extent, but once again it captures only part of what is important, and it may be misleading. Though Indian Buddhists did not think we should develop a theoretical ethical structure, they did have a focal point of concern. The diverse moral elements of their thought were always oriented toward overcoming suffering. This unifying orientation is not a feature of value pluralism as it is usually understood in philosophy today. For example, in a classic statement of pluralism, Thomas Nagel (1979) insists that there are incommensurably different kinds of value. In general, then, though there are certainly some affinities between Buddhism and some "antitheoretical" currents of contemporary Western moral philosophy, and though there may well be value in exploring these, it is important to keep in mind the distinctive nontheoretical stance of Indian Buddhist moral thought and to allow its own characteristic moral voice to guide our understanding of it.

3.4. Should the Absence of Moral Theory in Buddhism Perplex Us?

Keown (2006, p. 44) says that the absence of explicit moral theory is a "curious lacuna in Buddhist intellectual life." However, it may be that this absence is less perplexing than many people have supposed. To a very large extent, the idea that moral theory is important for living a morally good life began with Socrates. According to John Cooper (2012, p. 51), for Socrates, "the best life any actual human being is ever going to live" is one in which "we constantly and ceaselessly pursue wisdom through philosophical inquiry and discussion." This wisdom was specifically practical wisdom—some form of moral theory—about human goods and their comparative importance. As Cooper argues, this idea caught on and was developed in various ways by Plato, Aristotle, and the Hellenistic philosophers. In the Western world, from these ancient Greek roots until now, moral philosophy has been regarded as a standard part of philosophy (see Cooper, 2012, pp. 2–5). For those of us who work in philosophy today it is obvious that moral philosophy is a central part of the discipline, and, at least for many contemporary philosophers, it is also clear that moral philosophy can make an important contribution to living a morally good life. From this perspective it can seem perplexing that no tradition of moral philosophy developed in Indian Buddhism.

However, we should not lose sight of the innovative and radical nature of Socrates's proposal. Never before had it been suggested that living virtuously requires moral theory. Even today students in introductory philosophy classes, and colleagues in other disciplines, often need to be convinced—and in the end they are not always convinced—that moral theory has this kind of importance. The Buddha's and subsequent Buddhists' pragmatic orientation, that pursuing philosophical questions is worthwhile only if this contributes to enlightenment and overcoming suffering, meant that they would develop a moral theory only if something such as Socrates's proposal was accepted. No such notion was culturally available to them, and they had what they regarded as a plausible alternative: they thought that seeing the world aright in terms of Buddhist ideas about no-self and the like, something to which philosophy could contribute, went hand in hand with overcoming attachment and aversion, and that a person who has thus replaced the unwholesome with the wholesome roots of action would be in a position to deal properly with whatever moral complexities might arise. No moral theory would be needed. From this perspective we should not be perplexed that none was developed.[11]

But suppose that Socrates, who lived close to the time of the Buddha, had somehow been on the scene and, beyond this, that Buddhists had been aware of the development of moral philosophy in the ancient Greek world from the life of Socrates through the Hellenistic period. Would Buddhists have come to see the importance of moral theory? As a historical question, there is little that can be said about this. But as a philosophical question, there is a great deal that might be said. In effect, this is where we are today philosophically, in a world in which Buddhist thought and Western philosophy interact with one another in some significant ways. I have argued that, as a matter of historical interpretation, we should not assume that Indian Buddhists were committed to anything resembling Western moral theories. But it is another matter whether, in the contemporary world, it would be worthwhile to develop a Buddhist moral philosophy partly in terms of Western philosophical ideas. For the reasons I have given, there is a sense in which the Indian Buddhist tradition speaks against this. However, the development of such a Buddhist moral philosophy might nonetheless have a justification within the tradition. In particular, it might be seen as an application of skillful means, and in at least two senses.

First, it might be argued that, since Buddhism has now encountered a world in which the importance of moral theory is widely accepted, it would be valuable from a Buddhist standpoint to develop a moral theory so as to communicate its message within that world. Second, it might also be argued that, since a number of persons in the Western world find it natural to think in terms of moral theory, it would be worthwhile from a Buddhist perspective to develop a moral theory to bring its message to those particular persons. These are considerations that might be compelling now for developing a Buddhist moral theory as a form of skillful means, even though they were not compelling when Buddhism first developed in India. This would be an innovation, but, as is widely observed, Buddhism often developed in innovative ways when it entered a new cultural context.

Abbreviations

BCA   Śāntideva, *Bodhicaryāvatāra*. Translations from K. Crosby & A. Skilton in Śāntideva (1995).

MN   *Majjhima Nikāya*, volume and page in the Pali Text Society edition.

Notes

1. References to Buddhism should be understood to mean references to the Indian traditions of Buddhism, including both Theravāda and Mahāyāna forms. Those who have noted the absence of moral philosophy in Buddhism include Clayton (2006, pp. 21–22), Dreyfus (1995, p. 29), and Goodman (2009, p. 89).

2. For more details about these two parts of the paper, see Gowans (2015, Chapters 6, 7).

3. See Hursthouse (1999, pp. 26ff.). Of course these characterizations are quite simple; theories that are actually defended are typically more complex. But the characterizations are sufficient for the purpose at hand, which is to note that the theories differ primarily in their ordering of what is important.

4. A prominent example is Keown (1992).

5. A well-known example is Goodman (2009).

6. Goodman (2009, p. 89) claims that Śāntideva's texts "come closest to a worked-out ethical theory" in the Indian Buddhist tradition.

7. Such a hybrid interpretation is defended in Clayton (2009).

8. As Dancy (2004, pp. 5–7) sees it, this is a crucial difference between his view and that of W.D. Ross: Ross thinks that the fact that an action violates one of his prima facie duties always counts against performing the action (even if all things considered the action ought to be performed), and Dancy denies this. My

claim is that Indian Buddhists were not concerned with and were not committed to a position in this philosophical debate.

9. Garfield (2010, pp. 353–355) certainly affirms the importance of the metaphysics. My point is that this takes us outside the ordinary understanding of moral phenomenology in contemporary ethics.

10. Vélez de Cea (2010) argues that in the Pāli Nikāyas there is an irreducible plurality of values, but some of them are lexically ordered.

11. Keown (2006, p. 47) himself puts forward the possibility that we should be less perplexed about the absence of moral theory in Buddhism because it was unusual that what he calls "the sciences of ethics and politics" developed in ancient Greece (which he thinks is linked to the development of democracy there).

References

Aristotle. (2002). *Nicomachean ethics.* (C. Rowe, Trans.). Oxford: Oxford University Press.

Barnhart, M. G. (2012). Theory and comparison in the discussion of Buddhist ethics. *Philosophy East and West, 62*, 16–43.

Clayton, B. R. (2009). Śāntideva, virtue, and consequentialism. In J. Powers & C. S. Prebish (Eds.), *Destroying Mara forever: Buddhist ethics essays in honor of Damien Keown* (pp. 15–29). Ithaca, NY: Snow Lion.

Cooper, J. M. (2012). *Pursuits of wisdom: Six ways of life in ancient philosophy from Socrates to Plotinus.* Princeton, NJ: Princeton University Press.

Dancy, J. (2004). *Ethics without principles.* Oxford: Clarendon Press.

Dreyfus, G. (1995). Meditation as ethical activity. *Journal of Buddhist Ethics, 2*, 28–54.

Garfield, J. L. (2010). What is it like to be a bodhisattva? Moral phenomenology in Śāntideva's *Bodhicaryāvatāra. Journal of the International Association of Buddhist Studies, 33*, 333–357.

Goodman, C. (2009). *Consequences of compassion: An interpretation and defense of Buddhist ethics.* New York: Oxford University Press.

Gowans, C. W. (2015). *Buddhist moral philosophy: An introduction.* New York: Routledge.

Hursthouse, R. (1999). *On virtue ethics.* Oxford: Oxford University Press.

Keown, D. (1992). *The nature of Buddhist ethics.* New York: St. Martin's Press.

Keown, D. (2006). Buddhism: Morality without ethics? In D. Keown (Ed.), *Buddhist studies from India to America: Essays in honor of Charles S. Prebish* (pp. 40–48). London: Routledge.

Nagel, T. (1979). The fragmentation of value. In *Mortal questions* (pp. 128–141). Cambridge, UK: Cambridge University Press.

Ñāṇamoli, B., & Bodhi, B. (Trans.) (1995). *The middle length discourses of the Buddha (Majjhima Nikāya).* Boston: Wisdom.

Pincoffs, E. L. (1986). *Quandaries and virtues: Against reductionism in ethics.* Lawrence: University Press of Kansas.

Śāntideva. (1995). *The Bodhicaryāvatāra.* (K. Crosby & A. Skilton, Trans.). Oxford: Oxford University Press.

Velez de Cea, A. (2010). Value pluralism in early Buddhism. *Journal of the International Association of Buddhist Studies, 33,* 211–237.

Whitehill, J. (1994). Buddhist ethics in Western context: The "virtues" approach. *Journal of Buddhist Ethics, 1,* 1–22.

PART TWO

Constructing Buddhist Ethics

Chapter 4

Zen Buddhism and the Space of Ethics

Jin Y. Park

4.1. Introduction

What are the most important qualities to lead an ethical life in the context of Buddhism? Are there specific characteristics that distinguish Buddhist ethics from other ethical paradigms, and are there elements we need to pay special attention to in envisioning Buddhist ethics? An ethical theory is a practical branch of philosophy, and the nature of a philosophy and its ethical system are closely related. In this contribution, I hope to outline a Buddhist ethics without molding it to the parameters of existing Western ethical theories. I will do this in the context of Zen and Huayan Buddhism and consider what it means to practice Zen and Huayan Buddhist approaches to ethics in our daily existence.

4.2. Nonduality and Zen Buddhist Ethics

Since the introduction of Buddhism to American academia, Buddhism's capacity for ethics has been repeatedly questioned. Some have even claimed that the survival of Buddhism on American soil would depend on Buddhism's capacity to provide a clearer blueprint for its ethical paradigm (Whitehill, 2000; Palmer, 1997). Recently scholars working in the field of Buddhism and science have claimed that ethics should be one of the major contributions of Buddhism to this interdisciplinary study. That is, whereas science cannot say much about ethics, Buddhism can offer an ethical dimension of human beings' mental activities (Austin, 1999; Wallace, 2003, 2007). The contradictory evaluation of Buddhism's position in terms of ethics suggests that the concept of Buddhist ethics is still versatile and that scholarship on Buddhist ethics needs to clarify why this is the case and where this situation directs us in our discussion of the nature of Buddhist ethics.

The lingering suspicions about the possibility of Buddhist ethics could be evidence that Buddhist ethics cannot be properly outlined by employing dominant Western ethical paradigms. The structure of Buddhist philosophy is such that envisioning Buddhist ethics would require reorienting our ethical imagination to properly reflect the nature of Buddhist philosophy. This is especially the case with Zen and Huayan Buddhism of the Mahāyāna Buddhist tradition.

Precepts and Virtue Ethics

One of the fundamental theses of Zen and Huayan Buddhism is nondualism. In the context of Zen Buddhism, nondualism is the basis of the fundamental promise that the sentient being is the Buddha; it is also extended to the nonduality of *saṃsāra* and *nirvāṇa*. Even with these two theses of Zen Buddhism, the problem of nondualism as an ethical discourse seems clear. First, the nonduality of the sentient being (the current state of the subject) and the Buddha (the perfected state of the ethical agent) leads to ambiguity about the motivation of ethical behavior. If the sentient being were already a morally perfect being, why would one need an ethics? Second, the nonduality claim blurs the boundaries of traditional ethical categories such as good and evil or right and wrong, as they are said to be nondual. Third, the nonduality thesis also raises the question of the identity of the ethical agent: Is it the Buddha aspect that is the ethical agent or the sentient being aspect that should be the ethical agent in Zen Buddhist ethics?

Efforts have been made to use the nonduality thesis as a basis for a Buddhist ethical paradigm. According to this paradigm, since the sentient being and the Buddha are nondual, once the sentient being is awakened to its Buddha nature, the person should automatically and immediately perform moral action. James Whitehill (2000, p. 21) criticized this tendency as a "transcendence trap." Does an enlightened being automatically exercise compassion? I have argued against this in another work and have claimed that the exercise of compassion requires tremendous effort (Park, 2006).

Buddhist concepts of karma, *śīla* (precepts), and *nirvāṇa* have also been employed to envision Buddhist ethics. However, these concepts do not have the same function in Zen and Huayan Buddhism as they might have in other Buddhist traditions. This is so because the binary postulation of virtue and vice and their dualistic understanding do not always hold up well in the antinomian tendency of the Zen and Huayan traditions. Huineng (惠能 638–713), the sixth patriarch of Zen Buddhism, states it nicely in the following passage: "Darkness is not darkness by itself; because there is light there is darkness. That darkness is not darkness by itself is because light changes, becoming darkness, and with darkness light is revealed. They originate each from the other" (Huineng, 1924–1932, p. 343c; Yampolsky, 1967, p. 17).

The commonsense polar understanding of light and darkness loses its ground in Huineng's logic and thus in the logic of Zen Buddhism. In this logic, things exist only through mutual causation. The antinomianism of Zen Buddhism limits the possibility of identifying Buddhist ethics as virtue ethics. Proposing Buddhist ethics as a form of Aristotelian virtue ethics, Damien Keown (2001, p. 21) states that "ethical perfection is a central ingredient in the Buddhist *summum bonum*." He further suggests that cultivating "moral and intellectual excellence" corresponds to the Buddhist belief in the "potential in human nature in the absence of which no progress towards the goal could be made" (p. 21). Keown has been a leading scholar on Buddhist ethics. His vision of Buddhist ethics is based on early Buddhism, and when we examine Buddhist ethics in the context of Zen and Huayan Buddhism, we find that virtue ethics cannot completely respond to the Zen or Huayanist view of ethics and human flourishing.

As in early Buddhism, Mahāyāna Buddhism emphasizes the perfection of certain capacities of human beings. However, the process of training and the goal to be reached through this training have dimensions that are different from the goal that virtue ethics aims at. A general outline of virtue ethics would envision moral cultivation and self-transformation as a process of removing vice and replacing it with virtue. Paul Williams (2009) asks whether being a Buddha indicates being completely free from vice. A passage from Dōgen's *Shōbōgenzō* demonstrates the difference between moral cultivation of virtue ethics and Zen Buddhist cultivation.

In the well-known fascicle "Genjōkōan" (現成公案, Manifesting Suchness) in *Shōbōgenzō* (正法眼蔵), the Japanese Zen Master Dōgen (道元 1200–1253) describes the process of cultivation and the state of enlightenment as follows: "To learn the Buddha Way is to learn one's self. To learn one's self is to forget one's self. To forget one's self is to be confirmed by all dharmas. To be confirmed by all dharmas is to cast off one's body and mind and the bodies and minds of others as well. All trace of enlightenment disappears, and this traceless enlightenment continues on without end" (Dōgen, 2002, p. 51; Waddell and Abe, 2002, p. 41). Buddhist practice as described in this passage is a process of emptying one's individual characteristics by realizing the nonexistence of essence. A commentator to the Japanese version of this fascicle, Mizuno Yaōko, explains the "others" in this passage as "the others in the mind of oneself" (Dōgen, 2002, p. 51). This practice is to realize that the others in one's mind are one's construction and not the reality of others. Our daily self constructs our view of the self and others, and since the subject creates these, they have limitations. Virtue ethics aims to enhance practitioners' moral capacity, whereas the cultivation process proposed by Dōgen does the opposite. What does Zen Buddhism actually mean when it encourages the dropping of the mind and body of both the self and others? It seems that Zen Buddhists do not believe that what we call "morality" or "intellect" in the ultimate sense is conducive to human flourishing. Rather they could be and have been obstacles to real understanding of the self, others, and the world. But Zen Buddhists are not pessimists. They might not give as strong endorsement to human morality and intellect as we usually do, but they believe that all human beings have the capacity to attain freedom and lead a good life. What should we call this capacity? What are its characteristics if not morality or human intellect?

To answer these questions, let us go back to the nonduality thesis. The Zen Buddhist antinomian position does not negate the distinction between two poles in a dualist moral schema. As in Huineng's example of light and darkness, the two exist separately in one's experience, but their fundamental natures do not differ. Both light and darkness, as with vice and virtue or any other moral category, exist in a relationship of mutual causation. Here lies the paradox of Zen Buddhism in terms of moral theory. On one level, vice and virtue must remain separate; on another level, this separation should not attach intrinsic value to either, and cultivation aims at realizing their nonduality. This counterintuitive approach of Zen Buddhism with regard to commonsense moral categories is a good indication that moral cultivation in the Zen tradition takes a form that differs from that of any normative method.

The position of *sīla* (precepts, morality) in Mahāyāna Buddhism offers another way to explain the unique characteristics of Zen Buddhist ethics. While maintaining the importance of observing precepts, the literature on Mahāyāna bodhisattva precepts also warns against any tendency to substantialize precepts themselves. The seventh-century Korean Buddhist monk and thinker Wǒnhyo (元曉, 617–686), deals with this issue in his *Essentials on Observing and Violating the Fundamentals of Bodhisattva Precepts* (菩薩戒本持犯要記, Posal kyebon chibǒm yogi). In this essay, Wǒnhyo explains three different levels of the understanding and observance of bodhisattva precepts. The first level is to understand precepts according to the gravity of violation: there are "major" and "minor" offenses of the precepts. The second layer relates to how the same precepts can be interpreted differently depending on context.

This constitutes the difference between a "shallow" and a "profound" understanding of precepts. After laying out a basic understanding of the bodhisattva precepts, Wŏnhyo explains what it means in an ultimate sense to observe precepts. In a section entitled "The Ultimate Way of Observing and Violating Precepts," Wŏnhyo writes:

> The characteristics of offense are based on conditioned causality; so are those of precepts. The characteristics of precepts and offense are based on conditioned causality, and so are characteristics of human beings. Based on this understanding, if someone considers that because a precept does not exist [without conditioned causality], precepts do not exist at all, such a person will lose precepts forever, even though the person does not violate precepts by thinking so. That is so because the person denies the phenomenal existence of precepts. Also, based on this understanding, if someone claims that precepts do exist, even though that person is able to observe precepts, by observing precepts, the person violates them. That is so because the person violates the true characteristics of precepts. (Wŏnhyo, 1979, p. 1.585a; trans. in Park, 2009, 416).

The Buddhist worldview describes beings as existing through conditioned causality. Things exist through causes and conditions and not because of any essence belonging to them. The precepts are no exception. Precepts are means to guide practitioners in the path of cultivation, but like anything else, they do not have an independent essence: they are empty. Even though precepts are empty and do not have intrinsic value, this doesn't mean practitioners should ignore precepts. Thus, Wŏnhyo says, if one refuses to observe precepts because they are empty, one violates the precepts. However, Wŏnhyo warns, if, in observing the precepts, one thinks the precepts truly exist, *one violates precepts by observing them.* This is because one has failed to understand the fundamental worldview of Buddhist teaching that everything is empty. The rules are there to be observed, but while observing the rules, practitioners should be aware that in the end, the rules are the product of causal conditioning and do not have an independent self-nature. By the same token, moral principles have significance only insofar as they offer guidelines for the practitioner.

Karma and Consequentialism

The idea that Buddhist karma could provide a ground for an individual's ethical behavior is also problematic in the context of Zen Buddhism. Karma is not a concept that originated in Buddhism; Buddhism inherited it from an earlier

Indian tradition. Examinations of theories of karma in Buddhism demonstrate the concept's complexity, with scholars proposing different interpretations (Stcherbatsky, 1922/1994; Siderits, 1987; Reichtenbach, 1990; Kalupahana, 1994; Harvey, 2000; Bronkhorst, 2011). Once we put in parentheses those disputed and unresolved issues of karma, we find that scholars at least agree on the following as the fundamental aim of the theory of karma; that is, karma emphasizes (1) "the importance of human action and its effect" and therefore that (2) "people make their own 'destiny' by their actions" (Harvey, 2000, p. 23; also see Reichtenbach, 1990, pp. 13–23). Such an understanding of karma leads to an intention-focused rather than a consequence-focused concept of karma. This focus emphasizes the agent's proactive actions.

Karma in Buddhism underlines the individual's responsibility for his or her own actions and the impact of those actions on both self and others. That karma is about the effects of one's actions might lead someone to assume that consequentialism aligns with Buddhist ethics. However, the Buddhist way of understanding the relationship between intention and consequence is more nuanced than the linear and temporal logic of intention and its effect. Zen masters repeatedly emphasize that the idea that one *should* attain enlightenment becomes an obstacle for the practitioner to attain enlightenment. Such an obstacle is one of the last-stage obstacles in the path of cultivation. This suggests that utilitarianism or consequentialism cannot properly deal with the meaning of Buddhist ethics—at least, not in the Zen Buddhist tradition.

Buddhist Logic and Deconstructive Ethics

What, then, would be the ethical paradigm we draw from the Zen Buddhist nondualist thesis? Buddhist cultivation takes the form of constant and consistent self-deconstruction. One example of this form of cultivation appears in the *Diamond Sūtra*, a major scripture in Zen Buddhism. In this scripture, the Buddha teaches Subhuti how a bodhisattva—a Buddhist ethical person— should engage with sentient beings and practice compassion. The scripture teaches that when bodhisattvas practice compassion, if they believe they are helping sentient beings, they are actually going against bodhisattvic activities. That is because "when vast, uncountable, immeasurable numbers of sentient beings have thus been liberated, verily no sentient being has been liberated" (Kumārajīva, 1924–1932, p. 749a; trans. adapted from Price & Wong, 1990, p. 19). What does this paradox suggest? A bodhisattva is a being who has made a vow to lead unenlightened people to liberation, but the scripture says that even though bodhisattvas help unenlightened people, there are no unenlightened people who can be led to liberation. The Buddha explains this paradox as follows: If bodhisattvas have the idea that they are bodhisattvas rather than unenlightened people, they are not bodhisattvas since they have already reified the concept of bodhisattva and made a distinction between bodhisattvas and other sentient beings. Bodhisattvas are the epitome of ethical beings in Mahāyāna Buddhism. The *Diamond Sūtra* describes the quality of being a bodhisattva as a dual role of (1) helping others and (2) doing so without generating the awareness that one is helping others. The structure of the paradoxical relationship between the two components of bodhisattva activities constitutes a core of Zen Buddhist practice.

Shigenori Nagatomo (2000), a scholar of Japanese Buddhism, describes the logic of the *Diamond Sūtra* with the paradox "A is A and A is not A" (also see Kopf, 2005). A bodhisattva is a bodhisattva because a bodhisattva does not claim to be a bodhisattva. Bodhisattvas who claim to be bodhisattvas and differentiate themselves from sentient beings cannot be bodhisattvas because by assuming that identity, they are already reifying the concept of bodhisattva. By the same token, bodhisattvas who recognize the identity of those to whom they offer guidance as an unenlightened sentient being lose grounds for claiming to be bodhisattvas. By extension, one might say that from the Zen Buddhist perspective, moral people are moral not because they practice morality but because they are free from the constraints of morality. This logic is similar to Wŏnhyo's interpretation of how to observe precepts.

As I discuss elsewhere (Park, 2008), Zen Buddhist tradition employs language in order to deliver the message of Buddhist nonduality without getting caught up in the limits of linguistic structure. One such strategy is alternately affirming and negating the same claim, as we saw in the logic of the *Diamond Sūtra*. The effect is that the signification system is destabilized by the generation of irony and a dead end in cognitive function. Zen *gongan* case studies are especially filled with examples of such language (see Park, 2002). With the simultaneous use of affirmation and negation, Zen Buddhism brings the nonduality thesis into daily reality.

We can also employ the Buddhist ideas of conventional and ultimate reality to explain the *Diamond Sūtra*'s discussion of the bodhisattva path. A bodhisattva should lead sentient beings to liberation: this is conventional reality. However, there exist no sentient beings to be led by the bodhisattva: this is ultimate reality. When we propose nonduality as the foundation of the Zen Buddhist ethics, what is the outcome of that proposal? In commonsense logic, the first statement alone should be sufficient to construct an ethical paradigm. The imperative of moral action—that a bodhisattva should lead sentient beings to liberation—is already there. In the case of the *Diamond Sūtra* and Zen Buddhism, however, the first statement is not an ethical proposal without the second statement, which negates the action of the first statement. Acting on the first statement without at the same time acting on the second statement would be a case of what Wŏnhyo called "violating the precepts by observing them." The nonduality thesis, then, is the foundation for the Zen Buddhist ethical paradigm rather than the cause of Buddhism's conundrum with ethics since it is fundamentally geared toward the structure of moral action in Mahāyāna Buddhism. Why does Zen Buddhism require this extra level of ethical practice?

Moral norms based on rational thinking constitute the base of modernist Western normative ethics. Social norms are constructed and not given. Since norms are constructed, there exist authors who created those norms. The existence of the authors of the norms indicates that the norms are subject to the preferences of the creator, whether the creator be an individual, a group in a society, or a nation-state. In order for an ethical action to be beneficial to the general human population rather than only specific privileged groups, the moral agent needs to overcome a subjective perspective. The same applies to the subject of the action. When a bodhisattva exercises a moral norm created by a certain subject, the bodhisattva is already exercising his or her subjective perspective. Moral norms, then, have limited functions from the Zen Buddhist perspective.

4.3. Huayan Fourfold Worldview and Buddhist Ethics

Huayan Buddhism interprets the structure of nonduality through the Huayan fourfold worldview. The fourfold worldview is a step-by-step interpretation of how the Buddhist multilevel causal theory is manifested and understood in the lifeworld.

Imagine a classroom in which we see a professor, students, desks, chairs, blackboard, projector, and so on. When we first look around the room, what do we see? We see these diverse things, or beings. This is the world of individual beings. Huayan Buddhism calls this the reality realm of particularities, or *shìfǎjiè* (事法界) in Chinese. When we see those particular beings, however diverse they are, the mode of their ultimate existence is the same from the Buddhist perspective. They all exist through causes and conditions and not through their independent entity. Huayan Buddhism calls this the reality realm of the principle, or *lǐfǎjiè* (理法界) in Chinese. On the surface, the realm of particularities and the realm of the principle might look very different, but if we pay attention, we realize that the first level is a manifestation of the second level. They are two sides of the same reality. This realization constitutes the

third level of the Huayan fourfold worldview: the reality realm of the noninterference between the principle and individual events (*lǐshì wúài fǎjiè*, 理事
無碍法界). The fourth and final level applies this idea to individual existence
and posits that no conflict should exist among different beings, since they are
all empty. This is called the reality realm of the noninterference among individual events (*shìshì wúài fǎjiè*, 事事無碍法界).

The fourfold worldview does not claim that four different realms of reality actually exist separately. It is a hermeneutical device to explain the nature
and structure of existence by illuminating the nondual relationship between
the individual and total reality. The ultimate goal is to shed light on the reality of each particular existence. In appearance, particularities exist as a completely independent being; however, if the nature of existence is considered,
independent identity needs to retreat as the multilayered causes and conditions emerge as the foundationless foundation of existence. The structure
of the Huayan fourfold worldview is compatible with the *Diamond Sūtra*'s
strategy of alternating the use of affirmation and negation for the same claim.
Individuality exists at the first level, but it needs to give way to the negation
of separate identity at the second level. The final result is to see the relationship among different particularities without conflicts by virtue of their shared
ground of existence.

· Francis H. Cook, a scholar of Huayan Buddhism, claims that in Huayan
teaching, phenomenal diversity regained respectability after having been
marginalized in Mādhyamika Buddhism, which preceded the Huayan
school of thought (1970, p. 2). Cook considers this a major achievement of
Huayan Buddhism. Huayan Buddhism shares its understanding of total reality being emptiness with Mādhyamika Buddhism. However, it diverges from
Mādhyamika Buddhism in that it pays close attention to phenomenal realities
(or individual reality) as much as ultimate reality. As in the case of *Diamond
Sūtra* we discussed earlier, Huayan approach to ethics uses paradoxical relationship between total and individual realities, which Huayanists explain
through a series of hermeneutic tools, including the concepts of "mutual
identity" (*xiāngjí*, 相即), "mutual containment" (*xiāngrù*, 相入), "simultaneous arising" (*tóngshí dùnqǐ*, 同時頓起), and "simultaneous containment"
(*tóngshí hùshè*, 同時互攝).

Fazang (法藏, 643–712), the thinker mainly responsible for these Huayan
hermeneutic devices, expounded on the issue in detail in his *Treatise on the
Five Teachings* (*Wujiao zhang*, 五教章). In chapter 10 of the treatise, Fazang
explains the identity of a being in the phenomenal world: "In the perfect causation of the one vehicle of Samanthabhadra [Huayan Buddhism], the inex-
haustible dependent co-arising with the complete activities of intersubjectivity

is the stage of ultimate wisdom. The concepts of emptiness and existence make mutual identity possible; the concepts of function and non-function make mutual interfusion possible. The concepts of reliance and non-reliance on origination [dependent co-arising] make the same and different bodies possible. Based on these ideas, it is possible to put the entire world into a follicle of a hair" (Fazang, 1924–1932, p. 703a; trans. in Cook, 1970, p. 457). The idea that a follicle of a hair contains the entire world aptly expresses the Huayan concept of a being's identity. This seemingly nonsensical concept begins to make sense once we take examples from concrete reality. One such example Fazang uses is the numeric system 1 through 10. In understanding the numbers 1 through 10 (assuming that 1 through 10 represent the entire numeric system), we tend to think that each number has an independent identity. Hence 1 is not 2, 2 is not 3, and so on. Huayan Buddhism does not negate this individual identity but at the same time points out the other aspect of individual identity. The number 1 has its identity only when all other numbers up to the number 10 are included in the identity of the number 1. Without the numbers 2 through 10, the number 1 cannot function as the number 1. The number 1 therefore is number 1, which is different from other numbers, but at the same time number 1 is not just number 1, but within its identity it contains all other numbers to have the identity of the number 1. This applies to the rest of the nine numbers. An identity in the phenomenal world is constructed through "mutual penetration" and "mutual identity."

Fazang also explains this relationship with the coexistence of emptiness and existence. Number 1 exists separately from the other nine numbers, but number 1 becomes number 1 only when the other nine numbers exist; hence its identity is empty. Because a being contains the nature of both existence and emptiness, or identity and nonidentity, conflicts cannot occur between total reality and individual reality (or phenomena). The extension of this logic justifies the claim of the fourth level, that among different individual existences conflicts do not exist.

One would not have much of a problem conceptualizing that among the ten numbers that make up the numeric system 1 to 10 there would be no conflict. This, however, is not always the case when we think about other existences in the phenomenal world. For example, as Nāgārjuna states, a relationship between a father and a son is mutually dependent. As much as a father gives birth to a son, a son gives birth to the father, since without a child, one cannot be a parent (Garfield, 1995, III-7). However, unlike the ten numbers in the numeric system, which seem capable of coexisting without conflict, one cannot say that no conflict exists between a father and son. One does not need examples to understand this, and there will be numerous other occasions in which conflicts are understood as inevitable elements in inter-human relationships or in the relationship between human and nonhuman beings. How does the Huayan claim of noninterference explain this reality? What is the meaning of the Huayan vision that no conflict exists among different beings?

It is true that Huayan Buddhism emphasizes harmony envisioned through a state of no conflict, but serious discussion on the problem of conflicts is lacking in the tradition. Still, one can find indications that Huayanists were also aware of the problem of conflicts and considered a way of dealing with them. Statements made by Chengguan (澄觀, 738–839), the alleged fourth patriarch of Huayan Buddhism, offer us one such instance. In *Mirror of the Mysteries of the Realm of Reality in Huayan Buddhism* (*Huayan fajie xuanjing,* 華嚴 法界玄鏡), Chengguan states, "Phenomena [individual reality] basically obstruct each other, being different in size and so forth; noumenon [total reality, or the principle] basically includes everything, like space, without obstruction; merging phenomena [individual reality] with noumenon [total reality, or the principle], the totality of phenomena [individual events] is like noumenon [total reality, or the principle]—even a mote of dust or a hair has the capacity of including the totality" (Chengguan, 1924–1934, p. 672c; Cleary, 1994, p. 74, translation modified). Here Chengguan observes conflict as a fundamental nature of the phenomenal world by virtue of the physical reality of each existence. In this passage he seems to try to resolve the problem of conflicts by resorting to the nonconflicting reality at the ultimate level. This, however, cannot resolve the problem of conflicts on the phenomenal level, since as much as individual reality and total reality are nondual, individuals at the phenomenal level exist in separation from one another.

Chengguan must have realized this problem, and in a later section of the same text he readdresses the issue by employing two major teachings of Buddhism: wisdom and compassion. He submits that "contemplating phenomena [individual reality] involves compassion [in addition to wisdom] whereas contemplation of noumenon [total reality] is [related to] wisdom" (Chengguan, 1924–1934, p. 676b; Cleary, 1994, p. 91). Chengguan's statement brings the Huayan vision down to earth through its recognition of the fundamental difference between total reality and individual reality. Even though Huayan patriarchs take pains to expound on the nature of noumenon, or total reality, and its importance for understanding the diversity of existence in the phenomenal world, in the ultimate sense individual beings cannot be fully understood if approached from the perspective that is required to understand the total reality. Phenomena require an additional dimension, and Chengguan finds that dimension in the Buddhist concept of compassion.

Phenomena consist of beings that have individual identities characterized by boundaries; hence conflicts are an inevitable part of the existential mode in the realm of phenomena. Awakened to wisdom, one is awakened to total reality, but this awakening does not automatically remove the conflicts in the phenomenal world. The exercise of compassion, in this case, already implies that one is aware of the tension between the total and individual realities. As Keown (2001) duly notes, Buddhist ethics require the practice of both the cognitive and the affective faculties of human beings. Wisdom represents the former and compassion the latter. The relationship between the two is mutual enforcement. In envisioning Zen Buddhist ethics, we should not project a linear movement from the "wisdom" of understanding the dependent relationship among beings to the practice of compassion. Awareness of the mutual dependency should accompany compassionate action.

In the earlier stage of conceptualizing Buddhist ethics, the tendency to assume an automatic flow from wisdom to compassion generated an ethical impasse. The assumption was that once one is awakened to the reality of the world, this wisdom will naturally translate into compassionate actions. Zen Buddhism in this case was one of the factors most responsible for such an interpretation. Examining Zen literature, we find that the source of this interpretation does exist. The 12th-century Korean Zen master Pojo Chinul's (普照 知訥, 1158–1210) discussion of the relationship between practice and its result offers us one such example. In his essay *Encouragement to Practice* (*Kwŏnsu chŏnghye kyŏlsamun*, 勸修定慧結社文), Chinul explains that things do not have an essential nature; all arise through causes and conditions and thus are void. When one encounters various problems, Chinul teaches, one should investigate the roots of those problems, and one will find that they do not have any essence. With this realization, one should be able to stay calm without being influenced by external reality. Once one reaches that stage, "the entire body will be stabilized, and we will guard well the fortress of the mind. As we increase the quality of our insight, a calm refuge develops where our tranquility continues uninterrupted. At such a time, liking and disliking *naturally* weaken, compassion and wisdom *naturally* increase in clarity, wrong actions *naturally* cease, and meritorious conduct naturally improves" (Chinul, 1190/ 1979–1989, p. 699b; Buswell, 2012, p. 126, emphasis mine).

In this passage the correction of one's understanding of phenomenal reality is directly translated into moral actions. The question remains, however, whether realization of the ultimate reality would naturally induce moral or ethical actions when one faces everyday reality. In another of his works, *Excerpts from the Dharma Collection and Special Practice Record with Personal Notes* (*Pŏpchip pyŏrhaeng nok chŏryo pyŏngip saki*, 法集別行錄節要幷入私記), Chinul pays closer attention to this transition and underlines the necessity of making vows for wisdom to be translated into compassionate action: "Practitioners in our time often say, 'if one is able to look into one's Buddha-nature clearly, the vow and altruistic behaviors will naturally be realized.' I, Mokuja, do not think that is the case. To see clearly one's Buddha-nature is to realize that sentient beings and the Buddha are equal and that there is no discrimination between 'me' and others. However, I worry that if one does not make the vow of compassion, they will stagnate in the state of calmness" (Chinul, 1209/1979–1989, p. 755b; Buswell, 1983, p. 307). As Chengguan acknowledges the necessity of compassion *in addition to* wisdom for understanding phenomena, Chinul also points out that awakening to wisdom itself does not naturally translate into compassionate action. Without initial awakening, without realizing the nature of wisdom, one cannot practice compassion. Once the initial awakening takes place, however, one still needs incessant efforts to turn it into compassionate action.

The seventh-century Chinese Huayan thinker Li Tongxuan (李通玄, 635–730) emphasizes this aspect in his commentary on *Huayan Sūtra*. Li encourages the sentient beings to look for their own buddhahood. The sentient beings remain sentient beings as far as they are "ignorant" of their own buddhahood. However, since ignorance does not have essence, overcoming ignorance is possible with one's awakening to the fact of one's own buddhahood. Likewise even though sentient beings possess wisdom like the buddhas, since wisdom does not have essence of wisdom, it does not have guiding power, and the sentient beings remain sentient beings while their wisdom is shining brightly (Li, 1924–1932, p. 812b).

We once again encounter the nonduality thesis: the Buddha and sentient beings are nondual, but the actualization of nonduality requires specific efforts from sentient beings. This suggests a potential pitfall that one must face if Buddhist ethics solely focuses for its foundation on the emptiness of things or the nonduality of sentient beings and buddha. Recent scholarship on Buddhism and violence offers us historical evidence of this pitfall in cases where Buddhism emphasized the empty nature of things and became the cause of suffering instead of reducing the suffering of people (Victoria, 1997, 2003; Shields, 2011). What, then, is the quality needed for wisdom to be translated into compassionate action?

4.4. Ethics in the Everyday Lifeworld

In his *Buddhist Economics* (1992/1994), P. A. Payutto, a Thai Buddhist monk-scholar, explains how the Buddhist worldview of interdependency sheds light on the complexity of our economic activities. Here is Payutto's example: When one digs in the earth, the result of the action is a hole, if we follow his understanding of natural laws. According to the law of economics, the act of digging in the earth generates wages. It also generates petroleum, which then generates more profit. On the other hand, digging in the earth to produce petroleum also results in the loss of beings' natural habitats and probably contaminates the environment. Digging in the earth also results in increased production of cars and more wages, and at the same time causes global warming via the greenhouse effect. As Payutto states, "In nature, actions and results are not confined to isolated spheres" (pp. 18–19). Nevertheless people tend to see only a partial aspect of the results of their own actions.

The capacity to understand one's actions in the context of total reaction is the capacity to see the "emptiness" of things from the perspective of Buddhism. Emptiness, as it is repeatedly explained in Buddhist scriptures and by Buddhist thinkers, does not mean that things do not exist. It means that things do not have an isolated independent essence. If things are not "empty," the digger in the earth in a capitalist society will be able to think only about the material gains induced by the action of digging. But since things are empty and produce results that can be felt in every direction, seeing things exclusively from one thread of causality is ignorance. At this point an ethical question arises: What should a person do when he realizes that his job will not only bring him wages but will also potentially damage the environment? Producing petroleum and cars is necessary for maintaining people's current lifestyle. Becoming awakened to the totality of causal results is important, but it does not automatically produce a direction for ethical action.

In *The Wisdom of Forgiveness*, the Dalai Lama explains a Buddhist approach to forgiveness with a story about a Chinese boy. The boy was beaten to death by a Chinese soldier because the boy's father was a counterrevolutionary. On a first reading, the story is appalling; we feel that it lacks logic, justice, and ethical conscientiousness. Sensing this multilayered lack, we could easily jump to the conclusion that the Chinese soldier was wrong and behaved in an evil way. As in this case, our ethical judgment frequently relies on our capacity to explain and understand the situation at hand. Explanation and understanding, in turn, rely on one's position. From the Chinese soldier's perspective, a logical flaw may not exist in the development of this event. The causal connection of the event should be clear to the Chinese soldier: "The officer's action depends on his motivation; his motivation depends on propaganda. Because of propaganda, the counterrevolutionary father is seen as evil. Elimination of evil is something positive" (Dalai Lama & Chan, 2004, p. 111). The Dalai Lama was obviously not endorsing such logic, but he still demands that we forgive the Chinese officer: "We have to oppose bad action. But that does not mean we against [sic] that person, actor. Once action stopped, different action come [sic], then that person could be friend" (p. 111). The Dalai Lama's call for forgiveness could be disturbing to some people.

Reconsidering the incident with the Dalai Lama's call for forgiveness in mind, we come to understand that, in the ultimate sense, this story's message is not that both the Chinese solder and the boy are empty in the ultimate Buddhist sense, and so one needs to forgive the soldier. Rather the important lesson of this episode lies in the difficulty that is involved in the actual transference of wisdom (that both the Chinese soldier and his action are empty) into compassion (hence one needs to forgive the Chinese soldier). Even when one is aware of and awakened to emptiness, one resists and tries to justify one's incapacity to follow this Buddhist logic and the Dalai Lama's call for forgiveness. We might want to justify our unwillingness to grant forgiveness in the name of a higher justice. The Dalai Lama himself also suggests that we may find it difficult or even impossible to exercise compassion even after we have realized the emptiness of beings. The Dalai Lama states, "If I was on the spot and meet the Chinese soldier, the officer who beat that boy . . . If I was there, and I have gun . . . Such moment, I may shoot the Chinese" (Dalai Lama & Chan, 2004, p. 112). The Dalai Lama's response shocked his interlocutor, who asked how such an action could be possible for someone like the Dalai Lama. The Dalai Lama responded that sometimes action comes before thinking. I don't think anybody would take the Dalai Lama's statement literally. Instead we should remind ourselves of Chengguan's statement about total reality and individual reality (or phenomena) and try to understand it in a more nuanced way. Total reality can be understood through wisdom, and in that domain no conflict exists. However, on the phenomenal level, the conflict is more than real. The conflict between the counterrevolutionary father and the armed Chinese officer results in the death of a child. Will the awakening toward the total reality of the emptiness of all beings naturally lead to the compassionate action of forgiving the Chinese officer? Even if one forgives the Chinese officer, how would the forgiveness be a moral action to the dead child? The space between the awareness of total reality and the limitations of one's hermeneutic capacity to understand that reality is where a bud of compassion can emerge. What are the elements that we need for this bud of compassion to emerge and grow?

4.5. Zen Buddhism and the Space of Ethics

One way of characterizing this space is to use the concept of tension. I have discussed the notion of the ethics of tension in other works (Park, 2008,

2013). The basic idea is to think about ethics through the ethical agent's moral struggle instead of from a judgmental perspective. Mahāyāna Buddhism in general and Zen and Huayan Buddhism in particular do not negate the existence and necessity of moral and ethical norms. However, they bring out attention to the context of our existence in which moral norms exist. When we consider the diverse contexts in which an event or action takes place, moral and ethical norms can offer a contour of our judgment, but those norms cannot offer a final resolution to our moral questions. As in Payutto's example regarding the multiple results of digging a hole, or as with the Dalai Lama's story of the Chinese soldier and the boy, an event occurs through multifaceted causes and conditions, and our interpretation and understanding of those events vary depending on our position and our environments.

We can envision the ethical life by using an image of space. This is a space in which a moral agent constantly asks himself or herself about the best possible moral action based on the available information about the event and moral theories. A key to this approach to ethics is to be aware of the fact that seeing the totality of an event is not possible because of the multilayered conditions and causes that have generated the event. The moral agent's awareness of his or her limitation in seeing the full picture of the situation at hand should open up the space of ethics. This is the space in which the moral agent constantly struggles to find the most appropriate moral response to the situation at hand with an awareness of the venerability of his or her decision making. The limitations of the moral agent's hermeneutic capacity also imply that self-cultivation constitutes a foundation in envisioning Zen Buddhist ethics. Since there exists no one measurement to judge an action, and because a proper response to a situation always requires reflection on the diverse dimensions in which that situation locates itself, the moral agent's capacity to consider the invisible dimensions of an event, including the blind spot of the agent's own epistemic capacity, is crucial to ethical thinking. Buddhist tradition explains these ongoing efforts with the paradigm of sudden enlightenment and gradual cultivation (see Park 2006). Like the mutual illumination of wisdom and compassion, an awakening to the fundamental reality of the world (sudden enlightenment) should be complemented by constant and consistent cultivation (gradual cultivation).

The Six Perfections of Mahāyāna Buddhism constitute another example of underlining the importance of constant and consistent self-cultivation as a major quality of a moral agent. Dale S. Wright categorizes the Six Perfections into two groups. The first three—giving, morality, and perseverance (kṣānti)— are for anyone. The second three—energy, meditation, and wisdom—are for those who are more advanced. The Six perfections are "less like a set of principles or rules and more like a system of training," explains Wright (2009, p. 8).

Wright (2009, p. 30) continues, "Compassion is something we *learn to feel*"; it is not something that automatically takes place as a corollary of wisdom. (For the Western concept of compassion, see Nussbaum, 2001.) Just as our body needs nutrition from continuous activities of intake and excretion as well as the constant movement of our muscles and respiratory organs, so too does our mind require incessant activities without always reaching clear logic on the decisions made. Understanding ethics in the context of daily life requires this total capacity of human existence in which one is constantly and consistently aware of the differing possibilities and inevitable conflicts among the members of the world. As much as these conflicts are empty, they are real in one's daily life. Ethical life from the perspective of Zen and Huayan Buddhism demands the ethical agent to be aware of the two dimensions of understanding human existence: existence and emptiness. When one tries to make a moral decision, these two do not always harmoniously function in one's mind, but create conflicts, causing tension to the ethical agent. Zen Buddhism underlines the importance of maintaining this tension as a positive way of learning to live a life of total reality as it concerns the life of an individual.

References

Austin, J. H. (1999). *Zen and the brain: Toward an understanding of meditation and consciousness*. Cambridge, MA: MIT Press.

Bronkhorst, J. (2011). *Karma*. Honolulu: University of Hawai`i Press.

Buswell, R. E., Jr. (1983). *The Korean approach to Zen: The collected works of Chinul*. Honolulu: University of Hawai'i Press.

Buswell, R. E., Jr. (2012). *Collected works of Korean Buddhism*. Vol. 2: *Chinul: Selected works*. Seoul: Jogye Order of Korean Buddhism.

Chengguan 澄觀. (1924–1934). *Huayan fajie xuanjing* 華嚴法界玄鏡. *Taishō shinshū daizōkyō* 大正新脩大藏経. Vol. 45, no. 1883, pp. 672–683. Compiled by Takakusu, Junjirō, Watanabe Kaikyoku. Tokyo: Taishō issaikyō kankōkai.

Chinul 知訥. (1190). *Kwŏnsu chŏnghye kyŏlsamun* 勸修定慧結社文. *Han'guk Pulgyo Chŏnsŏ* 韓國佛教全書, vol. 4, pp. 698a–708a. Seoul: Tongguk taehakkyo ch'ulp'anbu, 1979–1989.

Chinul 知訥. (1209). *Pŏpchip Pyŏrhaeng nok chŏryo pyŏngip sagi* 法集別行錄節要幷入私記 *Han'guk Pulgyo Chŏnsŏ*, vol. 4, pp. 741a–767b. Seoul: Tongguk taehakkyo ch'ulp'anbu, 1979–1989.

Cleary, T. (1994). Mirror of the mysteries of the universe of the Hua-yen. In *Entry into the inconceivable* (pp. 69–124). Honolulu: University of Hawai'i Press.

Cook, F. H. (1970). Fa-tsang's treatise on the five doctrines: An annotated translation. PhD dissertation, University of Wisconsin.

Dalai Lama & Chan, V. (2004). *The wisdom of forgiveness: Intimate conversations and journeys.* New York: Riverhead Books.

Dōgen. (2002). Genjōkōan. In *Dōgen zenji zenshū* 道元禅師全集, vol. 1: *Shōbōgenzō* 正法眼藏. Tokyo: Shunjō-sha.

Fazang 法藏. (1924–1932). *Wujiao zhang* 五教章. In *Taishō shinshū daizōkyō*, vol. 45, no. 1866, pp. 477a–509a. Tokyo: Taishō issaikyō kankōkai.

Garfield, J. L. (Trans.). (1995). *The fundamental wisdom of the Middle Way: Nāgārjuna's Mūlamadhyamakakārikā.* New York: Oxford University Press.

Harvey, P. (2000). *An introduction to Buddhist ethics: Foundations, values, and issues.* Cambridge, UK: Cambridge University Press.

Huineng 慧能. (1924–1932). *Nanzong dunjiao zuishang dasheng mahe panruo boluomi jing: Liuzu Huineng dashi yu Shaozhou Dafansi shifa tanjing* 南宗頓教最上大乘摩訶般若波羅蜜經六祖惠能大師於韶州大梵寺施法壇經. *Taishō shinshū daizōkyō*, vol. 48, no. 2007, pp. 337a–345b. Tokyo: Taishō issaikyō kankōkai.

Kalupahana, D. J. (1994). *Ethics in early Buddhism.* Honolulu: University of Hawai`i Press.

Keown, D. (2001). *The nature of Buddhist ethics.* London: Palgrave.

Kopf, G. (2005, June). Critical comments on Nishida's use of Chinese Buddhism. *Journal of Chinese Philosophy, 32*(2), 313–329.

Kumārajīva 鳩摩羅什. (1924–1932). *Jingang bore boluomi jing* 金剛般若波羅蜜經. *Taishō shinshū daizōkyō*, vol. 8, no. 235, pp. 748c–752c. Tokyo: Taishō issaikyō kankōkai.

Li Tongxuan 李通玄. (1924–1932). *Xin huayan jing lun* 新華嚴經論. *Taishō shinshū daizōkyō*, vol. 36, no. 1739, pp. 721–1007. Tokyo: Taishō issaikyō kankōkai.

Nagatomo, S. (2000). The logic of the *Diamond Sutra*: A is not A, therefore it is A. *Asian Philosophy, 10* (3), 213–244.

Nussbaum, M. C. (2001). *Upheavals of thought: The intelligence of emotions.* Cambridge, UK: Cambridge University Press.

Palmer, D. (1997). Masao Abe, Zen Buddhism, and social ethics. *Journal of Buddhist Ethics, 4,* 112–137.

Park, J. Y. (2002). Zen and Zen philosophy of language: A soteriological perspective. *Dao: A Journal of Comparative Philosophy, 1*(2), 209–228.

Park, J. Y. (2006). Wisdom, compassion, and Zen social ethics: The case of Chinul, Sŏngch'ŏl, and Minjung Buddhism in Korea. *Journal of Buddhist Ethics, 13,* 1–26.

Park, J. Y. (2008). *Buddhism and postmodernity: Zen, Huayan and the possibility of Buddhist postmodern ethics.* Lanham, MD: Lexington Books.

Park, J. Y. (2009). Essentials on observing and violating the fundamentals of bodhisattva precepts: Wŏnhyo's nonsubstantial Mahāyāna ethics. In W. Edelglass & J. Garfield (Eds.), *Buddhist philosophy: Selected primary texts* (pp. 409–418). Oxford: Oxford University Press.

Park, J. Y. (2013). Ethics of tension: A Buddhist-postmodern ethical paradigm. *Taiwan Journal of East Asian Studies, 10*(1), 123–142.

Payutto, P. A. (1992/1994). *Buddhist economics: A middle way for the market place.* (Dhammavijaya & B. Evans, Trans.). Bangkok: Buddhadhamma Foundation.

Price, A. F., & Wong, M. (Trans.). (1990). *The Diamond Sūtra and the Sūtra of Hui-Neng.* Boston: Shambhala.

Reichtenbach, B. R. (1990). *The law of karma: A philosophical study.* Honolulu: University of Hawaiʻi Press.

Shields, J. M. (2011). *Critical Buddhism: Engaging with modern Japanese Buddhist thought.* Burlington, VT: Ashgate.

Siderits, M. T. (1987, April). Beyond compatibilism: A Buddhist approach to freedom and determinism. *American Philosophical Quarterly, 24*(2), 149–159.

Stcherbatsky, T. (1922). *The central conception of Buddhism.* Delhi: Motilal Banarsidass, 1994.

Victoria, B. (1997). *Zen at war.* New York: Weatherhill.

Victoria, B. (2003). *Zen war stories.* London: Routledge Curzon.

Waddell, N., & Abe, M. (Trans.). (2002). *The heart of Dōgen's Shōbōgenzō.* Albany: State University of New York Press.

Wallace, B. A. (Ed.). (2003). *Buddhism and science: Breaking new ground.* New York: Columbia University Press.

Wallace, B. A. (2007). *Contemplative science: Where Buddhism and neuroscience converge.* New York: Columbia University Press.

Whitehill, J. (2000). Buddhism and the virtues. In Damien Keown (Ed.), *Contemporary Buddhist ethics* (pp. 17–36). Richmond, Surrey, UK: Curzon.

Williams, P. (2009). Is Buddhist ethics virtue ethics? Toward a dialogue with Sāntideva and a footnote to Keown. In J. Powers & C. S. Prebish (Eds.), *Destroying Māra forever: Buddhist ethics essays in honor of Damien Keown* (pp. 113–137). Ithaca, NY: Snow Lion.

Wŏnhyo 元曉. (1979). *Posalkyebon chibom yoki* 菩薩戒本持犯要記. In *Han'guk Pulgyo Chŏnso,* vol. 1, pp. 581–585. Seoul: Tongguk taehakkyo ch'ulp'anbu.

Wright, D. W. (2009). *The six perfections: Buddhism and the cultivation of character.* Oxford: Oxford University Press.

Yampolsky, P. B. (1967). *The Platform Sūtra of the Sixth Patriarch: The text of the Tun-Huang manuscript.* New York: Columbia University Press.

Chapter 5

Buddhist Ethics

A PERSPECTIVE

*Graham Priest**

5.1. Introduction

Religions, and the metaphysics and ethics that go with them, often move from
one culture to another. When they do, they may gain features, features inherent in the older tradition but that are brought out by the new culture, or
just features plain added by the new culture. Conversely they may lose features, features to which the new culture is unsympathetic or with which it is
incompatible. Indeed to be successful in a new culture, the religion must have
this chameleon-like character.

Buddhism is no exception. It has moved from India to Tibet, Thailand,
China, and Japan, among other places. And each culture has shaped Buddhism
in different ways—sometimes more than one way. Thus the largely Theravāda
Buddhism of Thailand is different from Tibetan Buddhism, with its array of
tantric practices. Both are different from the fideistic Pure Land Buddhism of
China and Japan, not to mention Zen.

In the past 50 years we have witnessed Buddhism moving into "Western"
countries in North America, Australasia, and Europe. It can be expected to
evolve accordingly. How, it is too early to predict. But that this will happen is
all but certain.

This essay is about Buddhist ethics, and it is an attempt by one Westerner
to formulate a Buddhist ethics that makes sense to him. If, in the end, traditionalists say "This isn't really Buddhism," I don't really mind. I am more
interested in what seems to me to be true than in signing up to any "ism."[1]

---

* Dedicated with affection to Jay Garfield, on the occasion of his 2015th birthday.

In the first half of this essay I formulate what seems to me to be a plausible Buddhist, or Buddhist-inspired, ethics. In the second, I examine a number of objections and see what can be said by way of answer.[2]

5.2. A Buddhist Ethics
Buddhism

As I have already observed, there is not just one Buddhism; there are many Buddhisms. So what makes a view a Buddhist view? One might go about answering this question (and the similar question for Christianity or Islam) in a couple of different ways. One might hold that there are certain core Buddhist views essential to it; after this, there is a variety of "optional extras." Alternatively one might reject this essentialist position and hold the various Buddhisms to be connected by a web of similarities that form, in Wittgenstein's phrase, a family resemblance:[3] any two Buddhisms have some things in common, though there may be nothing common to all Buddhisms.

I shall not try to adjudicate the matter here. Whichever of the views one adopts, it seems clear that there are cultural accretions in Buddhism: things that were simply taken over from the ambient culture without argument. Abortion, for example, is deeply frowned upon in most Indo-Tibetan Buddhisms, but not generally in Japanese Buddhisms (Keown, 2005, Chapter 6). The reason, I presume, is that the Indo-Tibetan Buddhisms were influenced by Ayurvedic medical theory, according to which, as in the medieval Christian teaching, life begins at conception. Sino-Japanese medicine was quite different. Similarly Buddhism, like all major world religions, is patriarchal. It has its share of misogynistic texts; there has never been a female Dalai Lama; virtually all temple heads in Japan have been men; and so on. But there is nothing essentially patriarchal about Buddhism—quite the contrary: gender is of no theoretical importance whatever. So why the patriarchy? Simply because Buddhism evolved in times and places (India and China between about 500 BCE and 1000 CE) that were deeply patriarchal societies. The religion simply reflected this fact.

These two examples, it seems to me, are very clear cases of cultural accretion. With other things, matters are not so clear. One of these is the doctrine of rebirth. We will come to this in due course.

The Four Noble Truths

If there is a core to Buddhism, this must surely contain the Four Noble Truths—and if there isn't, there is yet, as far as I know, no form of Buddhism that has jettisoned these original teachings of the historical Buddha (see, e.g., Harvey, 2000, Chapter 1; Siderits, 2007, Chapter 2). These, it seems to me, form the framework of any Buddhist ethics.

The First Noble Truth is that life is *duḥkha*, a Sanskrit word that it is difficult to translate into English. The most frequent translation, "suffering," though it captures something of what is at issue, is quite inadequate. The word's connotations standardly include suffering, pain, discontent, unsatisfactoriness, unhappiness, sorrow, affliction, anxiety, dissatisfaction, discomfort, anguish, stress, misery, and frustration. The thought, whatever word one uses, is that all people get ill, suffer pain, age (if they are lucky to live long enough to do so), lose limbs, loved ones, jobs, treasured possessions—all of which gives rise to unhappiness, insecurity, mental dis-ease, and so on. This is not to say that there are not also times of happiness and joy. But like everything else in life, they are transient and so prone to occasion the unhappiness of loss.

I must confess that the first Noble Truth strikes me as pretty ungainsayable: "suffering" is a fact of anyone's life. There's not much to argue about here.

The second Noble Truth says that there is a cause of *duḥkha*. This is expressed by another of those words difficult to translate: *tṛṣṇā* (pronounced "trishna"). The common translation, "craving," suggesting as it does the feeling one has for water when one has had no fluid for four days, gives the wrong impression. Better is something like "attachment and aversion": a certain mental attitude connected with wanting something good to go on or wanting something bad to go away. The thought is that when we experience *duḥkha* it is caused by this attitude, the result of which is unpleasant, sometimes very unpleasant.

The truth of the second Noble Truth is, I think, less obvious than that of the first. But if one reflects on the times when one has been unhappy, I, at least, find it hard to think of one when this kind of attachment did not play a role. This is not, of course, to say that the mental attitude is the only cause of the unhappiness. Many causes have to conspire to bring about an effect. No doubt events of unhappiness can be brought about by cars crashing, stock markets collapsing, and so on. But of all the causes that conspire, our mental attitude is the only one that is significantly under our control. It makes sense, therefore, to single that out.

The third Noble Truth is but a corollary of the second. If you can get rid of the attitude of *tṛṣṇā*, you can get rid of the *duḥkha*.

The fourth Noble Truth is a series of suggestions as to how to get rid of the attitude—the Eightfold Noble Path: right view, right intention (wisdom); right speech, right action, right livelihood (ethical actions); right effort, right mindfulness, right concentration (mental states). When these suggestions are implemented in the appropriate way, they constitute what Foucault (1988) calls a technology of the self—though given the Buddhist view of the self (to which we will come in a moment), this is not a happy way of putting it. We might better say "personal technology": these are practices that bring about dispositional changes in a person. For the most part, when suitably spelled out, these strike me as good advice, though I'm sure there is much other good advice out there as well. Further details are not germane to the present inquiry, however.

The important point to take away from the preceding discussion is that the Noble Truths—especially the first and the second—serve to ground Buddhist ethics. When in doubt, it is by reference to these that we can seek guidance.

Rebirth

At this point an obvious thought arises: If the point of it all is to get rid of *duḥkha*, there is a very easy way to do so: kill yourself. That will certainly end it. Or if one is concerned with the *duḥkha* of other sentient creatures as well, nuke the planet. (Unlike committing suicide, this option is not practically available to most of us, but the thought experiment is still good.) Surely that cannot be right.

A standard reply will come immediately to most Buddhists (at least most Buddhists in the Indo-Tibetan tradition). Death won't work, because one is going to have to come back and do it all again: rebirth. One is locked into as many rebirths as it takes to get it right.

It might well have seemed that the doctrine of rebirth is simply a cultural accretion to Buddhism, just taken over from the general culture of India circa 500 BCE. The Buddhist canon certainly does not argue for it; it just takes it for granted. The preceding paragraphs might suggest that this is wrong, however. Rebirth is, in fact, integral to making the whole perspective coherent. But then again, rebirth plays little role in, say, Japanese Zen Buddhism. (Not that Zen Buddhists ever explicitly repudiated rebirth, to my knowledge; it just becomes strangely irrelevant to where the action is.) The matter, then, is at least moot.

Whatever one makes of this matter, however, let me put my cards on the table. I, like many Westerners, cannot endorse rebirth. There are, of course, problems about how even to conceptualize rebirth when there is no self to be reborn. (Here, Hindus, who believe in a self (*ātman*), have a much easier time.) Still, I think that one can, in fact, make sense of the notion in an appropriate way. The problem is simply one of lack of evidence. An old woman dies in downtown Melbourne in 2010. In the next year or two, hundreds of thousands of children are born all over the world. If rebirth is to mean any-thing, there must be something that makes one of them *her*. And there could be evidence for this. For example, if a child born in Osaka seems to remember Melbourne, and especially some of the things that no one but the old woman knew but that can be independently verified (say, that before her death she hid a box in a certain location), then we would have such evidence—especially if this sort of occurrence were common.

But we do not have such evidence. I see no more evidence for rebirth than for the existence of miracles in the Christian traditions. This does not, of course, show that rebirth is false. But the wise person, as Hume put it, pro-portions their beliefs according to the evidence.[4] Accordingly one should not believe it. In particular one most certainly should not base a system of ethics on such unsupported views.

Let me add that a rejection of rebirth does not mean a rejection of karma. Karma is the view that one's actions have effects, both good and bad, both for oneself and for others. In Indo-Tibetan Buddhism especially, the karma of one's actions plays an important role in how fortunate a human rebirth one has—indeed whether one has a *human* rebirth at all (see, e.g., Keown, 1996, Chapter 3). Clearly if one does not endorse rebirth, one will not endorse this. But the doctrine of karma makes perfectly good sense within one life. For example, if you go around being friendly to others, they are more likely to be friendly to you; if you go around being mean to others, they are more likely to be mean to you. And if you are constantly friendly, it will make you into a person with a friendly disposition; whereas if you go around being mean, it will make you into a person with a mean disposition. As Aristotle noted, we train ourselves into virtues and vices.[5] All this seems to me little more than plain naturalistic (commonsense) psychology.

Anyway, and to return to the question of the aim of a Buddhist ethics, if one cannot invoke rebirth, the suicide objection strikes me as a knock-down argument—as much as anything can be in philosophy. What it knocks down is the thought that a Buddhist ethics is simply about the elimination of the negative. It has to be about accentuating a positive. There must be something positive to promote. But what?

Ataraxia

The obvious candidate to someone who knows the Buddhist literature is peace of mind: equanimity. Most of us experience this sometimes, and we know when it happens that it is good. Of course most of us lose peace of mind when things go wrong. That's when the unhappiness kicks in, and we know it's bad.

The idea that ethics is about the promotion of peace of mind is not unique to Buddhism. It is a common thought in Hellenistic philosophy. The Greeks tended to call it *ataraxia*; the Romans *tranquillitas*. Buddhism itself has a name for it: *upekṣā*. Maybe these are not all exactly the same thing, but they are certainly in the same ballpark: a tranquil state of mind, not disturbed by unpleasant thoughts or emotions. I will use the word *ataraxia* in what follows.

It would be a mistake to think of ataraxia as emotional flatlining. It is quite compatible with peaceful joy, for example. Clearly, though, there are certain emotions that are incompatible with it. The obvious example is hatred. Hatred destroys peace of mind. Between these two extremes, however, there is a whole range of emotions where matters are not so clear. I once thought, for example, that sadness was not compatible with ataraxia. But there would seem to be a certain kind of sadness that is compatible with ataraxia. There is much beautiful Japanese Zen poetry, especially on the theme of the impermanence of things, that undeniably has an air of sadness about it. The Japanese term is *aware*, which is a sort of bittersweet sadness (or wistfulness) at the transience of things. This appears to be quite compatible with ataraxia.

There is surely more to be said about the nature of ataraxia, but that will do for the moment. I suggest that the goal of a Buddhist ethics is the promotion of this state. The Eightfold Noble Path can be thought of as steps in this direction.

Of course it needs to be said that one should not be *attached* to the goal of ataraxia. That would be self-defeating. Developing equanimity does not, moreover, mean withdrawing from the world. For a start, it is hard, probably impossible, to follow the Eightfold Path if one is starving, has no time to meditate, or whatever. Even if the aim is to transcend our material circumstances, material circumstances of the right kind are necessary to learn how to do this.

In what follows it will be convenient to have a word for the failure of ataraxia. Nothing particularly obvious seems to recommend itself. I will generally refer to this as *being troubled*. A corollary of these ethics, then, is that one should try to eliminate, or at least minimize, being troubled.

Compassion

So much for oneself. But what about others? Perhaps the central virtue of Buddhist ethics is compassion (*karuṇā*). The ethical steps of the Eightfold Path are, generally speaking, compassionate. In pre-Mahāyāna forms of Buddhism, compassionate behavior is good, but mainly because of its effect on the person who shows it. Later Buddhism, however, stresses compassion as a good in itself. So one should be just as much concerned with the ataraxia of others as one is with one's own. But why should this be?[6]

An answer is implicit in the early Buddhist view of the self, namely that there is none. Consider your car. It is just a bunch of parts that were put together at a certain time. They interact, some wear out and are replaced; and in the end they fall apart. It might be useful to give the car a name (like ABC 123), but this is no more than a matter of convenience. The parts of the car are interacting with all sorts of things (like the air and the road); it is just convenient to have a name for that particular *relatively* stable bunch of interacting bits.

Now, you are exactly like the car, except that your parts are psychobiological. And just as the car has no self, something that persists through all the changes and makes the car the very car it is, neither do you.

This is a paper on Buddhist ethics, and so not the place to enter into a discussion of the metaphysics of the self (see, e.g., Siderits, 2007, Chapter 3). Let us just grant this view here, for the sake of argument. If it is right, then a compassionate attitude would seem to follow. There are lots of psychobiological states of being troubled abroad. There is no sense in which some of these belong to *my* self and some belong to *other* selves: there are no selves in the relevant sense. Their badness, then, does not depend on *whose* they are. They are all equally bad. We should therefore be concerned to eliminate *all* troubled mental states.[7]

Why Be Moral?

I have now sketched a Buddhist ethics. Before we look at some objections to this, I will make a few further comments to round out the picture.

There is a standard conundrum about morality: Why should one be moral? If, for example, one were given the Ring of Gyges, which makes its wearer invisible, why should one not behave entirely out of self-interest? There are various standard answers to the question. I just point out here that the above account of ethics provides a very simple answer to the question. Ethical behavior *is* self-interest—though in the present context this has to be understood in a somewhat Pickwickian sense! Let me clarify.

For a start, why should a person behave in such a way as to develop their own ataraxia? This hardly needs an answer. A troubled state of mind is not a state we feel happy being in. Of course one would like to get rid of it. (You enjoy the headache? Okay, don't take the aspirin!) Why should one be concerned with the ataraxia of others? Because, in the last instance, the distinction between myself and another has no substance. One cannot even attribute a state of unease to *my* self and opposed to *your* self. There are no selves.

Morality is therefore self-interest, universalized by a denial of the self. Indeed one might say that self-interest in the narrow sense is irrational once one sees that there is no self. Perhaps, then, we should just say that ethical behavior is interest.

Application

Next, application. The above gives the framework within which ethical decisions are to be made. It does not, on its own, determine any particular ethical decision. Such decisions will depend on contingent facts concerning the outcomes of any particular action in its context and on natural laws of human (or, better, sentient) psychology.

Neither may making particular judgments be expected to be easy much of the time. Situations are always complex, and any action is likely to have both good consequences and bad consequences. The determination of the best course of action will therefore require an act of judgment, or *phronesis* (practical wisdom), as Aristotle put it.[8] This does not, of course, mean that all situations are unclear. In many situations the most important effects of a possible action will obviously be on a certain individual and those close to them. We should act in such a way as to promote their ataraxia. Thus it is quite clear that if, next time I am in class, I pull out a gun and shoot one of the students, that is not going to promote their ataraxia.

But life often presents hard moral choices. If I am a doctor, should I respect the wish of a parent not to give a blood transfusion to their child, even though I know that without it the child is very likely to die? Buddhist ethics provides no magic bullet in hard cases. *Phronesis* is required.

The Precepts

But what of the Precepts? In Buddhism there is a standard set of moral guidelines: Don't kill, don't lie, and so on (see Harvey, 2000, Chapter 2; Keown, 2005, Chapter 1). These look like pretty universal edicts. Violating them can certainly get one kicked out of the Sangha. However, in the Mahāyāna traditions, especially, it is recognized that it might be right to violate them sometimes. There are stories, for example, of the Buddha in an earlier rebirth killing someone because it was the best thing to do in the context. Nonetheless the edicts are enforced pretty rigidly. Don't expect to get away with breaking one if you are a much lesser mortal!

As is clear from what I have said, however, the Precepts can be at best rules of thumb, and they should never be promoted to thoughtless demands. This does not mean they are not generally good guidelines. Most of them probably are. But the effects of an action will always be context-dependent, and this must be taken into account. In particular it must be remembered that the Precepts were formulated at particular times and places and might well be heavily dependent on the sociohistorical contexts in question. And rules of thumb that were pretty good at one time may be disastrous at another. This should be borne in mind when reading Buddhist ethical texts.

For example, generally speaking, Buddhism has been down on gays and lesbians (and, being patriarchal, particularly down on male homosexuality; see Harvey, 2000, Chapter 10; Keown, 2005, Chapter 4). Now it may well have been the case that being gay in the India in the fourth century BCE was not a great strategy for leading a happy life. But in enlightened contemporary societies—or at least those parts that are enlightened—where sexual preference is not an issue, gay sexuality is no more (or less) problematic than straight sexuality.

Concluding the Outline

This concludes the outline of a Buddhist ethics that strikes me as plausible in a contemporary Western context. I have argued that the aim of ethics should be to promote one's own ataraxia and, with compassion, that of others. Before we pass on to possible objections, and so that we have it fresh in our minds, let me finish with a nice statement of what ataraxia—or to use its Sanskrit name, *upekṣā* (Pāli: *upekkha*)—is. This is from a contemporary Theravāda Buddhist monk, Bhikkhu Bodhi (1998):

> The real meaning of upekkha is equanimity, not indifference in the sense of unconcern for others. As a spiritual virtue, upekkha means equanimity in the face of the fluctuations of worldly fortune. It is evenness of mind, unshakeable freedom of mind, a state of inner equipoise that cannot be upset by gain and loss, honor and dishonor, praise and blame, pleasure and pain. Upekkha is freedom from all points of self-reference; it is indifference only to the demands of the ego-self with its craving for pleasure and position, not to the well-being of one's fellow human beings. True equanimity is the pinnacle of the four social attitudes that the Buddhist texts call the "divine abodes": boundless loving-kindness, compassion, altruistic joy, and equanimity. The last does not override and negate the preceding three, but perfects and consummates them.

5.3. Objections

So much for the outline. No ethical theory is without its problems. Nor is this one. Here I will formulate what (currently) strike me as the most interesting objections to the account and do what I can by way of giving answers. Some of the objections are reasonably easily answered; others are not. I will do my best.

The Bastards in Life

> Objection 1: You claim that one should work for the ataraxia of all things. But surely one should not work for the ataraxia of those things that cause others harm, such as colonies of malaria-bearing mosquitoes in Africa?

For a start, the only sorts of creatures that can have or fail to have ataraxia are sentient creatures. How far sentience goes down the evolutionary scale is debatable. But mosquitoes are too far down. Of course one should eradicate mosquitoes that cause much suffering.

I should note that some have suggested that Buddhist ethics are naturally an environmental ethics, concerned with the flourishing of all environments and species (see, e.g., Keown, 2005, Chapter 3). This is certainly not the case with the present view. It is sentience-centric. This is not to say, of course, that we should not care about the environment. What we are doing to it at the moment is very likely to cause a great deal of suffering for sentient creatures. But the environment is important because it has an instrumental value.

That is not an end to the matter, though. For there are certainly sentient beings—people, in particular—who cause others to suffer and destroy their ataraxia. How should one treat them? The exact answer in any particular case will depend on the context but should be determined by considerations of compassion. Violence is never good and should be avoided if possible. But sometimes it may be necessary to avoid greater suffering. Perhaps, if it had been possible to kill Hitler in 1933, this would have been the best thing to do.

It should be remembered that those who make others suffer are almost certainly suffering themselves. Plausibly this is the source of their desire to hurt others. At the very least I find it hard to see how someone in a state of ataraxia could want to perpetrate suffering on others. Ideally one should stop the suffering while helping the person causing it to develop ataraxia.

Goods Other than Ataraxia

> Objection 2: You say that the aim of ethics should be to promote ataraxia. Ataraxia is certainly a good, but there are many goods. Should these not be promoted too? Why single out just this one?

There are indeed goods other than ataraxia that are worth having. A Verdi opera, a bottle of wine with friends, an interesting philosophical discussion. These are quite compatible with ataraxia. But these goods are quite subjective. I love all the things just mentioned, but some people do not enjoy opera, wine, or philosophical discussion. And things that some others enjoy I most certainly do not: rap music, contemporary visual art, sodas. It seems to me that each individual can be safely left to choose their own goods of this kind. Such things are *ethically* neither goods nor bads; they are simply an area of "free choice."[9] It needs to be remembered, though, that *attachment* to any of these things will destroy peace of mind.

However, ataraxia is quite different. By its very nature it is something that all people would give to themselves if they could: no one likes being troubled. Moreover there is some sense in which all the other goods presuppose ataraxia. Suppose that you are listening to an opera or chatting with friends, but at the back of your mind there is a niggling worry about the pain you have been experiencing, what your kids are up to, or losing your job. The experiences of the moment will be marred. To enjoy them properly and experience these goods to the full, one needs to have ataraxia.

Goods Incompatible with Ataraxia

> Objection 3: There are goods such as love and the success of an ambition achieved. These are incompatible with ataraxia. Yet it is necessary to have them for a full life. Life without such things would be bland and boring. Ataraxia would ruin a full life.

I think that this is the hardest objection. One might pin something like it on Nietzsche. Interpreting Nietzsche is always a fraught task, but one may see him as painting a picture of life as a struggle. What gives it meaning is constantly facing challenges and overcoming them—and sometimes failing (see, e.g., Tanner, 1994, Chapter 4; Spinks, 2003, Chapter 1). Whether or not this was Nietzsche's view, it is not a foolish view.

In replying, let me start by reemphasizing that ataraxia is not emotional flatlining. It is not life after a lobotomy or constantly on Valium. It is quite compatible with joy, for example, just not with attachment to the joy. This is hardly even the start of a reply, though. Let us look more closely at love and aiming at a goal, in particular, to see if they really are incompatible with ataraxia.

Love is, at least for most people, a good in life. The joy of loving and being loved, whether it be love for a child or a partner, certainly enriches most people's lives (which is not to say that one cannot live a perfectly rich life without love). But as anyone who has loved knows, love normally comes with suffering: jealously, being rejected, the death of a child, and so on. Of course we all hope that our particular loves will not result in such things. But I have never yet known a love relation—mine or others'—which did not occasion some suffering.

Must it do so? Arguably the suffering is not caused by the love but by the state of attachment that normally goes with it. We suffer because we cling when our lover leaves or our child dies. We want the other person to be something, do something—often, perhaps very often, we want this in a self-centered way. But one can have the joy of the relationship without the clinging attachment. Indeed, arguably, a nonclinging love is better not only for oneself but also for the beloved and the thriving of the relationship itself.

I have heard it argued that this is impossible, that the experience of attachment is *phenomenologically constitutive* of love, at least the love of a partner. It's not really love if one does not want to possess and be possessed. I doubt this claim, though I certainly don't want to deny that love is often accompanied by this kind of possessiveness. But if it *is* constitutive in this way, what I am inclined to say is that there is something very much like love: the caring, the sharing, the giving, the receiving, which is not accompanied by possessiveness. Call this love*, if you like. And we are better off without love, but with love* instead.

What about achieving goals? Let's take sport as an example. Most people who play a sport do so with the aim of winning, sometimes at very high levels of performance. When they succeed, this brings them great joy. But in the process they fail often. (In fact the joy is often greater if winning has meant overcoming many failures.) And in most sports, training involves painful activities of physical endurance to build up strength, stamina, and so on.

But again the question is whether these things must entail suffering. For a start, physical pain is not suffering. Most athletes take on the pain of training gladly. It is certainly compatible with peace of mind. Suffering is something to do with the mental attitude we bring to bear on our pain (though one that, when it accompanies illness, is very hard to shake). And failure brings suffering only if one does not accept it with equanimity. If one fails, one should just accept it, pick oneself up, and carry on. On the other side, if one does succeed, one should accept this also with equanimity, enjoying the moment without clinging to something that is sure to pass.

Before we leave the subject of goods incompatible with ataraxia, there is another kind of example that might occur to you in this context. It is frequently claimed that there would be no great art—which is certainly a good for many of us—if there were no suffering, both in the process of creation and (sometimes) in that which is the subject of the art. As far as the latter goes, the first Noble Truth tells us that we are unlikely to run out of that very soon. If the thought is that one has to struggle to produce great art, which is no doubt true, the matter has already been addressed. There remains the claim that the artist must live in a garret, starve, go deaf, cut an ear off to produce great art. I see no real evidence of this. Bach, Picasso, and Shakespeare did not lead tragic lives. They were very successful people. This is not to deny that suffering can result in great works of art sometimes. But it does not seem to be necessary.

Making Others Suffer

> Objection 4: Suffering and making others suffer are goods in themselves.

I have already said that it may be right to stop people doing what they want to do, thereby making them unhappy, in the cause of compassion. For the same reason, one may even stop someone doing something for their own good: we do not let children do anything they want.

But Nietzsche sometimes suggests that suffering is not just good because it promotes good but is a good in itself. Not only that, but making others suffer can be a good in itself.[10]

I must confess that I find it very hard to have even a little sympathy with this view. As best I can understand it, the reason Nietzsche makes these extraordinary claims is that the surviving of suffering, and its infliction on others, is an exercise of the "will to power," which characterizes the "superior person" (Übermensch).

Now it is true that one who survives a tragic experience, such as a Nazi concentration camp, may well have had to develop an admirable strength of character, but it would have been better had it not had to be done in this way. The self-discipline required to develop a robust ataraxia is much to be preferred. And it must be said: for all that some people develop the strength to survive a tragic experience, such circumstances will just as often, if not more often, damage and crush people in the process—as the example of the Nazi concentration camps reminds us too clearly.

As for the need to valorize oneself by making others suffer, I can only regard this as a sign of a deeply troubled person. (Nietzsche, indeed, is not known for his untroubled psyche.) Why would one feel any need to do this unless one felt some deep sense of inadequacy and the *duḥkha* that goes along with it? There are better ways of dealing with this.

Nietzsche was contemptuous of those who had the mentality of sheep, who followed the herd and submitted passively. Whether or not he was right to be so (he wasn't), it should be obvious that ataraxia does not entail this. Compassionate action is often not easy—it often means *not* going along with the herd—and neither is nonviolent resistance of the kind sometimes undertaken by Buddhists (see, e.g., Keown, 2005, Chapter 7). Indeed compassion often requires as much strength of character as surviving suffering, and others do not come off worse as a result of it.

The Ethics Is Psychologically Unrealistic

Objection 5: This is psychologically unrealistic. How can one, for example, love a child without mourning her death (or struggle to win without an attachment to the project).

No one said that Buddhism is easy. It is a practice that may take much discipline. Perfection may even be unobtainable (unless one believes in *nirvāṇa*). But that does not mean that one should not work toward it. Moral ideals are often not fully realizable in practice.

Suppose one loves a child who is killed suddenly and tragically in a motor accident. If one did not grieve, would this not be the sign of some mental pathology? Indeed, yes, it normally would be. But if one has learned nonattachment, why should it be? No mental state can bring the child back or reverse the tragic events. The child themself does not benefit from the grief—and neither does the person who grieves. None of this means that the person could not have loved the child, cared for them, sought the best for them, enjoyed times together. But all things must pass, one way or another, sooner or later. Don't cling.[11]

The Ethics Is Theoretically Impossible

Objection 6: This is theoretically impossible. Standard belief/desire psychology tells us that one needs beliefs and desires to act at all.

Relinquishing all desires would result in no compassionate activity—indeed no activity at all.

Belief/desire psychology gives us the following picture:[12] I am thirsty and desire to alleviate the thirst. I believe that drinking a glass of water will do so. So I drink a glass of water. Without both the belief and the desire, I would have done nothing. Without the desire, I would have had no reason to drink the water; without the belief that this would be efficacious, I would not have known what to do. According to this account of action, desire is necessary for action because it provides the motor for action (and belief is necessary since it provides the method).

A couple of things need to be said about this. First, though desire may provide one kind of motive to act, it is not clear that it is the only thing that can do this. Arguably a belief that I *ought* to do something can itself motivate an act.[13]

Next, Buddhism is not about the elimination of desire—in one sense. There is nothing wrong with aiming to develop ataraxia or act compassionately. What is wrong is being attached to this aiming. This is the state of being mentally troubled until the aim has been fulfilled or after one has failed to fulfill it—desire in quite a different sense. Though these may normally go together, a Buddhist ethics teaches divorcing them.

5.4. Conclusion

Doubtless there is a lot more to be said on all these matters. There always is. But if one waited for all things to be resolved, one would wait till the end of time. One cannot wait untill then to act.[14]

Abbreviation

AN   *Aṅguttara Nikāya*, volume and page in the Pali Text Society edition.

Notes

1. As the Buddha himself says in the *Kālāma Sutra*, "Do not go upon what has been acquired by repeated hearing; nor upon tradition; nor upon rumor; nor upon what is in a scripture; nor upon surmise; nor upon an axiom; nor upon specious reasoning; nor upon a bias towards a notion that has been pondered over; nor upon another's seeming ability; nor upon the consideration, 'The monk is our teacher.' ... When you yourselves know: 'These things are good; these things are not blameable; these things are praised by the wise; undertaken

and observed, these things lead to benefit and happiness,' enter on and abide in them" (AN.i.190, trans. in Soma, 2010).

And as the first of the Fourteen Mindfulness Trainings, Thich Nhat Hanh says, "We are determined not to be idolatrous about or bound to any doctrine, theory or ideology, even Buddhist ones. Buddhist teachings are guiding means to help us learn to look deeply and develop our understanding and compassion" (Edelglass & Garfield, 2009, pp. 421–422).

2. Despite the fact that the paper is appearing for the first time here, it was, in fact, written in 2010, and I gave talks based on it in a number of places: a meeting of the Australasian Association of Philosophy in Sydney, July 2010; the Columbia Society for Comparative Philosophy in New York, October 2010; departmental seminars at the Universities of Melbourne, Tasmania, and Western Ontario; and the Student Philosophy Society at the University of St. Andrews. The original paper had another section, exploring the specifically Māhāyana justification for compassion. I have cut this here, since the matter is now covered in much greater details in Priest (2015). I drew upon this essay and that one to write chapters 14 and 15 of Priest (2014), which has now appeared before both of them.

3. Wittgenstein, *Philosophical Investigations*, sections 66ff.

4. Hume, *An Enquiry Concerning Human Understanding*, section 10, part 1, in Selby-Bigge (1902, p. 110).

5. Aristotle, *Nicomachean Ethics*, Book 2, Chapter 1.

6. The following is essentially an Abhidharma justification. For a quite different, Māhāyana justification, see Priest (2015).

7. These considerations are to be found, arguably, in perhaps the greatest Madhyamaka ethicist, the eighth-century Śāntideva, in chapter 8 of his *Guide to the Bodhisattva's Way of Life*. See Wallace and Wallace (1997). For further discussion, see the essays in Cowherds (2015), esp. Chapters 47, 12.

8. Aristotle, *Nicomachean Ethics*, Book 6, Chapters 5, 7.

9. But should an ethics not recommend the encouragement of a multitude of these to enhance the richness of life? No. If one wishes to become a monk and live a quiet, withdrawn life, this is a perfectly legitimate ethical choice.

10. E.g., Nietzsche, *Genealogy of Morals*, essay 2, section 5, and essay 3, section 28.

11. This does not mean, though, that one's immediate reaction should be to shrug one's shoulders when it happens. Why should one not cry? One can do this while accepting what has happened and not cling to the past—or to one's tears.

12. As found, for example, in Davidson (1963/2001).

13. See, further, Humberstone (1987).

14. Many thanks to all those who have heard me talk about the matters in the paper and given helpful comments and criticisms. Special thanks to Jay Garfield for many enlightening discussions.

References

Bodhi, B. (1998). Toward a threshold of understanding. BPS Newsletter. *Access to Insight.* Accessed January 15, 2007. Retrieved from http://www.accesstoinsight. org/lib/authors/bodhi/bps-essay_30.html.

The Cowherds. (2015). *Moonpaths: Ethics in the context of conventional truth.* New York: Oxford University Press.

Davidson, D. (1963). Actions, reasons and causes. *Journal of Philosophy, 60,* 685–700. Reprinted in *Essays on actions and events* (2nd ed., pp. 3–20). Oxford: Clarendon Press, 2001.

Edelglass, W., & Garfield, J. (Eds.). (2009). *Buddhist philosophy: Essential readings.* Oxford: Oxford University Press.

Foucault, M. (1988). Technologies of the self. In L. H. Martin, H. Gutman, & P. H. Hutton (Eds.), *Technologies of the self* (pp. 16–49). Amherst: University of Massachusetts Press.

Harvey, P. (2000). *Buddhist ethics.* Cambridge, UK: Cambridge University Press.

Humberstone, I. L. (1987). Wanting as believing. *Canadian Journal of Philosophy, 17,* 49–62.

Keown, D. (1996). *Buddhism: A very short introduction.* Oxford: Oxford University Press.

Keown, D. (2005). *Buddhist ethics: A very short introduction.* Oxford: Oxford University Press.

Priest, G. (2014). *One.* Oxford: Oxford University Press.

Priest, G. (2015). Compassion and the net of Indra. In Cowherds, *Moonpaths: Ethics in the context of conventional truth* (Chapter 12). New York: Oxford University Press.

Selby-Bigge, L. A. (Ed.). (1902). *Enquiries concerning the human understanding and concerning the principles of morals* (2nd ed.). Oxford: Clarendon Press.

Siderits, M. (2007). *Buddhism as philosophy.* Aldershot, UK: Ashgate.

Spinks, L. (2003). *Frederick Nietzsche.* London: Routledge.

Tanner, M. (1994). *Nietzsche: A very short introduction.* Oxford: Oxford University Press.

Soma, T. (Trans.). (2010). Kālāma Sutra: The instruction to the Kalamas. Accessed November 2010. Retrieved from Katinka Hesselink: Religious and Spiritual Wisdom website: http://www.katinkahesselink.net/tibet/kalama.html.

Wallace, V., & Wallace, A. (Trans.). (1997). *A guide to the bodhisattva's way of life.* Ithaca, NY: Snow Lion.

Chapter 6

Breaking Good

MORAL AGENCY, NEUROETHICS, AND
THE SPONTANEITY OF COMPASSION

Christian Coseru

6.1. Introduction

Although the credit for announcing the advent of "neural Buddhism" goes to the *New York Times* op-ed columnist David Brooks (2008)—who sees it as the natural outcome of a new wave of research into the neuroscience of religious experience—it is Nietzsche who most eloquently (and disquietingly) proclaimed its arrival more than a century ago. In *On the Genealogy of Morality*, Nietzsche (2006, p. 7) speaks of the morality of compassion and of the many (by his own estimation sinister) ways it has cast around "even wider to catch even philosophers and make them ill"—the philosophers' sickness being nothing but the symptom of a culture about to give birth to a new "European Buddhism."

Contemporary moral psychology lacks a systematic account of compassion.[1] Nonetheless a little over a century since Nietzsche's proleptic pronouncement, this genealogical quest for the roots of morality is giving birth to a new ethics—call it Buddhist neuroethics. As a specific domain of inquiry Buddhist neuroethics describes a constellation of moral and epistemological concerns about the exercise of practical reason in the age of brain science. As a taxonomical category, it simply functions in much the same way as Francisco Varela's "neurophenomenology" and Patricia Churchland's "neurophilosophy," terms coined to designate new domains of inquiry born from the relevance and applicability of neuroscientific research to traditional issues in phenomenology and philosophy of mind. In the broadest sense of the term,

Buddhist neuroethics stands for the collective (and concerted) effort to make different aspects of moral cultivation and contemplative practice receptive to the findings and conceptual resources of neuroscience. As such, it shares many features with programs in both neurophenomenology and neurophilosophy, as well as with newer programs in neuroethics (specifically, those concerned with how understanding the human mind, and our ability to predict, influence, and even control aspects of it, affects our moral views).

This paper addresses two specific and related questions the Buddhist neuroethics program raises for our traditional understanding of Buddhist ethics: Does affective neuroscience supply enough evidence that contemplative practices such as compassion meditation can enhance normal cognitive functioning? Can such an account advance the philosophical debate concerning freedom and determinism in a profitable direction? A satisfactory answer to the first question is simply a matter of identifying the relevant empirical evidence necessary to support a Buddhist neuroethics project.[2] The second question does not invite a straightforward answer. The long-running debate over the compatibility of freedom and determinism has moved mainly in two directions. Those approaching the problem from a metaphysical standpoint generally argue for some version of incompatibilism, on the grounds that, if determinism is true, it is incompatible with free will, and if it is false, we are left with an indeterminism that makes free will irrelevant. Those taking an empirical approach (and thus more sensitive to the findings of cognitive science) argue for some version of compatibilism. Specifically, certain versions of neocompatibilism are regarded as capable of accommodating freedom and determinism because they see its exercise as constrained by the very causal and conditioning factors that make freedom possible. Freedom is not free (so to speak) if it is not constrained by the reasons we give for choosing one way or another. Unconstrained freedom, at least on the neocompatibilist account, is a deeply incoherent notion.

In response to the first question, I will argue that dispositions such as empathy and altruism *can* in effect be understood in terms of the mechanisms that regulate affective cognition. Not only does such understanding make a good case for causal explanation, but it also reflects the generally naturalist outlook of Buddhist moral psychology; indeed, given that dispositions and reasons have an event structure (that is, they are constituted as mental states with specific intentional content) they are also causes, or at least are causally relevant for action.[3] But causal explanation is no substitute for understanding what it is about our capacity to choose that makes us moral agents. It seems as though at the most basic level choice is deeply embedded in mechanisms that regulate our capacity to discriminate and form judgments. If that is the case, then the roots of morality lie much deeper in the structure of conscious behavior than one might think.[4]

In response to the second question, I want to claim that moral agency is a type of achievement that comes with learning the norms of ethical conduct, which are not tractable by specifically neurobiological mechanisms and processes (though, once learned, such norms would have their neural correlates when enacted). We do not hold infants morally accountable for their actions, and we recognize that childhood is at best a setting stage for the development of a moral sense. And although we admit that only adults can be considered responsible for their actions, we recognize that their comportment too reflects norms and values that are both acquired and constitutive of their moral agency. In brief, if morality is an emergent property of a certain type of socialization and not simply an adaptive trait, at least some of its features should be easily accommodated by the dynamic of social and interpersonal relations.

Nonetheless, even as a late achievement responsibility-entailing moral agency still demands that cognitive mechanisms, specifically those that regulate an individual's capacity for self-monitoring, self-control, and self-correction, are in good working order. Indeed, conditions we typically associate with various psychopathies (and sociopathies) pose a challenge to this developmental account of moral responsibility. Likewise conditions associated with various forms of mental and moral cultivation suggest that introspective awareness and volitional control play a key role in modulating neuroplasticity (see Lutz, Dunne, & Davidson, 2007; Brefczynski-Lewis, Lutz, Schaefer, Levinson, & Davidson, 2008). At least for now the jury is still out on whether genetic, environmental, social, and interpersonal factors provide merely scaffolding for the development of a moral sense or are constitutive of it.

As I will argue, biological and neurobiological accounts of the origins and development of fine-grained affective responses can no longer be ignored in discussions about the nature of ethics in general and of Buddhist ethics in particular. Of course, neuroscience may not be able to tell us, solely on the basis of their neural signatures in the brain, why only certain feelings and dispositions should provide a basis for moral agency. For instance, a disposition to act in a way that shows concern for others, even if habitually acquired, cannot be deemed compassionate if it is not freely undertaken. But such empirical inquiries into the nature of morality *can* tell us whether the kind of moral judgment we associate with compassionate concern for others is primarily driven by affective or cognitive mechanisms.

Does the bodhisattva, the iconic representation of compassionate undertaking, act in a deliberate manner, or is his or her ethical conduct merely an embodied mode of coping with the situation at hand? Buddhist accounts of moral cultivation agree that for an action to be deemed compassionate it must have been freely undertaken (unlike selfish actions, which are rooted in insurmountable habitual and compulsive tendencies such as greed and delusion). Actions that do not possess the right sort of responsibility-conferring capacity, therefore, fall outside the moral domain. But here we run into a dilemma: insofar as bodhisattvas act compassionately on account of their training and cultivation (presumably they cannot do so otherwise), they can benefit sentient beings habitually or spontaneously (that is, without forming an intention to act in a deliberate manner).[5] Thus either the bodhisattva's compassionate deeds count as (freely undertaken) moral acts, or they are purely spontaneous, thus mysterious, unpredictable, and outside the framework of moral responsibility. But, of course, nothing can be "outside the framework of moral responsibility"—hence the reference in the title to the television series *Breaking Bad* that chronicles a spectacular example of moral downfall: to "break bad" in this context is to move decisively against the conventions of one's social environment to gain access to a larger nexus of action. By analogy, to "break good" is thus to enter a comprehensive and seemingly unfathomable arena of moral action.[6]

In what follows I will argue that the "spontaneity of compassion" picture we glean from the Mahāyāna ethical literature is problematic in light of the demands placed on our conceptions of moral agency by moral responsibility–entailing practices.[7] The question, then, is whether the achievement of moral ends requires a more robust conception of agency than the Buddhist no-self view can provide.

6.2. Virtue, Moral Agency, and Consequentialism

One of the most elaborate (and inspiring) accounts of the Buddhist path to moral and mental cultivation is found in Śāntideva's *A Guide to the Path to Awakening* (*Bodhicaryāvatāra*, hereinafter BCA), an immensely influential text that has been interpreted as advancing a version of either consequentialism or virtue ethics. While both ethical theories (and their variants) supply useful conceptual tools for unpacking this (broadly Mahāyāna) Buddhist ethical program, they cannot satisfactorily account for the meta-ethical principles that inform it. My intention is not to showcase the unique features of Buddhist ethics (such as they are) but to ask what Buddhist forms of moral and mental cultivation tell us about the nature of mind and how it can be altered (or, alternatively, about what moral agency is and how it is achieved).[8] If Buddhist neuroethics is concerned with the neural basis of enlightened moral agency (specifically the agency of those undergoing secular mindfulness and compassion meditation training), then established correlations between subpersonal processes (specifically those that regulate affective, retributive, and cognitive behavior) and first-person accounts (of what it is like to cultivate and exercise compassion, forbearance, or equanimity) ought to extend rather than limit the scope of moral agency. Indeed, any evidence that self-concern may be regulated by mechanisms that also monitor our interest in the well-being of others should provide sufficient ground for advancing a more robust account of the efficacy of compassion meditation practice.

Nietzsche's disquieting attitude toward the ethics of compassion notwithstanding, what explains the appeal of Buddhism in the West is precisely this emphasis on what may be deemed its cardinal virtues: nonviolence, compassion, and a general spirit of tolerance. Of course, these virtues are embedded in the theoretical structure of Buddhist ethics (itself part of the Buddhist path writ large)—a project whose characterization lacks scholarly consensus. I will not enter this debate here.[9] Instead, following recent work in neuroethics and cognitive moral psychology[10]—and its implication for analytic reconstructions of Buddhist ethics such as one finds, for instance, in Siderits (2008), Goodman (2009), and Flanagan (2011)—I will ask to what extent the view that moral principles are informed by emotionally driven intuitions rather than, say, deliberate moral reasoning can be said also to apply in the Buddhist context.

Containing what is perhaps the most developed account of moral and mental progress on the bodhisattva path—the iconic representation of a life dedicated to pursing enlightened knowledge for the sake of benefiting all sentient beings—*A Guide to the Path of Awakening* also showcases the centrality of compassion for Buddhist ethics. Although the cultivation of distinct moral sentiments is suggestive of a virtue-ethical approach, Śāntideva views compassion through what seems like a strongly consequentialist framework. Bodhisattvas with a well-developed character are called upon to exercise judgment when acting in the name of compassion. Thus "for the one who understands the work of compassion even the forbidden is permitted" (BCA 5.84). It is obvious from statements such as these that genuine compassion is accompanied by a level of discretion that permits the bodhisattva to act in peculiar ways; specifically it allows for breaking moral precepts like lying and killing without incurring the retributive effects of these acts (or, at the very least, without the threat of punishment).

That a well-developed character should be enough to mitigate the consequences of (seemingly unfathomable) compassionate acts has led some to propose that (Mahāyāna) Buddhist ethics is best understood as a type of character consequentialism: the value of generous acts depends on the value they confer upon all those involved, the agent as well as the beneficiary. If compassion is an outcome of character development, and Buddhist flourishing is essentially the embodiment of those perfections deemed essential for the bodhisattva to carry out his or her work in the world, then compassion is not agent-neutral. The generally consequentialist framework of Buddhist ethics, then, cannot be universalist, even though theoretically the bodhisattva is called upon to maximize happiness (and eliminate suffering) for all sentient beings.

As Charles Goodman (2009, p. 43) has quite convincingly argued, agent-neutrality makes consequentialism quite demanding; that is, it calls for great acts of self-sacrifice, which seems not only unrealistic but perhaps unachievable as well. How else is one to interpret Śāntideva's famous aspiration of bringing an end to suffering: "As long as space abides, as long as the world abides, / So long shall I abide, destroying the sufferings of the world" (BCA 10.55)? Whether the ethical ideals of the bodhisattva are suggestive of an agent-neutral framework, and whether that framework makes Buddhist ethics seem closer to consequentialism than to virtue ethics, is precisely what is at stake. For someone like Damien Keown (2001), positive accounts of pleasure and the pursuit of happiness for all sentient beings such as are found, for instance, in the *Sutra of Golden Light* (*Suvarṇaprabhāsa Sūtra*), suggest that the bodhisattva idea does fit the virtue-ethical model, where the ultimate good is a caring and compassionate love. Developing such obvious virtues as generosity, compassion, and insight is generally how one attains this ultimate good. But these virtues may be also regarded as having an instrumental value, insofar as they tend to counteract various defilements such as greed, hatred, and delusion and to promote progress toward Buddhahood. For Keown these virtues form an intrinsic part of the Buddhist conception of the good. A similar conception of Buddhist flourishing is articulated by Peter Harvey (2000, p. 354), who likewise notes the role certain attitudes and practices can have in fostering the cultivation of such virtues as generosity, compassion, and insight. Of course, insofar as the roots of the good here have instrumental value, this ethical model may also be viewed in character-consequentialist terms. Goodman (2009, p. 88) summarizes this view quite well when he writes that "happiness and the absence of suffering, as well as virtues and the absence of vices, are elements on an objective list that defines well-being."

How is this well-being achieved? And what sort of leverage does a bodhisattva (with well-developed character) have in maximizing happiness and minimizing suffering for all beings? It is certainly the case that individuals not only have different needs but also occupy different rungs of the moral ladder. It is here that the exercise of judgment takes precedence in mediating (or perhaps moderating) the disposition to act in a compassionate way. The Buddhist literature abounds with examples in which enlightened beings use deception to help beginners make progress on the path. (Some of the best examples are those from the *Lotus Sutra*: the Prodigal Son, the Burning House, and the Phantom City.)[11] What is the purpose of these examples of deception in the name of a (presumably) higher good? On the one hand, they reflect the specifically Mahāyāna demand that the early teachings of the Buddha be seen as provisory by comparison with such later teaching as one finds in Mahāyāna literature. On the other, they show the cardinal principle of excellence in means (*upāyakauśalya*) at work. For someone like Śāntideva, excellence in means is called for to explain why actions that are proscribed under general ethical precepts (like speaking the truth and causing no harm to others) *could* be permitted. Classic examples are found in such texts as the *Discourse on the Excellence in Means* (*Upāyakauśalya Sūtra*), where bodhisattvas are allowed to break standards precepts or rules so long as they are motivated by compassion.[12] On this account, the early teachings do not tell people what is the case, just what is most beneficial to them given their present situation. Such a view would be at odds specifically with Kantian views of morality, since for Kant deception, whatever its ultimate goal, disrespects human dignity. I will return to this issue when considering the Buddhist position on moral responsibility.

Given that Śāntideva does have an explicit position on whether and in what circumstances the interests of some may be weighted against the welfare of others, the expectation is that at least some of the classical features of consequentialism should apply in his case. Goodman identifies, specifically in a passage from the *Compendium on Trainings* (*Śikṣā-samuccaya*, hereinafter *ŚS*), not only some but by his count "all" the classical features of act-consequentialism: "the central moral importance of happy and unhappy states of mind; the extension of scope to all beings; the extreme demands; the absence of any room for personal moral space; the balancing of costs and benefits; and the pursuit of maximization" (Goodman, 2009, p. 97). The passage extolls the efforts of the bodhisattva who, "through actions of body, speech, and mind . . . makes a continuous effort to stop all present and future suffering and depression, and to produce present and future happiness and gladness, for all beings" (*ŚS*, in Goodman, 2009, p. 97).

Given the bodhisattva's extreme dedication to pursuing the welfare of all sentient beings, the framework of act-consequentialism must provide a way to account for the psychological and neuropsychological mechanisms that could underpin such ethical conduit. Indeed, it is not enough to say that Buddhist ethics is best captured by a specific theory—in this case, consequentialism. One must also ask whether this theory reflects a characteristically Buddhist understanding of the good (e.g., minimizing suffering and maximizing happiness) or simply represents a manifestation of the sort of psychological patterns that are integral to moral sentiments.

6.3. Evidence from Neuroimaging

The Buddhist ethical literature contains frequent references to characteristics like generosity, compassion, and insight that are considered beneficial or wholesome (kuśala) and thus conducive to achieving the ultimate ends that Buddhists seek. They are typically contrasted with traits like greed, hatred, and delusion, which constitute a major cause of suffering and thus an obstacle to achieving these ends. Both sets of characteristics are classified under the Abhidharma category of mental states (caitta). For moral psychologists who wish to get to the roots of morality, the question is this: Which of these mental states are to be understood primarily in affective and which primarily in cognitive terms (even as the classification of mental states in the Abhidharma literature admits of no such distinction)?[13] It is important to maintain this distinction, given its relevance to neuroimaging studies,[14] which take certain areas of the brain, primarily the dorsolateral surfaces of the prefrontal cortex and parietal lobes, to be associated with cognitive processes, while others, specifically the amygdala and the medial surfaces of the frontal and parietal lobes, track emotional states such as moods and gut feelings.[15]

To see whether moral judgments have an emotional component and in what circumstances (and whether) the emotional response may be overridden, let's briefly consider some empirical findings about entertaining the well-known hypothetical moral dilemmas of the trolley and the footbridge.

In the first instance, a runaway trolley is heading for five people gathered some way down a track, who will be killed if the trolley is not diverted onto a sidetrack. The only way to save these people is to divert the trolley. The problem is that there is one person on the alternate sidetrack, who, as a result, will end up being killed. What is one to do? Push the switch so that five people are saved at the expense of one? In the second instance, the same runaway trolley threatens to kill five people, but instead of proximity to a switch, you find yourself on a footbridge next to a large stranger standing right above the track with the runaway trolley. The only way to save the five people is to push this stranger off the bridge and onto the incoming trolley. The stranger will die as a result, but his body will stop the trolley in its tracks and save the five people. Again, what is one to do?

Neuroimaging studies of subjects presented with these dilemmas show a clear pattern of brain activity. Entertaining the more impersonal moral dilemma of the trolley corresponds to increased activity in brain regions associated with higher cognitive processes like complex planning (see, especially, Koechlin, Basso, Petrini, Panzer, & Grafman, 1999; Koechlin, Ody, & Kouneiher, 2003; Miller & Cohen, 2001) and deductive and inductive reasoning (Goel & Dolan, 2004). On the other hand, the footbridge dilemma activates brain regions associated with strong emotional response (Haidt, 2001; Greene and Haidt, 2002, and Greene et al., 2009). Furthermore engaging in characteristically consequentialist judgments leads to increased activity in those parts of the brain typically associated with higher cognitive functions such as decision making and executive control. The traditional approach to solving such dilemmas typically invokes the normative framework of ethics. The argument is that our response to these dilemmas should be judged relative to norms. Deontologists, for instance, might judge it wrong to harm someone in order to save someone else in all circumstances. The question, then, is not which ethical theory best fits the empirical data but rather what the empirical data tell us about the nature of morality.

As Joshua Greene (2008, p. 43) notes in reviewing the relevant neuroimaging studies, "People tend toward consequentialism in the case in which the emotional response is low and tend toward deontology in the case in which the emotional response is high." To support his hypothesis, Greene cites evidence from evolutionary history: "up close and personal" violence, for instance, reaches quite far back into our primate lineage by comparison with the types of impersonal harm (e.g., drone strikes) that demand complex forms of abstract reasoning. This hypothesis is further supported by reaction times, as it takes longer to ponder an impersonal moral dilemma (the trolley case) than dilemmas that elicit strong emotional response (the footbridge case). On this account, judging a personal moral violation appropriate (that is, judging that it is permissible to push the stranger to his death in the footbridge case) depends on the capacity to override the emotional response that such an up close and personal action would elicit.

What the evidence from neuroimaging so far suggests is that we are hardwired to have powerful innate responses to personal violence. We may regard these data as providing evidential support for the view that altruistic behavior is a natural kind. At the same time the capacity to override strong emotional responses implicit in judgments that deem personal moral violations appropriate casts a long shadow on any idea of an innate or intrinsic good.

On the grounds that the cultivation of compassion is essentially a normative aspect of Buddhist practice, we can now ask: Can a bodhisattva on the path of moral and mental cultivation undergo the kind of transformation that renders consequentialist thought immune to emotional response? The Buddhist literature is unambiguous on this point: compassion meditation has quite different effects on beginner bodhisattvas than on those who have advanced along the path. Beginning bodhisattvas are often portrayed as "overwhelmed by compassion" such that they may even be found crying. Progress along the path is such that the occasional outburst has gradually given way to equanimity.[16]

Do emotional responses, then, play any role in the generally consequentialist framework of Mahāyāna Buddhist ethics? In the case of prescriptions that sanction moral violations for a greater good, the presumption is that bodhisattvas would have developed the capacity to override their emotional responses, especially those typically associated with inflicting harm on a person judged to be committing some wrongdoing. (The bodhisattva cannot be plagued by an internal struggle to overcome such negative emotions as remorse.) However, such judgments of wrongdoing presuppose a normative framework and imply some notion of moral responsibility. And moral responsibility cannot be understood without addressing the issues of agency and free will.

6.4. Freedom and Human Responsibility

Whether something analogous to the Western notion of free will is found in Buddhism is an open question.[17] A notion of "the will"—in the sense of voluntary action (*voluntas*)—is indeed presupposed by the Buddhist concept of *cetanā*, variously translated as "volition," "intention," and "will." But at the most basic level, *cetanā* captures the dynamic aspects of the mind relative to objects or specific ends. The problem, then, is this: How can accounts of action and its consequences (karma) become part of an ethical framework given the standpoint of Buddhist reductionism?

Are free will and determinism compatible? Is there a way of reconciling our first-person account of volitional action with third-person perspectives of the underlying physical, biological, and now neurobiological processes? Is there another way of conceiving of humans or, indeed, of being human that demands a radical reassessment of our understanding of voluntary action and of the causal and motivational factors that inform, condition, and sanction our valuing judgments? More specifically for our purpose here, how has the relation between volitional and causal accounts of agency been understood in the Buddhist context?

The Buddhist account of this relation originates with Siddhārtha Gautama's experience of enlightenment. This experience becomes at once the source of the Buddhist metaphysical picture of reality and the culmination of all human aspiration for genuine freedom. Key to this metaphysical picture is the causal principle of dependent arising and a thoroughly reductionist account of persons, which takes volition to be but one of the many contributing factors that shape human identity and agency. In one of his earliest discourses, the Buddha declares that we ought to regard any form of sensation, attention, and consciousness, whether "past, future, or present; internal or external; manifest or subtle ... as it actually is... : 'This is not mine. This is not my self. This is not what I am'" (SN.iii.49). Of course the rejection of a permanent self as the agent of sensory, affective, and mental activity poses a significant challenge for Buddhism. If there is no agent, and if actions are merely transient events arising within a continuum of causally interconnected states, how is the intentional orientation of human actions to be understood? Even assuming, as the evidence from cognitive neuroscience seems to suggest, that we are psychologically hardwired to attribute agency and hold others responsible for their actions, the question why such agency-attributing capacities should be accompanied by a moral sense remains to be explained. I will return to this point in my conclusion.

Whether we take the Buddhist no-self view to be a theoretical construct or a descriptive account of the immediacy of lived experience, its picture of human nature and agency undermines (or is irrelevant to) the practical concerns of moral responsibility. Now, as some have suggested (most notably Siderits, 2008), there might be a conflict between the conventional practice of morality (to which the Buddha offers precepts, inspiring tales, and rules of conduct) and Buddhist metaphysical doctrine. The Kantian distinction invoked here, between the concerns of practical reason and theorizing about the nature of things, serves as a useful heuristic: the basic thrust of this broadly Kantian view is that when I engage in theoretical reasoning (of the sort that looks for causal explanation of events) there is no place for concepts like freedom and responsibility. But when I engage in practical reasoning (of the sort that asks "What should I do?" and then looks for the most justifiable course of action) there are good reasons to hold myself responsible for my actions. That is, regardless of whether or not theoretical reason is able to demonstrate freedom, practical reason must assume that freedom is possible for the purpose of action. Bringing this Kantian perspective to bear on the Buddhist account of human agency is motivated by the assumption that the kind of freedom we are supposed to consider (and perhaps criticize) is basically as described by libertarians, that is, as involving complete spontaneity. Furthermore, as the neuroimaging studies discussed above seem to suggest, the normative framework of deontology may have its roots in a basic tendency to avoid (and thus create circumstances that would minimize) the sort of comportment that is conducive to heightened emotional response.

Do freedom and responsibility, as artifacts of practical reason, belong in a discourse about causation in the natural world?[18] If the concerns of practical and theoretical reason are taken to be mutually entailing, then they do. On the other hand, if theoretical reason is seen to be at odds with our practical concerns about how best to live, then they do not. The Buddhist metaphysical picture of reality, as a product of theoretical reason, is devoid of any reference to selves and their concerns, or indeed to anything substantive. At least in principle, the no-self view would preclude any robust account of freedom and responsibility. Yet Buddhist practice requires the observance of certain norms and the valuation of certain types of thought, speech, and action that are considered beneficial. Chief among these is the restraint of unmitigated willful thought, speech, and action. However, this valuation, and the psychological terms in which it is expressed, is at odds with an impersonal account of the self and subjectivity in causal terms. Siderits's proposal is that some kind of Buddhist compatibilism is called for to solve this conflict. Can such an account, in effect, be offered?

Consider Śāntideva's extension of the permission to break moral rules to those who carry out "compassionate" actions. If such an injunction cannot be easily justified on a normative account of practical reason, then the largely consequentialist framework of compatibilism cannot give an adequate account of our moral institutions. (Such a framework is also indifferent to the concerns of practical reason.) Thus Mahāyāna ethicists are not concerned with the possibility of freedom in a causally ordered universe (such possibility is taken to be the modus operandi of all enlightened beings) but with minimizing suffering and/or maximizing happiness. This account of agency in the service of altruistic aims is partly the reason most interpreters have regarded Buddhist ethics as essentially utilitarian or consequentialist in scope.[19] The problem with this account is that it takes moral agency away from ordinary people, who come to be regarded as lacking an understanding of how things are and of the proper motivation for ethical action. (In some sense they are no better than children or the insane.)

Whether conventional morality and the antinomian character of the bodhisattva's conduct are perfectly comprehensible if, as Siderits argues, we take the Buddhist account of practical rationality in straightforwardly consequentialist terms is, indeed, open to debate. Siderits's (2008, p. 39) proposal is that we are dealing here with two versions of consequentialism: indirect consequentialism

for the common folk and act-consequentialism for the bodhisattva, whose enlightened perspective allows for all sorts of shortcuts that are simply not available to the rest of us. But the trust this view places in our capacity to account
for motivations that are inscrutable and for responsibilities that are intractable
makes the Buddhist view of practical rationality seem rather whimsical.

What, then, do the Buddhists debate when they talk about the Eightfold
Noble Path or the cultivation of perfections as an ethical program? And is this
seemingly virtue-ethical program compatible with the Buddhist metaphysical
picture of reality? It is tempting to say that what is at stake here is the so-called
mechanics of salvation, that is, whether or not the disciplined cultivation at
the heart of the Eightfold Noble Path guarantees the liberation from suffering
and cyclical existence that Buddhists aspire to. The question is this: Can disciplined cultivation take the place of practical reason?

Certainly the fact that ethical concerns occupy only the lower rung of the
Eightfold Path program would suggest that for the Buddhist moral norms are
conventional and ultimately they should be overcome or even discarded. What
does that mean for our understanding of the relation between freedom and responsibility? It is hard to say.[20] The idea that there are types of freedom, specifically freedom from suffering and rebirth, that are not responsibility-entailing
(at least not in terms of reasons for which actions might be held accountable)
seems to advocate a type of libertarian agency that is hard to reconcile with
Buddhist reductionism.

6.5. Conclusion

When Śāntideva allows for moral rules to be violated under the expediency
of a compassionate aim, he likewise undermines the traditional notion of responsibility.[21] Of course the absence of a strictly causal account of action poses
an even greater threat than does any notion of determinism. If prior conditioning does not determine our thoughts and actions, then they must be either
random or spontaneous. And indeterminism does not make things any easier
for the compatibilist than determinism does; quite the contrary (bumper-
sticker wisdom of the sort that urges us to "practice random acts of kindness"
notwithstanding). Neocompatibilist positions such as one finds, for instance,
in Flanagan (2002), address some of these challenges by showing how, if we
dispense with the incoherent notion of libertarian agency, some notion of
responsibility can be salvaged. For Flanagan and all neocompatibilists who
recognize the need to take cognitive science seriously, the main issue is that
our traditional notions of agency and responsibility are in need of revision.
Indeed, recent advances in the study of human cognition suggest that much

of our conscious mental life depends on subconscious cognitive processes. In setting out to offer an account of how the two pictures are compatible, neocompatibilists shift the dependency relation for freedom and responsibility from norms to facts. Critics of this sort of approach, and here I would include myself, point out that the results of cognitive science are subject to constant revision and that a notion of moral agency explainable in terms of, say, dispositions is provisory at best.[22] Indeed, the normative features of moral reasoning do not sit well with the revisionist methods of science, at least not as traditionally understood, even though there are no good reasons to exclude moral norms from the purview of empirical research.

Now, just as conscious awareness remains the single most puzzling and most difficult phenomenon to explain in reductive terms, the patterns exhibited by moral agency also resist the eliminative reductionism of certain types of scientific explanation. Some philosophers of cognitive science argue that human consciousness is inherently intersubjective, and therefore empathy must count as a precondition of consciousness (Thompson, 2001). This line of argumentation suggests that agency presupposes some degree of self-awareness and of concern for others, both of which resist impersonal causal explanation. Maybe the Buddhist ethicists have in mind a similar sort of resistance when they allow for the compassionate aspirations of the bodhisattva to trump psychological determinism. However, if the bodhisattva can attain a type of freedom that is unimpeded by karmic hindrances, the efficacy of his or her actions (outside the web of interdependent causation) becomes deeply mysterious. After all, as we noted above, tales of bodhisattvas who intervene, as if magically, to take humans out of the trap of cyclical existence abound in the Buddhist literature. Does that make the bodhisattva a sort of compassionate libertine? Perhaps. But in that case genuine compassion implies a kind of spontaneity that is not easily captured by notions of moral agency that depend only on the actual or foreseeable consequences of acts. Whether such compassionate spontaneity also possesses the right sort of responsibility-conferring capacity cannot be settled without further probing the mesh that is the bodhisattva's practical wisdom and skillful concern for others.

Abbreviations

BCA   Śāntideva's *Bodhicaryāvatāra*. Translations from K. Crosby & A. Skilton in Śāntideva (1995).

SN   *Saṃyutta Nikāya*, volume and page in the Pali Text Society edition. Translations from Bodhi (2000).

SŚ   Śāntideva's *Śikṣā-samuccaya*. In Śāntideva (2016).

Notes

1. The exception here is Nussbaum's (2001) comprehensive account of the cognitive structure of compassion in the context of an analysis of what she regards, borrowing a concept from Greek theater, as the tragic predicament of the human condition. Taking as her point of departure Aristotle's view of compassion—which, following Homer and Plato, he regards as a painful emotion directed at another person's misfortune—Nussbaum aligns herself with those who defend the centrality of compassion to any moral theory (e.g., Rousseau, Schopenhauer, and Adam Smith) against the opponents of emotion (e.g., the Greek and Roman Stoics, Spinoza, Kant, and Nietzsche). Noting the centrality of altruistic concerns to certain philosophical conceptions of morality (especially those that appeal to evolutionary theory to make the case that psychological altruism is true), Stich, Doris, and Roedder (2010) rightly identify compassion as the sort of "right emotion" for producing moral motivation. Nonetheless, they pay only scant attention to the role of compassion in explaining the link between moral motivation and voluntary action.

2. An extensive review of the literature on affective neuroscience and compassion is found in Davidson (2002). See also Lamm, Batson, and Decety (2007), Lutz, Brefczynski-Lewis, Johnstone, and Davidson (2008), and Mascaro, Rilling, Tenzin Negi, and Raison (2012) for studies that showcase high empathic responses in individuals who undergo a form of secularized analytical compassion meditation.

3. See Coseru (2012, Chapter 3.3). Note that "intentional content" here is broadly conceived to include both what the mental state is a state of (its object) as well as its own operations. Of course, whether intentional content is distinct from the objects intended by such mental acts as perceiving or judging is a controversial topic. For more on this debate, see Zahavi (2004).

4. Wilson's (1998, p. 54) suggestion that "causal explanation of brain activity and evolution" suffices as an explanation of moral behavior may be unwarranted in light of the fact that moral judgment has the capacity to alter conditioned behavior in substantive ways; being made aware, for instance, that one is evolutionarily conditioned to favor members of one's group over outsiders can, on reflection, lead to adopting a more egalitarian view. Although tracing the history of moral behavior is notoriously difficult, its roots are generally assumed to lie in an innate biological altruism (which is found in many species). It is this biological altruism that underpins the more complex psychological altruism at the heart of our so-called 'ethical project' (cf. Kitcher, 2011). Indeed only the latter can explain how we come to care for the welfare of others not for our but for their own sake.

5. For an argument in favor of the spontaneity of compassion, see Williams (2009, pp. 116–117). In his discussion of BCA 9.34–35, Williams takes the view that buddhas are disposed to help precisely because they lack reifying and modal propositional attitudes.

6. I owe this suggestion to Sheridan Hough, who explores the causal aspects of agency and intersubjectivity in her essay on *Breaking Bad*; as she points out (Hough, 2016, p. 218), the series creator, Vince Gilligan, "denies the discrete or independent reality of the objects and persons within the causal structure." As Gilligan himself puts it: "I like to believe . . . that karma kicks in at some point, even if it takes years or decades to happen" (quoted in Hough, 2016, p. 218).

7. I explore this issue at length in Coseru (2016), where I also address the tension between the Buddhist account of the irreducibility of the mental and the tendency to confine freedom and responsibility to the domain of social convention. If the Buddhist's ultimate ontology contains phenomenal primitives, then freedom and responsibility cannot be mere artifacts of conceptual proliferation.

8. While the secondary literature of Buddhist ethics has grown considerably in recent years, with few exceptions (notably Keown, 1996; Siderits, 2008; Goodman, 2009; Garfield, 2010; Finnigan, 2011), most treatments are still exegetical in scope and anchored in specific texts and/or traditions. Surveys that address the relevance of Buddhist ethical principles to a wider range of topics, including such controversial issues as human rights, animal rights, ecology, war, and abortion, are found in Cooper and James (2005) and Keown (2007).

9. Readers may consult the excellent surveys in Harvey (2000), Keown (2001), Clayton (2006), and Goodman (2009). I address some of the same issues in Coseru (2016).

10. See, especially, Farah (2005), Gazzaniga (2005), Greene and Haidt (2002), and Greene (2008, 2009).

11. For a close look at the expedient role of these parables, with specific reference to the Prodigal Son, in the *Lotus Sutra*, see Lai (1981).

12. An ethics of compassionate violence, as Stephen Jenkins (2010, p. 326) has convincingly argued, works by "removing the possibility that any action is essentially inauspicious." Such an ethics, then, coupled with the (metaphysical) notion that the workings of karma are generally inconceivable, not only engenders ambiguity about the bodhisattva's ethical program but also diminishes the capacity for moral certainty.

13. See Dreyfus (2002) for an illuminating account of the difficulties of cross-cultural approaches to mental typologies with specific reference to the dialogue between Buddhism and cognitive science.

14. See, especially, Koechlin, Ody, and Kouneiher (2003), Miller and Cohen (2001), and Ramnani and Owen (2004).

15. See, especially, Adolphs (2002), Maddock (1999), and Phan, Wager, Taylor, and Liberzon, (2002).

16. Contrast, for example, BCA 2.50, "In despair, I cry out for help to protector Avalokiteśvara, who acts compassionately and inerrantly, begging him to protect my vicious self", with BCA 10.2, "Whoever is suffering distress of body or

mind in any of the ten directions—may they obtain oceans of happiness and joy through my good actions."

17. See Dasti and Bryant (2014) and Repetti (2016), and contributions therein.

18. Addressing a similar issue, but with respect to the moral implications of advances in neuroscience, Hilary Bok (2007) concludes that learning about the many ways freedom can be undermined (by phobias, compulsions, failures of self-control, etc.) offers an opportunity to conceive of freedom in more effective terms. Bok proposes that we understand freedom as a "capacity for self-governance" rather than as a type of choice-driven action (p. 559).

19. Proposals that advance a utilitarian interpretation of Buddhist ethics are found in, among others, Pratt (1928), Kalupahana (1976), and Goodman (2009).

20. I do, however, venture a response to this question in Coseru (2016).

21. See BCA 5.83 and ŚS 168.11, and discussion in Clayton (2009, p. 23).

22. Stich, Doris, and Roedder (2010) reach the same conclusion about employing evolutionary theory to intervene in the empirical debate between altruists and egoists: useful as it may be, in the end, neither camp makes a convincing case.

References

Adolphs, R. (2002). Neural systems for recognizing emotion. *Current Opinion in Neurobiology, 12*(2), 169–177.

Bodhi, B. (Trans.). (2000). *The connected discourses of the Buddha.* Boston: Wisdom.

Bok, H. (2007). The implications of advances in neuroscience for freedom of the will. *Neurotherapeutics: The Journal of the American Society for Experimental NeuroTherapeutics, 4,* 555–559.

Brefczynski-Lewis, J. A., Lutz, A., Schaefer, H. S., Levinson, D. B., & Davidson, R. J. (2007). Neural correlates of attentional expertise in long-term meditation practitioners. *Proceedings of the National Academy of Sciences, 104,* 11483–11488.

Brooks, D. (2008, May 13). The neural Buddhists. *New York Times.*

Clayton, B. R. (2006). *Moral theory in Śāntideva's Śikṣāsamuccaya: Cultivating the fruits of virtue.* New York: Routledge.

Clayton, B. R. (2009). Śāntideva, virtue, consequentialism. In J. Powers & C. S. Prebish (Eds.), *Destroying Mara forever* (pp. 16–29). New York: Snow Lion.

Cooper, D. E., & James, S. P. (2005). *Buddhism, virtue, environment.* Burlington, VT: Ashgate.

Coseru, C. (2012). *Perceiving reality: Consciousness, intentionality, and cognition in Buddhist philosophy.* New York: Oxford University Press.

Coseru, C. (2016). Freedom from responsibility: Agent neutral consequentialism and the bodhisattva ideal. In R. Repetti (Ed.), *Buddhist perspectives on free will* (pp. 92–105). London: Routledge.

Dasti, M., & Bryant, E. F. (Eds). (2014). *Free will, agency, and selfhood in Indian philosophy*. New York: Oxford University Press.

Davidson, R. (2002). Toward a biology of positive affect and compassion. In R. Davisdon & A. Harrington (Eds.), *Visions of compassion: Western scientists and Tibetan Buddhists examine human nature* (pp. 107–130). New York: Oxford University Press.

Dreyfus, G. (2002). Is compassion an emotion? A cross-cultural exploration of mental typologies. In R. Davisdon & A. Harrington (Eds.), *Visions of compassion: Western scientists and Tibetan Buddhists examine human nature* (pp. 31–45). New York: Oxford University Press.

Farah, M. J. (2005). Neuroethics: The practical and the philosophical. *Trends in Cognitive Sciences, 9,* 34–40.

Finnigan, B. (2011). How can a Buddha come to act? The possibility of a Buddhist account of ethical agency. *Philosophy East and West, 61*(1), 134–160.

Flanagan, O. (2002). *The problem of the soul: Two visions of the mind and how to reconcile them*. New York: Basic Books.

Flanagan, O. (2011). *The bodhisattva's brain: Buddhism naturalized*. Cambridge, MA: MIT Press.

Garfield, J. (2010). What it is like to be a bodhisattva? Moral phenomenology in Śāntideva's *Bodhicaryāvarāta. Journal of the International Association of Buddhist Studies, 33*(1–2), 333–358.

Gazzaniga, M. S. (2005). *The ethical brain: The science of our moral dilemmas*. New York: Dana Press.

Goel, V., & Dolan, R. J. (2004). Differential involvement of left prefrontal cortex in inductive and deductive reasoning. *Cognition, 93,* B109–B121.

Goodman, C. (2009). *Consequences of compassion: An interpretation and defense of Buddhist ethics*. New York: Oxford University Press.

Greene, J. (2008). The secret joke of Kant's soul. In W. Sinnott-Armstrong (Ed.), *Moral Psychology* (vol. 3, pp. 35–79). Boston: MIT Press.

Greene, J. (2009). The cognitive neuroscience of moral judgment. In M. S. Gazzaniga (Ed.), *The Cognitive Neurosciences* IV. Cambridge, MA: MIT Press.

Greene, J., Cushman, F. A., Stewart, L.A., Lowenberg, K., Nystrom, L. E., & Cohen, J. D. (2009). Pushing moral buttons: The interaction between personal force and intention in moral judgment. *Cognition, 111,* 364–371.

Greene, J., & Haidt, J. (2002). How (and where) does moral judgment work? *Trends in Cognitive Sciences, 6*(12), 517–523.

Haidt, J. (2001). The emotional dog and its rational tail: A social intuitionist approach to moral judgment. *Psychological Review, 108*(4), 814–834.

Harvey, P. (2000). *An introduction to Buddhist ethics*. Cambridge, UK: Cambridge University Press.

Hough, S. (2016). "We are responsible to all for all": an intersubjective analysis of *Breaking Bad*. In Decker, K. S., Koepsell, D. R., & Arp, R., (Eds.), *Philosophy and Breaking Bad* (pp. 217–232). Palgrave Macmillan.

Jenkins, S. (2010). On the auspiciousness of compassionate violence. *Journal of the International Association of Buddhist Studies, 33*(1–2), 299–332.

Kalupahana, D. (1976). *Buddhist philosophy: A historical analysis.* Honolulu: University Press of Hawaii.

Kant, I. (1993). *Grounding for the metaphysics of morals.* (J. W. Ellington, Trans.). Indianapolis: Hackett.

Keown, D. (1996). Karma, character, and consequentialism. *Journal of Religious Ethics, 24*(2), 329–350.

Keown, D. (2001). *The nature of Buddhist ethics.* London: Macmillan.

Keown, D. (2007). Buddhism and ecology: A virtue ethics approach. *Contemporary Buddhism, 8*(2), 97–112.

Kitcher, P. (2011). *The ethical project.* Cambridge, MA: Harvard University Press.

Koechlin, E., Basso, G., Petrini, P., Panzer, S., & Grafman, J. (1999). The role of the anterior prefrontal cortex in human cognition. *Nature, 399,* 148–151.

Koechlin, E., Ody, C., & Kouneiher, F. (2003). The architecture of cognitive control in the human prefrontal cortex. *Science, 302,* 1181–1185.

Lai, W. (1981). The Buddhist "prodigal son": A history of misperceptions. *Journal of the International Association of Buddhist Studies, 4*(2), 91–98.

Lamm, C., Batson, C. D., & Decety, J. (2007). The neural substrate of human empathy: Effects of perspective-taking and cognitive appraisal. *Journal of Cognitive Neuroscience, 19*(1), 42–58.

Lutz, A, Brefczynski-Lewis, J., Johnstone, T., & Davidson, R. J. (2008). Regulation of the neural circuitry of emotion by compassion meditation: Effects of meditative expertise. *PLoS ONE, 3*(3), e1897.

Lutz, A., Dunne, J., & Davidson, R. (2007). Meditation and the neuroscience of cognition. In P. Zelazo, M. Moscovitch, & E. Thompson (Eds.), *The Cambridge handbook of consciousness* (pp. 499–554). Cambridge, UK: Cambridge University Press.

Maddock, R. J. (1999). The retrosplenial cortex and emotion: New insights from functional neuroimaging of the human brain. *Trends in Neuroscience, 22,* 310–316.

Miller, E. K., & Cohen, J. D. (2001). An integrative theory of prefrontal cortex function. *Annual Review of Neuroscience, 24,* 167–202.

Mascaro, J. S., Rilling, J., Tenzin Negi, L., & Raison, C. L. (2012). Compassion meditation enhances empathic accuracy and related neural activity. *Social Cognitive & Affective Neuroscience, 5,* 1–8.

Nietzsche, F. (2006). *On the genealogy of morality.* (C. Diethe, Trans.). Cambridge, UK: Cambridge University Press.

Nussbaum, M. (2001). *Upheavals of thought: The intelligence of emotions.* Cambridge, UK: Cambridge University Press.

Phan, K. L., Wager, T., Taylor, S. F., & Liberzon, I. (2002). Functional neuroanatomy of emotion: A meta-analysis of emotion activation studies in PET and fMRI. *Neuroimage, 16,* 331–348.

Pratt, J. B. (1928). *The pilgrimage of Buddhism.* New York: Macmillan.

Ramnani, N., & Owen, A.M., (2004). Anterior prefrontal cortex: insights into function from anatomy and neuroimaging. *Nat Rev Neurosci, 5,* 184–194.

Repetti, R. (Ed.). (2016). *Buddhist perspectives on free will: Agentless agency?* London: Routledge.

Stich, S., Doris, J. M., & Roedder, E. 2010. Altruism. In John M. Doris & The Moral Psychology Research Group (Eds.), *The moral psychology handbook* (pp. 147–205). Oxford: Oxford University Press.

Śāntideva. (1995). *The Bodhicaryāvatāra.* (K. Crosby & A. Skilton, Trans.). Oxford: Oxford University Press.

Śāntideva. (2016). *The Training Anthology of Śāntideva: A Translation of Śikṣā-samuccaya.* (C. Goodman, Trans.). New York: Oxford University Press.

Siderits, M. (2008). Paleo-compatibilism and Buddhist reductionism. *Sophia, 47,* 29–42.

Thompson, E. (2001). Empathy and consciousness. *Journal of Consciousness Studies, 8*(5–7), 1–32.

Williams, P. (2009). Is Buddhist ethics virtue ethics? In J. Powers & C. S. Prebish (Eds.), *Destroying Mara forever* (pp. 114–137). New York: Snow Lion.

Wilson, E. O. (1998, April). The biological basis of Morality. *Atlantic Monthly, 53–70.*

Zahavi, D. (2004). Husserl's noema and the internalism-externalism debate. *Inquiry, 47*(1), 42–66.

PART THREE

Karma and Rebirth

Chapter 7

Modern and Traditional Understandings of Karma

Charles Goodman

7.1. Introduction

Karma is dead; long live karma! The traditional understanding of karma as a cosmic force that makes the world fair, matching destinies to actions over the course of innumerable lives in the cycle of existence, does not seem to be tenable in the context of a scientific worldview. Meanwhile, Buddhist modernists are developing an understanding of karma as a distinctive psychological process that frequently leads harmful actions to evolve into experiences of suffering and helpful actions to evolve into experiences of happiness. If we shift to this kind of understanding of karma, the effect on Buddhist ethics will be quite significant. In this essay I explore the relations between the old and the new understandings of karma and between this issue and the broader question of the theoretical structure of Buddhist ethics.

7.2. Between the Lines of the *Śikṣā-samuccaya*

Many of the great systematic Buddhist treatises from India and Tibet contain detailed discussions of karma and its results. One such discussion, closely based on scriptural sources, can be found in chapter 4 of the *Training Anthology* (*Śikṣā-samuccaya*, or ŚS) of Śāntideva. Here Śāntideva, drawing primarily on the *Sūtra on the Application of Mindfulness to the Holy Dharma*, lays out what he takes to be the karmic consequences of the Ten Bad Courses of Action (*daśa-akuśala-karma-pātha*). This presentation of karma lays great stress on the gruesome and terrifying nature of the results of the worst actions. In particular the description of the "Bird Terror Wing" of Avīci hell is enough to make the most determined skeptic shudder.

And yet, even in the midst of this hellfire-and-brimstone passage, which rivals the most lurid of Christian sermons, we can find hints and indications of a counternarrative. Much of what Śāntideva says about hell can be understood, with very little interpretive license, to refer to the ways in which actions carried out in this life produce karmic results in this same life, either by their effects on our external circumstances or, more frequently, by their effects on how we perceive the world around us. That is, it is not only possible but natural to read the text along the lines of the psychological interpretation of karma presented in Buddhist modernist works such as Ken McLeod's (2002) *Wake Up to Your Life*.[1]

Now, not everything that features in this part of the *Training Anthology* is best interpreted in the way I am suggesting. Much of the text seems based on a rather crude form of poetic justice. But to the extent that the kind of interpretation I favor gives us the best explanation of at least some of what Śāntideva says, we may be justified in regarding the modern account of karma as continuing at least a major strand that was already present in the Indian Buddhist tradition and that may be the most viable aspect of the traditional theory of karma for a worldview of today.

Let's begin by considering the passage, quoted from the *Sūtra on the Application of Mindfulness to the Holy Dharma*, that explains the results of stealing, or in Buddhist terminology, taking what is not given:

When he goes to the end of that ruinous action, [the thief] sees an illusion that appears to be a great collection of wealth—gems, clothing, money, and grain—but is in fact like a wheel of flames, a city of gandharvas, or a mirage. Overcome by greed and deluded by karma, he thinks, "This is mine!" Deluded in this way, the wrongdoer crosses over a blazing fire of dry dung and hot coals, and runs up to that wealth. There Yama's men, who are created by karma, seize him, and in a blaze of swords, cut his body in pieces. Then they burn the body, leaving only the bones. But even though it has brought him to a situation like this, the greed that has existed in him for beginningless time does not diminish. (ŚS 71)

What can we find in this passage that might be relevant to the modern interpretation? The thief in the passage is deluded in two ways. First, he takes the wealth to be real when it is in fact illusory. Of course the wealth that we observe people stealing is in fact illusory in more than one important sense: they emotionally take it to be permanent, whereas it is actually impermanent; they emotionally take it to be the key to true satisfaction and happiness, whereas it is actually deeply unsatisfactory. In addition to the fact that the wealth is illusory, the wrongdoer also mentally regards it as his own. In our world, thieves often tell themselves some kind of absurd story about how the things they are going to steal rightfully belong to them, in order to justify the actions they will need to take to get what they think they need.

Because of his fundamental errors, the thief accepts great pain (in the allegory, due to having to cross a fire) in order to obtain this wealth. But in the end he is caught by the agents of the state—in this case, guardians of hell—and subjected to painful punishment. In fact this passage does a fairly good job of representing in symbolic form the basic errors and the inevitable destiny of those who, in the world of our ordinary experience, try to live by stealing.

Another passage, dripping with ascetic misogyny, is just as well-suited to express, in the language of hellfire and damnation, a certain kind of Buddhist view about how our own world works. This is the general presentation of the karmic results of sexual misconduct:

> When he somehow gets out of [the region called] Beset with Swords, the one who has acted vilely crosses the fire of dry dung and hot coals. Driven to wander by karma, he arrives at a region named Deceptive Appearance. He sees women created by karma; he has seen others like them before, but has lost his memory. When he sees them, the fire of attraction that has been habituated in him since beginningless time flares up, and he runs towards those women. But they are made of iron, created that way by karma. They seize him, and starting with the lips, they devour him, leaving nothing behind, not even [a remnant] the size of a mustard-seed. He is born again, and again he is eaten. He experiences harsh, unbearable sensations, but because of them, the fire of attraction does not cease; instead, he runs towards those women even more, and the pain he suffers doesn't interfere with the fire of attraction. Those women of iron and adamant, their bodies burdened with blazing garlands, crush that hell-being like a handful of sand. He is born again, and so on as before. (ŚS 71–72)

I'm sure there are quite a few men who would find that this passage resonates with something in their experience—and, for that matter, quite a few women who could substitute blazing iron men and get a description that fits their lives, if anything, even better. Surely this is not a coincidence; it seems obvious the anonymous author or authors of the *Sūtra on the Application of Mindfulness to the Holy Dharma* intended it to be possible to make this kind of connection.

The description of the results of murder that begins the discussion from which I am quoting is highly complex, but at least part of the description fits well into the modern framework: "When, by some rare chance, he gets out of there, wandering around in great pain, seeking protection, seeking refuge, seeking rescue,[2] he goes toward a second region, named Fallen Into the Abyss. He is surrounded on all sides by eleven masses of flames, friendless, bound by the noose of karma, encircled by enemies, in a disastrous situation. In great distress due to the multitude of hell-beings everywhere around, he runs toward the region named Fallen Into the Abyss. At every step his foot is consumed by fire" (ŚS 70). I see in this passage a strong emphasis on the murderer as alone and friendless. And this fits with the modern interpretation in several ways. Quite obviously, once you start murdering people, the number of friends who will stand up for you and help you diminishes rapidly, while the number of enemies you have (starting with the SWAT team) increases just as rapidly. Even more significant, the murderer comes to perceive the world as a hostile and threatening place, full of enemies. No one can be trusted; anyone could stab you in the back at any time. This world, in this life, becomes a harsh realm of conflict, full of fire and demons. The murderer comes to perceive the Earth as a hell.

However, not everything in Śāntideva's presentation of the Ten Bad Courses of Action can be related so neatly to the modern interpretation. There are other thematic forces that shape the way karma is presented here. Consider, for example, the alleged results of the evolution of lying:

> Yama's men seize him, and forcing open his mouth, pull out his tongue. By the power of karma, as the result of that lie, his tongue becomes five hundred leagues long. As soon as it comes out, Yama's men force the tongue down onto the ground of blazing iron. A thousand ploughs appear, made of blazing iron. Mighty oxen propel them onto his tongue. Rivers of oozing pus and blood, full of worms, flow out. ... And that tongue is very tender, just like the eye of one of the gods. He groans, cries and calls out weakly from the pain, but none of his pain is relieved. As he experiences unbearable sensations in this way, his tongue is ploughed for many hundreds of thousands of years, until somehow he gets his tongue back into his mouth. (ŚS 72)

This passage seems to have much more to do with a kind of poetic justice than with the sophisticated psychology I see at work in other parts of the same discussion. The tongue is used to lie, so the tongue is the focus of the punishment, which is made as gruesome as possible. There is no clear way to relate this vivid description to any significant aspects of the external or internal this-worldly consequences of lying.

At the same time, how plausible would it be to try to believe that this passage expresses the literal truth about what happens to liars? The grim, relentless onslaught of the *sūtra*'s account of the karmic consequences of murder is well suited to induce a fearful doubt in the reader: What if this is really true? Could this happen to me? But on the other hand, who is really going to believe in a hellish destiny involving a five-hundred-league-long tongue? If we read the passage as suggesting in general, through vivid, imagistic language, that lying brings adverse consequences and that these consequences are often appropriate and poetically fitting to the nature of the offense, won't it be far easier to take the text's message seriously? And such a reading would be entirely consistent with taking karma to be a psychological process within us, operating in this life, rather than an exceptionless law of nature, operating primarily between lives.

Six Realms

A central structural feature of the modern interpretation of karma, as McLeod articulates it, is a psychological reading of the Six Realms of Buddhist cosmology. These realms, or destinies, have traditionally been understood as the forms of existence into which a sentient being can be reborn. They are the hell realm, the hungry ghost realm, the animal realm, the human realm, the titan realm, and the god realm. Many texts posit a complex and opaque relationship between the types of actions and motivations that one might commit and the realm in which one would be reborn as a result. But there is a teaching—associated, perhaps, most closely with the bKa' rgyud and the rNying ma lineages of Tibetan Buddhism—which connects each of the realms with a particular reactive emotion (Skt. *kleśa*, Tib. *nyon mongs*). Pride is said to give rise to the god realm; competitiveness, to the titan realm; desire, to the human realm; blind instinct, to the animal realm; greed, to the hungry ghost realm; and anger or hatred, to the hell realm. A teaching of this kind can be found, for example, in the *Prayer of Great Power* (see Kapstein, 2000, 197–201, especially 199–200).

Once we make this kind of association, the way is open for us to understand the Six Realms psychologically, as the imagined worlds projected by each of these reactive emotions. Under the influence of emotional confusion, we see the world in distorted ways; the descriptions of the realms found in the texts, though at least partly intended originally as cosmology, can also be read as analyses of how these distorted perceptions appear and the further actions to which they then tend to lead.

This account of how our minds work should have testable implications. It implies that when people carry out wrong actions under the influence of the various reactive emotions, those actions lead to predictable changes in how they perceive the world around them. It should be possible to design psychological experiments to attempt to measure these effects. If such experiments were done, this account might well turn out to be false or oversimplified. But it may nevertheless be interesting to explore what the ethical implications of adopting such an account might be.

7.3. Implications

If this modernist, revisionist understanding of the Law of Karma is correct, what, if anything, would follow about the theoretical structure of Buddhist ethics? I submit that the modern account of karma has important implications both for the virtue ethics interpretation and for the consequentialist interpretation, which I take to be the two most important proposals about how to read Buddhist ethics. Relative to a standard materialist worldview, the modern account will go some distance toward justifying eudaemonism—but not nearly as far as the traditional account. Moreover, the modern account will provide the consequentialist with some resources for dealing with difficult cases, such as Rawls's notorious problem about utilitarian persecution. The net effect, I think, will be to weaken the virtue ethics interpretation and strengthen the consequentialist interpretation. But let me discuss the two arguments in more detail.

At the heart of most forms of virtue ethics is a view called eudaemonism. To advocate eudaemonism is to assert a very tight connection between virtuous action, on the one hand, and the well-being of the agent, on the other. The locus classicus of eudaemonism is, of course, Aristotle's *Nicomachean Ethics*. In that work Aristotle (1999, p. 9: *NE* 1098a10) actually defines eudaemonia, "happiness" or "human flourishing," as "activity of the soul in accord with virtue . . . in a complete life." For some form of eudaemonism to be true, the connection between virtuous action and well-being does not necessarily have to be definitional. But it will have to turn out, for some reason or other, that we cannot improve our well-being by acting wrongly.

This claim would turn out to be true automatically if virtue were the only component in well-being, so that good fortune, success, and subjective pleasure had nothing whatsoever to do with how well anyone's life goes. And some might well be tempted to base an interpretation of Buddhist ethics on a claim like this. After all, Aristotle (1999, p. 117: *NE* 1153b20) expressed one ground of his disagreement with the virtue-only view as follows: "Some maintain, on the contrary, that we are happy when we are broken on the wheel, or fall into terrible misfortunes, provided that we are good. Whether they mean to or not, these people are talking nonsense." It's actually not difficult to find passages in Buddhist texts that assert more or less exactly what Aristotle thought was nonsense. In the *Training Anthology*, for example, we read:

> There is, Blessed One, a meditative absorption called Everything is Covered with Happiness. Bodhisattvas who attain this feel only happy feelings towards all objects they are aware of, with no feelings of suffering or unhappiness. Even while feeling the pains of the torments of hell, they think only happy thoughts. Even while suffering all the harms of the human condition, such as having their hands, feet or noses cut off, they think only happy thoughts. Even while being beaten with canes, half-canes or whips, they have only happy thoughts. . . . If their bones are being pulled out, or they are impaled on stakes, or led away to be killed, or their heads are cut off, they have only happy thoughts, not thoughts of suffering, nor thoughts that are neither happy nor suffering. (ŚS 181–182)

Unlike Aristotle, Mahāyāna Buddhists such as Śāntideva held that happiness could exist without any contribution from favorable external circumstances. This claim creates the possibility of holding that only the virtue that makes this special kind of happiness possible has any value at all.

On the other hand, a view that regards only virtue as valuable is subject to devastating objections. Notably, Nussbaum's famous critique of the ancient Greek and Roman Stoics will apply to Buddhist ethics if read this way. In *The Therapy of Desire*, among other works, Nussbaum (1994/2009) has pointed out that the Stoic account of well-being as consisting only of virtue seems to undermine the content of any plausible account of the virtues themselves. If physical injury, degradation, and misery are not bad for people, then why should it be any part of virtue to refrain from inflicting them on others? And if those who suffer these alterations of fortune at the hands of others have not been harmed, then what can justify setting up elaborate social institutions to prevent them, or participating in the functioning of those institutions?[3] The view that assigns value to nothing but virtue seems to drain all content out of both our ethical and our political theories, leaving nothing but a sterile form behind.

In addition to the substantive problem raised by Nussbaum, there is a serious interpretive problem with reading Buddhist ethics in this way. Unlike the Stoics, Buddhists have among their most important virtues both loving kindness, the wish for others to be happy, and compassion, the wish for others to be free from suffering. In the preceding sentence, "happy" includes the kind of worldly pleasures that, according to the view we are examining, are totally valueless. So try this claim on for size: Among the most important goods in existence are the wish for others to be in a state of no value and the wish for others to be free from a condition that is not bad for them! Such a view would be simply laughable.

Those who accept the traditional understanding of karma and its results need not go anywhere near such an absurd view. They can assign some positive value to worldly pleasures and some disvalue to the pain and suffering produced by unfavorable circumstances in cyclic existence. They can then claim that pleasure results from right actions, in this or in previous lives, whereas pain results from wrong actions.

Meanwhile, they can hold a view of the emotions that shares many claims with that of the Stoics but disagrees on certain crucial points. Buddhists of this kind can and should agree with the Stoics that ordinary reactive emotions, such as anger, resentment, contempt, or a desire for vengeance, are entirely inappropriate responses to the suffering, pain, and wrongdoing of others. People who are overcome by emotions of this kind show thereby that they don't understand how things are. Their emotional reactions are based on a sense of self and on relating external events to their sense of self—very much as in Nussbaum's preferred account of the emotions. But it is possible to have an appropriate emotional response to the misfortunes, wrongdoing, and suffering of others. This is compassion, a nonreactive emotion that is not organized around a sense of self. Thus a Buddhist view, while radically revisionary in its picture of the appropriateness of emotions, does not entail that all emotions without exception must be extirpated.

Those who endorse the traditional understanding of karma can then go on to endorse eudaemonism. On this view, when someone is considering doing what is wrong, she needs to recognize not only that the wrong action will move her further away from being awake but also that there will inevitably be adverse worldly consequences that more than outweigh any temporary gains that could be produced by acting wrongly. So morality and self-interest will coincide; there will be no conflict between doing the right thing and doing what is best for the agent's own well-being. And such a claim will create a hospitable descriptive background for a virtue ethics interpretation.

The modern understanding can do some of this work, but only some. In many instances, it's clear on ordinary grounds that crime doesn't pay; violating moral norms appears to be beneficial to the agent only because of foolishness and self-deception. In many other cases of wrongdoing, although the action may superficially appear to offer a real chance of net benefits to the agent, appropriate consideration of the psychological consequences of the action will reveal that there is really no chance of the agent's well-being increasing as a result. Social psychologists and other empirical researchers may be able to establish through experiment the existence of at least some of these additional consequences; others may be revealed through the introspective examination of the process of suffering carried out by highly trained and dedicated Buddhist meditators.

But will these claims hold in all possible cases of wrongdoing? It seems very hard to resist the claim that there will be at least certain rare cases of spectacularly profitable wrongdoing that will supply the perpetrator with plentiful material resources for life, with relatively little chance of failure or of being caught. In these cases, a credible understanding of the nature and scope of the psychological ill effects of wrongdoing is unlikely to imply that the perpetrator's well-being will be reduced by carrying out such an act. So if there is nothing more to karma than the workings of our psychology, as the modern view claims, then morality and self-interest will sometimes fail to coincide. The cases in which they diverge are likely to be rare; unfortunately, potential criminals will probably perceive them as diverging far more often than they actually do. But the theoretical point remains: Absent some heroic defense that has yet to be provided, on the modern understanding of karma, eudaemonism is false.

Of course there are non-eudaemonistic versions of virtue ethics, and one of those could still be adopted even in the descriptive environment I am sketching. Certainly it will be the case that profitable wrongdoing will not be an example of action in accord with virtue, and so this type of virtue ethicist will still have the moral resources to reject it. It seems, though, that it would be very helpful to have consequentialist or deontological considerations to bring in at this juncture. If we are no longer able to say that such actions impair the well-being of the agent, we will want to be able to say that profitable wrongdoing must be avoided either because it harms others or because it violates others' rights.

So much, then, for the effect of the modern understanding of karma on the virtue ethics interpretation. Let us proceed to consider the relevance of the modern understanding to consequentialism and to consequentialist interpretations of the structure of Buddhist ethics. On this kind of ethical view, karma is not intrinsically normative at all, but is part of the descriptive background against which moral reasoning takes place. Karmic consequences are some of the consequences that actions have and, as such, need to be taken appropriately into consideration in deciding whether an action would promote what is good. Now if we draw on the modern understanding of karma in this way, we may be able to answer important objections against consequentialism.

Rawls (1971, pp. 30–31) pointed out that according to utilitarianism, "social welfare depends directly and solely upon the levels of satisfaction or dissatisfaction of individuals. Thus if men take a certain pleasure in discriminating against one another, in subjecting others to a lesser liberty as a means of enhancing their self-respect, then the satisfaction of these desires must be weighed in our deliberations according to their intensity, or whatever, along with other desires." Of course there will be many countervailing considerations; discrimination of this kind will have all sorts of negative social effects. But philosophers such as Jeremy Waldron (1988, p. 12) have been willing to take Rawls's point one step further, arguing that "when one section of a population takes pleasure in persecuting another, that satisfaction may conceivably be taken as decisive in justifying on utilitarian grounds a decision not to extend social protection to the persecuted group."

The main reason this objection has been so influential is that it seems quite realistic. It won't work for large minorities, since, for a utilitarian, the suffering of one person who is being subjected to persecution clearly outweighs the prideful delight of one person who is rejoicing in the persecution of others. But it is easy to imagine a society in which a small minority, only 0.9% of the population, is hated with a ferocious passion by 90% of the population. Now if the pleasure gained by each member of the majority at seeing the tiny minority "put in their place" significantly exceeds 1% of the suffering experienced by each minority group member as a result of their subjugation, then a utilitarian would seem to be compelled to endorse the arrangement as one that increases social utility relative to a liberal system of legal equality.

To use a distinction drawn by Rawls (2005) in *Political Liberalism*, this example is a serious objection to utilitarianism whether it is considered as a comprehensive doctrine or as a political theory. It is not plausible that this kind of persecution is a reasonable way to organize our social life, nor should we find it acceptable for a theory about what is truly good in life to endorse as morally valuable the persecution of small, unpopular minorities.

What happens if we introduce the modern doctrine of karma? On this assumption, one can predict that the hate-filled attitudes and choices of the majority in this example generate psychological traces that mature into suffering for the majority group members. We do not even have to appeal to long-term social consequences, such as the disadvantages for economic development of a closed-minded, intolerant attitude. We can say that even though the majority group may believe they are happier as a result of their policy of persecution, the subconscious functioning of karma will make it turn out that, on the whole, they are far less happy than they would be if they could learn to live with the minority on fairer terms. This new utilitarian calculation will not be reversed by turning up the intensity of the majority's hatred and the strength of their preference for persecution. The more they hate the minority, the more powerful the adverse karmic consequences of persecution will be. It is conceivable that with great ingenuity, we could devise a bizarre case in which persecution would increase total utility even given the modern account of karma. But this objection against utilitarianism will lose most of its force if it turns out not to be based on a highly realistic and indeed occasionally actual social state of affairs, but instead on a far-fetched and speculative scenario.

I offer this reply in defense of a Buddhist form of utilitarianism as a comprehensive doctrine, not as a political theory. I find it objectionable to propose coercing non-Buddhists on the basis of assumptions about karma that they would reject. But the modern account of karma will allow us to say, from within a Buddhist comprehensive doctrine whose ethics are understood to be utilitarian, that it would be morally wrong for the majority to persecute a small minority out of intense hatred. By drawing on arguments similar to those offered by Mill in *On Liberty*, the Buddhist comprehensive doctrine can then form part of an overlapping consensus that justifies a system of liberal rights and freedoms. Non-Buddhists may choose to join the consensus for other reasons, and a constitutional prohibition against persecuting unpopular minorities can then be justified by the political norms endorsed in the public sphere as part of the consensus.

The same strategy may help with other objections to utilitarianism that have a similar structure to the objection from persecution. So, for example, Waldron (1993, pp. 260–261) rejects utilitarianism as a theory of justice largely on the ground that it might endorse slavery as a means of increasing average utility, and that the slaves would not be willing or able to consent to the social arrangements that were victimizing them, despite the fact that those arrangements maximized the average welfare of all the members of society. Now given what we know about the economic inefficiency of slavery—at least when the interests of the slaves are taken into account—such a scenario seems quite unlikely. But however strong the generic utilitarian case against slavery may be, a Buddhist utilitarian case could be considerably stronger. Though there is some controversy about the correct analytical definition of slavery as a social category, a widespread consensus exists that actual violence is central in maintaining any slave system.[1] Now if anything at all generates karmic consequences that lead to suffering, so does enforcing the enslavement of others through physical cruelty. So if the modern account of karma has any truth to it, it will be even less likely that utilitarianism could ever justify a slave system.

A Buddhist consequentialist theory gets these improved results by sacrificing a feature of Western utilitarian views that has been a source of much of their appeal but that also lies at the root of many of their problems. In practice the Buddhist version no longer treats all preferences or sources of enjoyment as equal, since some of them are regarded negatively in virtue of being sources of negative karma. The effect is to make the resulting theory much better suited as a comprehensive doctrine of the good and perhaps somewhat worse suited as a political theory that can be the object of universal agreement in a diverse modern society.

Though the strategy of appealing to the karmic consequences of malevolent preferences and violent social arrangements may save utilitarianism from some embarrassing apparent implications that have been raised against it, such a strategy cannot defend against all such implications. It will be entirely unhelpful, for example, in Williams's famous case of Jim and the Indians, in which visiting botanist Jim must decide between killing an innocent man or allowing an army sergeant to murder twenty innocent people.[5] Jim can certainly count the bad karma he could suffer as one of the consequences of the action of carrying out one killing himself, but he must also count the greater bad karma the sergeant stands to incur as a reason against allowing him to perpetrate twenty killings. Indeed given that Jim's motivation would be to save nineteen lives, and the sergeant's motivation would be to serve the goals of a repressive military dictatorship, the karmic consequences faced by the sergeant might be more than twenty times worse than those faced by Jim, giving Jim an even stronger reason to kill than in the more usual understanding of the case. But though we may feel an understandable horror at such a morally difficult situation, it is far from clear in any case that killing the one to save the twenty would actually be wrong; whereas many of us feel that slavery or the persecution of minorities is undoubtedly wrong, and the only issue is to find a moral theory that does not threaten to endorse such wrongs.

The modern account of karma also has a different set of attractive normative features that, though entirely compatible with a consequentialist theory, are independent of any particular thesis about the theoretical structure of Buddhist ethics. The modern account, it turns out, has just the structure that you need in order to practice engaged Buddhism. As other essays in this volume may have suggested to the reader, what attracts engaged Buddhists to the doctrine of karma is that it provides self-interested reasons to refrain from harming others. The modern doctrine of karma can fill this role—perhaps not quite as well as the traditional account, but still to a significant degree. What concerns engaged Buddhists about karma, on the other hand, is that it may carry with it the implication that downtrodden and socially disadvantaged groups actually deserve the miseries inflicted upon them, a claim that could seriously undermine our reasons to bring about social change. Now the modern account of karma is not committed to reincarnation and rejects the project of explaining every form of suffering as due to karmic causality. Therefore the modern account simply doesn't imply this problematic view. Sometimes oppressed people do make bad choices that make their problems even worse, and these choices may well bring bad karma into play. But often, on the modern view, the explanation of the suffering of marginalized people simply won't have much to do with their own karma and should be sought in the overall political or economic structure of society.[6]

Adopting the modern account of karma can't solve all of consequentialism's problems, but it can help with a certain range of problematic cases. I draw the same lesson from this discussion as I did from a consideration of related issues in my book (Goodman, 2009). I argue not only that the best version of Buddhist ethics is consequentialist, but also that the best version of consequentialist ethics is Buddhist. Drawing connections between contemporary utilitarianism, with its successes, challenges, and problems, and the very different problematic of Indian Buddhist texts such as the *Training Anthology* is of more than merely historical interest. It may actually help in the formulation of a certain kind of modern Buddhist ethics, well suited to form part of an overlapping Rawlsian consensus through which people of all faiths and philosophical perspectives can come together to meet the pressing issues of today.

Abbreviations

NE   Aristotle's *Nicomachean ethics*. Translations from T. Irwin in Aristotle (1999).

SŚ   Śāntideva's *Śīkṣā-samuccaya* (*The Training Anthology*). Translations are my own, in Śāntideva (2016). For a recent edition of the Sanskrit see Vaidya & Tripathi (1999).

Notes

1. McLeod (2002, esp. Chapter 5). For a discussion of Buddhist modernism as a historical and intellectual phenomenon, see McMahan (2008). The understanding of karma that I am presenting is a form of "minimal karma" in Dreyfus's sense; it could also be considered a form of "tamed karma," in the sense defined by Flanagan.
2. Thus Skt. *paritrāṇa*, "rescue;" but Tib. has *dpung gnyen*, "a friend to help."
3. See, for example, Nussbaum ([1994] 2009, pp. 414–419).
4. "To ensure good behavior, the slaveholder relies on the whip; to induce proper humility, he relies on the whip; to rebuke what he is pleased to term insolence, he relies on the whip; to supply the place of wages, as an incentive to toil, he relies on the whip; to bind down the spirit of the slave, to imbrute and destroy his manhood, he relies on the whip" (Frederick Douglass, *My Bondage and My Freedom*, 1855, quoted in Farnsworth, 2011, p. 40). One influential definition of slavery is found in Patterson (1982, p. 13): "Slavery is the permanent, violent domination of natally alienated and generally dishonored persons."
5. As discussed in Smart and Williams (1973).
6. As it happens, we could also reject the "you deserved it" claim by changing our understanding of the role of free will in Buddhism. I argue for this perspective in chapter 8 of Goodman (2009), but I understand that some of my readers may not be convinced by my arguments there.

References

Aristotle. (1999). *Nicomachean ethics*. (T. Irwin, Trans.). Indianapolis: Hackett.
Farnsworth, W. (2011). *Farnsworth's classical English rhetoric*. Boston: David R. Godine.
Goodman, C. (2009). *Consequences of compassion: An interpretation and defense of Buddhist ethics*. New York: Oxford University Press.
Kapstein, M. (2000). *The Tibetan assimilation of Buddhism: Conversion, contestation, and memory*. Oxford: Oxford University Press.
McLeod, K. (2002). *Wake up to your life: Discovering the Buddhist path of attention*. San Francisco: HarperCollins.
McMahan, D. L. (2008). *The making of Buddhist modernism*. Oxford: Oxford University Press.
Nussbaum, M. (1994/2009). *The therapy of desire: Theory and practice in Hellenistic ethics*. Princeton, NJ: Princeton University Press.
Patterson, O. (1982). *Slavery and social death: A comparative study*. Cambridge, MA: Harvard University Press.
Rawls, J. (1971). *A theory of justice*. Cambridge, MA: Harvard University Press.
Rawls, J. (2005). *Political liberalism* (2nd ed.). New York: Columbia University Press.

Śāntideva. (2016). *The Training Anthology of Śāntideva: A Translation of the Śikṣā-samuccaya.* (C. Goodman, Trans.). New York: Oxford University Press.

Smart, J. J. C., & Williams, B. (Eds.). (1973). *Utilitarianism: For and against.* Cambridge, UK: Cambridge University Press.

Vaidya, P. L., and Tripathi, Sridhar, (Eds.). (1999). *Śikṣā-samuccaya of Śāntideva.* Darbhanga, India: Mithila Institute.

Waldron, J. (1988). *The right to private property.* Oxford: Clarendon Press.

Waldron, J. (1993). *Liberal rights.* Cambridge, UK: Cambridge University Press.

Chapter 8

Buddhism without Reincarnation? Examining the Prospects of a "Naturalized" Buddhism

Jan Westerhoff

8.1. Introduction

The relationship between Buddhism and contemporary science has been surprisingly cordial, characterized by a mutually beneficial exchange of ideas. This is especially (though not exclusively) the case for the modern sciences of the mind, neurobiology and cognitive science. Studies on the physical effects of meditative practices abound (see, e.g., Benson, Lehmann, Malhotra, Goldman, Hopkins, et al., 1982; Austin, 1999; Lutz, Brefczynski-Lewis, Johnstone, Davidson, & Baune, 2008; Singer & Ricard, 2008); there are investigations of how Buddhist spiritual exercises can help to overcome destructive emotions (Goleman, 2003), development of mindfulness-based stress-reduction techniques derived from Buddhist practices (Kabat-Zinn, 1982), research on Buddhist meditation and lucid dreaming (LaBerge, 2003), and more.

In addition to these cross-disciplinary research projects many researchers also see a considerable theoretical agreement between the Buddhist conception of the mind and views being developed in contemporary cognitive science. The central point of contact is the Buddhist notion of non-self (*anātman*) and the modern idea that our sense of self is a brain-based simulation (Metzinger, 2010), a "user illusion" (Nørretranders, 1999), a mistaken assumption of a "Cartesian theatre" (Dennett, 1991), a centerless memetic complex (Blackmore, 2000). The underlying idea here is that because we do not find any neurobiological functional unity in the brain that acts as a unifier of incoming sensory information or locus of control, but rather a complex of spatiotemporally spread-out processes, our belief that such a unifier (namely the self) exists is a higher-level superimposition, not a reflection of the fundamental architecture of the mind. This agrees with the understanding in Buddhist texts of the person as wholly decomposable into a group of physical and mental factors, though none of them can individually function as a self. The self or ego is something projected onto the collection of these factors, but nothing that is fundamentally real.

Yet despite this agreement there appears to be a fundamental incongruity between the contemporary and the Buddhist conception of mind, an incongruity which, even though quite obvious, is frequently ignored.[1] The incongruity results from the fundamental tension between the naturalist presuppositions that form the basis of the modern conception of mind and clearly non-naturalist notions underlying the Buddhist view.

According to the predominant, scientifically informed contemporary conception of the mind, mental processes are either identical with or at the very least existentially dependent on physical processes, in particular on neurobiological events that take place in our brain. If these events were not to take place, mental processes would not be taking place either, and as a consequence there would be no mind. As the neurobiological events that support the existence of minds cease at death, our minds too cease at death.

The Buddhist view of mind disagrees with all of this. First of all it does not agree with the claim that the continuity of our mental existence is broken when our body ceases to exist. Mental processes carry on despite the destruction of our brain and the rest of our body at death. Moreover mental processes are subsequently associated with new bodies and new brains—this is the doctrine of rebirth. Finally, the kinds of experiences the old minds have in the new bodies are to a significant extent dependent on the intentions and actions that characterized these minds in previous bodies—this is the doctrine of karma.

Once the opposition between the modern and the Buddhist view of mind has been set out like this, there are two possible positions to adopt. The first understands the Buddhist and the contemporary scientific view of the mind as two mutually inconsistent theoretical systems. At most one of them can be true, and while there is of course room for a debate between the two, there are no prospects for any kind of synthesis. One needs to make a choice about which view one wants to adopt.

The second view assumes the superiority of the contemporary view but argues for a cherry-picking approach that accepts only those parts of Buddhist theory and practices that are consistent with naturalist assumptions or can at least be reinterpreted in such a way. Even though no naturalist could take on Buddhism in its full form, this view maintains, particular parts (such as the theory of non-self and mindfulness-based meditative techniques) can be fruitfully adopted. Interpretations of this approach vary; some regard it as a kind of cafeteria-style eclecticism that adopts parts of the theory and practice of a variety of traditions; others conceive of it as resulting in a "tamed" or "secularized" Buddhism purged of supernatural "hocus pocus" that preserves as much of the Buddhist teachings as is compatible with the naturalist outlook commonly attributed to members of WEIRD (Western educated industrialized rich democratic) societies.[2]

Neither of these positions seems to be wholly satisfying. The former, never-the-twain-shall-meet approach cuts off any discussion before it even gets started, while the latter, eclectic position faces the danger of ending up as a hodgepodge of theory fragments, none of which makes much sense outside of the context in which it was devised.

It is therefore necessary to develop a more nuanced view of relations between the Buddhist and the contemporary theory of mind. In this essay I focus on one particular difficulty for naturalized Buddhism (the "suicide argument") and discuss some possible responses.

8.2. The Suicide Argument

In the *Sāmaññaphala Sutta* the views of a materialist philosopher, Ajita Kesakambalī, are related to the Buddha. His position is the following:

> There is nothing given, bestowed, offered in sacrifice, there is no fruit or result of good or bad deeds, there is not this world or the next, there is no mother or father, there are no spontaneously arisen beings, there are in the world no ascetics or Brahmins who have attained, who have perfectly practised, who proclaim this world and the next, having realised them by their own super-knowledge. This human being is composed of the four great elements, and when one dies the earth part reverts to earth, the water part to water, the fire part to fire, the air part to air, and the faculties pass away into space. They accompany the dead man with four bearers and the bier as fifth, their footsteps are heard as far as the cremation ground. There the bones whiten, the sacrifice ends in ashes. It is the idea of a fool to give this gift: the talk of those who preach a doctrine of survival is vain and false. Fools and wise, at the breaking-up of the body, are destroyed and perish, they do not exist after death. (DN.i.55)

This view is regarded as erroneous, for later in the *sūtra* the Buddha speaks of the power of clairvoyance (*dibba-cakkhu*, the divine eye) developed through meditative practice that allows one to see the "passing away and arising of beings." In particular one perceives that some beings "at the breaking-up of the body after death ... are reborn in a lower world, a bad destination, a state of suffering, hell. But these [other] beings, on account of good conduct of body, speech or thought, of praising the Noble Ones, have right view and will reap the karmic reward of right view. At the breaking-up of the body after death they are reborn in a good destination, a heavenly world" (DN.i.82).

It appears as if the tenets of materialism as expounded by Ajita Kesakambalī are incompatible with the insights obtained on even a relatively low level of realization. There seems to be at least a tension between being both a Buddhist and a materialist (or physicalist). One particularly important point is summed up well by Richard Hayes (1993, p. 128): "If there is no rebirth, then the very goal of attaining nirvāṇa, understood as the cessation of rebirth, becomes almost perfectly meaningless. Or rather, nirvāṇa comes automatically to every being that dies, regardless of how that being has lived."

More specifically the problem is the following. The central goal of the Buddhist path is the complete and permanent eradication of suffering (*duḥkha*). If there is no continuity of mind after the decay of this physical body, and if the existence of our mind depends on the existence of our body, the third Noble Truth, the truth of the cessation of suffering, would be to put an end to the existence of this body, and the fourth Noble Truth, the way to this cessation, would be suicide. This would lead to the permanent destruction of the complex of the five *skandha*s, the physic-psychological elements that make up the person, thereby leading to the complete elimination of suffering.

In this case none of the three trainings of ethics, meditation, and wisdom would be necessary for the cessation of suffering, but the simple act of destroying the body would be sufficient. I regard this as a reductio ad absurdum of a specific kind of attempt of naturalizing Buddhism, that is, of one that rejects all Buddhist tenets not compatible with naturalism. The defenders of this naturalizing endeavor would have to establish that their view does not in fact entail this peculiar consequence.[3] On the other hand, if this consequence is entailed it seems hard for the naturalist to make sense of most of what the Buddha taught as the Buddhist path. What would be the point of even obtaining the first of the four stages of enlightenment, that of a stream-enterer (*sotāpanna*), which guarantees that one does not have to be reborn for more than seven times if nobody is reborn in any case? What is the point of meditative practice if the ultimate instrument for the destruction of suffering is the destruction of the present body?

In order to get around this absurd consequence the defenders of naturalism need a reply to the suicide argument. So let us consider what a (hypothetical) naturalized Buddhist might bring forward to establish that even if there is no mental continuity after the destruction of our physical body, we should still not kill ourselves.[4]

8.3. Possible Responses

Suicide Violates Key Principles of Buddhism

Within the Pāli canon we find the Buddha stating various key principles and precepts that appear to be in clear conflict with even a permissive attitude toward suicide.[5] These include the principle of nonharm (avihiṃsā, ahiṃsā);[6] the first of the five precepts (pañca-sikkhāpada), which entails abstaining from taking life (pāṇātipātā); and the third "defeat" (pārājika), taking the life of a human being, which leads to expulsion from the community of monks.

The difficulty for the naturalized Buddhist in responding to the suicide argument by recourse to the precepts is that he will presumably not accept them just on the basis of the Buddha's authority but only because they serve a particular purpose within the Buddhist system of thought. Their purpose is arguably to prevent behavior that continues to bind us to the cycle of saṃsāra. As such they are of limited use in convincing somebody who doubts the existence of this cycle in the first place.[7]

Compassion Argument (Synchronous Version)

Even though our death might mean the complete cessation of our suffering (since there is no subject to be suffering subsequently), our suicide may cause suffering for the people around us. Since our goal is to eliminate suffering independent of the bearer, out of concern for the suffering of the people around us we should not kill ourselves. Suicide deprives the world of the potential good influence of the persons killing themselves.[8]

This argument is unlikely to convince the skeptic, since its consequences are even more extreme than those of the original position. If suffering should be eliminated in general, and if suffering can be eliminated by the destruction of the bodies of the beings who are suffering, we should strive to kill not just ourselves but all other beings as well.

Switching from a Theravāda perspective focusing on individual liberation to a Mahāyāna one that emphasizes the liberation of all living beings does not refute the suicide argument but makes its consequences more extreme. If "nirvāṇa comes automatically to every being that dies," we might be tempted to kill ourselves to speed up the obtaining of liberation, but if we believe that we should liberate all beings, the suicide argument can be transformed into an argument for universal homicide.[9] Indeed if there is a way of bringing about the simultaneous complete extinction of all living beings we should bring it about, for in this way all beings can attain *nirvaṇā* simultaneously. Needless to say, anybody who had his doubts about the suicide argument is unlikely to be convinced by this argument for universal homicide.

Compassion Argument (Diachronous Version)

Instead of emphasizing the presumed good consequences not killing ourselves has for others right now, the naturalist might argue as follows: "Whether or not we believe in the continuity of the mental stream after death, there is no question that the actions we carried out in this life form part of causal chains that continue even a long time after our death. The more wholesome actions we carry out, the more positive consequences there will be in the future. This is a reason against killing ourselves now. Of course as our mind ceases at the death of the physical body, we will not experience the good consequences of our actions. But other beings, who are alive then, will do so. And by the familiar Buddhist arguments from no-self we should value their happiness as much as we value our own."[10]

This attempt at providing a naturalistically acceptable version of mental continuity after death and karma is an interesting proposal,[11] but unfortunately it fails to address the key issue of the suicide argument. If the first Noble Truth holds, and all experiences are fundamentally suffused by *duḥkha*, then whatever positive consequences our present actions have for beings living after us will be little more than honey on a razor blade of existential suffering,[12] falling well short of the final liberation of *nirvāṇa*. The obtaining of this final liberation, however, does not require any effort and will happen automatically, if we are to believe the naturalist. As such the support for a moral purpose in our staying alive for the benefit of our contemporaries and descendants appears to be rather thin.

Pascal's Wager

In Āryaśūra's *Jātakamālā* we learn of a king skeptical of the possibility of rebirth who tries to convince the future Buddha of a highly dubious investment scheme: You pay me 500 ounces of gold now, and I'll return them with 100% interest in my next life (Halbfass, 2000, p. 199).[13] It is unlikely that we would be very interested to invest our money in this scheme, but how about the following variant: You pay me 500 dollars (or any finite sum) now, and I will pay you back an *infinite* amount of money in the next life. Following the argument we find in Pascal's wager, even if there is just a small possibility of continuity of mind after death, the possibility of an infinite reward makes the present finite investment worth the effort. This argument could therefore be used against any proponent of the suicide argument who agreed that there is a small chance that he might be wrong and that mental continuity would not stop at death. By committing suicide he would deprive himself of the opportunity of practicing the dharma, and thus of the chance of winning an infinite reward (or rather that of avoiding an infinitely bad negative result: being stuck in cyclic existence for ever).

Unfortunately criticisms of Pascal's wager abound, and a problem often regarded as the most serious one is also a problem here: the many gods objection. Assume some religion promised an infinite reward in the next life on the condition of performing a large number of animal sacrifices in this life. It would be rational to enter into this bet as well, but the conditions for betting in each case (dharma practice, animal sacrifice) are not compatible. Yet the wagers don't give you any criteria for choosing between them.

Present Benefits Argument

This approach suggests that the suicide argument overlooks that Buddhist practice produces great benefits even in this life.[14] Buddhism can be practiced profitably without the presupposition that it yields specific consequences after the death of our present body. The proponent of this approach points out that in fact the Buddha himself raises the possibility of the nonexistence of rebirth and karma in the *Kālāma Sutta* when he speaks of the "four assurances," the second of which is this: "If there is no other world, and if there is no fruit and ripening of well-done and ill-done deeds, still right here, in this very life, I will live happily, free from enmity and ill will" (AN.i.193).

So we could argue that the aim of Buddhist practice is to live happily in this life, independent of whether or not there is a continuity of mind after death. This is an argument we encounter frequently in the contemporary Buddhist literature. Here is one example: "The most important thing . . . is to live a skilful, compassionate life. If we do this, we need not worry about what may or may not happen after death, since if there is rebirth we will have established a wholesome foundation for our next existence, and if there is no rebirth it won't concern us. We need not rely on the possibility of some 'reward' after death because there are great benefits to be gained here and now through spiritual practice" (Nagapriya, 2004, p. 139). Yet the difficulty with the present benefits argument is that even a practitioner's life will not be free from the three kinds of suffering: the suffering of birth, old age, illness, and death (*dukkha-dukkha*); the suffering of change (*viparināma-dukkha*); and the fundamental unsatisfactoriness underlying all conditioned phenomena (*saṅkhārā-dukkha*). So for the Buddhist naturalist the choice appears to be between a reduced amount of suffering (through practice) or a complete and permanent removal of all suffering (through suicide). It is difficult to see why the former should appear to be the more attractive option.

It is worthwhile to note in this context that the present benefits argument is also employed by the Buddhist naturalist in a slightly different context. Apart from being appealed to as a reason not to kill ourselves it is also used to address the worry that if there is no mental continuity after death, all religious practice will have been a waste of time. If the time of our life is so strictly limited and the outcome uncertain, why spend time on strenuous and time-consuming observances?

It is clear that this is not the point the suicide argument is making. According to this argument, the problem is not that the outcome of our religious practices is uncertain, but that it is as certain as it can be. It is just that its certainty is independent of our practice. If physicalism is true, the complete cessation of our mental stream, and with it the complete and irrevocable cessation of suffering experienced within this stream, will obtain for each living being when it dies. To the extent that this permanent cessation of suffering is the highest goal of Buddhist practice, all special efforts to achieve it appear strictly pointless. Whether or not dharma is its own reward, to the extent that there are "great benefits to be gained here and now", it plays no role in the final liberation from suffering. If this liberation is the objective, the defender of the suicide argument points out, it is by suicide, not by spiritual practice, that we are going to arrive at this goal in the most speedy manner.

But is the present benefits argument at least a good answer to the it-might-all-be-a-waste-of-time worry? I have my doubts, at least regarding the way this answer is usually presented.

Consider the following scenario: You set out to travel to the remote country of Obscuristan, and I try to sell you a large quantity of a fairly expensive snake-oil mosquito repellent to protect you from mosquito-borne diseases. When you ask me whether there really are all these aggressive mosquitoes in Obscuristan I reply, "I don't really know whether there are any mosquitoes there or not. But if there are, you'll be happy you bought my snake-oil, and if there aren't—well, in that case I can *guarantee* that you won't have any problems with mosquitoes."

You can be excused for thinking that the snake-oil salesman is trying to take you for a ride. It is not sufficient that the defender of the dharma-is-its-own-reward response to the it-might-all-be-a-waste-of-time worry shows that the practice of dharma has some benefits; he has to show that the benefits are higher than the costs. The Buddhist writers are clear in their statements that this is the case. Śāntideva notes in the *Bodhicaryāvatāra*, "This limited suffering of mine, the means to perfect Buddhahood, is like the pain of extraction when getting rid of the agony of an embedded thorn. All doctors use painful treatments to restore health. It follows that to put an end to many sufferings, a slight one must be endured" (BCA 6.22–23). In the context in which Śāntideva is arguing we can straightforwardly use the example that the benefit of the absence of future thorn-induced pain is higher than the cost that is the pain felt at extraction to argue that the effort invested into spiritual practice is well spent. But then this is a context that presupposes rebirth.[15] Whether this argument can be replicated in a this-life-only context is far from obvious (and very much depends on what kinds of spiritual practices are envisaged).

Nirvāṇa Properly Understood Cannot Be Attained by Suicide

We might argue that the notion of *nirvāṇa* employed here fails to take into account the full complexity of the concept.[16] *Nirvāṇa* is not just total extinction; it is also qualified by a variety of positive attributes. Some predicates attributed to *nirvāṇa* in the Pāli canon include "peace" (*santa*), "wonderful" (*acchariya*), "marvellous" (*abbhuta*), "purity" (*suddhi*), "ultimate bliss" (*paramaṃ sukhaṃ*), and "unshakeable bliss" (*acalaṃ sukhaṃ*).[17] As it seems clear that *this* kind of *nirvāṇa* is not the mere extinction obtained by killing oneself, the defender of the suicide argument might be described as barking up the wrong tree.

Yet consider the fact that as the Buddhist path is conceived as a reaction to the first Noble Truth, the truth of suffering, its aim is the complete elimination of this suffering. When liberation is achieved, there is no more suffering. For the naturalist, there is no more suffering after death, since suffering requires a conscious subject that can suffer, and with the destruction of the body this subject ceases to exist. So liberation-for-the-Buddhist and death-for-the-naturalist share this property.

So all the naturalist is able to say is that liberation-before-death may have properties over and above the extinction of suffering, but the state a liberated being and a nonliberated being are in after death is the very same.[18] She may then argue against the suicide argument by pointing out that liberation-before-death is better than liberation-after-death (which for her is coextensive with death), on the grounds that it is better to be alive than to be dead. As such, those striving for liberation should not plan to achieve that goal by killing themselves.

The difficulty with this approach is that it necessitates a radical reconceptualization of the enlightened state. According to the traditional view, a key benefit of enlightenment lies in the fact that it is the only alternative to being stuck in the painful loop of cyclic existence forever. Yet according to the view just described, the alternatives to consider are no longer liberation versus remaining in *saṃsāra* forever but *n* years of enlightened existence versus *n* years of unenlightened existence (where *n* stands for the number of years up to our death). But if *these* are the alternatives to choose from, whether enlightenment is a goal we choose depends on how involved the practices are that are supposed to get us there. Since being endlessly trapped in *saṃsāra* is such an unattractive prospect, any amount of temporal investment, whether it takes up the whole of this life or even a large number of future lives, can be considered justified. But in the naturalist scenario this is no longer the case. It would be hard to justify, for example, a set of practices that took up nearly our entire life span since the period during which we could remain in liberation-before-death would be so very short.

This entails that enlightenment can no longer be considered an unconditional good for all living beings, but only a conditional good, a good for some beings in some circumstances. Suppose that for most beings achieving enlightenment took ten years of dedicated practice. In this case it would be something to be recommended to a man of 30 since he could afterward remain in liberation-before-death for 35 years (assuming a life span of 75 years), but not to a man of 70, as he would be more likely to die before achieving liberation, thereby paying the costs (spiritual practice) without reaping any of the benefits (liberation-before-death).

I would argue that the resulting shift of enlightenment to a conditional good is sufficiently severe to make the Buddhist naturalist question whether the two chariots he is riding at the same time are not drifting apart to such an extent that it is time to decide which one to relinquish.[19]

Suicide Results from an Unwholesome Mental State

We might argue that the act of suicide always results from an unwholesome mental state of self-aggression and that, since unwholesome mental states should be avoided, the act of suicide should be avoided as well. The impulse to kill others arises from an unwholesome emotion (such as anger), and directing this impulse at ourselves does not change its fundamental moral quality.

It is doubtful whether any act of suicide is necessarily accompanied by an unwholesome mental state (the Stoics would disagree with this), but let us grant this point for the sake of argument. The difficulty that remains is that the unwholesomeness of a mental state like anger is a direct consequence of the state's unwholesome consequences in the future, not a fact about the state's intrinsic nature. But this also implies that the emotion occurring at the last moment of one's mental stream could not be unwholesome (or, for that matter, wholesome) because after the stream terminates there are no more consequences, since any potential experiencer of consequences of that mental state has disappeared. Even presupposing that the act of suicide is always preceded by a mental state phenomenologically very much like the states we usually subsume under the term *anger*, we could not argue that this state should be avoided because of its unwholesome quality, as this unwholesomeness is only relationally defined in terms of the consequences the state has for succeeding mental states of the same person.

One way to rescue this argument would be to argue for the intrinsic unwholesomeness of the mental states in question. Quite apart from any worries the Buddhist philosophers raise about qualities belonging to an object intrinsically (*svabhāvatas*), to say that a certain mental state has a (moral) quality intrinsically also means that it has this quality independent of its consequences. But reconciling a theory that assesses states of mind independent of their karmic consequences with Buddhist ethics as we know it seems to be a task that is unlikely to succeed.

An alternative (and more promising) response would be to argue that a particular mind-moment (of, say, anger) is unwholesome not because of the way it relates to some future state (possibly after rebirth) but because of the way it relates to the rest of our psychology right now. Consider the initial verses of the *Dhammapada* (Dhp. 1–2):[20]

1. Mind precedes all mental states. Mind is their chief; they are all mind-wrought. If with an impure mind a person speaks or acts suffering follows him like the wheel that follows the foot of the ox.
2. Mind precedes all mental states. Mind is their chief; they are all mind-wrought. If with a pure mind a person speaks or acts happiness follows him like his never-departing shadow.

This seems to support the idea that it is the purity or impurity of a mental state that determines the consequences, not the other way around. We are unable to ascribe a negative moral valence to the last mind-moment before suicide only if we assume that these valences arise in a fundamentally consequentialist manner. As the naturalist assumes that the last mind-moment before death has no consequences because it has no successor, it should not be assigned any karmic valence.

Whether Buddhist ethics is to be best conceptualized along consequentialist lines is of course very controversial.[21] One argument sometime raised against this interpretation is that it would imply that we have no indication as to how we should be living now, since the full complexity of karmic consequences is knowable only to a Buddha, a consequence that would be difficult to reconcile with such characterizations of the Buddha's teachings as *sandiṭṭhiko* (Sanskrit: *sāṃdṛṣṭika*), amenable to examination, and *ehipassiko* (Sanskrit: *ehipaśyika*), being such that each can see the truth of the teachings for himself.

This in itself does not appear to present much of a difficulty for the consequentialist interpretation, as we would need to know only some, not *all*, of the consequences of a particular action to be able to assess its karmic valence. Even if we agree that only a fully enlightened being can survey all the karmic implications of a particular action, just with limited insight into actions and their consequences we know that actions like those of the serial murderer Aṅgulimala will not be conducive to a happy and peaceful state of mind.

A greater difficulty for consequentialist theories appears to be the role Buddhist theory assigns to intention (*cetanā*) in the determination of karmic valence. If this undermines the attempt to interpret Buddhist ethics in a purely consequentialist manner, there appears to be an opening for attacking the suicide argument by pointing out that the mind-moment before suicide would be unwholesome because it involves an unwholesome intention of anger, despair, desire for annihilation, and so forth. And if the avoidance of unwholesome mind-moments is a fundamental ingredient of Buddhist practices, this provides us with a good reason against committing suicide. For this reply it is not necessarily problematic that intention is a mental state directed (via anticipation) at future mental states. Even if certain mental states have nothing they are directed at in this way (because they are the last mind-moment), their quality as present anticipation might still be unwholesome. This unwholesomeness manifests in these mental states being experienced as painful in the present. Any action leading to suicide would be in direct contradiction with the Buddhist path aiming at the cultivation of wholesome present mind-moments, mind-moments that by their particular quality determine their ethical valence, not by the future consequences of the actions associated with them.

The difficulty with this otherwise very interesting response is that it presupposes that we give up not only a consequentialist interpretation of Buddhist ethics but also a consequentialist interpretation of karma. Karmic consequences are not understood as positive or negative results we obtain at a later time or during a future life, but as the wholesome or unwholesome, joyful or painful quality of an intentional state here and now. This "instant karma" view suffers from its apparent implausibility: while forming the intention to lie or to steal, the liar and the thief do not necessarily undergo great mental pain. (Otherwise, why would they act the way they do?) The defender of this approach might reply that the quality of instant results is apparent only to beings with sufficiently trained faculties of observation. But this leaves us with the question to what extent we are dealing here with an ethical theory applicable to the majority of human beings and their actions, and not just to a small group of highly trained meditators.

A second difficulty with this approach is that it was not taken up within the Buddhist philosophical tradition in places where it would have constituted a very natural fit. If we assume (as many Buddhist schools did) that the mind consists of instantaneous mind-moments in rapid succession, how to make sense of karmic consequences (which stretch a multitude of such mind-moments) becomes an obvious problem. In this context, adopting the instant-karma view would have been an equally obvious solution. There would have been no need for something like the Sarvāstivāda concept of *avijñapti-rūpa*, the Sautrāntika notion of seeds (*bīja*), or the Yogācāra *ālaya* to tie together the present mind-moment having a certain intention and a later mind-moment reaping the karmic result (Dowling, 1979, p. 85; see also Walser, 2005, pp. 194–203). Instead the present moment would be simultaneously sowing the karmic seed and reaping the karmic fruit.

The fact that proponents of momentariness did not take up the instant-karma view to resolve this problem but developed a variety of complex theories to account for karmic "traces" should make us suspicious that perhaps they did not understand karma in this presentist, nonconsequentialist way.[22]

I WILL LEAVE the discussion of the suicide argument at this point. Having surveyed a variety of responses the Buddhist naturalist can provide in defense, it still appears as if the suicide argument continues to constitute a considerable difficulty for a naturalized form of Buddhism that rejects mental continuity after death.

Assuming the naturalist has no satisfactory answer to the suicide argument, where would this leave us? Would we simply have to assume that any form of Buddhism has to reject contemporary insights into the biological basis of mental processes and retreat to a form of dualism, as found in the theory of the five *skandhas*? I believe that neither this nor starting from the contemporary naturalist view of the mind in order to determine how much of the traditional Buddhist conception can be deemed to be acceptable is likely to be successful. Instead, taking the reverse approach might yield more fruitful results.

This approach would begin with a careful analysis of the Buddhist doctrinal position on mental continuity, rebirth, and karma and would subsequently try to determine which of the positions in contemporary cognitive science and the philosophy of mind might be compatible with it, and which would be most suited to explaining the view of the mind the Buddhist thinkers developed.

What would these positions be? Unfortunately considerations of space do not allow us to discuss this matter more fully, so some pointers have to suffice. Two obvious candidates to explore are functionalism, with its idea that mind can be instantiated by a variety of underlying bases,[23] and panpsychism, which assumes that what we consider to be matter is at its very basis in some way conscious (Blamauer, 2011; Strawson, 2006; Skrbina, 2005). Other useful theoretical avenues to explore in this context are the Madhyamaka idea of universal constructivism (Westerhoff, 2009), Madhyamaka-inspired transcendental arguments against eliminativism (Tillemans, 2015), and the observation that a brain-based view of the world must regard the brain as a brain-based construct as well (Westerhoff, 2015). Starting from approaches such as these to explain, analyze, and expand the Buddhist view of mental continuity after death is, I believe, more likely to yield interesting results than any attempt to streamline the Buddhist tradition in the light of contemporary forms of naturalism.[24]

Abbreviations

AN   *Aṅguttara Nikāya*, volume and page in the Pali Text Society edition. Translations from P. Harvey (2009).

BCA   Śāntideva, *Bodhicaryāvatāra*. Translations from K. Crosby & A. Skilton in Śāntideva (1995).

Dhp.   *Dhammapada*, verse number. Translations from A. Buddharakkhita (2013).

DN   *Dīgha Nikāya*, volume and page in the Pali Text Society edition. Translations from M. Walshe (1995).

MN   *Majjhima Nikāya*, volume and page in the Pali Text Society edition. Translations from Nyanaponika (1988/2013).

Notes

1. Flanagan (2011) is an exception.
2. The terms "tamed," "secularized," and "hocus pocus" come from Flanagan (2011).
3. I am thus not addressing the view that it is really the case that the result of the Buddhist path can equally (and with less effort) be reached by suicide—and so much the worse for the Buddhist path. Clearly the argument I am considering here can be regarded as presenting a difficulty for naturalism only if we do not think that the effects of *nirvāṇa* without remainder and suicide are one and the same.
4. Not entirely hypothetical, though. A group of practitioners referring to themselves as "secular Buddhists" claim to avoid any "consideration of the supernatural or reincarnation" while regarding this as "an attempt to return to the original teachings of the Buddha." See secularbuddhism.wordpress.com.
5. There is a considerable literature on the "suicide" problem in Buddhism (see, e.g., Wiltshire, 1983; Keown, 1996; Harvey, 2000), which concerns the question if, and if so under which circumstances, it is permissible for Buddhists to kill themselves. In the Pāli canon we read of several cases of monks who kill themselves, often during the course of a degenerative and fatal illness. The case of Channa (see Keown, 1996, for a detailed discussion) is particularly relevant since it appears to involve an example of the Buddha condoning or at least exonerating Channa's action. Much hinges here on the translation of the term *anupavajja*, which the Buddha uses; it can be understood to mean "blameless" or "without reproach," or along the lines of the synonyms given in the commentaries: *anuppattika*, "without further arising," and *appaṭisandhika*, "not leading to rebirth" (p. 22). In the latter case it can be argued that the Buddha was not actually commenting on the moral quality of Channa's act but was pointing out that (either because Channa was already an Arhat or because he became one at the moment of death) he would not be reborn again. Even though of related interest, this is not a question that concerns us here. I am investigating the question whether for a "naturalized Buddhist" who rejects rebirth suicide might not be just permissible but in fact desirable.
6. See, e.g., *Sallekha Sutta*: "Others will be harmful; we shall not be harmful here" (*pare vihiṃsakā bhavissanti mayamettha avihiṃsakā bhavissāmāti*; MN.i.42). *Dhammapala*'s Majjhimanikāyaṭika comments on this passage: "But why is harmlessness (or nonviolence, *ahiṃsā*) mentioned at the very beginning? Because it is the root of all virtues; harmlessness, namely, is a synonym of compassion. Especially, it is the root-cause of morality because it makes one refrain from immorality which has as its characteristic mark the harming of others" (Nyanaponika Thera, 1988/2013 note 17).
7. Note that the naturalized Buddhist would not have problems accepting the Buddha's ethical pronouncements in general, though not for the reason of the

Buddha's authority. Killing harms both other beings and ourselves and is therefore to be avoided. In the case of suicide, however, neither the self-harm nor the
harm to others resulting from the act is evident to one rejecting continuity after
death, and for this reason the justification of the precepts in this particular instance is subject to doubt.

8. See Mahā-Kassapa's reply to Pāyāsi at DN.i.330–331: "The longer such moral
   and well-conducted ascetics and brahmins remain alive, the greater the merit
   that they create; they practise for the welfare of the many, for the happiness of
   the many, out of compassion for the world, for the profit and benefit of devas
   and humans."

9. It is worth noting in passing that advocates of homicide as a means to liberation
   may well have had predecessors in ancient India. The Ghaṭacaṭakas ("pot-break-
   ers") are described as a sect that "taught 'immediate liberation through breaking
   the pot' (*jhaṭiti ghaṭacaṭakamokṣaḥ*), implying that the body is a kind of container
   from which an imprisoned soul ought to be liberated" (Halbfass, 1991, p. 98).
   The Saṃsāramocakas ("liberators from saṃsāra") are considered to be "a special branch of materialists" defending killing on "the assumption that 'final release' takes place when the body is destroyed, coinciding with the destruction of
   the 'soul' contained in it" (p. 99). It should be noted, however, that determining
   the tenets of these schools is far from straightforward. (Halbfass, 1991, pp. 97–
   102 offers a good discussion.) In particular, whether the Saṃsāramocakas were
   materialists is unclear. Advocating homicide as a means to liberation certainly
   does not imply materialism, as the tantric notion of *sbyor sgrol* demonstrates (on
   this see McKay, 2003, p. 6).

10. See, e.g., Śāntideva's BCA 8.102: "All sufferings are without an owner, be-
    cause they are not different. They should be warded off simply because they
    are suffering. Why is any restriction made in this case?" (*asvāmikāni duḥkhāni
    sarvāṇyevāviśeṣataḥ | duḥkhatvādeva vāryāṇi niyamastatra kiṃkṛtaḥ*).

11. For a similar approach see Johnston (2011).

12. To use Śāntideva's metaphor from BCA 7.64.

13. The future Buddha replies that this attitude will take the king straight to hell,
    and it will be difficult for his debtors to collect the payment from there. The de-
    scription of the suffering of hell finally causes the king to change his mind.

14. This is the reason for the Buddha's teachings being described as *akāliko*, imme-
    diate, that is, bestowing results here and now, not just in some future state.

15. "I shall be cut up, sliced open, burned, and split open for innumerable billions
    of aeons, and still there will be no awakening" (BCA 6.21).

16. "Robert Caesar Childers, in his famous and still useful Pali dictionary (1875),
    devoted a whole long article, in fact a short treatise, to proving to his own satis-
    faction that Nibbana implies total extinction, and this view, though certainly er-
    roneous, is still to be met with among some Western scholars. And yet, it would

be odd indeed if Buddhists were supposed to have to tread the entire path right up to the attainment of Arahantship merely in order to finish up with that total obliteration which the materialists, and many ordinary people today, assume to occur for all of us, good, bad and indifferent, at the end of our present life" (Walshe, 1995, pp. 27–28).

17. Pasanno and Amaro (2009, p. 30); Dhammapada 15 6; Udāna 2, 8,10.

18. So for the naturalist either the positive properties of liberation are not essential (as these properties presuppose a conscious subject, and since there is no such subject after death liberation must still be liberation without them) or liberated beings stop being liberated after they die (there would then be no *parinirvana* and the Buddha, for example, could not be regarded as liberated, since he is not alive any more).

19. It is for this reason that I do not discuss here attempts of responding to the suicide argument that involve a radical reconceptualization of *nirvāṇa*, understanding it as the reduction of self-constructed cravings, a regulative ideal that nobody actually attains, a minimization of the suffering in this world, or other approaches that view *nirvāṇa* as a somehow improved *saṃsāra*. Such reconceptualizations make it doubtful, I would argue, whether we are still speaking about a naturalized form of Buddhism, and not simply about a kind of naturalism.

20. Dhp. 1.1–2: "*Manopubbaṅgamā dhammā manoseṭṭhā manomayā | Manasā ce paduṭṭhena bhāsati vā karoti vā | Tato naṃ dukkhamanveti cakkam'va vahato padaṃ|| Manopubbaṅgamā dhammā manoseṭṭhā manomayā | Manasā ce pasannena bhāsati vā karoti vā | Tato naṃ sukhamanveti chāyā'va anapāyinī.*"

21. The matter continues to be debated in contemporary literature. See Goodman (2009) for a consequentialist interpretation, Keown (1992) for one in terms of virtue ethics, and Hallisey (1996) and Garfield (2010) for pluralist interpretations.

22. Of course there is still the possibility of arguing that all these thinkers misunderstood what karma is all about. Yet given the prominence of theories accounting for diachronic karmic potentialities in the Buddhist philosophical literature, this raises the question whether what we are dealing with here is an explication of the *Buddhist* conception of karma.

23. The assumption that minds can exist in the absence of brains is also made by some kinds of transhumanism that consider the possibility of "mind uploading" (the transfer of the information contained in a human brain to a computer). See Sandberg and Boström (2008, p. 7). Given that a computer is fundamentally an abstract structure, the step from this position to one that accommodates the existence of minds without a material basis appears not to be too great.

24. I would like to thank audiences at Columbia University, both at the 2011 conference Contemporary Perspectives on Buddhist Ethics and at the Columbia Society for Comparative Philosophy, for useful discussion of these matters.

Special thanks are due to Jake Davis for bringing a variety of important points to my attention that allowed me to develop the discussion of the suicide argument further.

References

Austin, J. H. (1999). *Zen and the brain: Toward an understanding of meditation and consciousness.* Cambridge, MA: MIT Press.

Benson, H., Lehmann, J. W., Malhotra, M. S., Goldman, R. F., Hopkins, J., & Epstein, M. D. (1982, January). Body temperature changes during the practice of gTum mo yoga. Letter to the editor. *Nature, 295,* 234–236.

Blackmore, S. (2000). *The meme machine.* Oxford: Oxford University Press.

Blamauer, M. (2011). *The mental as fundamental: New perspectives on panpsychism.* Frankfurt, Germany: Ontos.

Buddharakkhita, A. (2013). Yamakavagga: Pairs (Dhp I). *Access to Insight (Legacy Edition),* 30 November 2013. http://www.accesstoinsight.org/tipitaka/kn/dhp/dhp.o1.budd.html.

Dennett, D. (1991). *Consciousness explained.* London: Penguin.

Dowling, T. (1979). Karma doctrine and sectarian development. In A. K. Narain (Ed.), *Studies in Pāli and Buddhism: A memorial volume in honor of Bhikkhu Jagdish Kashyap.* Delhi: B. R. Publishing.

Flanagan, O. (2011). *The bodhisattva's brain: Buddhism naturalized.* Cambridge, MA: MIT Press.

Garfield. J. (2010). What is it like to be a bodhisattva? Moral phenomenology in Śāntideva's Bodhicaryāvatāra. *Journal of the International Association of Buddhist Studies, 33*(1–2), 333–357.

Goodman, C. (2009). *Consequences of compassion: An interpretation and defense of Buddhist ethics.* Oxford: Oxford University Press.

Goleman, D. (2003). *Destructive emotions: A scientific dialogue with the Dalai Lama.* New York: Bantam Books.

Halbfass, W. (1991). *Tradition and reflection: Explorations in Indian thought.* Albany: State University of New York Press.

Halbfass, W. (2000). *Karma und Wiedergeburt im indischen Denken.* Munich: Diederichs.

Hallisey, C. (1996). Ethical particularism in Theravāda Buddhism. *Journal of Buddhist Ethics, 3,* 32–43.

Harvey, P. (2000). *An introduction to Buddhist ethics.* Cambridge, UK: Cambridge University Press.

Harvey, P. (2009). The approach to knowledge and truth in the Theravāda record of the discourses of the Buddha. In W. Edelglass and J. Garfield (Eds.),

Buddhist philosophy: essential readings (pp. 175–185). New York: Oxford University Press.

Hayes, R. (1993). Dharmakīrti on rebirth. In Egaku Mayeda (Ed.), *Studies in Original Buddhism and Mahāyāna Buddhism* (pp. 111–129). Kyoto: Nagata Bunshodo.

Johnston, M. (2011). *Surviving death*. Princeton, NJ: Princeton University Press.

Kabat-Zinn, J. (1982). An out patient program in behavioral medicine for chronic pain patients based on the practice of mindfulness meditation: Theoretical considerations and preliminary results. *General Hospital Psychiatry, 4*(1), 33–47.

Keown, D. (1992). *The nature of Buddhist ethics*. New York: Palgrave.

Keown. D. (1996). Buddhism and suicide: The case of Channa. *Journal of Buddhist Ethics, 3*, 8–31.

LaBerge, S. (2003). Lucid dreaming and the yoga of the dream state: A psychophysiological perspective. In A. B. Wallace (Ed.), *Buddhism and science: Breaking new ground* (pp. 233–255). New York: Columbia University Press.

Lutz, A., Brefczynski-Lewis, J., Johnstone, T., Davidson, R. J., & Baune, B. (2008). Regulation of the neural circuitry of emotion by compassion meditation: Effects of meditative expertise. *PLoS ONE 3*(3), e1897.

McKay, A. (2003). *History of Tibet: The medieval period: c850–1895. The development of Buddhist paramountcy*. London: RoutledgeCurzon.

Metzinger, T. (2010). *The ego tunnel: The science of the mind and the myth of the self*. New York: Basic Books.

Nagapriya. (2004). *Exploring karma and rebirth*. Birmingham, UK: Windhorse.

Nørretranders, T. (1999). *The user illusion: Cutting consciousness down to size*. London: Penguin.

Nyanaponika, T. (2013). The Simile of the Cloth & The Discourse on Effacement: Two Discourses of the Buddha. Edited with Introduction and Notes by Nyanaponika Thera. *Access to Insight (Legacy Edition)*, 30 November 2013. http://www.access-toinsight.org/lib/authors/nyanaponika/wheel061.html. Originally published as *The Wheel* Publication No. 61/62 (Kandy: Buddhist Publication Society, 1988).

Pasanno, A., & Amaro, A. (2009). *The island: An anthology of the Buddha's teachings on nibbāna*. Redwood Valley, CA: Abhayagiri Monastic Foundation.

Sandberg, A., & Boström, N. (2008). *Whole brain emulation: A roadmap*. Technical Report #2008-3. Future of Humanity Institute, Oxford University.

Śāntideva. (1995). *The Bodhicaryāvatāra*. (K. Crosby & A. Skilton, Trans.). Oxford: Oxford University Press.

Singer, W., & Ricard, M. (2008). *Hirnforschung und Meditation: Ein Dialog*. Frankfurt am Main: Suhrkamp.

Skrbina, D. (2005). *Panpsychism in the West*. Cambridge, MA: MIT Press.

Strawson, G. (2006). Realistic monism: Why physicalism entails panpsychism. *Journal of Consciousness Studies, 13*(10–11), 3–31.

Tillemans, T. (2015). On minds, Dharmakīrti, and Madhyamaka. In K. Tanaka, Y. Deguchi, J. Garfield, & G. Priest (Eds.), *The moon points back* (pp. 45–66). New York: Oxford University Press.

Walser, J. (2005). *Nāgārjuna in context: Mahāyāna Buddhism and early Indian culture.* New York: Columbia University Press.

Walshe, M. (1995). *The long discourse of the Buddha: A translation of the Dīgha Nikāya.* Boston: Wisdom.

Westerhoff, J. (2009). Costruzioni senza fine? Un problema per il costruttivismo Goodmaniano. *Rivista di estetica, 41*(2), 101–107.

Westerhoff, J. (2015, August 18). What it means to live in a virtual world generated by our brain. *Erkenntis*, 1–22. Online.

Wiltshire, M. (1983). The "suicide" problem in the Pāli canon. *Journal of the International Association of Buddhist Studies, 6*(2), 124–140.

Chapter 9

The Problems and Promise of Karma from an Engaged Buddhist Perspective

Sallie B. King

9.1. Introduction

Engaged Buddhism (also known as Socially Engaged Buddhism) is a contemporary movement found throughout the Buddhist world made up of Buddhists of all sects who engage with the problems of their society—inclusive of political, social, economic, racial, gender, environmental, and other problems—on the basis of their Buddhist worldview, values, and spirituality. Insofar as Engaged Buddhists construct their theory and practice on the basis of traditional Buddhist ideas, since karma is such a fundamental principle of traditional Buddhism, it looms large as well in Engaged Buddhism, both as an asset and as a difficulty.

This paper presents an overview of the place of karma in Engaged Buddhist thought and action. There are four parts to this overview: (1) ways in which Engaged Buddhists make use of karma; (2) ways in which karma is a problem for Engaged Buddhism; (3) ways in which Engaged Buddhists have attempted consciously to overcome the difficulties associated with traditional ideas about karma; and (4) concluding thoughts.

9.2. Ways in Which Engaged Buddhists Make Use of Karma

There are many examples of Engaged Buddhists who make constructive use of beliefs about karma and rebirth in their thinking. Many traditional

Buddhists feel that without beliefs in karma and rebirth, people will have no motivation to be good; they believe people behave well because they want to avoid the suffering of a painful future existence and want to earn the reward of a future happy life. There are also those who see karma as a dam that holds back the flood of ethical relativism; they believe that karmic processes demonstrate the existence of objective, cosmic standards of right and wrong. Some Engaged Buddhists feel this way as well. Sarvodaya Shramadana founder A. T. Ariyaratne expresses both of these views: "The biggest blunder Western culture has made is that there is no standard to measure good and bad. It is lost in liberal thinking. In other words, there is nothing called sin and merit. You are not accountable because you do not know whether you will be reborn or not. In Sri Lanka, we believe in rebirth. We believe in sin and merit" (quoted in Ingram, 1990, p. 132). For Ariyaratne, it is necessary that every human society have an objective standard of right and wrong and a system of accountability. Belief in karma and rebirth satisfies this need.

Some Engaged Buddhists use karma as a mechanism that aids in preventing the development of hatred and violent behavior. For example, Tibetan Buddhist activists associated with the Dalai Lama sometimes say the Chinese invasion and occupation of Tibet is the karmic result of an unspecified occasion in the past when Tibetans did something similar to the Chinese. Geshe Sopa has said, "Why did the Chinese attack Tibet? It was a karmic result. We believe that this is due to karma, our collective karma. Sometime in our past lives we as a group did something terrible to the Chinese; our suffering now at the hands of the Chinese is the result" (quoted in King, 2006, pp. 208–209). Here the implication is that one has brought the present unhappy state of affairs upon oneself by one's own actions in the past; one must swallow the bitter pill of the consequences of one's own behavior.

It is important to note that while this interpretation of karma might mitigate hatred of the Chinese, it does not in any way absolve or morally excuse the actions of the Chinese. This speaks to the moral implications of karma: even if, in some karmic way, the Tibetans' behavior in earlier lives was the karmic seed of their present suffering at the hands of the Chinese, that does not mean the Chinese behavior is morally justified. The Chinese are fully responsible for *their own* behavior now, whatever the karmic past, and that behavior is morally reprehensible, as the Tibetans often point out; indeed, one of the Tibetans' concerns is that the Chinese are earning themselves terrible karmic retribution by their violent and oppressive behavior in Tibet.

Similarly in Cambodia, it is striking that there was no bloodbath of revenge following the Khmer Rouge genocide. I once had the opportunity to ask Dith Pran, the subject of *The Killing Fields*, why this was so. He answered, "They don't want to suffer any more."[1] In other words, karma. The Cambodian people knew that a violent act on their part would bring more violence raining down upon them in the future, so for their own sakes, and their children's, they restrained themselves. The famous Cambodian Engaged Buddhist leader Maha Ghosananda (1992, p. 27) took this view a step further. He incorporated the fifth verse of the *Dhammapada* into a "Prayer for Peace" that he composed, reminding the people, "Hatred is never appeased by hatred. Hatred is appeased by love. This is an eternal law." His message to the Cambodian people was that if they wanted to be rid of the hatred—and hateful, violent acts—of the Khmer Rouge, they should not hate them or act out their hatred by seeking vengeance, but forgive them, let it go, and move on.

Engaged Buddhists throughout the Buddhist world often cite this passage from the *Dhammapada* to argue against the view that force or violence is able to resolve problems. They see violence as, at best, providing quick, short-term answers to problems but leaving behind not only the seeds of new conflict but also the issues that led to the original conflict, issues that have temporarily been silenced, but not resolved, by one side's victory. Thus cause and effect, and karma, are the foundation of the Engaged Buddhists' justification of their nonviolent approach to conflict resolution. In response to those who say his devotion to nonviolence is impractical, the Dalai Lama (1999, p. 202) says, "Actually, it is far more naïve to suppose that the human-created problems which lead to violence can ever be solved through conflict." Why? Within the law of karmic cause and effect, those unresolved, underlying problems will continue to stimulate unwholesome states of mind of resentment, anger, and so on, which will eventually manifest in renewed violent actions. Nonviolence is the only way out.

Western Buddhist activists engaged in working with the prison population make particularly powerful and constructive use of the doctrine of karma. A crucial step in this work is for prisoners to accept responsibility for their actions that resulted in their imprisonment. Some activists, notably S. N. Goenka, teach prisoners Vipassana meditation in intensive 10-day retreats. This practice allows them to begin to see how their minds work, how their minds generate feelings and actions, and what patterns these thoughts, feelings, and actions tend to fall into.[2] This practice, in other words, allows the inmates to see in an intimate way the workings of karma in their own lives: the causal links between their thoughts, their actions, and the people they have made themselves into. Seeing all of this often makes them able, for the first time, to accept responsibility for what they have done. Anthony Stultz, an American Buddhist prison minister, has developed a liturgy the prisoners chant, which includes the words, "We take complete responsibility for our own life and all of our actions" (Parkum & Stultz, 2003, pp. 240–241).

Accepting responsibility for their actions and seeing the connection between their thoughts and their actions makes it possible for the prisoners to realize that they have the power to choose to think and act differently. This use of ideas about karma is concerned only with the linkage of cause and effect as it plays out in a person's life; rebirth is not a concern. We should note in passing that in contrast to the complaints of some regarding some of the disempowering implications of karma, this way of using ideas about karma is entirely empowering and clearly liberating for the prisoners who engage it.

9.3. Ways in Which Karma Is a Problem for Engaged Buddhism

(1) In the Buddhist world, karmic beliefs have often resulted in stigmatizing attitudes toward disabled people. Popularly, many Buddhists have felt that disabled persons have brought their disability on themselves by bad actions in a past life, and therefore they morally "deserved" to be born in a disabled body. This is a very real way in which beliefs about karma have themselves played a direct role in causing devastating suffering on a vast scale over the centuries.

This attitude is particularly difficult because it is based on words attributed to the Buddha himself. The *Cūlakammavibhanga Sutta* (Majjhima Nikāya 135) records the following exchange. A student asks the Buddha:

> "Master Gotama, why is it that human beings are seen to be inferior and superior? For people are seen to be short-lived and long-lived, sickly and healthy, ugly and beautiful, without influence and influential, poor and wealthy, low born and high born, stupid and wise. Why is it, Master Gotama, that human beings are seen to be inferior and superior?"
>
> [The Buddha replies,] "Student, beings are owners of their actions, heirs of their actions; they originate from their actions. . . . It is action that distinguishes beings as inferior and superior." . . .
>
> [The Buddha goes on to give specifics of this karmic link:]
>
> "Here, student, some man or woman is given to injuring beings with the hand, with a clod, with a stick, or with a knife. Because of performing and undertaking such action, on the breakup of the body, after death, he is reborn in a state of misery. . . . But if instead he comes back to the human state, then wherever he is reborn he is sickly. This is the way, student, that leads to sickliness, namely, one is given to injuring beings with the hand, with a clod, with a stick, or with a knife." (MN.iii. 202–204)

William Bodiford (1996, p. 15) quotes a verse with similar sentiment that has been commonly recited in Sōtō Zen sermons in Japan:

> *Short lifespans come from butchering animals.*
> *Ugliness and sickness come from ritual impurities.*
> *Poverty and desperation come from miserly thoughts.*
> *Being crippled and blind come from violating the Buddhist precepts.*[3]

In short, it is a traditional Buddhist view that karma is in this way a justice mechanism: one is punished in a later life for crimes committed in an earlier life. I have met people who work with the disabled in Buddhist countries who are furious with Buddhism and perceive it as their enemy. These people believe that Buddhism caused their societies to dismiss the sufferings of the disabled and to leave them on their own to get along as best they could—not only without any help but also without compassion from those around them. One who believes that sickliness—or bodily or mental disability—is a matter of purely physiological processes with no relation to moral desert will regard the teaching that disability is a matter of moral desert as a doctrine that blames the victim, adds to his or her suffering, and is itself unwarranted, harmful, and unjust.

(2) A very similar situation obtains for the Indian class that calls itself "dalit," the class formerly known as the "untouchables" or "outcastes" in the rigidly hierarchical Hindu caste system and who are regarded as occupying the lowest level of that system.

In the *Majjhima Nikāya sutta* cited earlier, the Buddha also explains the status of persons who are "low born," without influence, and poor in a way very similar to the way he explained the status of those born sickly or disabled. Thus, with regard to "low birth," he says, "Here, student, some man or woman is obstinate and arrogant; he does not pay homage to one who should receive homage, does not rise up for one in whose presence he should rise up ... and does not honor, respect, revere, and venerate one who should be honored, respected, revered, and venerated. Because of performing and undertaking such action ... he is reborn in a state of misery. ... But if instead he comes back to the human state, then wherever he is reborn he is low born" (MN.iii.205). Similarly one who "envies, resents, and begrudges the gains, honor, respect, reverence, salutations, and veneration received by others" will be reborn, if as a human, "without influence." One who "does not give food, drink, clothing, carriages, garlands, scents, unguents, beds, dwelling, and lamps to ascetics or brahmins" will be reborn, if as a human, in poverty. These passages are open to interpretation as a Buddhist explanation for why one is

born in a low caste or outcaste condition (a "low birth" condition, without influence and poor): one earned this life condition by one's actions in a past life.

Dr. B. R. Ambedkar (1891–1956), the great leader of India's untouchables,
led his followers in converting from Hinduism to Buddhism as a religio-social
act of self-liberation from Hinduism's caste system. Though he embraced
Buddhism, he nevertheless clearly dissociated himself, and the Buddhism
that he passed on to his followers, from the notion that caste status or physical
health could be the karmic result of actions in past lives. He writes, "The basis
of the Hindu doctrine of past karma as the regulator of future life is an iniqui-
tous doctrine. What could have been the purpose of inventing such a doctrine?
The only purpose one can think of is to enable the state or the society to escape
responsibility for the condition of the poor and the lowly. Otherwise such an
inhuman and absurd doctrine could never have been invented" (Ambedkar,
1957, bk. IV, pt. II, sec. II).

(3) Engaged Buddhists sometimes point to karma being used to justify or rationalize immoral and unfair traditional practices. These are concerns around
what the West calls justice, though Engaged Buddhists seldom use that term.
For example, the Thai lay Engaged Buddhist Sulak Sivaraksa writes of a common situation in Southeast Asia, where landlords often charge the landless
peasants 70% of the harvest in order to work the land. Sivaraksa argues that
this amount is exorbitant and plainly immoral. It continues, he says, partly
because of its justification by karma: "Establishment Buddhism ... explains
this oppression as the working of *karma*, saying that both peasants and the
landlord are reaping the results of their actions in former lives; the peasants of
bad deeds and the landlord of merit achieved by building temples and images
of the Buddha" (Sivaraksa, 1999, p. 198). In other words, the peasants are
conditioned by karmic teachings to accept this system as fair and their consequent poverty as inevitable, and therefore they do not insist upon a change in
this fundamental social structure. In this way, what from another perspective
may be seen as an unfair and immoral social system continues on and on. We
note in passing Sivaraksa's implicit rejection of what he calls "establishment
Buddhism" and its role in justifying these moral wrongs.

(4) Another important area of concern around karma for Engaged
Buddhists is that it promotes fatalism and passivity. For example, Aung San
Suu Kyi (1997, p. 124) has said, "Some people think of *karma* as destiny or
fate and that there's nothing they can do about it. It's simply what is going to
happen because of their past deeds. This is the way in which *karma* is often
interpreted in Burma." This kind of belief about karma is very widespread in
the Buddhist world. From this perspective, there was no sense, for example, in
risking one's life in the struggle to end the dictatorship in Burma (Myanmar);

the wise thing to do was to lie low and wait until the karma that brought the dictatorship to power was exhausted (in accordance with the Buddhist doctrine of conditioned origination that teaches, "When the fuel is removed, the fire will go out"), when it would be replaced by the fruition of other karmic forces. The outcome of this way of thinking is indeed fatalism and passivity. Gene Sharp (1973, pp. 19–24), the great theoretician of nonviolent power, points out that cultural and religious factors are elements contributing to the success or failure of efforts to work with nonviolent power. It is impossible to estimate how much traditional beliefs about karma hampered the Burmese Buddhist effort to end that country's dictatorship, but it is clear that a set of beliefs that promote fatalism and passivity would not be an asset to such a struggle.

(5) A final area that combines most of these concerns about karma is the problem of karma-related beliefs about gender. It is a widespread belief in both Hinduism and Buddhism that women have inferior karmic inheritance compared to men. This is considered obvious: if those born as women had had better karma, they would have been born as men, a clearly more desirable birth. A specific context in which such beliefs play a tremendously harmful role is the prostitution and sex industry in Thailand. The Thai Engaged Buddhist laywoman Ouyporn Khuankaew (2012), who works to heal and empower Asian women, writes that girls in the sex industry are often sold into it by extremely poor rural families. The girls themselves are deeply ashamed of what they have become but tell themselves that such is the fate of women with women's poor karma and this kind of work at least gives them a way to repay their parents for their care. Here beliefs about karma promote fatalism and passivity: such is the fate of girls; if they had had better karma they would have been born male. These beliefs justify and rationalize traditional social and economic structures, preventing even the perception of the structural violence of gender discrimination in Thailand.

It is important to note that "establishment Buddhism" itself participates in the structural violence of Thai gender discrimination to the extent that there has never been an option for Thai girls to become *bhikkhunī*, fully ordained nuns. It is a crucial outlet for poor, rural boys to be able to join the Sangha, earning their parents merit—good karma—in so doing and also getting access to an education and an escape from rural poverty. Alternatively, Thai boys may temporarily ordain, an act that also is believed to earn their parents merit (Khuankaew, 2012; see also Khuankaew, 2009, pp. 199–224). Girls and women have not been able to participate in this form of merit making, a fact that both reinforces and perpetuates beliefs about females' comparatively lowly karmic condition.

9.4. Engaged Buddhist Efforts to Overcome the Difficulties Associated with Karma

(1) B. R. Ambedkar is relatively radical among Engaged Buddhists in his response to the perceived problem of karma. Ambedkar by no means rejects the notion of karma in toto. On the contrary, he writes in his major Buddhist work, *The Buddha and His Dhamma*, "To believe that Karma [*sic*] is the instrument of Moral Order is Dhamma." However, what he accepts as the workings of karma is considerably narrower than the usual Buddhist understanding: "By speaking of the law of Kamma what the Buddha wanted to convey was that the effect of the deed was bound to follow the deed, as surely as night follows day. . . . Therefore, the Buddha's admonition was: Do Kusala Kamma so that humanity may benefit by a good moral order which a Kusala Kamma helps to sustain; do not do Akusala Kamma for humanity will suffer from the bad moral order which an Akusala Kamma will bring about." Thus, for Ambedkar, "The Law of Kamma has to do only with the question of general moral order. It has nothing to do with the fortunes or misfortunes of an individual" (1957, Book III, Part III, Section VI).

In particular, Ambedkar objects strenuously to the notion that an individual's actions in previous lives bear fruit in subsequent lives. This doctrine, in its Hindu form, has been used for centuries, if not millennia, to justify the base status to which the untouchables were relegated in Hindu society, the view being that untouchables had earned a low birth through their actions in past lives. To leave this status behind was Ambedkar's primary motive in converting from Hinduism to Buddhism and in advocating that his followers do the same. He had no intention of embracing the same set of ideas in a Buddhist form.

In *The Buddha and His Dhamma*, Ambedkar argues that the idea of past-life karma causing present-life consequences is a logical impossibility in Buddhism: "The Hindu Law of Karma is based on the soul. The Buddhist is not. In fact there is no soul in Buddhism. The Brahminic Law of Karma is hereditary. It goes on from life to life. This is so because of the transmigration of the soul. This cannot be true of the Buddhist Law of Karma. This is also because there is no soul. . . . For these reasons the Buddhist doctrine of Karma cannot be and is not the same as the Hindu doctrine of Karma." Ambedkar further argues that Buddhist scriptural passages that teach what he sees as pernicious karma doctrines (such as the *Majjhima Nikāya* passages cited above) misreport the words of the Buddha and thus misrepresent the Buddha's teaching. His main argument on this point is based on the fact that initially the teachings of the Buddha were not written down but transmitted orally. The Bhanakas (reciters of the Buddhist canon), he wrote, were known to have made many errors, such errors being inevitable given the large volume of material to be memorized. Thus scriptural "cases of misreporting are common with regard to karma and rebirth" inasmuch as "these doctrines have also a place in the Brahminic religion [and] consequently it was easy for the Bhanakas to incorporate the Brahminic tenets into the Buddhist Religion" (1957, bk. IV, pt. II, sec. II).

Ambedkar goes on to say that since one cannot trust that everything reported to be the word of the Buddha is in fact the word of the Buddha, one needs tests to sort the reliable from the unreliable. He proposes three such tests, the first two of which apply most clearly here. First, "if there is anything which could be said with confidence it is: He was nothing if not rational, if not logical. Anything therefore which is rational and logical, other things being equal, may be taken to be the word of the Buddha" (1957, bk. IV, pt. II, sec. II). As we have seen, Ambedkar argued that the Buddha's teaching of no soul, *anātman*, is logically incompatible with the teaching of the soul's transmigration. This justifies his rejecting the notion of past-life karma causing present-life suffering as being the teaching of the Buddha, according to his first test.

Ambedkar's second test is this: "The Buddha never cared to enter into a discussion which was not profitable for man's welfare. Therefore anything attributed to the Buddha which did not relate to man's welfare cannot be accepted to be the word of the Buddha." Since Ambedkar regards the notion of past-life karma causing present-life suffering as a view that is greatly inimical to human welfare, this second test would also reject this teaching as being the teaching of the Buddha. As he writes, "It is impossible to imagine that the Buddha who was known as the Maha Karunika [the Greatly Compassionate One] could have supported such a doctrine" (1957, Book IV, Part II, Section II).

(2) A second approach, and one more common among Engaged Buddhists, is to advocate for the reform of traditional Buddhism. We saw that Sivaraksa has criticized "establishment Buddhism," which he sees as bogged down in traditional culture, and in the Thai case, in nationalism and militarism as well. He advocates instead what he calls "small b" Buddhism, a reformed Buddhism that does not simply perpetuate traditional teachings but is ready to challenge those teachings that conflict with what he sees as core Buddhist values. Regarding the case of the poor peasants who had to pay exorbitant rents to the landowners, Sivaraksa (1999, p. 199) goes on to write, "Non-establishment Buddhism, with a small b, is against this trend of wrong teaching. If the landlord understands and practices *dana* [giving] he will know that it is wrong to take 70% of the harvest when the workers do not have enough to sustain them. ... At the same time ... out of *metta* [loving-kindness] and

compassion people will share whatever extra they have." In this example, traditional Buddhist values and practices are placed against a traditional Buddhist idea in order to reform the latter.

Engaged Buddhists may also advocate for changes in traditional *practices* surrounding the idea of karma, especially practices concerning the earning of merit. The practice of Theravāda Buddhism by the laity has traditionally emphasized earning merit, or good karma, by giving to Buddhist temples and monks. Many Engaged Buddhists advocate adjusting such traditional practices. They promote the idea of earning merit by giving funds to the temple that the temple will use not for itself but instead will use for a rice bank, or for microloans for a village bank, or to plant fruit trees that will be used to reforest and to provide income for the entire village. In this way the villager is secure in earning merit since the funds are given to a temple, but the funds are put directly to use in reducing poverty. Such programs have become very popular in rural Thai Buddhism thanks to advocacy by Thai "development monks."

Another example of Engaged Buddhist efforts to reform traditional thought and practice around karma focuses on the female ordination issue. The Venerable Dhammananda, an Engaged Buddhist and Buddhist scholar, was the first Thai woman to be fully ordained as a Theravāda *bhikkhunī*. With this groundbreaking act, her advocacy in scholarly writings and in public media for the reestablishment of the Theravāda *bhikkhunī* order, and her training of many young women as *bhikkhunī*, Ven. Dhammananda has brought the *bhikkhunī* option to Thai women. There are now about 100 fully ordained *bhikkhunī* in Thailand.[4] In addition, since 2009, Ven. Dhammananda has made temporary ordination available to girls and women for the first time ever. Both temporary and permanent ordination for girls and women open the door for them to earn their parents merit and also profoundly challenge traditional notions of what a female's karmic inheritance is.

That this is a very small incursion into a massive issue is obvious. However, the great symbolic power of a woman wearing the saffron robes and its potential for powerfully impacting gender issues in Thailand should not be underestimated. Before Ven. Dhammananda's ordination, one frequently saw many men and women bowing before monks in Thailand, but a man never publicly bowed down before any woman. In that situation, one *performed* gender discrimination, whether one liked it or not. With women now wearing the saffron robe, one now sees many women and men (laypersons) bowing before some women and some men (*bhikkhus* and *bhikkhunī*s), removing the subliminal but powerful suggestion that gender (determined by karmic inheritance) might be a factor in meriting such veneration.

In sum, many Engaged Buddhists are in favor of retaining the idea of karma and merit but changing its interpretation in such a way that the practice of earning merit, which is of great interest to most traditional Theravāda laypeople, can be harnessed as a vehicle for social and economic change.

(3) Engaged Buddhists often argue that traditional, popular understandings of karma are incorrect. In particular they insist that in thinking about karma it is important to turn away from a focus on the past and focus instead on the present and the future; they emphasize that karma means action, coupled with a belief in the openness of the future, and the determination to act. That is, Engaged Buddhists simply do not accept any implication of passivity in karma. We saw that Aung San Suu Kyi has said, "Some people think of *karma* as destiny or fate and that there's nothing they can do about it. It's simply what is going to happen because of their past deeds." She continued, "But *karma* is not that at all. It's doing, it's action. So you are creating your own *karma* all the time. Buddhism is a very dynamic philosophy and it's a great pity that some people forget that aspect of our religion" (1997, p. 124).

The Engaged Buddhists are on firm ground here. The Buddha expressly negated the teaching that everything we experience is due to our past karma. He said that our karma plays a role in what happens to us, but so do many other factors. Moreover he emphasized that this view is particularly pernicious insofar as it promotes passivity. He said, "When people take the kamma that they have done as the essential cause [of present experience], then proper resolve (*chanda*), effort, and 'this should be done—this should not be done' do not exist'" (Payutto, 1995, p. 147).[5] In short, if one believes that everything that happens to one is due to one's past karma playing out, one will resignedly wait for that karma to play out and not make any effort. A consequence is that one will not make an effort to practice the Dharma. To the Buddha this was one of the most destructive views one could hold.

Contemporary Tibetan activists provide a good example of an alternative approach that is in harmony with the Buddha's teachings. It would have been very easy for the Tibetans to conclude that since they (or their Tibetan ancestors) did something terrible to the Chinese in the past and the Chinese occupation of Tibet is the result, they should accept their fate quietly. This is the attitude Aung San Suu Kyi complains of in Burma (Myanmar). But the Tibetans have not accepted the Chinese occupation as their fate; on the contrary, they have consistently struggled against it. This is easily justified: even if what happens to oneself or one's group is the result of karmic seeds sown in the past, the present and the future are still open. The Tibetans believe that karma, as action, means that we should take care to make very intelligent, skillful actions now in order to construct a better future for ourselves and our group. Consequently, Tibetans strive to act energetically but skillfully and nonviolently in their response to the Chinese occupation in order to gradually transform the situation and create a positive outcome, while avoiding sowing negative karmic seeds (e.g., through violent acts) that would only create new problems for the future.

(4) A fourth way in which Engaged Buddhists respond to problems around karma is by simply advocating the position that *mettā* (loving-kindness) and compassion trump all. We saw this when Sivaraksa argued against those who referred to karma to justify the peasants paying 70% of their harvest to use the landowner's fields. Sivaraksa's counterargument did not even mention karma. It just pointed to the suffering of the peasants and said, in effect, that this suffering required a response of *dāna, mettā*, and compassion. This is a very common approach in Engaged Buddhism, where *mettā* and compassion trump all. Geshe Sopa similarly refers to the idea that the Chinese occupation is due to the Tibetans' karma. But when it comes time to discuss what to do about the situation, compassion is the determinant: "The main thing is to have compassion for mistakes made from an egocentric viewpoint, from ignorance. Sometimes you have a wrong view that fills you with hatred and you do something out of hatred that earns you negative karma. That must be subject to our compassion, our love. The Chinese are now earning terrible karma for what they are doing to us. We must feel compassion for all who are suffering, on both sides" (quoted in King, 2006, pp. 208–209). It is noteworthy that since what is emphasized here is the compassionate *response*—that is, action in the present—the focus is not on the past karma, but on present actions creating future karma.

(5) A final conundrum surrounding karma must be mentioned: the question of individual versus social responsibility. That is, if a person commits a crime, is that person responsible for the crime, or should we say that social factors, such as poverty or racism, are responsible for the crime? In his famous poem, "Please Call Me by My True Names," when Thich Nhat Hanh (1987, p. 62) writes of the pirates who preyed upon the Vietnamese boat people, he pointedly avoids condemning them and even identifies himself with them:

> I am the 12-eyar-old girl, refugee on a small boat,
> who throws herself into the ocean after being raped by a sea pirate,
> and I am the pirate, my heart not yet capable of seeing and loving.

In his discussion of the poem, Thich Nhat Hanh explained that if he had been born into the kind of poverty the pirate had been born into, he himself might well have become a pirate (64).

Thich Nhat Hanh has been criticized for this stance insofar as it seems to absolve the pirate and other criminals from personal responsibility for their crimes, yet we know that he is right insofar as poverty can lead to crime. The Buddha implied much the same thing in the *Cakkavatti Sīhanāda Sutta* (Dīgha Nikāya 26, in Walshe, 1987/1995, pp. 395–405), where he identifies poverty as a cause of crime. Is blaming crime on the individual criminal, then, another case of blaming the victim?

Some activists have resolved the issue of individual responsibility versus social responsibility for crime by making use of Buddhist nondualism: responsibility for criminal behavior is *both* individual *and* social. The American Buddhist laywoman Melody Ermachild Chavis works as a mitigation lawyer for felons facing a possible death sentence. Karma is fundamental to her outlook and her work. On the one hand, like Stultz and others who work with prison inmates, she sees the acceptance of personal responsibility as an essential and inevitable part of the process of prisoners working on themselves. She writes, "I've seen, so many times, people avowing their karma. That's our chant, that's our vow, and it happens. We realize what we've done, we really get it, and we begin to transform it" (Chavis, 2001, pp. 17–21).

On the other hand, looking at the lives of those eligible for the death penalty, she again and again sees karmic patterns that are larger than the individual: "More than anything else, the truth of the law of karma is what I have learned from my job, from my long investigation into why people do terrible things. ... And we're not just saying: Because this child was in a homeless shelter, was poor, had an alcoholic mother, and so on, that is why he might have killed a police officer. That's way too simple. We're talking about the whole huge swirl of karma, including a group of youngsters, a gun, a car, even police brutality. There are a lot of causes, 10,000 causes" (Chavis, 2001, pp. 17–21).

For Chavis, the law of karma is true, but interdependence is true too. It's not accurate to treat karma as a single line of individual responsibility, divorced from everything else; this is not reality. Interdependence is reality. Both individual responsibility and social responsibility are realities, and they are both integral parts of karma playing out in an ocean of causes and conditions. Seeing the playing out of cause and effect on this vast scale does not change the fact that one does see the thread of one's choices and their consequences and the necessity of accepting full responsibility for all of one's actions. However, it supports a measure of understanding and mercy for offenders (e.g., no death penalty), and it supports efforts to eliminate the social causes of crime.

9.5. Concluding Thoughts

One of the biggest problems associated with karma is the objection that karma blames the victim. Because of this, Buddhism is sometimes criticized as immoral. This is an especially difficult problem because the Buddhist public often does blame the victim, as in the cases of the dalits and the disabled. The attitude, to be blunt, is "You deserved it!"

To this attitude I proffer three possible responses that remain within the worldview of Buddhism. (1) The first replies to "You deserved it!" by asking, "Who is this 'you'?" According to the Buddhist teaching of *anātman*, or no-self, the person who is suffering at present is *neither the same as nor different from* the person who did the deed that sowed the karmic seed of the present suffering. There is continuity, but there is also change between these two persons. The later person exists as he or she does partly because of the deeds of that earlier person, but also because of many other causes and conditions, including present life choices and environmental factors. *The Questions of King Milinda* (46:5ff, in Warren, 1979, pp. 234–235) famously teaches that the relationship between a former and a subsequent human life is like the relationship between a mango hanging in a tree and the mango seed that sprouted that tree. A mango presently hanging in the tree is a consequence of the planted mango seed, but it is certainly not identical to it. There is no principle of identity between them and, importantly, nothing that carries over in identical form from the earlier mango to the subsequent one. There is continuity between the two mangoes, but there are also differences between them, due, in the mangoes' case, to different environmental conditions of soil, nutrients, water, and sunlight. The same is true of the sequence of persons in a karmic chain: there is continuity between them but also variation in environmental factors (vastly more variation for humans than for mangoes, of course) and, for humans, different personal choices made in the previous and subsequent lives. "You deserved it"? Not insofar as there is continuity, but also change, and *no identity* between the two.

(2) Second, if one wants to be guided on social issues by the Buddha's teachings, one should look to the Buddha's *social* teachings for instruction. In the *Cakkavatti Sīhanāda Sutta* (Dīgha Nikāya 26), the Buddha teaches a king that poverty should not be allowed to exist and that a wise government will see to it that poverty is eliminated. In the *Vāseṭṭha Sutta* (Majjhima Nikāya 98, in Ñāṇamoli & Bodhi, 1995, pp. 798–807), the Buddha teaches that the Hindu caste system is an arbitrary social convention that has no basis in reality and that a person's standing in life should be based on his or her actions, not his or her birth. All this implies that, for the Buddha, the possibility of birth into

a low caste or poverty ideally should not even *exist*. If the Buddha believed that such a birth should not even exist, we can hardly conclude that he was teaching us to regard it as an appropriate working out of karma.

(3) The third response to the "You deserved it!" attitude we have seen already: compassion trumps all. Let us look to the example of the Buddha's actions. The Buddha says that a person is born sickly or in a low social class because of previous life deeds, but he does not say that we should therefore condemn or dismiss such people with a moralistic "You deserved it" and that it therefore is right for his followers to turn their backs on them. On the contrary, the Buddha welcomed low-caste and untouchable people, men and women, into the Sangha and treated them with the same compassion with which he treated everyone else. He refused to speak to a group of villagers until they fed a hungry man. He himself nursed a sick disciple. The Buddha showed with his actions that the proper response to suffering and need is compassion and appropriate practical help.

Again we can look to the example of the ordained Sangha. Despite popular views on the subject, the Sangha has been involved extensively in caring for disabled people and mentally or physically ill people throughout the history of Buddhism in many parts of the world. The practice of medicine is, of course, one of the great traditional contributions of the Sangha to their societies. Normatively the Sangha's attitude toward the sick and suffering has not been dismissal or negative judgment, but compassion and practical help.

In conclusion, as a consequence of their work with the concrete social and economic problems of their societies, Engaged Buddhists are keenly alert to a number of negative implications and consequences of karma theory. They have responded by pioneering a variety of ways to resolve these problems. While Ambedkar's response would seem to require extensive rethinking of ideas foundational to Buddhist thought and practice, other Engaged Buddhists respond by rejecting misunderstandings of karma, calling for reinterpretations of karma, inventing new practices built upon belief in karma, or rebalancing the idea of karma with other Buddhist teachings and values. These latter approaches remain well within established Buddhist norms and do not require fundamental rethinking of Buddhist thought and practice.

Abbreviations

AN   *Aṅguttara Nikāya*, volume and page in the Pali Text Society edition.
MN   *Majjhima Nikāya*, volume and page in the Pali Text Society edition. Translations from Bodhi (2005).

Notes

1. Dith Pran, in a private conversation at James Madison University, Harrisonburg, Virginia, October 1995. The quotation is from notes made immediately after the conversation and is not precise.
2. See the film *Doing Time, Doing Vipassana* by Ayelet Menahemi and Eilonia Ariel, Karuna Films, 1997.
3. Japanese terms omitted here.
4. Venerable Dhammananda, email, August 27, 2015.
5. Quoting AN I, 173.

References

Ambedkar, B. R. (1957). *The Buddha and his Dhamma.* Accessed May 18, 2012. Retrieved from http://www.ambedkar.org/buddhism/BAHD/45D.Buddha%20and%20His%20Dhamma%20PART%20IV.htm#a24 (sentence numbers removed).

Aung San Suu Kyi. (1997). *The voice of hope: Conversations with Alan Clements.* London: Penguin Books.

Bodhi. (Ed.). (2005). *In the Buddha's words: An anthology of discourses from the Pāli canon.* Boston: Wisdom.

Bodiford, W. (1996). Zen and the art of religious prejudice: Efforts to reform a tradition of social discrimination. *Japanese Journal of Religious Studies, 23*(1–2), 1–27.

Chavis, M. E. (2001). The 10,000 causes of crime. *Turning Wheel* (Summer).

Dalai Lama. (1999). *Ethics for the new millennium.* New York: Riverhead Books.

Ghosananda. (1992). *Step by step: Meditations on wisdom and compassion.* Berkeley, CA: Parallax Press.

Ingram, C. (1990). *In the footsteps of Gandhi: Conversations with spiritual social activists.* Berkeley, CA: Parallax Press.

Khuankaew, O. (2009). Buddhism and domestic violence: Using the four noble truths to deconstruct and liberate women's karma. In J. S.Watts (Ed.), *Rethinking Karma: The Dharma of Social Justice* (pp. 199–224). Chiang Mai, Thailand: Silkworm Books.

Khuankaew, O. (2012). Thai Buddhism and patriarchy. Unpublished manuscript.

King, S. B. (2006). *Being benevolence: The social ethics of Engaged Buddhism.* Honolulu: University of Hawaii Press.

Ñāṇamoli & Bodhi. (Trans.) (1995). *The middle length discourses of the Buddha: A new translation of the Majjhima Nikāya.* Boston: Wisdom.

Parkum, V. C., & Stultz, J. A. (2003). Symbol and narration in Buddhist prison ministry. In C. Queen, C. Prebish and D. Keown (Eds.), *Action Dharma: New Studies in Engaged Buddhism* (pp. 237–250). New York: RoutledgeCurzon.

Payutto, P. P. (1995). *Buddhadhamma: Natural laws and values for life.* (Grant A. Olson, Trans.). Albany: State University of New York Press.

Sharp, G. (1973). *The politics of nonviolent action. Part one: Power and struggle.* Boston: Porter Sargent.

Sivaraksa, S. (1999). Buddhism and human rights in Siam. In S. Sivaraksa (Ed.), *Socially Engaged Buddhism for the new millennium: Essays in honor of the Ven. Phra Dhammapitaka (Bhikkhu P. A. Payutto) on his 60th birthday anniversary* (pp. 195–212). Bangkok: Sathirakoses-Nagapradipa Foundation and Foundation for Children.

Thich Nhat Hanh. (1987). *Being peace.* Berkeley, CA: Parallax Press.

Walsh, M. (Trans.). (1987/1995). *The long discourses of the Buddha: A translation of the Dīgha Nikāya.* Boston: Wisdom.

Warren, H. C. (Trans.). (1979). *Milindapañha (The questions of King Milinda).* In *Buddhism in translations* (pp. 234–238). New York: Atheneum.

PART FOUR

Mindfulness, Memory, and Virtue

Chapter 10

Ethical Reading and the Ethics of Forgetting and Remembering

Sara McClintock

10.1. Introduction

This paper is an experiment in reading Buddhist narratives in a way I shall call *ethical reading*, that is, reading that engages texts with openness to the possibility that one may be ethically transformed by the encounter. This characterization of ethical reading reflects my understanding of ethics as a form of autopoiesis in which individuals fashion and refashion their subjectivity in relation to both self and world through a process of more or less conscious reflection on issues of moral significance.[1] Understanding ethics like this means rejecting that ethics is primarily a matter of the rational justification of particular actions or principles—even while acknowledging that issues of justification arise for individuals engaged in ethical autopoiesis. But any study of ethics that focuses on questions of justification while neglecting processes of ethical autopoiesis is at grave risk of losing touch with ethics itself. Instead one will be left studying the scaffolding of ethics, the arguments and principles that serve to support the ethical work of fashioning and refashioning one's subjectivity, but that can neither substitute for that work nor fully describe it. My interest in ethics is thus here decidedly not in *meta-ethics* but rather in *ethics itself*—that is, in the actual and ongoing work of ethical self-refashioning and transformation. And this interest applies both in terms of my desire to understand diverse traditions of Buddhist ethics and in terms of the ethics of my own reading of Buddhist texts.[2]

10.2. Ethical Reading

In recent years there has been some controversy surrounding the ethics of reading. The question of *what* we read, and the equally important question of *how* we read, have each been recognized as having profound ethical implications. Numerous strategies have been prescribed for avoiding ethical pitfalls, all meant to protect various actors from what appears to be the nearly inevitable violence of interpretation. Most of these strategies end up being variations on a hermeneutics of recovery and a hermeneutics of suspicion. Many argue for the need to combine both interpretative strategies, using a hermeneutics of recovery to find what is of value within the text and a hermeneutics of suspicion to discover its hidden agendas.[3] The ethical import of these considerations is clear, as is the power of hermeneutical strategies to perpetuate or ameliorate forms of harm that may arise in reading. I think it obvious that consideration of all these concerns and strategies belongs under the broad rubric of the ethics of reading, where ethics includes questions of the justification of various actions, attitudes, interpretations, and so on.

Here, however, I point to a different performative arena. That is, my concern is not directly about the effects our reading may have on others or on the world. Instead I am interested in the effects our reading may have on our own self-fashioning such that we may ultimately become *different kinds of actors* in the world (thus, however, also contributing to making *a different kind of world*). The theoretical backdrop to this kind of ethical reading relies on a performative understanding of meaning as an unstable, momentary event that takes place in a virtual space created by the conjunction of an unstable reader and an unstable text.[4] Meaning, on this view, is neither fixed nor lying hidden in a text waiting to be discovered by a reader, no matter how informed that reader may be.[5] Instead meaning emerges or is produced from a reader's encounter with a text—an encounter we call reading—and as it emerges both reader and text are changed. Each new encounter produces a new, more or less slightly altered meaning, as well as a new, more or less slightly altered reader and a new, more or less slightly altered text. Since my interest in ethical reading concerns ethical autopoiesis, the fact that each reading produces a new, more or less slightly altered reader is important to me. This new reader will understand and experience himself or herself differently in relation to both self and world, and this is the mark of ethical self-refashioning. And this, in turn, may affect how such readers act in the world.[6] Ethical reading is not reading undertaken in order to decide on general principles that will help one choose the best course of action in particular kinds of circumstances. Even less is it about finding reasons to justify such general principles. Such concerns are the domain of meta-ethics. Ethical reading is the actual enactment of *ethics itself* through the process of ethical autopoiesis via a reader's encounter with a text.

Buddhist narratives are fertile soil for ethical reading for several reasons. First, Buddhist stories deliberately *showcase* instances of Buddhist ethical auto-poiesis, providing a window onto the ways in which a colorful range of characters refashion themselves as the result of their engagement with Buddhist and non-Buddhist persons, practices, locales, objects, stories, and ideas. Second, Buddhist tales may be understood as seeking to *provoke* processes of ethical autopoiesis in their listeners or readers; attending to the mechanisms by which such stories appear designed to bring about ethical transformation in their audiences gives powerful insight into the nature of Buddhist ethics itself. Together these two features of Buddhist narratives provide compelling motivation to plunge deeply into these narrative worlds as part of any exploration of the nuances of Buddhist ethics itself. But there is another step one can take, and that is to open oneself to the possibility of one's own ethical transformation through the encounter with Buddhist stories. I want to argue that there are good reasons for taking this third step, reasons that are independent of whether or not one considers oneself to be a Buddhist.

10.3. Forgetting and Remembering

Describing ethical reading is important, but we also need examples of it in order to understand better what it is and to consider whether we may find it of value to ourselves as ethical beings. In what follows I attempt to engage in the ethical reading of three narratives from the *Divyāvadāna* (Vaidya, 1959).[7] Each narrative touches on the themes of forgetting and remembering in its own way. The stories of course contain much else that is of interest both to the historian of religion and to the ethical reader. My decision to focus on the themes of forgetting and remembering reflects my own interests and is not an attempt to represent an exhaustive interpretation of these extremely rich tales. Indeed inherent in the process of ethical reading is the recognition that one's own reading is always a partial, biased, and evanescent event. I therefore make no claims to completeness or any other kind of exhaustive interpretation. What I offer instead is an account of my own encounter with these narratives and the kind of ethical autopoiesis they seem to have produced.

Forgetting and remembering had been on my mind for some time— specifically the question of what we have forgotten about our own past selves, and also how we sometimes unexpectedly remember those forgotten things.

I also have had an ongoing scholarly and philosophical interest in the question of how living with the assumed reality of an infinite number of previous lives contributes to the ethical autopoiesis of individuals from Buddhist cultures past and present. Pivotal for me has been Charles Hallisey and Anne Hansen's (1996, p. 319) work on narrative, sub-ethics, and the moral life, in which the authors portray the moral condition of Buddhists as a matter of *karmic opacity* (see also Heim, 2014, pp. 205–212). Karmic opacity describes the situation in which a person knows that his or her present life is the result of actions undertaken in previous lives but has no knowledge of the details of those previous lives. According to Hallisey and Hansen, it is karmic opacity that allows Buddhists to reconcile the clear innocence of a present life with responsibility stemming from a past life. It is what allows a person to feel, even after hearing of the unjust assassination of an indisputably virtuous minister, "*Innocent Bandhula got what he deserved*" (Hallisey & Hansen, 1996, p. 318). The idea is that everything about my current situation can be causally explained—just not by me, not at this time.

Many Buddhist narratives, including those from the *Divyāvadāna*, pivot around the discovery of events from a character's past life. The discovery helps the character as well as the reader to understand more about the character's present life. But it does something else as well: it provides the reader with an impetus to contemplate what he or she may have forgotten about the past that is exerting a powerful influence on what is happening right now. For readers from cultures where the reality of past lives is accepted as a matter of course, such a contemplation could easily lead to a sense of wonder at the complexity of the karmic web. But even for those for whom past lives are not a given, there is ample room for considering what one has forgotten within the confines of this life alone. In recognizing the enormity of what one has forgotten, there is the possibility that one may experience an aesthetic shock that takes the form of a trembling (*saṃvega*) in the face of the implications of that amnesia.[8]

It is precisely this kind of heightened state that can provoke ethical autopoiesis. In the stories that follow, there are particular moments that provoked a kind of trembling for me as a reader. These were moments in which I recognized with inescapable clarity the limits of my knowledge of my own past, and of the past of others, and through which I was impelled to reflect upon the reality that I could not even begin to give a full account of the causal factors that had led me to my current situation. This in turn led me to reconsider how I regard others in my day-to-day life and to begin to refashion my way of being in the world in this regard. But I am getting ahead of myself. First I must tell the stories, though in necessarily brief and condensed form.

10.4. The Story of a Good-for-Nothing

I start with the story of Panthaka, whose unfortunate life is made exceedingly difficult due to his birth as an idiot and a fool. His elder brother is a brilliant ritualist and scholar who becomes a Buddhist monk, eventually attaining the state of an arhat with many disciples. Panthaka decides that he too would like to take ordination. His brother, Mahāpanthaka, performs the ordination and then gives Panthaka a simple verse to learn. After three months of study, however, Panthaka still is unable to remember the verse and must rely on local cowherds to remind him of its content. At a gathering of the monks, some miscreant monks goad Panthaka into asking his brother for another text to study. Mahāpanthaka, with the supernormal powers of an arhat, sees that his younger brother has been put up to making the request; he sees also that his brother will learn best if he is chastised rather than encouraged. So the elder brother throws the younger brother out of the monastery, telling him that he is an idiot and a fool.

Outside the monastery, Panthaka weeps. Just then, along comes the Buddha. The Buddha requests his attendant Ānanda to teach Panthaka. But finding that teaching Panthaka is extremely time-consuming, Ānanda returns to the Buddha, stating that he does not have time. Now the Buddha himself gives Panthaka a terse text of two lines to study and memorize: "I remove filth. / I remove impurity" (Rotman, 2014, p. 254; Cowell & Neil, 1886, p. 491). Stating that Panthaka's bad karma needs to be destroyed, the Buddha assigns him to clean the sandals of the other monks. While cleaning the sandals, Panthaka recites the verse. Eventually he manages to remember the two lines.

One day, at dawn, Panthaka has a sudden doubt: he wonders whether the verse he has been reciting refers to filth on the inside or to filth on the outside. As soon as Panthaka has this thought, three verses he has never heard before suddenly present (*āmukhīpravṛtta*) themselves to his mind. The three verses connect the filth of the slogan with the afflictions of attachment (*rāga*), hate (*dveṣa*), and delusion (*moha*); note that filth (*raja*) here definitely does not mean ordinary dirt (*reṇu*). With this understanding in place, Panthaka is now suddenly able to exert himself, and he quickly becomes an arhat, endowed with knowledge of his previous lives and living his final existence in *saṃsāra*.

The narrative goes on to present seven more stories, two concerning events in Panthaka's present life and five relating to events in previous lives. These substories are immensely entertaining, but unfortunately I do not have room to tell them here. Instead I will focus just on one, concerning twelve nuns who are offended that the Buddha has sent the fool Panthaka to give them teachings. Not realizing that Panthaka is an arhat, they set up a pretentious lion throne for him to sit upon, hoping to humiliate him. Panthaka sees through the trap, however, and brings the throne down to a more appropriate level. He preaches the dharma, and thousands benefit. The Buddha explains, "Not only now, but in the past as well, they were determined to ruin him" (Rotman, 2014, p. 271). He then tells the story of twelve evil daughters-in-law and how they attempt to poison their blind father-in-law but inadvertently end up curing him so that he sees their attempts to undo him! Of course the twelve daughters-in-law are the twelve nuns, and the blind father-in-law is Panthaka in a past life. Space does not permit me to relate the amusing details of this narrative, but we can appreciate how, in addition to providing an explanation for why these particular twelve nuns are behaving so childishly toward Panthaka, the tale also reminds us that our forgetfulness about our past tends to make us blind to the patterns of behavior that we keep on repeating in the present.

10.5. The Story of Dharmaruci

Structurally the narrative of Dharmaruci is simpler than that of Panthaka, though it still contains four major story lines. It starts with the tale of a close call that a group of merchants have with a giant sea monster named Timitingila, who very nearly swallows their ship in one gulp. When this creature rises from the depths of the ocean and opens his great jaws, it causes a large volume of water to enter his mouth at extreme speed, pulling the merchants' ship toward the monster's mouth. Terrified, the merchants call on the gods to whom they usually pray, but Śiva, Kubera, Varuṇa, and the others are unable to stop the tide. At this point a lay disciple of the Buddha recommends that since they are going to die, they should collectively say "Praise to the Buddha!" so that they will at least die with their minds focused on the Buddha and thus have a fortunate rebirth.

Apparently with no other option, the merchants collectively voice their praise of the Buddha. Far away in the Jeta Grove, the Buddha hears their cry with his divine ear. The Buddha then makes it such that Timingila is able to hear the prayer. The prayer makes a great impact on the sea creature, and he becomes uneasy. Thinking it would be wrong to eat food after hearing the Lord Buddha's name, and recognizing that the ship is in danger of being swallowed, he gently closes his mouth to avoid causing harm. Overcome with relief and gratitude, the merchants decide to offer their treasures to the Buddha. The Buddha, however, turns down the offering and instead invites the merchants to become monks in his order. They distribute the treasure to their families and friends, take ordination, and eventually all become arhats.

Meanwhile, having heard the word *Buddha*, Timitiṅgila becomes unable to take food and, after some time, dies of starvation. His giant carcass floats ashore, and its bones are picked clean by birds and animals. Timitiṅgila is reincarnated in the womb of a Brahman woman. As soon as the woman conceives, she becomes wracked with hunger pains. This continues until the baby is born, after which she is cured, but the baby becomes insatiable. The only time he seems satisfied is when monks and nuns come to the house to beg food and, having eaten, tell a "roundabout story."[9] During that time he would stop experiencing thirst and hunger pains and would stop crying. Noting that the child relishes the dharma, they name him Dharmaruci (literally, "Relishes the Dharma").

When he grows up, his parents give Dharmaruci a begging bowl so he can collect alms, but even after collecting alms all day, he still is not satisfied. A lay disciple of the Buddha sees him and urges him to go forth as a monk in the Buddha's order, which Dharmaruci does. After ordination Dharmaruci remains unable to eliminate his hunger, and soon his instructor and the other monks are giving him food from their own bowls. Still he is not satisfied. One day the Buddha and his monks are invited to a householder's place for a meal. The Buddha appoints Dharmaruci to oversee the monastery while the other monks are gone. But another householder has decided to bring to the monastery food for 500 monks. Arriving there, he finds only Dharmaruci. Although disappointed, the layman decides that he can at least feed this one monk. He offers him food, but he sees that the monk still is not satisfied. Politely he asks whether the monk would eat some more, and politely Dharmaruci accepts the offer of more food and drink. But having eaten a second generous helping, he remains unsatisfied. The householder again offers him food and drink, giving him even more this time. Soon Dharmaruci has eaten all the available food—enough for 500 monks! The householder is convinced that Dharmaruci is a demon. Terrified, he quickly runs back to the city. A monk sent by the Buddha now returns to the monastery with a single serving of food, and with this serving Dharmaruci finally is satisfied.

As the householder is entering the city, the Buddha and his retinue of monks, who are returning to the Jeta Grove, encounter him. The householder tells the Buddha the story of the monk who ate food for 500. The Buddha praises the householder, proclaiming that Dharmaruci has finally been satisfied and that he would soon attain the state of an arhat. Returning to the Jeta Grove, the Buddha asks Dharmaruci if he ever has seen the ocean. Dharmaruci says that he has not, and the Buddha then instructs him to hold on to the edge of the Buddha's robe. Using his magical powers, the Buddha transports Dharmaruci to the edge of the ocean, to the place where Timitiṅgila's skeleton is resting. The Buddha instructs Dharmaruci to contemplate the skeleton without telling him what it is. The skeleton is so huge that Dharmaruci cannot even determine where it begins and where it ends. Confounded, he asks the Buddha about the object. The Buddha says, "This is a skeleton." Then he utters this exhortation: "Rejoice, Dharmaruci, in the different states of existence! Rejoice in the means that lead to these states of existence! This is your skeleton" (Rotman, 2014, pp. 20–21; Cowell & Neil, 1886, p. 240). When Dharmaruci understands that the immense object in front of him is his own skeleton, he is suddenly and mightily affected by a trembling terror.[10] After instructing Dharmaruci to concentrate on the skeleton, the Buddha departs. Motivated by his fear, Dharmaruci passes through all the stages of the path and becomes an arhat with extreme alacrity. Having attained awakening, he turns his attention to his previous lives and sees hundreds of them. He then returns to the Jeta Grove using his own newfound magical powers.

When Dharmaruci returns as an arhat, the Buddha greets him in such a way as to imply that they have known each other for a very long time. He then relates three past life stories to the assembled monks. Each story features two characters, one the past life of Dharmaruci and the other the past life of the Buddha. The narratives tell of their evolving relationship over the eons and help to explain how it is that one of them is now the Buddha while the other one is his disciple. They also explain why the sea monster Timitiṅgila was unable to swallow the merchants' ship upon hearing the name *Buddha*. The stories serve to show the monks, as well as the readers of the tale, the past causes and conditions for the monk Dharmaruci's current life—causes and conditions that become clear to Dharmaruci when he meditates on the skeleton of his former body. It is this new knowledge that allows Dharmaruci to finally understand not only his previous insatiability but also the futility of his attempts to satisfy himself with anything short of the complete destruction of delusion, attachment, and hate.

10.6. The Story of Svāgata

As in the first two stories, meditation practice again plays a key role as a catalyst for the remembrance of previous lives in the final story I will present, the story of Svāgata, "The One Who Is Welcome." Here the theme of forgetfulness is explicitly addressed, becoming one of the tale's primary leitmotifs. Again the Buddha intervenes, both as an active agent in the main character's current life and as a source of clarity concerning causes from the distant past.

The trouble begins when the wife of a wealthy householder conceives a son. From the moment of conception, misfortune descends on the householder and his family. Soothsayers attribute the problems to the unborn child, but the householder refuses to abort the fetus, stating that the child is *svāgata* ("welcome"). After Svāgata is born, however, the householder's misfortunes increase. His wealth is exhausted, and both he and his wife soon die. The house and fields are destroyed in a fire, and soon even the servants are expiring. Those who do survive run off until there is no one left but the boy and one elderly maid. Curious about the cause of all this misfortune, she reflects that it must be either her fault or the fault of Svāgata. To find out, she cooks some rice in Svāgata's name and it goes bad. She then cooks some rice in her own name and it turns out fine. Deciding that he must be the cause of the problems, she takes whatever of any value is left and flees.

When Svāgata returns to the house, he finds it empty. Being hungry and alone, he goes to a relative's home, but as soon as he arrives they begin to quarrel. The relatives decide that he is the cause of their fighting. Proclaiming that he is not welcome, they throw him out, dubbing him Durāgata, "The One Who Is Unwelcome." Having no choice, Svāgata eventually joins up with some beggars. No sooner does he join their group, however, than their luck dries up. Unable to collect alms as usual, they decide to test who is at fault. Breaking up into two groups, they enter the city. The group with Svāgata in it returns empty-handed. Next, that group is broken into two, and again Svāgata's group returns empty-handed. The beggars proceed in this way until it is down to two beggars. At the end of the day, when Svāgata returns with no food, it is clear that he is the ill-fated one. The beggars beat him, break a begging bowl over his head, and throw him out.

Svāgata moves on and soon encounters a merchant who is an old family friend. Recognizing the boy, the merchant gives him two coins, telling him to take care of himself with the money until the merchant can return. Svāgata ties the coins into the hem of his ragged clothes and promptly forgets about them. Meanwhile the merchant himself forgets about Svāgata. After a while the merchant sets off on a trading journey with a large number of other merchants, taking the role of the caravan leader. Unbeknownst to him, Svāgata joins the caravan. Soon both the caravan members and even the bulls start quarreling. One of the caravan members has the idea to check the caravan, saying, "That Durāgata better not have come here!" Checking the caravan, they find Svāgata, and they beat him and kick him out. The caravan leader comes to see what is going on and again recognizes Svāgata. Seeing that the other caravan members refuse to go on if Svāgata is allowed to be in the party, the merchant secretly tells Svāgata to follow behind the caravan at a distance. The merchant then leaves food for Svāgata in the bushes and the trees, but the food is always eaten by animals before Svāgata can get to it.

Somehow, however, Svāgata manages to make it all the way to Śrāvastī, the caravan's destination and the home of his sister, who is married to the wealthy Buddhist householder Anāthapiṇḍada. A servant of his sister recognizes him and tells her that her brother has arrived in miserable condition. The sister sends along expensive clothes and coins, with the idea that he should clean himself up and then present himself at the rich layman's home. Svāgata immediately goes off to get some food but ends up buying liquor instead. After imbibing the alcohol, he passes out drunk in a park. Some thieves come across him and rob him of the expensive clothes and coins so that he wakes up with his same old clothes and no money. Meanwhile his sister is worried that he has not shown up. A maidservant goes off to investigate and finds Svāgata in his same miserable state. She goes back to the sister, who reflects that it is her brother's fault that her father's home was destroyed and that he is truly a force for disaster who must not be allowed to enter her home.

At this point Svāgata forgets about his sister. Once again he joins a group of beggars, and once again the beggars find themselves abused and unable to obtain alms. This group of beggars too splits into two, gradually zeroing in on the bearer of bad luck. When they realize it is Svāgata, they beat him, break his begging bowl over his head, and throw him out. Meanwhile the householder Anāthapiṇḍada has invited the Buddha and his monks for a meal, and he instructs his doorkeeper not to let any beggars come in for food until after the Buddha and the monks have finished eating. The beggars, who are used to relying on Anāthapiṇḍada (literally, "Almsgiver to the Poor"), suspect that "The One Who Is Unwelcome" is responsible for this rejection. They search him out, and when they find him they beat him again, this time breaking his skull with a begging bowl and throwing him upon a pile of refuse.

So there lies Svāgata, a pitiful sight, when along comes the Buddha on his way to partake of the meal offered by Anāthapiṇḍada. The *avadāna* describes the encounter:

> The Blessed One saw Svāgata lying on that pile of garbage. His fingers were rough and dirty, his hair was long, and his body was smeared with dirt; he was skinny, with hardly any strength, and he was wearing dirty, tattered clothes. Blood was streaming from his broken head, as flies attacked the wounds all over his body. At the sight of him, the Blessed One addressed the monks: "Rejoice, monks, in rebirths in all realms of existence! Rejoice in the means for rebirth in all realms of existence! For this is the condition of a being in his last existence." (Rotman, 2008, p. 301; Cowell & Neil, 1886, p. 177)[11]

The Buddha then asks Svāgata if he would like to have the leftover food from an alms bowl. Svāgata says yes, and the Buddha tells his attendant Ānanda to set aside some food from his bowl for Svāgata. Then the Buddha, Ānanda, and the rest of the monks go to the place where Anāthapiṇḍada is offering the meal, leaving Svāgata behind.

Once the Buddha has finished his meal, Ānanda picks up the Buddha's bowl and sees that he has left some food aside for Svāgata. Mortified, Ānanda realizes that he himself has forgotten to set aside any food as the Buddha had instructed him to do, and he begins to cry. The Buddha, however, reassures Ānanda that his oversight was not his fault. Rather his forgetfulness can be attributed to the deeds that Svāgata has committed in former times.[12] Then the Buddha tells Ānanda to go and call for Svāgata. But when Ānanda does so, using the name Svāgata ("Welcome"), many people respond. Of course Svāgata has forgotten about the promise of food and has even forgotten his old name. Ānanda asks the Buddha what to do, and the Buddha tells him to go and call for "Svāgata, the son of the householder Bodha of Śuśumāragiri." When he hears this, Svāgata suddenly remembers his own name. He goes forward and eats the food from the Buddha's bowl. Although it is only a little bit of food, he is able to eat until he is satisfied.

After this, Svāgata, who is now referred to by the narrative as "that being who was in his last existence," follows the Buddha back to the monastery. Venerating the Buddha, he then sits down at a respectful distance. The Buddha addresses him, asking him if he has any coins. Svāgata says no, but the Buddha directs him to look in the hem of his clothes, where he finds the two coins he had sewn in there much earlier. The Buddha instructs Svāgata to take the coins to the gardener Gaṇḍaka and to get some blue lotuses. Svāgata does as he is told and comes back with the blue lotuses. The Buddha instructs him to distribute the lotuses to the monks. The monks do not wish to accept the flowers, but they do so when Buddha says, "His [bad] karma must be destroyed by what he sees" (Rotman, 2008, p. 305; Cowell & Neil, 1886, p. 180).[13]

It turns out that in a previous life Svāgata had practiced blue *kṛstna* (Pāli *kasiṇa*), a type of stabilization meditation in which the practitioner focuses one-pointedly on a blue disk. Now in the presence of the monks, Svāgata looks at the blue flowers and suddenly has a strong experience of this blue *kṛstna*. The Buddha asks him if he would like to go forth as a monk, and Svāgata says yes. Under the tutelage of the Buddha, Svāgata progresses in his studies and meditation until he becomes an arhat.

Further adventures unfold—including one in which the arhat Svāgata subdues a troublesome water spirit (*nāga*) with a magical display of such awesomeness that many lay disciples mistake Svāgata for the Buddha himself, and another in which the arhat becomes inadvertently drunk. But unfortunately all this narrative goodness cannot detain us here. Instead I will consider the ethics of remembering and forgetting in relation to these Buddhist stories.

10.7. May We Always Remember Our Former Lives!

In each of these stories, a character who is ignorant about his past attains awakening as an arhat and remembers his past lives through a trigger event orchestrated by the Buddha. For Panthaka, the key moment came as he was cleaning sandals and had sudden knowledge of three verses he had never heard before. For Dharmaruci, realization and memory dawned while contemplating the huge skeleton from his previous life as a sea monster. For Svāgata, things began to change when his memory was jolted upon seeing the blue color of the lotus flowers he was distributing to the monks. The visual component in each of these events is notable and confirms Andy Rotman's (2009) analysis of the importance of visual experience in the *Divyāvadāna* and related literature. As readers, however, our knowledge of the past lives of these characters unfolds through the narratives themselves, and it is intriguing to consider how the narrative structure of the stories seems to provoke moments of aesthetic shock or recognition that can spark ethical autopoiesis in us as readers. In this concluding section, I will attempt to make good on my promise to perform an ethical reading by sharing some of the insights and transformations that have occurred to me through my study of these tales.

But before doing so I want to make a brief detour into the scholarly literature on the remembrance of past lives in the Buddhist tradition. As Donald Lopez (1992) documents, scholars such as André Bareau, Paul Demiéville (1927), and Mircea Eliade have sought explanations for the Buddhist tradition's emphasis on the remembrance of previous lives as a component of the awakening of the Buddha and of many arhats, with no general agreement to be found. At stake is the question of the *purpose* of this memory, the first of three special kinds of knowledge (*trividyā*) held to have been attained by the Buddha during the night of his awakening. For Lopez, the primary puzzle is that this first special knowledge would appear to be rendered superfluous by the third special knowledge—the knowledge of the destruction of the defilements—according to which the Buddha would have had a radically de-subjectivating insight into the absence of any unchanging self (*ātman*) that could serve as an enduring identity that connects all these memories. Lopez's proposal is to see the Buddha's remembrance of his previous lives as similar to a Freudian "screen memory," in which trivial details of the past are remembered so as to provide a "screen" for more traumatic, repressed memories. On Lopez's reading, the Buddha's formulaic account of his previous lives is a banal reconstruction that allows him to destroy all personal identification with that past. In this way, Lopez (1992, p. 23) considers "whether the Buddha needed to remember in order to forget, whether the vision of his former lives served to digest the past so that he could eliminate it and be freed from its effects." Such a theoretical position has its advantages, including that it goes some way (though not all the way) toward addressing Paul Griffiths's (1989, 1992) qualm about how the Buddha, with his utter absence of the conceit of "I" (*asmimāna*) could remember his previous lives. Griffiths's worry is one of a larger species with which the Buddhist tradition has dealt in various ways, namely, the question of how a Buddha can engage with ordinary, erroneous, conventional, or conceptual knowledge. These are interesting theoretical problems, but they are not my questions here.

Lopez's solution has a certain eloquence, but it does not take into account another, more obvious reason for the Buddha's memories of his own past lives. That is, it is only because the Buddha can remember both his and others' pasts that he is able to narrate the *jātaka*s and *avadāna*s, stories that give ordinary people critical insight into their existential situation as one of being conditioned by previous, unremembered karma. Gregory Schopen (1983) gets at some of the significance of this in his study of the phrase *jātismara* (literally, "remembrance of births") in a wide variety of early and medieval Indian Mahāyāna texts. He notes that, unlike the remembrance of previous lives associated with the Buddha and arhats, *jātismara* in these texts is said to be obtained by ordinary persons as a result of contact with the Buddha and his teachings. For example, people are said to gain *jātismara* by hearing, copying, or reciting certain scriptures; by seeing, making, or worshipping certain images; and by hearing, remembering, or having faith in certain names. The importance of *jātismara* for the ordinary practitioner is further underscored by the presence of many aspirational prayers in which practitioners pray to remember their former lives, as in the verse from the *Bhadracaripraṇidhāna*, which states, "And may I, practicing the practice for enlightenment in all rebirths be possessed of the memory of my former births" (Schopen, 1989, p. 113). Many similar verses can be found, including in the well-known *Bodhicaryāvatāra* of Śāntideva, which states, "May I always obtain recollection of my former births and the going forth" (Schopen, 1983, pp. 113–114). As Schopen makes clear, the *purpose* of this memory to bring about a "radical restructuring of behavior and attitude" such that one is henceforth able to avoid the negative actions that would result in taking rebirth as a hell realm being, an animal, or a ghost (p. 138).

In short, on Schopen's reading the aspiration to remember one's past lives and the purpose of remembering them is all for the sake of ethical autopoiesis. A question here is how *jātismara* functions to bring about transformation. Clearly there is fear of the suffering of the lower realms, and there is mortification and shame in the face of one's prior bad behavior. Both these are attested in Schopen's texts. But I want to suggest another way in which *jātismara* might function to provoke ethical autopoiesis, and this is a way that can happen through an encounter with narratives like the *jātakas* and *avadānas*. Here *jātismara* should be understood not as the remembrance of specific past lives but rather as the remembrance (one might even say mindfulness) of the fact that one has forgotten most of the formative actions that have brought one to one's current situation. This existential situation of karmic opacity is one that we easily forget or ignore, imagining that we know and can easily understand the causes and conditions of our lives. In my case, the stories of the *Divyāvadāna* have encouraged me to adjust my way of being in the world in recognition of my ignorance of the past. Let me explain.

With the story of Panthaka, I recognized the shock that Panthaka and the twelve unkind nuns must have felt in learning that their current situation had a parallel in the distance past. In particular I was reminded of a recent encounter with an old friend whom I had not seen in many years, who reminded me of an incident from my own past that I had long since forgotten. What was disturbing about the experience was how clearly I saw that certain mistakes I had made in my past were so similar to mistakes I was continuing to make in the present. Recognizing how little I understood about the repetitive nature of my errors opened my eyes to the importance of examining my behavior for destructive patterns. In addition I was struck by Panthaka's seemingly miraculous contact with three previously unheard verses. This narrative episode triggered in me an awareness of the possibility that a kind of epiphany could arise for me coming from previous insight, training, or study or from contact with a special person. As a result of this insight, I feel that I became simultaneously more critical and more accepting of myself as I currently am, knowing that I am deeply flawed in ways conditioned by my past while also recognizing that I have the capacity for deep insights, also rooted in work in the past. I further reflected that such insight might come, as it did for Panthaka, while performing with single-pointed attention a mundane task for the benefit of others. I therefore resolved to devote myself wholeheartedly to any task I might undertake for others.

With the story of Dharmaruci, I recognized the shock that the monk must have felt upon realizing that the huge object before him was his own skeleton from his previous life as a sea monster. This made me think about the ways I often encounter the detritus of my earlier life and how I often do not recognize the mess as a mess that I myself have created. I resolved to become more observant in trying to see my hand in the messes of my current life. In addition, in the three past life stories that the Buddha told to explain his relationship with Dharmaruci over eons, I was jolted into realizing how many relationships with important people I must have forgotten even in the course of this single life. Thinking more deeply, I realized that there have been thousands of people—friends, teachers, relatives, strangers, confidants—who have helped me or shown me some kindness but the memory of whom is not available to me. Even within a relatively short time, I have certainly forgotten—if I ever recognized—the assistance of many relatives, friends, and strangers. I therefore resolved to be more attentive to the kindness of others and to remember that anyone I meet could be a person who has helped in the past, whose help I have forgotten.

Finally, with the story of Svāgata, I recognized the shock the monks must have felt upon being told by the Buddha that the starving, bleeding, nearly dead beggar sitting on a garbage heap was a being in his final existence. This story, in a manner that was quite visceral, prompted me to consider the fact that anyone I might meet, no matter how apparently lacking in qualities, could be on the verge of some great attainment. Not knowing the past of others means that we do not know how close they may be to greatness, even if their current manifestation appears unfortunate. The Buddha could see Svāgata's greatness because the Buddha understood all the past causes and conditions that brought Svāgata to that place. But we cannot see the fullness of causes and conditions that have brought others to the places where they are, and so we must refrain from assuming to understand or know their capacities and limitation. I therefore resolved to relinquish such judgments and to proceed with the understanding that anyone could become my teacher.

Reading these stories from the *Divyāvadāna* became ethical reading for me when I allowed myself to be touched by them in ways that provoked ethical autopoiesis. The stories gave me a taste of *jātismara*, not only because they explicitly discuss the past lives of their characters but, more significantly, because they motivated me to become more mindful of the importance of the past—and here *jāti* or "birth" can be understood not only as a past life but also as the production of a previous moment in the current life—for the unfolding of the present while simultaneously driving home deeply my inability to know that past in anything close to the fullness of its complexity. In short, these stories from the *Divyāvadāna* have served to make me remember that I have forgotten my past lives or, perhaps better, that I have forgotten the pasts of my life. This is rather different from Lopez's theory that the Buddha remembers so that he can forget. Here, rather, as an ordinary being, I am reminded that I have forgotten. These stories help me to do so, and they help in such a way as to open me up to a sense of humility concerning the limits of my knowledge, an intensified appreciation of the unrecognized kindnesses of others, and a genuine optimism concerning the capacities of both myself and others to transform ourselves ethically even in the face of great challenges and obstacles. May we all always remember our former lives thus!

Notes

1. *Autopoiesis* is a term coined by the philosophers and biologists Humberto Maturana and Francisco Varela to refer to the continual process of self-production characteristic of the organization of living systems. See Thompson (2007, pp. 97ff) for an overview of the theory of autopoiesis and autopoietic organization.

2. See Heim (2014, pp. 2–6) for an eloquent application of the ideas of the philosopher Pierre Hadot to the project of "learning how to read," a project that involves both carefully situating texts within their historical and discursive contexts and carefully attending to the subjective meanings that texts provoke in us.

3. Susanne Mrozik (2007, pp. 117–121) makes an excellent argument for the need to combine both these approaches. See also Ricoeur (1970, pp. 20–36).

4. The instability of the text is here taken as axiomatic insofar as the text can never be encountered the same way twice. See Barthes (1974) for a masterful demonstration of this reality.

   From this point forward I will use the term *reader* since the encounter with the text in contemporary times is generally via the written word. In ancient India, these Buddhist texts would have often been encountered aurally, and there the term *listener* is more appropriate.

5. See Iser (1978, pp. 3–19) for an analysis of some of the problems with the conception of meaning as hidden within the text by reference to Henry James's short story "The Figure in the Carpet."

6. See Attridge (2004, p. xii): "A literary work is not an object of a thesis; literature *happens* (and not only in the texts we call 'literary'). The event of the literary work can have powerful effects on its readers, and through them, on the cultural and political environment; but these can never be predicted in advance."

7. My reading of these stories is greatly indebted to Andy Rotman's lively translations.

8. The affect or emotion *saṃvega* plays a central role on the Buddhist path, as does its counterpart *prasāda* (Pāli, *pasāda*), meaning "clarity." The first, described by Coomaraswamy as an "aesthetic shock," represents the jolt one receives when one recognizes one's folly in continuing to lead an unexamined life in the face of certain mortality. The second represents the clarity that settles upon one once one recognizes what needs to be done in the face of certain death and impermanence. See Coomaraswamy (1943) on *saṃvega* and Rotman (2009) on *prasāda*.

9. On the significance of the roundabout story (*parikathā*), see Rotman (2008, pp. 24–25), who states that a roundabout story appears to be similar to a "dharma story" (*dharmīkathā*), that is, a story about people listening to a story about the dharma. In such stories, one discovers the karmic bonds (*karmaploti*) that serve as the thread (*ploti*) that ties together a karmic history. The *avadāna* seems here to recognize its role in provoking ethical autopoiesis.

10. The Sanskrit here is *atīvasaṃvignaḥ* (following the reading in Vaidya, 1959, p. 148; Cowell & Neil, 1886, p. 240 have *ativasaṃvignaḥ*). The word *saṃvigna* is the past passive participle from the verbal root *saṃvij*, which means "to tremble" or "to startle with fear." It is the same verbal root from which is derived *saṃvega*, discussed in note 8 above.

11. Note the similarity to the Buddha's statement to Dharmaruci, where, however, Rotman has translated the verb *tṛp* as "be satisfied" rather than "rejoice."

12. The impact of Svāgata's memory problem on others is a fascinating affirmation, found elsewhere in the *Divyāvadāna* also, that karma is not a solitary affair but has a strong intersubjective aspect. Ryan Kuratko (2013) describes Svāgata as a "field of *pāpa* (or demerit)," analogous to the well-known idea of monks and enlightened beings as "fields of merit" (*puṇyakṣetra*).

13. See also Rotman (2008, p. 434n654).

References

Attridge, D. (2004). *J. M. Coetzee and the ethics of reading: Literature in the event.* Chicago: University of Chicago.

Barthes, R. (1974). *S/Z: An essay.* (R. Miller, Trans.). New York: Hill and Wang.

Coomaraswamy, A. K. (1943). *Saṃvega*: Aesthetic shock. *Harvard Journal of Asiatic Studies, 7*(3), 174–179.

Cowell, E. B., & Neil, R. A. (Eds.). (1886). *The Divyāvadāna: A collection of early Buddhist legends.* Cambridge, UK: University Press.

Demiéville, P. (1927). Sur la mémoire des existences antérieures. *Bulletin d'Ecole française d'extrême-Orient, 27*, 283–298.

Griffiths, P. J. (1989). Why buddhas can't remember their previous lives. *Philosophy East and West, 39*(4), 449–451.

Griffiths, P. J. (1992). Memory in classical Indian Yogācāra. In J. Gyatso (Ed.), *In the mirror of memory: Reflections on mindfulness and remembrance in Indian and Tibetan Buddhism* (109–131). Albany: State University of New York Press.

Hallisey, C., & Hansen, A. (1996). Narrative, sub-ethics, and the moral life: Some evidence from Theravāda Buddhism. *Journal of Religious Ethics, 24*(2), 305–327.

Heim, M. (2014). *The forerunner of all things: Buddhaghosa on mind, intention, and agency.* Oxford: Oxford University Press.

Iser, W. (1978). *The act of reading: A theory of aesthetic response.* Baltimore: Johns Hopkins University Press.

Kuratko, R. (2013). A field of disaster: The reverse sides of mercantile karma and *Prasāda* in the *Svāgata-avadāna.* Unpublished manuscript.

Lopez, D. S., Jr. (1992). Memories of the Buddha. In J. Gyatso (Ed.), *In the mirror of memory: Reflections on mindfulness and remembrance in Indian and Tibetan Buddhism* (pp. 21–45). Albany: State University of New York Press.

Mrozik, S. (2007). *Virtuous bodies: The physical dimensions of morality in Buddhist ethics.* Oxford: Oxford University Press.

Ricoeur, P. (1970). *Freud and philosophy: An essay on interpretation.* New Haven, CT: Yale University Press.

Rotman, A. (Trans.). (2008). *Divine stories: Divyāvadāna.* Part 1. Boston: Wisdom.

Rotman, A. (2009). *Thus have I seen: Visualizing faith in early Indian Buddhism.* Oxford: Oxford University Press.

Rotman, A. (Trans.). (2014). Divine stories: *Divyāvadāna.* Part 2. Unpublished manuscript.

Schopen, G. (1983). The generalization of an old yogic attainment in medieval Mahāyāna Sūtra literature: Some notes on *Jātismara. Journal of the International Association of Buddhist Studies, 6*(1), 109–147.

Thompson, E. (2007). *Mind in life: Biology, phenomenology, and the sciences of mind.* Cambridge, MA: Belknap Press of Harvard University Press.

Vaidya, P. L. (Ed.). (1959). *Divyāvadāna.* Buddhist Sanskrit Text, no. 20. Darbhanga, India: Mithila Institute of Post-Graduate Studies and Research in Sanskrit Learning.

Chapter 11

Mindfulness and Ethics

ATTENTION, VIRTUE, AND PERFECTION

*Jay L. Garfield**

11.1. Introduction

If there is any domain in which Buddhism can contribute significantly to cognitive science—one in which Buddhist insight is arguably well in advance of contemporary theory in the West—that is moral psychology. Buddhist ethics has always been grounded in a sophisticated moral phenomenology, connecting suffering and vice to attachment and aversion, those to deep confusion about the fundamental nature of reality and in particular to the self and subjectivity, and these in turn to deep primal fear.

Moral progress in turn has been understood as a transformation of one's comportment toward the world, comprising both a transformation of moral and metaphysical vision and an elimination of the profound fear of death, enabling our pervasive subconscious awareness of impermanence to become a source of joy and compassion rather than a source of fear and grasping (Garfield, 2010–2011, 2015; Finnigan & Tanaka, 2010). The phenomenological reflection that underlies this moral psychology as well as the recommendations it entails for moral development involve both deep introspective engagement and a powerful transcendental reflection on what we have come to know since Heidegger's *Being and Time* as *dasein* and *mitsein*. While aspects

*Thanks to Nalini Bhushan, Nic Bommarito, Bronwyn Finnigan, Maria Heim, Susan Levin, Guy Newland, and Sonam Thakchöe for helpful comments on an earlier draft. I also thank members of the Upper Valley Zen Center for helpful questions and comments. Special thanks to the ven Geshe Damdul Namgyal for a searching critique and for discussions that have led to substantial improvements. Many errors remain, and they are all mine.

of these insights have emerged in the West, principally in the work of Freud and more recently in the discipline of cognitive behavior therapy, there is little either in ethical theory or in the psychology of ethical thought and action that approaches Buddhist ideas, particularly as articulated by such philosophers as Śāntideva, in sophistication.

Buddhist reflection indicates to us the ways our perception of ourselves, of those around us, and of the world of animate and inanimate objects to which we relate are conditioned by ideology and by affect. It also indicates the plasticity of that perception, of our preconscious ideology and of our affect, albeit also the difficulty of exploiting the plasticity in daily life. And it holds open the prospect that the application of a cognitive understanding of the fundamental nature of reality—including the pervasiveness of impermanence and interdependence—and of the technique of mindfulness can effect the transformation that takes us from fear to contentment and from egocentric misery to altruistic joy.

This is, of course, the burgeoning science of positive psychology and of ethical development, science that may succeed in redrawing the map of the domain of moral experience, motivation, and action through empirical investigation. And this investigation has been and will continue to be theoretically and clinically fecund. It involves straightforward experimental and imaging paradigms of the kind used to examine motivation, affect, perception, and moral reasoning already, turning our gaze on phenomena such as fear versus equanimity, egoism versus altruism, compassion versus indifference and their connection to the perception of independence versus interdependence, permanence versus impermanence, and so on. Not rocket science, but potentially more valuable to humankind than much that is. And a domain in which Buddhist *theory*, as well as practice, has much to contribute to contemporary cognitive science.

11.2. Mindfulness

Mindfulness is regarded by all scholars and practitioners of all Buddhist traditions as essential not only for the development of insight but also for the cultivation and maintenance of ethical discipline. The English term denotes the joint operation of what are regarded in Buddhist philosophy of mind as two cognitive functions: *sati/smṛti/dran pa*, which we might translate as "attention" in this context (although the semantic range of these terms also encompasses "memory" and "recollection") and *sampajañña/samprajanya /shes bzhin*, which I will render here as "introspective vigilance."[1] The first function involves the fixation of attention on an object, and the second the careful maintenance of that attention and of the attendant attitudes and motivations.[2] When we bring attention and introspective vigilance to bear on an object, we can be said to be mindful of it.

Indeed—and this is no news to Buddhist scholars or practitioners, though it is sometimes surprising to non-Buddhist ethicists—the cultivation of ethical discipline is generally regarded in the Buddhist philosophical tradition as a necessary condition of the cultivation both of mundane insight into conventional reality and of the wisdom that allows us to understand ultimate reality. For that reason, not only is there an important reciprocal relation in this tradition between the cognitive and the moral, but mindfulness per se lies at the foundation of *everything*. In the Pāli canon, particularly in the *Satipaṭṭhāna-Sutta* but also in such places as the *Vitakkasaṇṭhāna-Sutta*, the *Sekha-Sutta*, the *Ānāpānasati-Sutta*, and the *Kāyagatāsati-Sutta* and even the *Mahāsuññata-Sutta*, we encounter admonitions to train in mindfulness as the foundation of all Buddhist practice and direct connections between the practice of mindfulness and the cultivation of morality.

In the best-known and most sophisticated text on ethics of the Mahāyāna tradition, Śāntideva's *Bodhicāryāvatāra*, mindfulness is taken up as the very foundation of all of moral practice and development. This foundational role was emphasized beautifully in one of the most instructive and eloquent dharma talks I ever had occasion to hear: the Most Venerable Khamtrul Rinpoche explained to my students how easy it is to practice the Buddhist path perfectly for one second—just for one second, right action, right speech, right livelihood, and so on, and how easy it is to continue for one more second— but that only with mindfulness can that practice be preserved continuously, moment after moment.

I use the English term "mindfulness" to translate the joint operation of *smṛti/samprajanya, dran pa/shes bzhin* because it nicely captures the broad semantic range that the pairs of Sanskrit and Tibetan terms enjoy, bringing together what we would characterize in English as memory, as well as attention. "Mindfulness" in this unusually felicitous Buddhist-hybrid-English sense captures the unification of these cognitive functions under the rubric of *calling to mind* and vigilantly *retaining in mind*. This is not, I emphasize, to say that these functions are identical. They are not. It is one thing to attend and another to guard that attention with vigilance, but it is important to note that these functions are cooperative, each enabling and reinforcing the other.

Śāntideva emphasizes that mindfulness is constituted by the union of these functions in the following verses, in which he first introduces the need to care for the mind, and then cashes out that care in terms of these two functions:

> Those who do not understand the secret of the mind,
> Which is the innermost essence of phenomena,
> Although they wish to achieve happiness and avoid suffering:
> They just wander aimlessly.
> Therefore, I should maintain and care for
> This mind well.
> If the vow to care for the mind is not maintained,
> What is the point of maintaining any of the other vows?
> . . . .
> I therefore beg those who wish to care for their minds:
> Always, assiduously,
> Care for your
> Attention and introspective vigilance! (BCA 5.17–18, 23)[3]

Here Śāntideva emphasizes first the primacy of mindfulness as a whole—that care for the mind is the foundation of all other virtuous activity, as well as the foundation of the possibility of happiness, the release from suffering, and a meaningful life. But he concludes this passage by emphasizing that this care amounts to the union of attention and introspective vigilance. That is the essence of mindfulness.

Thinking about the role of mindfulness in ethics as it is articulated by both Śāntideva and Khamtrul Rinpoche—as the necessary mechanism for focusing the mind on the morally relevant dimensions of situations and on one's own moral responsibility—calls to my mind two prima facie contrary streams of thought about the relationship between mindfulness and moral experience, setting up interesting tensions that arise both outside of the Buddhist tradition and within it: Aristotle's account of virtuous action, Theravāda and Mahāyāna accounts of a buddha's enlightened action, and the Chan/Zen account of action without thought. These tensions are also relevant to contemporary life, as we try to imagine the goals and methods of values education in our schools and our individual practice as ethical agents and as mentors to young people in their ethical development.

Each of these traditions—albeit in ways different from one another—emphasizes both the importance of *conscious attention* in moral conduct and the importance of nondeliberate *spontaneity*. This emphasis on spontaneity and on noncognitive engagement at least appears to be in tension with an emphasis on the deliberate, conscious focus suggested by the Pāli *suttas* and indeed in the Chan meditation tradition, by the *Bodhicāryāvatāra*, and by Aristotle in the Western tradition. How can one be at the same time fully mindful in one's conduct and appropriately spontaneous? In the end, I think these two strains of thought are not only consistent but mutually illuminating. Reflection on just why this is the case and on how to reconcile the demand for spontaneity and the demand for mindfulness leads to deeper insight into each.

I will first discuss briefly why mindfulness is so important in Buddhist ethics. I will then shift gears and discuss the importance of spontaneity, first in the Aristotelian and then in the Zen tradition. I will close by showing why spontaneity can be understood as desirable only if infused by the kind of mindfulness philosophers such as Śāntideva recommend, and why mindfulness can be morally efficacious only if it suffuses our perception and action so as to render them spontaneous.

11.3. The Importance of Mindfulness

Why is mindfulness so important? Śāntideva puts the point in the following memorable way at the beginning of chapter 5 of *Bodhicāryāvatāra*:

> One who wishes to protect his practice
> Should be careful to protect his mind.
> If one does not protect one's mind
> It is impossible to protect one's practice.
> The elephant of the mind
> Causes much harm and degradation.
> Wild, mad elephants
> Do not cause so much harm.
> Nonetheless, if the elephant of the mind
> Is restrained by the rope of mindfulness,
> Then all fear is banished,
> And every virtue falls into our hands. (BCA 5.1–3)

Śāntideva here argues that the cultivation of a moment-to-moment awareness of one's own cognitive and emotional states is central to leading an awakened life.[4] The "practice" with which he is concerned here (*bslab pa/śikṣa*) is of course the bodhisattva's training in moral perfection. Without mindfulness, he insists, morality is impossible to achieve or to maintain. That is because it is possible to remain utterly inattentive to one's own moral life, failing to notice situations that call for moral response, failing even to recognize one's own moral attitudes, dispositions, and motivations, even if one is obsessed with the *idea* of morality. Indeed the obsession with the idea of morality in the context of inattention to the moral landscape is a common phenomenon in the modern world, evident in persistent public discourse about moral principles alongside regular blindness to the pervasiveness of poverty, oppression, and preventable hunger and disease, not to mention the destruction of the ecosystem that sustains life.

The three fundamental *kleśas* of confusion, attraction, and aversion function in the first instance as distracters, leading us away from the attention that is necessary if we are to live effectively, insightfully, and compassionately; awakening consists in part in replacing that inattention with mindfulness. Awakening, and the moral development that facilitates it, Śāntideva emphasizes in the first two chapters of *Bodhicāryāvatāra*, also requires the conquering of fear, as fear—in particular the fear of death—conditions attachment, aversion, and confusion so deeply. Hence the remark that mindfulness banishes fear.[5]

There are several other important issues to note here. These opening verses emphasize the fact that mindfulness is necessary to combat the natural tendency to *mindless* action driven not by the compassionate motivation and insight that Śāntideva extols in this text, but rather by blind passion and confusion. That mindfulness, as the connotations both of *smṛti* and *samprajanya* suggest, need not involve explicit reflection. Indeed, as we shall see, in the end they had better *not*, although this kind of reflection may be needed at the outset of moral development in order to stabilize them. But there is much of which we are aware and to which we attend, on which we do not explicitly *reflect*. Consider, for instance, our awareness of the position of our body as we sit or move through space, or of the goings-on on the road that guide our driving even when we are absorbed in conversation or listening to a news broadcast or music on the radio, or, more to the point, of the activities of others on the sports field that guide an expert athlete's actions. There is neither the time nor the resources for reflection in this kind of expert performance, but there is the need for supremely refined attention and awareness and constant guiding by well-practiced knowledge.

Without attention to our motivation as well as to the situations in the context of which we act, moral conduct is impossible. Later in the same chapter, using the metaphors of Buddhist hell imagery, Śāntideva emphasizes a second *moral* dimension of mindfulness: that mindfulness is necessary for us not only in order to directly alleviate the suffering of *others* but also in order to extirpate the deep existential suffering in ourselves that leads us to moral failing in virtue of our inability to see beyond our own misery. He emphasizes that this suffering is entirely endogenous and that moral development is entirely mental cultivation:

> *Who so purposefully forged*
> *The implements of sentient beings' hell?*
> *Who constructed the floor of burning iron?*
> *And whence have those women come?*
> *The Sage has explained that*
> *The vicious mind gives rise to all of these.*
> *So, there is nothing whatever in the triple world*
> *More terrifying than the mind.* (BCA 5.7–8)

Because our own *maladaptive* mental activity is the root of primal confusion, it is the root of the other root vices of attraction and aversion, and so of all vice, and so of all suffering. Because our own *effective* mental activity is the only possible root of insight and understanding, it is the only possible root of compassion, of virtue and so of liberation. Left to its own devices, the mind is the mad elephant and the architect of hell. But mindfulness of what we can, on reflection, endorse as cogent and beneficial can tame it, and it can become the disciplined instrument of our own and others' happiness. Without mindfulness, even carefully considered and endorsed reflective knowledge is not efficacious in action, just as a carefully memorized score cannot guide a musician's skillful performance without the cultivation of its action-guiding force, or a playbook guide a basketball player without assiduous practice, not only of the play itself, but also of the perceptual and motor skills that enable its effective execution in the moment of play. Mindfulness, from this perspective, is therefore important because without it no other virtue can be manifest and because with it, all other virtue emerges.

Attention to these issues is not novel in the Mahāyāna, but begins in the earliest stratum of Buddhist texts. Consider these important remarks from the Pāli canon, which are taken only as representative. There are many such admonitions spread throughout that corpus. In the *Satipaṭṭhāna Sutta* we read, "And how does a bhikkhu abide contemplating mind-objects as mind-objects in terms of the five hindrances? Here, there being sensual desire in him, a bhikkhu understands: 'There is sensual desire in me'; or there being no sensual desire in him he also understands how there comes to be the arising of unarisen sensual desire, and how there comes to be the abandoning of arisen sensual desire, and how there comes to be the future non-arising of abandoned sensual desire" (MN.i.60). The point is clear: the cultivation of mindfulness is what makes it possible in the first place to abandon the attachment and aversion (sensual desire) that the Buddha argues in the *Dhammacakkappavatttana Sutta* are the root of suffering and of action conditioned by the *kleśas*. In the *Vitakkasaṇṭhāna Sutta* this mindfulness that allows the abandonment of attachment and aversion is given a more directly ethical direction:

> Here, bhikkhus, when a bhikkhu is giving attention to some sign, and owing to that sign there arise in him evil unwholesome thoughts connected with desire, with hate, and with delusion, then he should give attention to some other sign connected with what is wholesome. When he gives attention to some other sign connected to what is wholesome, then any evil unwholesome thoughts connected with desire, with hate, and with delusion are abandoned in him and subside. With the abandoning of them his mind becomes steadied internally, quieted, brought to signlessness, and concentrated. Just as a skilled carpenter or his apprentice might knock out, remove, and extract a coarse peg by means of a fine one, so too ... when a bhikkhu gives attention to some other sign connected with what is wholesome. ... His mind becomes steadied internally, quieted, brought to signlessness, and concentrated. (MN.i.119, ellipses in original translation)

Here we see a representation of the reciprocal relation between mindfulness and morality. Mindfulness enables the abandonment of the causes of immorality, and a return to ethical engagement facilitates increased mindfulness. The *Sekha Sutta*, after an eloquent discussion of the aspects of cultivation, draws this direct connection between mindfulness and the cultivation of ethical sensibility:

> Having arrived at that supreme mindfulness whose purity is due to equanimity, this noble disciple recollects his manifold past lives.... Thus with their aspects and particulars he recollects his manifold past lives. This is the first breaking out like that of the hen's chicks from their shells.
>
> Having arrived at that same supreme mindfulness whose purity is due to equanimity, with the divine eye, which is purified and surpasses the human, this noble disciple sees beings passing away and reappearing. ... He understands how beings pass on according to their actions. This is his second breaking out like that of the hen's chicks from their shells.
>
> Having arrived at that same supreme mindfulness whose purity is due to equanimity, by realizing for himself with direct knowledge, this noble disciple here and now enters upon and abides in the deliverance

of mind and deliverance by wisdom that are taintless with the destruction of the taints. This is his third breaking out like that of the hen's chicks from their shells. (MN.i.357–358)

This *sutta* continues to emphasize that the roots of all other virtues are grounded in mindfulness and the capacities of moral perception it enables. The *Ānāpānasati Sutta* and the *Kāyagatāsati Sutta* ground the cultivation of this awareness firmly in the focus on the breath and on the nature of the body, respectively, with the *Kāyagatāsati Sutta* in particular arguing that relinquishing the attachment to sensual pleasures that ground immorality is grounded in the mindfulness of the similarity of the body to a corpse (MN.iii.91–92), concluding:

When mindfulness of the body has been repeatedly practiced, developed, cultivated, used as a vehicle, used as a basis, established, consolidated, and well undertaken, these ten benefits may be expected. What ten?

One becomes a conqueror of discontent and delight, and discontent does not conquer oneself; one abides overcoming discontent whenever it arises.

One becomes a conqueror of fear and dread, and fear and dread do not conquer oneself; one abides overcoming fear and dread whenever they arise. (MN.iii.97)

Given the role of attraction and aversion in the genesis of *saṃsāra* and the role of fear in propelling vice in Buddhist moral phenomenology (Garfield, 2015), this is a very direct connection indeed between the cultivation of mindfulness and the cultivation of moral perfection. Finally, in this sampler of passages from the Pāli *suttas*, consider the *Mahāsuññata Sutta*, one of the earliest explicit discussions of emptiness in the Buddhist canon:

Then that bhikkhu should steady his mind internally, quiet it, bring it to singleness, and concentrate on that same sign of concentration as before. Then he gives attention to voidness internally. When he is giving attention to voidness internally, his mind enters into voidness internally and acquires confidence, steadiness, and decision. In this way he has full awareness of that.

... He gives attention to voidness internally and externally. ... He gives attention to imperturbability. While he is giving attention to imperturbability, his mind enters into imperturbability, and acquires confidence, steadiness, and decision. When that is so, he understands thus: While I am giving attention to imperturbability, my mind enters into imperturbability and acquires confidence, steadiness and decision. . . .

When a bhikkhu abides thus, if his mind inclines to walking, he walks, thinking: "while I am walking thus, no evil or unwholesome states of covetousness and grief will beset me." In this way he has full awareness of that. And when a bhikkhu abides thus, if his mind inclines to standing, . . . sitting, . . . lying down, . . . thinking: "while I am lying down thus, no evil, unwholesome states will beset me." In this way, he has full awareness of that.

When a bhikkhu abides thus, if his mind inclines to talking, he resolves: "Such talk as is low, vulgar, coarse, ignoble, unbeneficial, and which does not lead to disenchantment, cessation, peace, direct knowledge, enlightenment and Nibbāna, . . . such talk I shall not utter. . . ."

But he resolves: "Such talk as deals with effacement, as favours the mind's release, and which leads to complete disenchantment, dispassion, cessation, peace, direct knowledge, enlightenment, and Nibbāna . . . such talk I shall utter. In this way, he has full awareness of that. (MN.iii.112–113)

So here, in one of the very earliest discussions of emptiness in the entire Buddhist canon, we already have an emphasis on the need to cultivate mindfulness of emptiness and an articulation of the intimate connection between that mindfulness and moral cultivation, a connection made possible only by the union of *smṛti* and *samprajanya*—by not only attending to the emptiness of self and others but also ensuring that that attention is constant and action-guiding. Āryadeva, Candrakīrti, and Śāntideva were to explore this connection in rich detail much later.

11.4. Spontaneity

So far, so good. But as I anticipated, there is another narrative about mindfulness in ethical discourse, one we find in both Western and Buddhist sources. Let us begin by examining how that narrative arises in the Western tradition, with its origins in the *Nicomachean Ethics* of Aristotle (1962, 1105a17–1105b8). Aristotle, in distinguishing between *virtuous* action and action *merely in accordance with virtue*, addresses himself, as would any Buddhist moral theorist, to the relation between the action and the state of mind that gives rise to it. Actions that are merely in accordance with virtue are those a virtuous person would perform but that are performed not with virtuous motivation but by accident, under compulsion, under the instruction of another, out of desire for praise or gain, and so on. Virtuous actions, by contrast, are performed voluntarily, with pleasure, as a consequence of one's character, *spontaneously*.[6]

Aristotle draws a number of important distinctions between virtuous action and action merely in accordance with virtue, prominently including the role of a stable character as well as the relation between pleasure and pain and the role of practical wisdom. But an important aspect of this complex distinction—and the one most relevant to the present issue—concerns the spontaneity of action in the Aristotelian sense. The "one thought too many problem" (Williams, 1981) brings out this aspect very nicely. You are ill. I visit you in the hospital. You thank me for coming. I reply that there is no need to thank me. I came only because I knew that it was the virtuous thing to do, and I wanted to be good. Suddenly what looked like an act of kindness turns out to be hollow, ironically because it was done from an impulse to be kind. If I were truly kind, I would have visited you out of concern for *you*, not out of concern for my moral state. The Aristotelian insight that a kind action is an action performed spontaneously *because one is kind* as opposed to one done *in order to be kind* captures this feature of virtue.

We can connect this more directly to the character of mindfulness and the distinction between mindfulness and reflectiveness. Virtuous action in this case requires that one *has internalized and is guided by* the relevant habits of moral perception and action and that these are steady features of one's ethical engagement. Being so guided—having these *embedded in one's mind*—determines that one's actions are motivated by friendship and compassion. On the other hand, the very need for reflection—for the extra vitiating thought—indicates a *failure* of the kind of mindfulness we expect in the morally mature agent, akin to the failure that would be represented by the basketball player having to remind himself to get into position, or the pianist asking herself what notes come next in midperformance. In this case one attends not to one's friend but to the demands of morality themselves, and that indicates a *failure* of the kind of attention represented in true mindfulness, not a refinement of it. Reflection is necessary in the context of training, of justification, or of explanation; it gets in the way in the context of expert action.[7]

The Aristotelian account of moral development reinforces this picture. *Paideia*, or moral cultivation,[8] on Aristotle's account involves teaching a child to perform virtuous actions as well as to take pleasure in those actions. The goal is a mature moral agent with a stable character constituted by the virtues as well as a set of desires, perceptual ability, practical skills, and strength sufficient to enable activity inspired by those virtues, who performs virtuous actions not because *those actions* are virtuous but because *she* is virtuous, spontaneously, joyfully, without having to think first about whether this is the right action.[9]

A different model of spontaneity—but a model of spontaneity in the moral domain nonetheless—emerges in Chan Buddhism, partly through an inheritance of ideals of *wu wei*, or effortless action, from the Daoist tradition that partially informs it in China (Hansen, 1992, 2011; Kasulis, 1981; Garfield, 2006, 2011; Cowherds, 2010; Finnigan, 2011; Finnigan & Tanaka, 2011, in press). Here the driving idea is the suspicion of conceptual thought common to Buddhists and Daoists. Such discursive mental activity always involves the superimposition of unreal universals upon reality. In the case of action this leads to an ideal of moral agency in which perception guides action mediated by compassion and skill, but not by conceptual representation, not by thought.

Spontaneous action on this model is also nondual in an important sense connecting directly to the role of mindfulness in morality. Spontaneous action is characterized by an absence of subject-object duality in phenomenology. In awakened action, there is no awareness of self as subject or actor, no awareness of action as action, of instrument as instrument, or of object as object. The absence of the objectification (*ālambana/dmigs pa*) of agent, instrument, action, and object is a hallmark of action emanating not from egoistic involvement but from awakened awareness.

We can now see more clearly the tension to which I alluded earlier in the characterization of morally mature action. On the one hand, we demand of ourselves and others, as moral agents, a certain degree of mindfulness, of consciousness and attention. Moral agency is not robotic. On the other hand, we demand a certain degree of spontaneity. Moral agency is not calculating. The task is to find the middle ground between the viciously mindless and the psychopathically deliberate. This is the task, I might add, not only of moral theory, but also of moral education. It is to the resolution of this tension and the search for the middle way—*madhyama pratipad*—in morality that we now turn.

11.5. Digression on the Way to a Solution: Deliberation and Intention

Before seeking a complete resolution of the tension between the demand for greater attention to the moral domain and the need for less explicit reflection about it implicit in the accounts we have been scouring, let us first deepen that tension through attention to two technical terms, one Aristotelian, one Buddhist: *bouleusis*, or "deliberation," and *cetanā/sems*, or "intention." Consideration of the role of these concepts in their respective domains complicates matters in interesting ways but also shows us the way to resolution.[10] Let us begin with the Greek context.

As we have seen, the Aristotelian ideal of spontaneous virtuous action involves an agent acting voluntarily and from character. Nonetheless the manifestation of virtue in action requires not only the possession of *moral* virtue but also two essential auxiliary character traits: *enkrates*, or "moral strength," the role of which we can set aside for present purposes, and the *intellectual* virtue of *phronēsis*, or "practical wisdom," to which I now turn. Aristotle emphasizes that for virtue to manifest as virtuous action, we need to know *how* to act. The impulse to generosity, for instance, must be mediated by the practical knowledge of how to give, to whom to give, and in what amount to give, and this is a kind of *knowledge*, albeit practical knowledge.

This knowledge is realized in the process of *deliberation*, culminating in the *choice* (*proharesis*) of a particular action appropriate in a particular situation. Deliberation begins when an end is given and terminates when the means to that end are selected, with the choice of action. *Phronēsis* is excellence in deliberation. The importance of *phronēsis*, and hence the need for *deliberation*, complicates the account of moral spontaneity. If truly virtuous action is mediated by deliberation, we should pause before we take spontaneity to entail a retreat from mindfulness. Even mature virtue does not entail that virtuous action is completely *thoughtless*, at least not for Aristotle.

We encounter a parallel complexity when we consider the role of *cetanā*, or "intention," in Buddhist moral psychology.[11] *Cetanā* is central to karmic formation because it is our intentions that have the greatest effect on who we subsequently become. Aristotle would have agreed. It is for this reason that it is important to develop positive intentions, intentions that are morally beneficial. And of course *cetanā* is *cognitive, conceptual*.[12] So, just as in the Aristotelian framework, Buddhist accounts of spontaneous action must be modulated. Morally positive action, however free from duality we might hope it can become, is, at least initially, *intentional*, hence *conceptualized*, hence implicated with subject-object duality, objectification, always conditioned by ignorance, and therefore, in the end, with *saṃsāra*.[13]

The point here is that even appropriate conception is *conceptual*; even positive karma is *karma*, and it is important for Buddhist soteriological theory that a buddha does not generate karma, does not objectify, does not engage conceptually. A buddha therefore acts without *cetanā, nonintentionally*. This is difficult stuff—the idea is not simply that a buddha acts without *reflection* of the one-thought-too-many kind, but that a buddha acts without any conceptuality, or intention, at all. Now a great deal of debate about how to understand the subjectivity and agency of a buddha without the category of intentionality has been generated by this conundrum.[14]

We need not venture into that fraught terrain for present purposes, for what concerns us here is the role of mindfulness in *human* action—path, not fruition—and we are concerned in our lives and in the present context with the cultivation of our own moral development and that of our fellow citizens. It is therefore important to note that Buddhist theory of the path to awakening must make room for action that is *intentional* in the full sense, on the way to action that *is not*, or at least to action that is intentional in a *different sense*, a distinction encoded, for instance, in Śāntideva's important distinction between *aspirational* and *engaged bodhicitta*[15]—between an altruistic commitment that is conceptually mediated and that which is direct and spontaneous, whose necessary condition is the cultivation and development of its conceptual precursor.[16]

All of this is to say that whether we see the landscape from Pagan Greece, from Buddhist Asia, or from the standpoint of our own modern reflection on the nature of human action, we must acknowledge that *even if our ideal of action is one of spontaneity* there is room for attention, thought, deliberation, in short, for mindfulness, at least if we are talking about action undertaken by *persons* as opposed to buddhas or divinities, whatever they may be like. After all, even in the most spontaneous expert action, such as that in sport, virtuoso musical performance, or intimate human association, while explicit calculation may well be absent, attentive responsiveness is essential.

The soccer player does not deliberate, but she is aware of what is going on around her when she crosses the ball to the spot where the striker will arrive; the saxophone soloist is attentive to the piano and the bass, but he is not thinking about music theory; the mother is focused attentively on her child but is not deliberating about whether to embrace him. Each, however, acts in a way that reflects an internalization of principles that, while not present in consciousness, nonetheless direct consciousness, allowing us to be more mindful not of those *principles* but of the *immediate objects* that determine action, and to be mindful of those ways in a sense that neither objectifies self, nor object, nor action but that allows action to flow spontaneously.[17]

11.6. Mindful Spontaneity and Spontaneous Mindfulness

There are lessons to be gained from this cross-cultural excursion for the relationship between mindfulness and spontaneity in traditions that valorize both. First, it is worth noting that spontaneity, whether it is conceived in the Buddhist or the Aristotelian tradition, is not *randomness*. Any spontaneity in action worth cultivating in the first place emerges from training, and much of that training requires the cultivation and maintenance of mindfulness, mindfulness of moral principles and of the moral situation.[18] In the training situation, that mindfulness will even involve a great deal of explicit meta-awareness, as is necessary in the development of any expertise.

Mindfulness is also implicated with spontaneity in morally salutary action. For the cultivation of mindfulness is the cultivation of a particular spontaneous response: that of being mindful. This cultivation is the very point of mindfulness meditation. Here we must remember that mindfulness is not simply an *accompaniment* to or a *quality* of actions or of perceptual sets; being mindful is *itself* an action, and training in mindfulness makes being mindful, being *attentive*, a spontaneous way of taking up with the world.[19]

Mindfulness—a spontaneous disposition to be aware that has become *embedded in the mind*—is therefore that which makes spontaneous action skillful as opposed to random. Mindfulness also confers a kind of *freedom* to our actions—not freedom in the Augustinian sense, that is, the freedom of a causeless will, but the ability to be genuinely *responsive* as opposed to being merely *reactive*,[20] the ability to mobilize our own moral sensibilities and understanding in action as opposed to being driven by unmodulated reflexes. This freedom is the freedom of *authorship* of our lives, as opposed to handing over our actions and our lives to be buffeted about by external events and the actions of others. Śāntideva puts it this way:

> *Since it is only the basis of coming and going,*
> *Think of your body as a vessel;*
> *Let it be your wish that your body*
> *Achieves the purposes of sentient beings.*
> *In this way one becomes free.*
> *And with a perpetual smile.*
> *Forgoing scowls and dark countenance,*
> *And becomes a sincere friend to all beings.* (BCA 5.70–71)

Śāntideva emphasizes here that when mindfulness becomes spontaneous we gain control of our emotional and interpersonal lives. That control issues not in freedom from the interests of *others* but in freedom from our *own* destructive reactive habits that lead not to spontaneity but to heteronomy—a freedom *to* advance the welfare of all, and a freedom manifested both in skillful responsiveness and in genuine joy.

I am reminded here of a wonderful interview of the great jazz pianist Hank Jones by the journalist Terry Gross (2005/2010). She asked him whether, when he plays, he knows what he will play next, expecting, in a suitably romantic mood, the answer that the music just comes out of its own accord, without any thought or intention. Jones responded, "What do you think all of those years of practice are *for?* I may not be consciously aware of what my fingers are doing now, but I am certainly thinking hard about the next two measures." Great jazz, Jones emphasizes, may be *spontaneous,* but it is not *random.* And it certainly requires responsiveness to those with whom and for whom one is playing, a responsiveness that itself must be spontaneous, not labored, albeit the product of countless hours of deliberate labor.

So what do *you* think all of those years of practice are for? To become a mindless robot, or to become a virtuoso human agent? Mindfulness— deliberate, metacognitive attention—makes training possible, but the goal of that training is to abandon that attention in the context of mature perception and action. Yet we train not to become mindless but to become more spontaneously mindful in a deeper sense, mindful of ourselves, of others, of the moral landscape, and of our actions so that we can act with the effortless virtuosity of a jazzman bodhisattva.[21]

To paraphrase Candrakīrti on compassion: Mindfulness is important at the beginning, the middle, and the end; it is the seed that gives rise to morality, the rain that nurtures its cultivation, and the harvest in skillful spontaneous interaction that is the hallmark of moral sensibility.

Abbreviations

BCA   Śāntideva, *Bodhicaryāvatāra.* All translations from *Bodhicāryāvatāra* are my own, from the sDe dge Tibetan edition, Śāntideva (1999).

MN   *Majjhima Nikāya,* volume and page in the Pali Text Society edition. Translations from B. Ñāṇamoli & B. Bodhi (1995).

Notes

1. See Shulman (2010) for an excellent discussion of the interpretation of *sati/ smṛti/dran pa* and its roots in Pāli literature.

2. Hallisey (2010) translates the Pāli cognate *satisampajañña* as "moral discernment" or "prudence" (p. 141), while recognizing its sense as "mindfulness and awareness of the way things are" (p. 144) in nonmoral contexts. The examples he offers as reasons for this translation, however, are not entirely compelling. In each case, the second translation would be felicitous. It appears that Hallisey is motivated in part by a discomfort with the moral import of *mindfulness.* I hope my case for its moral import in this context should set this worry to rest.

3. All translations are from Śāntideva (1999).

4. There are two aspects to this mindfulness, as Śāntideva mentions, marked by the difference between *smṛti/dran pa* on the one hand, and *shes bzhin/sampra-janya* on the other. The first pair, which can often denote *memory* as well as *retention*, connotes a *keeping in mind* of moral motivation, morally relevant information, and so on. The second connotes *attention* or *moment-to-moment awareness*. The *smṛti/dran pa* aspect of mindfulness is cultivated as the basis of the *shes bzhin/samprajanya* aspect. But they form a coherent whole, a psychological state in which one is guided by moral attention and in which that guiding consciousness is not permitted to lapse. (See Shulman, 2010)

5. I explore this issue at length in Garfield (2012).

6. As we will see, this spontaneity may well nonetheless require deliberation and choice in order to be effective. But the act of deliberation may itself be undertaken spontaneously, of course.

7. On Aristotle's account of *paideia* (education, upbringing, cultivation), early moral *paideia* involves a great deal of explicit attention guided by a moral expert, but no deliberation or choice and no infusion of moral conduct by genuine virtue (*aretē*) or practical wisdom (*phronēsis*). These traits of character emerge only with maturity, at which point one becomes *attentive* to the demands of morality but not necessarily, in the context of action, *reflective*. On the other hand, on the Aristotelian view, as we will see, there certainly are cases in which moral decisions require explicit reflection and the deployment of explicit deliberation. In this respect we cannot map the Aristotelian framework directly on to the Buddhist framework. These are, in this respect and in others, very different approaches to morality. See Garfield (2015) for more on this.

8. The parallel Sanskrit term would be *śikṣa*, again connoting teaching, but teaching *how* or *cultivating*.

9. Once again the picture will become more complex once we attend to the role of *deliberation* in Aristotle's moral psychology.

10. I emphasize that in considering these terms together I am *not* suggesting that *cetanā* is synonymous with *boulesis* or indeed any other Aristotelian ethical term, and I am certainly not suggesting in this essay that Buddhist and Aristotelian ethics are structurally analogous. (See Garfield, 2015, for more on this.) I am only suggesting that there are good heuristic reasons for thinking about these terms at the same time because, despite the differences in their semantic range, and despite the structural differences between the theories in which they are at home, similar problems arise.

11. This term is notoriously difficult to translate, partly because of its broad semantic range in Pāli and Sanskrit and partly because of the incommensurability of Buddhist and Western moral psychology (Heim, 2003). Gombrich (2005) uses *intention*; Keown (1991) prefers *choice*; Rhys Davis (1898) likes *volition*; other translations are *choice* (Karunaratna, 1979), *decision*, and, felicitously, *intending* (Myers, 2010).

12. For an exceptionally clear treatment of the role of *cetanā* in Buddhist theory of action, see Myers, 2010.

13. This is why the relevant distinction, as is so often the case in Buddhist epistemology, is that between *perception* and *reflection* or *conceptual thought*. When we perceive, we engage directly with particulars, and hence with *reality*. When we reflect, we *conceive*, and apprehend unreal universals. For unawakened human beings, the morally salutary finger pointing to the moon of perfection remains, for all that, a finger.

14. See Griffiths (1994), Siderits (2011), Finnigan (2011), Finnigan & Tanaka (in press), Garfield (2011), and Myers (2010) for some recent moments in these debates. Buddhaghosa attempts to resolve the conundrum of a Buddha's motivation being at the same time intentional but not karmic by introducing a new neutral kind of intention and karma that characterizes the Buddha's and arhat's actions: *kirīyakarma* or *kirīyacetanā*, which are neither the fruits of other karma nor generative of future fruits. This karma is also called "path karma" (*maggakarma* or *maggacetanā*). This device is picked up by Vasubandhu in *Abhidharmakośa* as well. This move to something that is supposed to be just like an intention, directing action to its object, only without objectification or conceptualization, does appear rather desperately ad hoc, only emphasizing the difficulty and the importance of the problem.

15. I draw this distinction differently from the way it is typically drawn in the Tibetan tradition. Most in that tradition take aspirational *bodhicitta* to be the aspiration to take the bodhisattva vows and to be only that *bodhicitta* that inspires one to engage in the bodhisattva path, with engaged *bodhicitta* arising the moment one takes the vow, well before nonconceptual engagement with phenomena arises at the higher bodhisattva grounds. But I prefer to take the metaphor Śāntideva employs—that of the distinction between those who have merely read guidebooks and want to travel and those who have traveled—more seriously and to see this distinction as encoding the distinction between an inferential or conceptual motivation and a perceptual or direct motivation, arising from the direct perception of the nature of suffering made possible by transcendental wisdom. So I see aspirational *bodhicitta* as operative until the achievement of the perfection of wisdom, and engaged *bodhicitta* as operative only after the direct apprehension of emptiness. I think this makes better sense of the role of the ninth chapter in *Bodhicāryāvatāra* as well as of the initial metaphor. I do realize that this is heterodox.

16. Once again we might note a difference between the Aristotelian and the Buddhist accounts of *paideia/śikṣa*, and hence of moral majority. For Aristotle the development of a moral student into a full moral agent involves, inter alia, the development of conceptual, reflective capacities, such as skill in deliberation; for Śāntideva the development of a bodhisattva from aspirational *bodhicitta* involves the abandonment of conceptual mediation in favor of direct perception.

17. This idea of spontaneous but mindful flow is articulated elegantly by Csikszentmihalyi (1990).

18. One might at this point ask whether training is *essential* or *accidental* to the cultivation of mindful spontaneity. Suppose, as Nic Bommarito has suggested to me, a surgeon could simply inculcate mindful spontaneity in me without training. Wouldn't this be a good thing? It would, but unfortunately, that is not the way *human* moral development works, and I am addressing the human condition here. (Of course *tantra* might involve just such a shortcut, but that is beyond the scope of this paper.)

19. And of course if it could not become spontaneous, as Nic Bommarito has pointed out to me, a vicious regress of mindfulness would emerge.

20. I thank Geshe Damdul Namgyal for this happy distinction.

21. See *Bodhicāryāvatāra* 1:19, where Śāntideva remarks that the effects of the cultivation of mindfulness are evident even in sleep or when one is distracted:

> From that moment on,
> Even when one is asleep or inattentive
> An uninterrupted continuum of merit
> Limitless, like the sky, constantly proceeds.

Of course Śāntideva is really emphasizing here the role that the vow plays in the psychological continuum as an ever-present substantial cause of merit. But it cannot fulfill this function if the vowed mindfulness itself is not maintained in some form as an aspect of consciousness even when attention is not explicit.

References

Aristotle. (1962). *Nicomachean ethics.* (M. Ostwald, Trans.). Indianapolis: Library of Liberal Arts.

The Cowherds. (2010). *Moonshadows: Conventional truth in Buddhist philosophy.* New York: Oxford University Press.

Csikszentmihalyi, M. (1990). *Flow: The psychology of optimal experience.* New York: Harper and Row.

Finnigan. B. (2011). How can a Buddha come to act? The possibility of a Buddhist account of ethical agency. *Philosophy East and West, 61*(1), 143–159.

Finnigan, B. and K. Tanaka. (2010). Ethics for Mādhyamikas. In Cowherds, *Moonshadows: Conventional truth in Buddhist philosophy* (pp. 221–232). New York: Oxford University Press.

Finnigan, B., & Tanaka, K. (in press). Don't think. Just act! In G. Priest & D. Young (Eds.), *Philosophy and the martial arts.* Chicago: Open Court Press.

Garfield, J. (2006). Why did Bodhidharma go to the East? Buddhism's struggle with mind in the world. *Sophia, 42*(2), 61–80.

Garfield, J. (2010–2011). What is it like to be a bodhisattva? *Journal of the International Association of Buddhist Studies, 33,*(1–2), 327–351.

Garfield, J. (2011). Hey, Buddha! Don't think! Just act! *Philosophy East and West*, *61*(1), 174–183.

Garfield, J. (2012). Mindfulness and morality. In German as "Achtsamkeit als Grundlage fur ethisches Verhalten" in M. Zimmermann, C. Spitz, & S. Schmidt (Eds.), *Achtsamkeit* (pp. 227–250). Stuttgart: Hans Huber.

Garfield, J. (2015). *Engaging Buddhism. Why it Matters to Philosophy*. New York: Oxford University Press.

Gombrich, R. (2005). *How Buddhism began: The conditioned genesis of the early teachings*. London: Routledge.

Grifiths, P. (1994). *On Being Buddha*. Albany: State University of New York Press.

Gross, T. (2005/2010). Remembering Hank Jones. Retrieved from *Fresh Air*, NPR: http://www.npr.org/templates/story/story.php?storyId=126884916.

Hallisey, C. (2010). Between intuition and judgment: Moral creativity in Theravada ethics. In A. Pandian & D. Ali (Eds.), *Ethical life in South Asia* (pp. 141–152). Bloomington: Indiana University Press.

Hansen, C. (1992). *A Daoist theory of Chinese thought*. Cambridge, MA: Harvard University Press.

Hansen, C. (2011). Washing the dust from my mirror: The deconstruction of Buddhism—A reply to Bronwyn Finnigan. *Philosophy East and West*, *61*(1), 160–173.

Heim, M. (2003). The aesthetics of excess. *Journal of the American Academy of Religion*, *71*(3), 531–554.

Karunaratna, W. (1979). *Cetanā*. In G. P. Malesekara (Ed.), *Encyclopedia of Buddhism*, (vol. 4, pp. 86–97). Columbo: Sri Lanka Department of Government Printing.

Kasulis, T. (1981). *Zen action: Zen person*. Honolulu: University of Hawai'i Press.

Keown, D. (1991). *The nature of Buddhist ethics*. New York: St. Martin's Press.

Myers, K. (2010). Freedom and self control: Free will in South Asian Buddhism. PhD dissertation, University of Chicago Divinity School.

Ñāṇamoli, B. & Bodhi, B. (Trans.). (1995). *The middle length discourses of the Buddha: A new translation of the Majjhima Nikāya*. Boston: Wisdom.

Rhys Davids, C. A. F. (1898). On the will in Buddhism. *Journal of the Royal Asiatic Society of Great Britain and Ireland*, 47–59.

Śāntideva. (1999). *Byang chub sems kyi las spyod pa*. Sarnath, India: Gelukpa Student Welfare Committee.

Shulman, E. (2010). Mindful wisdom: The *Sati-Paṭṭhāna-Sutta* on mindfulness, memory and liberation. *History of Religions*, *49*(4), 393–420.

Siderits, M. (2011). Buddhas as zombies. In M. Siderits, E. Thompson, & D. Zahavi (Eds.), *Self, no self? Perspectives from analytical, phenomenological and Indian philosophical traditions* (pp. 308–332). Oxford: Oxford University Press.

Williams, B. (1981). Persons, character and morality. In *Moral luck and other essays* (pp. 1–19). Cambridge, UK: Cambridge University Press.

Chapter 12

"When You Know for Yourselves"

MINDFULNESS, WISDOM, AND
THE QUALITIES OF HEART

Jake H. Davis

12.1. Introduction

The early Buddhist dialogues of the Pāli Nikāyas and the Chinese Āgamas
take as the primary focus of ethical evaluation an agent's emotional motivations, qualities such as hatred or friendliness, craving or equanimity—what
I will call Qualities of Heart. These dialogues emphasize that one can develop
wisdom through the establishment of mindfulness (*satipaṭṭhāna*), a practice
of becoming more fully and accurately aware of both internal and external
stimuli. I bring these two theses together to offer a naturalistic reconstruction of early Buddhist ethical theory. I draw on empirical and philosophical
considerations to argue for the plausibility of a thesis that lies at the heart of
Buddhist ethics: that certain Qualities of Heart are unskillful (*akusala*) and to
be abandoned (*pahātabbaṃ*); that other Qualities of Heart are skillful (*kusala*)
and to be cultivated (*bhavitabbaṃ*); and that we can come to discern the difference for ourselves.

A number of Buddhist theorists may be interpreted as grounding the
goodness of acting selflessly in a metaphysical argument that there is no self
(Goodman, 2009; Siderits, 2003). The idea is that the perception of ourselves
as selves is a basic and universal perceptual error, due to unwholesome states
such as ignorance and craving. By correcting this error one comes to see all
suffering everywhere as equally to be prevented. Goodman argues that various
Buddhist traditions are best understood along these consequentialist lines,
as adopting approaches on which what makes an action or rule or mental

state skillful is that it minimizes *dukkha*: unease and suffering. The early discourses agree insofar as they emphasize that getting wrong how one ought to live is one result of a basic and universal perceptual error and in relating the correction of this error to a proper understanding of *dukkha*. However, in the *Sabbāsava Sutta*, both the view that there is a self and the view that there is no self are taken to result from inappropriate attention. In contrast, to attend appropriately is to notice "this is *dukkha* . . . this is the origination of *dukkha* . . . this is the cessation of *dukkha* . . . this is the path leading to the cessation of *dukkha*" (MN.i.9). As I will suggest, the form of perceptual distortion most directly relevant to the accuracy of ethical judgments has to do with not seeing accurately which ways of being, and in particular which ways of being motivated, bring ease and which bring unease. Moreover, the Pāli Nikāyas reject the assumption that there is a finite universe within which *dukkha* can be minimized (see, e.g., MN.i.483), an assumption that consequentialist ethical theories depend on (Davis, 2016). Even for a form of welfare consequentialism that takes motives as the primary unit of evaluative focus (e.g., Adams, 1976), what makes it the case that a certain motive is a good one are consequences for aggregate welfare that could be known only from a God's-eye view. Although both welfare-consequentialism and the reading of Buddhist ethics that I propose here are grounded fundamentally in pleasure and pain, my proposal differs in grounding ethical claims directly in features that can be known by human beings, each for themselves, from a first-person perspective.

12.2. Attention, Affect, and Buddhist Ethics

Although the early dialogues do not examine in detail the metaphysics or epistemology of ethical claims, they do raise the philosophical question of how we can know what is right and wrong, given the evident diversity of human ethical judgment. In one dialogue recorded in the *Aṅguttara Nikāya*, the Kālāma townspeople find themselves visited by many spiritual teachers, each claiming their own system of values to be the right one and all others to be false. When in turn the Buddha comes to visit, the Kālāmas ask of him which of the many claims they have heard about the right way to live are true. "When you know for yourselves [*yada attanāva jāneyyātha*]," the Buddha replies, "these qualities are wholesome [*kusalā*] . . . blameless [*anavajjā*] . . . praised by the wise [*viññuppasatthā*]," leading to welfare and ease, then cultivate those (AN.i.189–190). However, as Bhikkhu Bodhi (1988) rightly points out, in precisely the same terms as the discourse famously counsels against going on faith in a cultural tradition or in a teacher, it also discounts the authority of appeals to logic (*takkahetu*), appeals

to inference (*nayahetu*), considering appearances (*ākāraparivitakka*), sympa-
thies toward a considered view (*diṭṭhinijjhānakkhantiyā*), and the appearance
of probability (*bhabbarūpatāya*). The discourse leaves us with the question of
what avenue remains when both appeals to authority and also logical reason
are dismissed as means of knowing how one ought to live. Indeed it does not
explicitly address what makes it the case that certain ways of being are wholesome and others unwholesome, nor how precisely we can discern for ourselves
the difference.

Drawing on other texts from the Nikāyas, I propose that the establishment
of mindfulness can develop this kind of wisdom, functioning as a means for
any human being to come to know for herself how any human being ought to
live. In a certain surprising way, it is by developing full and accurate perceptual awareness of internal as well as external stimuli that we come to know
the truth of the Buddha's normative claims. If this account is cogent, it helps
make sense of a stock refrain in the Nikāyas to the effect that the whole of
Buddha's teaching—the *Dhamma*—is "to be experienced by the wise for
themselves" (*paccattaṃ veditabbo viññūhi*).

If in the early Buddhist dialogues being criticized by the wise is one characteristic of unwholesome qualities, this suggests that what makes a certain
Quality of Heart wholesome or unwholesome must be features that can be
known from the perspective of human experience. The wise ones portrayed
throughout the Nikāyas point out that when we feel pleasure, we normally react
by grasping onto it, craving more of the same. When we meet with unpleasant experience, we normally react by pushing away the experience, craving
for something—anything—other than the unpleasant way things actually are
in that moment. Thus either pleasant or unpleasant experience can be the
cause for an emotional response of craving to arise, craving for things to be
some particular way rather than another. This connection between the affective valence of an experience (termed *vedanā*) and emotional responses based
in craving (*taṇhā*) is the central link in the theory proposed in the Nikāyas for
understanding how human suffering is perpetuated, the theory of dependent
co-arising (*paṭicca-samuppāda*). For that reason, uncoupling the link between
the affective valence of an experience and emotional responses of craving and
aversion can be seen as the ultimate aim of every teaching in the Nikāyas—
every prescription, admonition, and evaluative claim put in the mouth of the
Buddha and his disciples in these early dialogues. The possibility of uncoupling *vedanā* from *taṇhā* is not merely a theoretical one, according to modern
teachers such as Nyanaponika Thera. He suggests that by being continuously
and carefully mindful of the affective valence of experience, a meditator "distinctly realizes that a pleasant feeling is not identical with lust and need not be

followed by it. . . . By doing so, he makes a definite start in cutting through the chain of dependent origination at that decisive point where feeling becomes the condition for craving. . . . It will thus become the meditator's indubitable experience that the causal sequence of feeling and craving is not a necessary one" (Nyanaponika, 2000, p. 174).

This suggestion by Nyanaponika sums up two central Buddhist claims that I draw on to suggest a way forward for Western philosophical debates over the ground of ethical claims. First, there is a distinction to be made between the pleasant or unpleasant affective valence of an experience and the emotional reaction to it, whether compassion or hatred, craving or equanimity. Second, one can come to see the difference between these two on an experiential level through the establishment of mindfulness. A third claim is implicit in this quote from Nyanaponika but is more explicit in the dialogues of the Nikāyas: it is not just that through mindfulness we see that we do not have to react to pleasure with craving; the further suggestion is that to the degree one establishes mindfulness, and thereby comes to know fully and accurately how unpleasant it is to react with craving or hatred, one simply cannot want oneself or others to perpetuate such states.

According to the *Vipallāsa Sutta* (AN.ii.52), perceptions, thoughts, and views can be distorted (*vipallāsa*). In the *Māgandiya Sutta* (MN.i.501ff.) and its parallel version in the *Madhyama-āgama*, the Buddha illustrates this with an analogy: one with distorted perceptions due to leprosy might want to burn his flesh over hot coals, but on being cured he could not be induced to touch the coals by any means (Anālayo, 2011, p. 410). In the same way, to those with perceptions distorted by craving, aversion, and delusion, the pursuit of sensual pleasure will appear enjoyable. But such distortions can be corrected.

Employing the broad Indian notion of morally valenced action, *karma*, but modifying it to suit his own distinctive approach, the Buddha says in a well-known passage from the *Aṅguttara Nikāya*, "It is *cetanā* (intention or motivation) that I call *kamma*" (AN.iii.415). The point of the leper simile may not be so much that sensual pleasures themselves are painful; after all, even the most enlightened beings cannot avoid feeling the pleasure of a beautiful vista, of a pleasant taste, or of good friends. Rather, as I take it, the point is, first, that the craving and like motivations that motivate the pursuit of sensual pleasures are in fact painful emotional motivations to have and, second, that we normally fail to see this.

Recent research has distinguished two separable psychological systems involved in human moral judgment, the first responsive to an action's outcomes, and the second responsive to the agent's intentions. One can get a handle on the distinction conceptually by considering cases of moral luck, such as the difference between a drunk driver who accidentally runs over a small bush and an otherwise identical drunk driver who accidentally runs over a small child. Cushman (2008) demonstrates that in such cases of accidental harm adults tend to assign punishment based on outcomes but to make judgments of moral wrongness and of moral character based on perceived intentions. Recent work by Inbar, Pizarro, and Cushman (2012, p. 57) suggests more precisely that in morally evaluating intentions, subjects respond to "perceptions of desires for a harmful outcome" even in a case where no actual harm was precipitated.

The question remains to what degree these perceptions and ethical judgments of various motivational desires and intentions have some universal ground, some justification for judging desire for a harmful outcome as worse than the desire for a beneficial outcome. The suggestion I want to draw from the early Buddhist texts is that by establishing mindfulness one comes to be a reliable judge of the particular ethical valence of motivations such as friendliness or hatred, craving or equanimity, what I am calling Qualities of Heart. The basic intuition behind the proposal is this: to the degree any human being were to fully feel what it is like to be motivated by care versus what it is like to be motivated by hatred, they will *know* which is a better way to be. I read the early Buddhist texts as committed in this way to the claim that to the degree that human beings become wise, they will converge in their ethical judgments about which sorts of Qualities of Heart human beings ought to act out of and which we ought not to.

12.3. Emotional Awareness and the Qualities of Heart

The early Buddhist account does not suggest that all human beings agree about whether we ought to cultivate hatred or instead cultivate friendliness. On the contrary, the central proposal is an account, first, of how it is that many of us, much of the time, get such evaluative judgments wrong. If we are subject to many various sorts of distortions, it is to be expected that our perceptions, thoughts, and views about which ways of living are good and right will be distorted in many varied and opposing ways. But to say that we can get such evaluative claims wrong is also to say that we could get them right. The early Buddhist texts hold out the possibility that by correcting the psychological forces that lead to distorted perceptions, by coming to see what is actually painful as painful, we can come to know for ourselves what is wholesome and what is unwholesome for all of us.

Drawing on recent empirical evidence, Evan Thompson and I have proposed that mindfulness training functions both to increase a generalized level of alertness to internal and external stimuli and to attenuate affective biases of attention and memory (Davis & Thompson, 2013, 2014). For instance, mindfulness training has been associated with increased reportability not only of subtle and fleeting external stimuli such as in rapid serial visual presentations (Slagter et al., 2007) but also of subtle somatosensory stimuli involved in emotional reactions (Silverstein, Brown, Roth, & Britton, 2011; Sze, Gyurak, Yuan, & Levenson, 2010). Moreover the development of general alertness may counteract biases of attention by broadening awareness to include incoming stimuli that attention would otherwise have been biased away from. Recent results suggest that mindfulness decreases such emotional proliferation and rumination by attenuating affective biases of attention and memory that cause our stream of thought to return again and again to mental images that spark negative affect (Roberts-Wolfe, Sacchet, Hastings, Roth, & Britton, 2012; van Vugt, Hitchcock, Shahar, & Britton, 2012). Mindfulness may decrease not only negative affective biases but also biases toward positively valenced stimuli, the kind of narrowing of attention that leads to wishful thinking by preventing us from seeing negative aspects. In accord with this suggestion, Ortner, Kilner, and Zelazo (2007) found that decreases in arousal to negative images were common to both mindfulness training and a relaxation training control group, but that decreases in arousal to positive images were unique to mindfulness training. Thus, establishing mindfulness can be seen as a practice of increasing alertness and attenuating the affective biases of attention and memory that narrow one's awareness. This process of becoming more Wide Awake, in the sense of being more alert and less biased, thereby allows individuals to perceive more accurately both negatively and positively valenced objects of awareness.

In these terms, then, the early Buddhist proposal I want to defend is that to the degree individuals are Wide Awake, they will converge in their ethical judgments about which sorts of Qualities of Heart human beings ought to act out of and which we ought not to. The function of mindfulness practice in making individuals more fully and accurately aware of internal and external stimuli is a first step toward justifying this claim. The second step starts from an assumption that at least some human Qualities of Heart, hatred and care, for instance, have physiological and affective profiles that are both distinct enough from each other and also similar enough across human beings that to the degree any of us are feeling fully what it is like to experience these, we will converge in our preferences regarding which Qualities of Heart we would rather our actions be motivated by. It might be, for instance, that to the degree individuals are Wide Awake enough to feel what is actually painful as painful, they will converge in preferring to be motivated by hatred rather than by care. I think the converse hypothesis vastly more likely, however: that to the degree people are Wide Awake enough to feel what is actually painful as painful, they will converge in preferring to be motivated by *care* rather than by *hatred*. I mean this as an empirical claim, subject to disconfirmation by future scientific research.

A judgment that hatred is a bad Quality of Heart will also count against types of actions that could be motivated only by hatred, such as perhaps hate crimes. Conversely, if those who are Wide Awake will converge on judging the motivational state of friendliness to be praiseworthy, then they will also converge on judging as morally praiseworthy the sorts of compassionate actions that would be done by anyone who was in this state. On the other hand, the theory does not imply any convergence on the moral value or disvalue of types of action, except by implication from the moral value or disvalue of the particular Qualities of Heart behind particular actions. Nonetheless, this gives us a sketch of how establishing mindfulness might lead to convergence in moral judgments of various human Qualities of Heart, despite radically diverging cultural mores. What remains is to show how this psychological claim could bear on the normative claim that we ought to agree with the consensus of those who are Wide Awake about how human beings ought to live, if there were to be such a consensus.

12.4. Acting Wide Awake

In describing the state of being fully and accurately aware as correcting distortions of perception, thought, and view, my reconstructed approach follows Buddhist tradition in implicitly appealing to a general epistemic norm that privileges knowledge over ignorance. The claim I draw from the early Buddhist texts is that to the degree individuals attenuate affective biases of attention and memory, and are thereby more fully conscious of various aspects of external and internal stimuli, they will be better judges than they were before of the relative ease and unease characteristic of various Qualities of Heart. The basic project of avoiding unease is a concern built into the affective systems of human psychology, and perhaps more broadly animal psychology as well. It is a concern that we can plan to override in certain specified cases, of course. However, if it is affective valence that serves as the basic currency of human and animal motivation, then we can only override the motivational pull of the affective valence of a particular emotional state, for instance, by employing an opposing affective force, of a certain thought, for example. The ascetic who plans to deny himself every sensual pleasure must use a thought of some end to do so, a thought that must itself have enough affective force to beat out the opposing affective pulls on his motivational system. The thought of some eternal reward might be pleasant, but at the very least the thought of giving in to the pursuit of sensual pleasures must have for him a stronger negative affective valence than the thought of not giving in in this way, however he conceives of those two. If so, it is practically inconsistent to plan to override the motivational force of affective valence in every case.

The sorts of beings that take sides in the ethical debates we get into, human beings, are each subject to the motivational force of ease and unease. The value of this project of avoiding unease therefore is a shared premise on both sides of any such debate. Moreover, to the degree I recognize that I sometimes do badly at knowing how to live, to be internally consistent with our shared human project of avoiding unease requires deciding to rely on those who are better at such judgments. We ought to agree with the consensus of those who are Wide Awake about how human beings ought to live, if there were to be such a consensus, because these are the judgments we ourselves would come to, to the degree we were Wide Awake. Even if I am not on my own motivated to act as the wise do, I can use their example as a motivation. And even if I am not intuitively inclined to make the same judgments about how to live that they are, I can decide to defer to the judgments they make, since these are the judgments I myself would make in a moment of wisdom. In short, we can *act* Wide Awake, even when we are not. The ethical claims entailed by the theory I have outlined has force for all human beings because, given our shared project of avoiding unease, any internally consistent plan for a human life will be one that requires us to act as if we were Wide Awake.

I have suggested that all human beings, or at least all human beings with whom we can conduct our practices of moral judgment and debate in the normal way, value living in ways that are characterized by ease rather than by unease. And I have suggested that to the degree one establishes mindfulness one can come to be a better judge of which states are which. Suppose that two human beings have equal epistemic access to the external world; in particular, suppose they know all the same facts about the impacts of their own actions on others' welfare and suffering. Still, on my account, they may make different judgments about which sorts of actions ought to be done if they are not equally alert and unbiased, because they may not have the same preferences regarding various Qualities of Heart. One who favors compassion may express this attitude in positive moral evaluation of actions intended to bring about welfare and not harm, whereas one who prioritizes other Qualities of Heart may not agree. The point of the arguments sketched above is that we all ought to privilege the judgments of those who are more fully and accurately aware of which Qualities of Heart are characterized by ease over the judgments of those who are less Wide Awake in this way, all else being equal, because the project of avoiding unease is one we all share.

One might object to this proposal on the grounds that it represents a sort of enlightened egoism, that it falsely takes the aim of ethics to be the (at best) morally neutral project of decreasing one's own suffering rather than the morally praiseworthy project of decreasing the suffering of all. My own interpretation is that the position of the early Buddhist texts is to bite this bullet. That is, the path to the end of *dukkha* is a path to the end of *dukkha* in one's own world of experience. It is not a path to the end of *dukkha* in the external world, the world conceived from a third-person perspective as populated by other beings, a finite universe within which it would be meaningful to think of decreasing or eliminating suffering overall. In general the states that are characterized by ease internally, such as care rather than hatred, are those that lead to benefiting others rather than harming them. Nonetheless external effects are not what make morally praiseworthy states morally praiseworthy, as I read the early Buddhist account. Although ethical reflection does involve concern for others, the foundational reasons an ethical theory gives for why this concern for others matters ethically need not themselves appeal to considerations about others. Moreover perhaps it is not—not directly, at any rate—the fact that the states described as wholesome in the early Buddhist texts are characterized by relative freedom from *dukkha* that makes them wholesome. Rather I have suggested that states such as care are morally praiseworthy states because they are the states we ourselves would praise to the degree we were Wide Awake.

12.5. Further Objections

Although it is suggested in general terms that the establishment of mindfulness leads to wise understanding of what is wholesome and unwholesome, nonetheless the discourses of the Nikāyas do not offer any precise psychological account of how the one leads to the other. I have drawn on empirical studies to suggest one way the increased alertness and decreased affective biases characteristic of those with established mindfulness could lead to systematic shifts in ethical judgments about which Qualities of Heart ought to motivate our actions. As I have reconstructed the claim, the judgments converged on by those who are Wide Awake have force for the rest of us just because we share a common human experience of various emotional motivations. Both in the course of the cultural evolution of moral judgment and also in the contemporary context, it is with other human beings and only with other human beings that we make and debate ethical claims. For this reason, it is plausible to think that our practices of moral judgment might include an implicit if defeasible assumption of a distinctly human practical point of view, one that all human beings share in virtue of our shared neurobiological makeup.

Nonetheless this appeal to human nature also raises a question about the aptness of Acting Wide Awake as an interpretation of Buddhist ethics. It is inaccurate and irresponsible to construe the early Buddhist dialogues as neatly compatible with a modern naturalistic worldview. These dialogues relate the Buddha's interactions with many sorts of spirit beings, such as devas and more elevated beings, including the god Brahma, who is said to have originally convinced the Buddha to begin teaching what he had discovered for the sake of those beings who would be able to understand, those "with little dust in their eyes." We have no reason to suppose that such spirit beings would share the particular neurobiology that makes the state of hatred an unpleasant one for us human beings, if it is one. And yet these dialogues clearly take it to be the case that states of craving, hatred, and delusion are present among spirit beings and unwholesome for them just as for human beings. So to the degree one takes this cosmology seriously as truth-apt metaphysical claims rather than as stories that are apt instead as powerful motivation for human beings to live wisely, then this worry could be a serious one for my interpretation of Buddhist ethics. It is worth noting, however, that whatever sorts of beings the stories in the dialogues are told *about*, these stories are nonetheless told *for* a human audience. If so, a practical perspective that is distinctly human can nonetheless be assumed as a invariant aspect of any performative context in which the Buddhist dialogues are told, including whatever evaluative claims are made about craving and hatred.

A further worry has been raised by Westerhoff.[1] It will be noted that my reconstruction of Buddhist ethics has made no mention of the doctrine of rebirth that figures so prominently in traditional Buddhist culture and also in the stories of the Nikāyas. Westerhoff suggests that attempts to naturalize Buddhist ethics fail in principle because without this cosmological picture, one cannot make sense of the notion of karmic consequences that is so central to Buddhist ethical teaching. Given a naturalistic picture on which there is no rebirth, there could be no karmic consequences for an action done just before death, for instance. And if one assumes a consequentialist reading of Buddhist ethics, Westerhoff's objections to naturalization may hold. But on one natural reading of the early Buddhist view, an action is not unwholesome because it has bad karmic consequences in the future; rather an action has bad karmic consequences in the future because it was unwholesome at the time it occurred. In particular, I have suggested that early Buddhist ethics is best understood as taking the states that give rise to actions, not the consequences of actions, as the primary unit of evaluative focus (Davis, 2016). On this line of thought, the ethical quality of actions done just before death is determined in the same way as actions at any other time, by the quality of the motivating intention. Moreover, taking intentions as determinative of ethical valence helps make plausible, in the way I have shown, a second thesis evident throughout the Nikāyas: that by increasing awareness and decreasing bias on the perceptual level, one can become wise, a reliable judge of how one ought to live. This way of grounding ethics is meant to have force independently of whether one accepts or rejects the doctrine of rebirth, or remains uncommitted.

The proposal offered in this chapter thus not only serves as an example of how a naturalistic reconstruction of early Buddhist ethics could be executed; the particular naturalized account on offer may also serve to help make Buddhist ethics safe for naturalization. In return, the distinctive approach of early Buddhist ethics offers a novel and powerful contender among contemporary naturalistic approaches. In particular, it offers a means for establishing a certain circumscribed set of truths about whether we ought to be motivated by hatred or instead by care. These are truths that hold even for human beings socialized in radically opposed systems of value, because they are entailed by the set of values we are all born into in virtue of shared features of human experience. It is this that allows the theory to adjudicate the sorts of debates over questions of how to live that human beings get into with one another, and the debates we each get into within ourselves.

Abbreviations

AN   *Aṅguttara Nikāya*, volume and page in the Pali Text Society edition. Translations are my own.

MN   *Majjhima Nikāya*, volume and page in the Pali Text Society edition. Translations are my own.

Note

1. See this volume, chapter 8.

References

Adams, R. M. (1976). Motive utilitarianism. *Journal of Philosophy, 73*(14), 467–481.

Anālayo, B. (2011). *A Comparative Study of the Majjhima-nikāya.* Taipei, Taiwan: Dharma Drum Publishing.

Bodhi. (1988). A look at the Kalama Sutta. *BPS Newsletter, 9.* Retrieved from http://www.accesstoinsight.org/lib/authors/bodhi/bps-essay_09.html.

Cushman, F. (2008). Crime and punishment: Distinguishing the roles of causal and intentional analyses in moral judgment. *Cognition, 108*(2), 353–380. doi:10.1016/j.cognition.2008.03.006.

Davis, J. H. (2016). "The scope for wisdom": Early Buddhism on reasons and persons. In S. Ranganathan (Ed.), *Indian ethics* (pp. 127–153). New York: Bloomsbury Academic.

Davis, J. H., & Thompson, E. (2013). From the five aggregates to phenomenal consciousness: Towards a cross-cultural cognitive science. In S. M. Emmanuel (Ed.), *A companion to Buddhist philosophy* (pp. 585–597). Hoboken, NJ: John Wiley & Sons.

Davis, J. H., & Thompson, E. (2014). Developing attention and decreasing affective bias: Toward a cross-cultural cognitive science of mindfulness. In K. W. Brown, J. D. Creswell, & R. M. Ryan (Eds.), *Handbook of mindfulness* (pp. 585–597). New York: Guilford Press.

Goodman, C. (2009). *Consequences of compassion: An interpretation and defense of Buddhist ethics.* New York: Oxford University Press.

Inbar, Y., Pizarro, D. A., & Cushman, F. (2012). Benefiting from misfortune: When harmless actions are judged to be morally blameworthy. *Personality and Social Psychology Bulletin, 38*(1), 52–62. doi:10.1177/0146167211430232.

Nyanaponika, T. (2000). *The vision of dhamma: Buddhist writings of Nyanaponika Thera.* (B. Bodhi, Ed.). (enlarged 2nd ed.). Onalaska, WA: Pariyatti.

Ortner, C. N. M., Kilner, S. J., & Zelazo, P. D. (2007). Mindfulness meditation and reduced emotional interference on a cognitive task. *Motivation and Emotion, 31*(4), 271–283. doi:10.1007/s11031-007-9076-7.

Roberts-Wolfe, D., Sacchet, M., Hastings, E., Roth, H., & Britton, W. (2012). Mindfulness training alters emotional memory recall compared to active controls: Support for an emotional information processing model of mindfulness. *Frontiers in Human Neuroscience, 6*(15), 1–13. doi:10.3389/fnhum.2012.00015.

Siderits, M. (2003). *Personal identity and Buddhist philosophy: Empty persons.* Burlington, VT: Ashgate.

Silverstein, R. G., Brown, A.-C. H., Roth, H. D., & Britton, W. B. (2011). Effects of mindfulness training on body awareness to sexual stimuli: Implications for female sexual dysfunction. *Psychosomatic Medicine, 73*(9), 817–825. doi:10.1097/PSY.0b013e318234e628.

Slagter, H. A., Lutz, A., Greischar, L. L., Francis, A. D., Nieuwenhuis, S., Davis, J. M., & Davidson, R. J. (2007). Mental training affects distribution of limited brain resources. *PLoS Biol, 5*(6), e138. doi:10.1371/journal.pbio.0050138.

Sze, J. A., Gyurak, A., Yuan, J. W., & Levenson, R. W. (2010). Coherence between emotional experience and physiology: Does body awareness training have an impact? *Emotion, 10*(6), 803–814. doi:10.1037/a0020146.

van Vugt, M. K., Hitchcock, P., Shahar, B., & Britton, W. (2012). The effects of mindfulness-based cognitive therapy on affective memory recall dynamics in depression: A mechanistic model of rumination. *Frontiers in Human Neuroscience, 6*(257), 1–13. doi:10.3389/fnhum.2012.00257.

PART FIVE

Intention and Action

Chapter 13

The Dynamics of Intention, Freedom, and Habituation according to Vasubandhu's *Abhidharmakośabhāṣya*

*Karin L. Meyers**

13.1. Introduction

In his *Abhidharmakośabhāṣya*, Vasubandhu insists that karma[1] is nothing other than intention (*cetanā*; AKBh iv.1a–3c, in Śāstrī, 1998, pp. 447–455). Ancient and modern interpreters alike have taken this or similar Buddhist statements[2] to imply a thorough psychologization of karma (discounting physical and other factors external to the agent's mind from playing a role in the mechanics of karmic cause and effect) or a radically intentionalist ethics (an ethics wherein the ethical quality and karmic result of an action are determined exclusively by the intention with which it is performed).[3] But this does not fit Vasubandhu's or many other South Asian Buddhists' typically realist and objectivist understanding of karma and its results. Modern interpreters have also taken such statements to imply that karma is voluntary (subject to conscious control) or deliberate (subject to reflection and decision), or, more generally, that free will and moral responsibility are central features of Buddhist ethical theory.

While Vasubandhu's view has implications for the voluntary and deliberate nature of karma, his concerns about intention do not map as easily onto those

* This essay is a revised and abridged version of Meyers (2010, Chapter 5).

of Western ethical theory as interpreters have assumed.[4] In order to demonstrate how and why this is the case, this essay outlines some of the key features of Vasubandhu's theory of intention and action (sections 13.2–5) and then examines how this informs his understanding of the dynamics of freedom and habituation in the cultivation of the Buddhist path (sections 13.6–7)

13.2. Karma as Intention

In chapter 4 of the AKBh, Vasubandhu defines all three varieties of karma (bodily, vocal, and mental) as intention (*cetanā*) in response to the Vaibhāṣika definition of mental karma as intention but bodily and vocal karma as "manifest action" (*vijñapti*)—meaning the configuration of the body and vocal utterance, respectively (AKBh iv.2, in Śāstrī, 1998, p. 448). Vasubandhu claims that bodily and vocal karma are simply intentions that have the body or the voice as their focus (*adhiṣṭhānam*; AKBh iv.3c, in Śāstrī, 1998, p. 455).[5] This claim follows on the heels of several statements that appear to suggest a comprehensive psychologization of karma. For instance, in chapter 2, in a typical Buddhist appropriation of the Brahmanical idea of sacrificial action as constructing (*abhisaṃs√kṛ*) temporal existence, Vasubandhu defines intention (*cetanā*) as "a mental action that shapes/constructs the mind" (*citta-abhisaṃskāra*; AKBh ii.24, in Śāstrī, 1998, p. 147).[6] In chapter 3 he explains that "rebirth is projected owing to a mind that is intending, and again in that projected existence, there is production from the potential [*bīja*] of consciousness, infused by karma" (AKBh iii.41cd, in Śāstrī, 1998, p. 392). In other words, he claims that consciousness (*vijñāna*) is the medium through which an intention creates the potential for rebirth and from which a new existence is projected. Then, just prior to critiquing the Vaibhāṣika definition of karma and insisting that all three kinds of karma are intention, he opens chapter 4 with the claim that the external variety of the world and the variety of sentient beings in the world are produced not from any divine intelligence but from karma (AKBh iv.1ab, in Śāstrī, 1998, p. 447).

On the basis of these claims, one might conclude that Vasubandhu believes all karmic results and, indeed, all of temporal existence is determined by the conscious aim or purpose with which one acts. But, as I will demonstrate, he clearly takes intention to come in conscious and unconscious,[7] voluntary and involuntary, as well as deliberate and nondeliberate varieties. Moreover he understands the objective qualities of the object, end, or person toward which an action is directed as well as other external and internal factors to affect both the ethical quality and the result of that action. Given all this, his definition of karma as intention cannot be understood as endorsing any wholesale psychologism or intentionalism.

Nevertheless Vasubandhu does take a strong interest in the psychological dynamics of karma in the AKBh and in his Yogācāra works,[8] a fact that is made evident in his critiques of the Vaibhāṣika theory on grounds of both scriptural infidelity and theoretical inadequacy. With respect to scripture, he objects to the way the Vaibhāṣikas invoke and then reify various theoretical entities (*dharmas*) not attested in *sūtra* and, in particular, to the fact that they attribute ethical qualities to matter (*rūpa*). Thus in his *Karmasiddhiprakaraṇa*, he punctuates his discussion with the refrain "Buddhists do not assert that tangible things [or smells or colors, etc.] are wholesome [*kuśala*] or unwholesome" (KSP 137ab).[9] With respect to theory, Vasubandhu demonstrates how the various entities the Vaibhāṣikas invoke in order to explain karmic cause and effect are unnecessary or conceptually incoherent or both, but his strongest argument is that the Vaibhāṣika theory fails to provide a coherent account of the psychology of action and habituation involved in the cultivation of the Buddhist path. In order to better appreciate this argument (see section 13.5) and its implications for the cultivation of freedom (section 13.6), it will be helpful to first examine some of the particularities of his theory of intention (sections 13.2–4), especially the ways in which it does not always correspond with modern sensibilities.

13.3. Action versus Accident, Moral Realism, and the Intentional Structure of Karma

An intention (*cetanā*) is not just any mental activity, not just "thinking," as its etymology might suggest, but a mental orientation or movement toward a particular end or object subject to ethical qualification.[10] In some cases, an intention is directed toward a specific deed. In other cases, it is simply the movement of a mind toward an object conducive to wholesome (or unwholesome or neutral) action, such as delighting in the presence of the Buddha. Thus *cetanā* can have the ordinary English sense of "intention" as a kind purpose or design, a technical phenomenological sense of being directed toward an object,[11] or both. It is this intentional structure (being directed toward an ethically qualified end or object) that makes karma wholesome (*kuśala*), unwholesome, or neutral and that creates the potential for a pleasant or painful result.[12]

Vasubandhu understands this intentional structure to be critical for the distinction between karma and a mere happening or accident, and this is why he objects to the Jain notion that "there is vice [adharma] for an agent who strikes a being without prior reflection [abuddhipūrva], just as there is burning from contact with fire" (AKBh iv.73, in Śāstrī, 1998, p. 541). He argues that by the same logic there would be bad karmic consequences (prasaṅga) in such cases where a doctor inflicts pain in the course of treating a patient, for a murder victim insofar as he is physically connected to the act of murder, or for a house when it collapses and kills its occupants (AKBh iv.73, in Śāstrī, 1998, pp. 541–542). Rhetorically this serves as an oblique attack on the Vaibhāṣika definition of bodily and vocal action as a kind of ethically qualified matter. Taken more broadly, it suggests that it is absurd to regard any object or movement lacking an intentional structure as ethically qualified.

Given that he describes the Jain position as discounting prior reflection (buddhipūrva) and cites conscious, purposeful actions as the paradigmatic examples of karma, it is easy to suppose that Vasubandhu understands intention to imply conscious purpose or design. But according to the Abhidharma theory to which he subscribes, intention of some variety is present in all conditioned mental states (citta), including sleep and nondiscursive states of meditative absorption. This entails that karma of some kind (much of it mental karma) is found in all such states and that its essential characteristic is the fact that it is a mental activity directed toward a particular object or end, not the manner in which it becomes so oriented, although the latter does—contra the Jain theory—affect the gravity of the karmic result. (See section 13.3 for a discussion of forethought.)

While defining karma in terms of intention does not entail that karma is always conscious, voluntary, deliberate, and so on, it does support a kind of moral realism in which objective factors play a significant role in determining its ethical quality and result—a fact that ancient and modern interpreters alike have sometimes overlooked. In the Jain text the Sūyagaḍa, for example, Buddhists are ridiculed for holding that a person who mistakenly believes that he is eating a child but actually eats an oil cake will experience the repercussions of killing a living being, while the person who eats a child believing it to be a oil cake will not (Bronkhorst, 2007, p. 19). Similarly, after claiming that "Buddhist morality is in principle intentionalist," de La Vallée Poussin (1927/2001, p. 127) opines that the Buddhist doctors (namely, Vasubandhu and his Vaibhāṣika interlocutors) were not entirely consistent because they also considered external factors, such as the material execution of the action or the virtues of the recipient of an action (the field of merit), to affect its result.

However, if the quality and result of action were entirely dependent on an individual's aim or belief, regardless of objective fact, this would compromise the objectivity and universality of the "law of karma" presumed by most

South Asian Buddhists as well as their non-Buddhist interlocutors—which is the Jain critic's point. Moreover one of the central soteriological problems to which Buddhism responds is that persons unwittingly engage in unwholesome actions and then suffer the consequences of these because their attitudes, beliefs, and desires are informed by a variety of delusions and wrong views. This is why beings require guidance in the form of moral precepts and why Buddhist texts offer detailed accounts of how objective and external factors contribute to karmic results.[13]

For his part Vasubandhu explicitly rejects the notion that the three intentions expressed as "I will kill him," "I kill," and "he has been killed" amount to the offense of killing or a "course of action" of taking life (AKBh iv.4ab, in Śāstrī, 1998, pp. 461–462). He explains that when a murder is successful and the intended victim is killed, there is a subtle change or transformation (*pariṇāma*) of the mental series (*santati*) of the person who had the intention to take a life, and this is the case regardless of whether he performs the action himself or by proxy (AKBh iv.4ab, in Śāstrī, 1998, pp. 461–462).[14] He further explains that in the case of murder by proxy, there might be an intention to kill and a belief that the murder has been a success, but so long as the victim has not died, there is no offense of killing. This is not to say that there are no karmic repercussions. To the extent that there was an intention to murder, there is inappropriate conduct (*asamudācāra*) —and presumably a result commensurate with the mental karma of intending to take a life (AKBh iv.4ab, in Śāstrī, 1998, pp. 461–462). Thus the person who cooks, eats, and enjoys an oil cake believing it to be a child will likely experience the negative consequences of intending to eat a child but will not experience the weighty karmic repercussions of actually killing and eating a child. In sum, in the case of physical (or vocal) action, the intention to do X is not sufficient to bring about the same result as actually doing X.

That said, an intention to do X is a *necessary* condition for the karmic result of doing X, and in the context of discussing the grave action of killing, Vasubandhu emphasizes that it must also be free from cognitive error. He says, "To take life is the non-mistaken slaying [*abhrāntimāraṇa*] of another, with forethought [*sañcintya*]," explaining that the murderer first determines (*saṃjñāya*) "I will kill him" and then proceeds to kill that person and not another by mistake (AKBh iv.73, in Śāstrī, 1998, p. 540).

In a context where mistaken views are the norm, deciding what counts as cognitive error can be a bit tricky, but there is a distinction between simple cognitive error and delusion or false view. Vasubandhu's subcommentator Yaśomitra illustrates this with the example of a mortal transgression of matricide or patricide on the part of a Persian who kills a parent thinking this to be meritorious (SV, Śāstrī, 1998, p. 522). While the Persian may have perverted views, he is not mistaken with respect to the identity of his victim. By contrast, Vasubandhu explains that a person who intends to kill his mother but kills someone else by accident will not experience the repercussions of matricide (AKBh iv.103a–d, in Śāstrī, 1998, pp. 575–577). Thus it appears that cognitive or perceptual error mitigates the heavy karmic weight of a grave action, while holding a mistaken view about the ethical nature of that action does not.

So it looks like the Jain author of the *Sūyagaḍa* was partially right: the confused person who eats a child with the intention of eating an oil cake will not accumulate the karmic result of taking life. He failed, however, to note the asymmetry, that intention is only a *necessary* and not a *sufficient* condition with respect to a particular karmic result: a person who eats an oil cake with the aim of eating a child will also not experience the karmic repercussions of murder.

While he denies the brand of moral realism he sees in the Jain theory—one in which the quality and results of action are measured exclusively in terms of the external, objective, and material qualities of an action—objective factors *do matter* for Vasubandhu. At various places in the AKBh, he elaborates how the particular qualities of the object and the recipient of an action and even one's relationship to that recipient affect its ethical quality and result. For example, he accepts that a material gift is more meritorious than mere devotion (*bhakti*; AKBh iv.121, in Śāstrī, 1998, pp. 590–591); a gift of superior material quality is more meritorious than a lesser quality gift (AKBh iv.114cd, in Śāstrī, 1998, p. 586); a superior field[15] will yield a more extreme result even when the intention is weak (AKBh iv.55ab, in Śāstrī, 1998, p. 522),[16] while a poor field may yield a negligible result even when the intention is good (AKBh iv.121, in Śāstrī, 1998, p. 591);[17] harm toward a Buddha or arhat accrues more demerit than would harm to an ordinary being;[18] there is more merit in giving alms to a monk who subsequently attains one of the four immeasurables than one who does not (AKBh iv.4ab, in Śāstrī, 1998, p. 461);[19] and, as mentioned, matricide involves killing one's own mother, not someone else's mother. Barring any perceptual or cognitive error, such objective factors affect the result of action even when one is not aware of the recipient's special qualities or activities; in other words, an agent may benefit or suffer from the *unintended* effects and features of his actions.

At first blush this may appear to contradict the distinction between action and accident, but in the case of giving alms to a monk who subsequently attains one of the four immeasurables, for example, the monk's meditative attainment is merely the proximate cause of a "definitive transformation" (*pariṇāmaviśeṣa*) in the mental series of the donor that gives rise to unexpected good results.[20] The intention to give is still the necessary condition that makes such transformation possible: "It is the way of things [*dharmatā*] that insofar as the gifts of the donors are enjoyed, the mental series of the donors—which are infused [*paribhāvita*] by the intention of giving and have the recipient as their object, obtain a subtle definitive transformation as a result of the particular virtues [*guṇa*] and favors [*anugraha*] of the recipient, even when the minds [of the donors] are differently occupied [at a later time]. By this [transformation] those [series] are able to manifest a greater quantity of results in the future" (AKBh iv.4ab, in Śāstrī, 1998, p. 461).[21]

In sum, without intention, without a mind oriented toward a specific object or end, there is no karma. Contrary to the Jain theory, material objects cannot perform ethical actions, and accidents (in which there is no intention directed toward X, or there is an intention directed toward Y instead of X) do not constitute the karma of doing X or yield its karmic results.[22] On the other hand, objective factors external to the agent's series do affect the results of action, even when the agent does not know of these or has mistaken views about them.

13.4. Forethought, Habituation, and the Accumulation of Action

While intentions, which are present in every conditioned mental state, are not always voluntary or deliberate, the degree to which an action is subject to forethought is, according to Vasubandhu, one of the primary factors contributing to the gravity of its result. This is made clear in his account of the distinction between an action that is accumulated (*upacita*)—meaning it has a determinate ethical quality and decisive existential result (i.e., in terms of rebirth)—and one that is merely performed (*kṛta*). Vasubandhu explains that an action is accumulated when it is done intentionally (*sañcetanataḥ*),[23] that is, "performed with forethought [*sañcintya kṛta bhavati*], not without prior reflection [*abuddhipūrvam*], i.e., not in haste [*sahasā*]" (AKBh iv.120, in Śāstrī, 1998, p. 589). By contrast, an action performed without any prior reflection may be ethically neutral and thus have no positive or negative karmic result or have an ethical quality but negligible karmic result.

Aside from forethought, the other key condition for the accumulation of an action is whether it is complete (*samāpati*). This includes not only its material success but also the performance of preparatory (*prayoga*) actions and related subsequent (*pṛṣṭha*) actions.[24] Additional factors include whether it is followed by repentance (*kaukṛtya*) and application of antidotes (*pratipakṣa*) such as confession—which mitigate against accumulation—as well as its attendant mental qualities (*parivāra*), such as a relishing in its accomplishment (AKBh, iv.120, in Śāstrī, 1998, pp. 589–590).

Elaborating on this distinction between accumulation and mere performance of an action, Yaśomitra gives the example of false speech owing to habit or repetition (*abhyāsa*).[25] This does not constitute the accumulation of false speech but is merely an "unwholesome performance" (SV in Śāstrī, 1998, p. 589). Here, presumably, there is intention—some degree of mental activity directed toward the utterance—but since it is not accompanied by forethought or followed by similar actions it is not accumulated and will not by itself yield a decisive existential result.

Because the correlation between the deliberate quality of an action and its karmic result corresponds nicely with our intuitions about the distinction between action and accident and the conditions for moral responsibility, it is easy to forget that not all intention (or action) involves forethought: recall that according to the Abhidharma, *all* conditioned mental states include intention. Thus even actions performed without prior reflection can have an ethical quality,[26] and, as indicated earlier, they can have a decisive existential result when *combined with* actions of similar quality. This is important as it would seem that most actions fall into this category: actions that are not particularly deliberate and perhaps not strongly wholesome or unwholesome. But from a Buddhist perspective it stands to reason that they should have some role in shaping one's future existence and experience.

In the context of discussing the merit accruing to nonmaterial works, Vasubandhu explains, "Even in dreams [*svapna*] there are intentions that follow from the constant repetition [*abhyāsa*] of intentions that have [Tathāgatas and their disciples] as their object" (AKBh iv.4ab; Śāstrī, 1998, p. 461).[27] In contrast to the case of false speech owing to unconscious habit or repetition (*abhyāsa*), here the repetition is a kind of conscious cultivation (*bhāvanā*), and thus the subsequent intentions that arise during sleep do not have negligible results; they add something like compound interest to the merit accrued by the waking intention. Of course the extreme virtue of the field—the Tathāgata or his disciples—adds to this interest as well.

The general principle seems to be that although an action performed without any immediate prior reflection may be wholesome or unwholesome, its effect on rebirth is negligible when it is not a function of a generally wholesome or unwholesome character or connected with similar actions, especially when these are consciously cultivated.[28] This is consistent with other views expressed in the AKBh: that the quality and result of action is affected by whether it is performed with intense defilement or purity (*tīvra-kleśa-prasāda*) or continually (*sātatya*; AKBh iv.54, in Śāstrī, 1998, p. 522); that an unwholesome course of action bears a result according to the way it practiced (*āsevita*), cultivated (*bhāvita*), and developed (*bahulīkṛta*; AKBh iv.85, in Śāstrī, 1998, pp. 561–562); and that the enjoyable fruits of giving are contingent upon the faith (*śraddha*), training (*śīla*), learning (*śruta*), and so on of the donor as well as the devotion (*satkṛtya*) with which he gives (AKBh 115ab, in Śāstrī, 1998, p. 586).

All of this suggests that an intention is existentially significant not only when it is subject to conscious control or issues from a deliberative process but also when it is the result of conscious cultivation or is consistent with one's general character, such that even involuntary or nondeliberate intentions may have an ethical quality and contribute to pleasant or painful existential results. Given that forethought is not always a factor, the next section examines how intention inclines toward its object.

13.5. How Intention Inclines toward Its Object

While Vasubandhu recognizes forethought and absence of cognitive error as key factors in determining the weight of a karmic result, when he analyzes the etiology of action he tends to focus on memory and conative and affective factors as its most salient conditions.[29] For example, in the ninth chapter of the AKBh, in the context of discussing how karma arises without a self (*ātman*) serving as its agent (*kartṛ*), he explains, "From memory [*smṛti*] comes desire [*chandas*], from desire applied thought [*vitarka*] and from applied thought effort [*prayatna*], and from effort a wind [*vāyu*], and from that there is action" (AKBh ix, in Śāstrī, 1998, pp. 952–953). Here applied thought (*vitarka*) is equivalent to intention.[30] This intention may involve or proceed from a deliberative process, but if so, Vasubandhu does not say.[31] Instead he focuses on the affective and conative elements of the process. Similarly in the *Karmasiddhiprakaraṇa* he explains that bodily karma is distinct from autonomic processes (*so so pa'i nus pa*) owing to the factor of exertion (*rtsol ba*, *vyāyāma*, KSP 145a4).

Although he cites memory, desire, and effort as salient conditions for action and exertion as its distinguishing feature, Vasubandhu says little else about how an intention comes to be oriented toward a particular object or end. In his commentary on the *Triṃśikā*, however, Sthiramati offers a provocative analogy: "Intention is the shaper of the mind [*cittābhisaṃskāra*], a mental stirring [*ceṣṭā*]. Where it is present, it is like the movement [*praspanda*] of a mind toward an object, like the movement [*praspanda*] of iron under the power of a lodestone."[32] This seems to suggest that intention shapes the mind insofar as it is pulled by the force of affection for its object—a theme that is found throughout Buddhist thought. However, the latter portion of the Tibetan translation reads a bit differently: "Where [intention] is present, it moves the mind toward an object, like iron is moved by the power of lodestone."[33] Instead of taking the *object* to function like a lodestone upon *intention*, as in the Sanskrit version, the Tibetan suggests *intention* functions like a lodestone upon the *mind*. I suspect this slight difference in the interpretation of the analogy (regardless of its philological provenance) can be attributed to the fact that whereas an intention may be compelled by the force of affection for an object and habit (in ways that are both wholesome and unwholesome), it also actively shapes the mind as it fixes upon and moves toward this object. As is the case with the other conditioning factors (*saṃskāra*), intention is both that which is constructed and that which constructs, both product and process.

Whichever way it is read, the analogy of the lodestone is consistent with the notion that the essential characteristic of intention is its movement toward an object or end. As we have seen, such movement may be the result of prior thought or deliberation or the result of force of habit or affection, and in many cases may be the result of both. Indeed the fact that it has an intentional structure and that this can be expressed verbally (e.g., "I will give alms to the monk") explains how an action can be sensitive to thought about and even sustained reflection upon its object or end, as well as to affection and habit. This is what creates the space for rational reflection and the cultivation of affection and moral sentiment that constitute the foundation of the Buddhist path. Before drawing some conclusions about the dynamics of freedom and habituation therein (section 13.7), a brief examination of his critique of the Vaibhāṣika theory of karma will help illuminate Vasubandhu's understanding of the relation between intention and habituation.

13.6. Intention, Transformation, and Habituation

As we saw, the Vaibhāṣikas define bodily and vocal karma as manifest actions (*vijñapti*) issuing from intention. This definition plays a key role in their explanation of the transmission of karmic results and the changes brought about by the practice of the path. The basic problem they seek to address is how to explain such enduring effects of action given the variable ethical quality and intermittent operation of the minds in a series of aggregates—how to explain, for example, the change brought about by the wholesome discipline (*saṃvara*) of observing a monastic vow when the current mental state may be neutral or unwholesome or when there is no mental state (as in certain meditative attainments or unconsciousness).[34] According to their theory, a manifest bodily or vocal action (*vijñapti*), such as the formal vocal utterance of assent that constitutes taking a monastic vow,[35] creates a series of imperceptible (*adarśana*), nonresistant (*apratigha*), and thus nonmanifest (*avijñapti*) material forms (*rūpa*) that have an ethical quality similar to the manifest action and are subsequently possessed by the aggregate series (AKBh iv.4ab, in Śāstrī, 1998, pp. 456–459). By attributing the effect of taking a monastic vow to this kind of unmanifest matter they make it a kind of metaphysical state divorced from the psychological dynamics of the mental series.

With respect to the problem of the transmission of karmic results, Vasubandhu finds the Vaibhāṣika theory inelegant, bloated with explanatorily unnecessary and scripturally or metaphysically dubious phenomena.[36] He finds the notion of unmanifest matter in particular conceptually incoherent, but the thrust of his argument is that it fails to account for the *psychological effects* of cultivating the path, such as the effects of taking a monastic vow. He argues that such effects as well as the objective transmission of karmic results can be sufficiently explained in terms of various modifications or transformations of the mental series engendered by intention, and thus solely in terms of the phenomena (*dharmas*) attested in *sūtra* (as per his "Sautrāntika" orientation).

In the case of karmic fruition (as we saw in section 13.3), intention infuses the mental series with a potential for a "definitive transformation" (*pariṇāmaviśeṣa*) to which other internal and external factors may contribute in order to give rise to a karmic result. Vasubandhu defines "transformation" (*pariṇāma*) simply as the fact of change (*anyathātva*) within the series (AKBh ii.36d, in Śāstrī, 1998, p. 171) but generally reserves the term "definitive transformation" for the mechanism of karmic fruition. However, he first mentions the concept of transformation in the context of discussing a more fundamental transformation of the series: the radical alteration of the personality or constitution (*āśraya-parāvṛtti*) that distinguishes a spiritually mature from an ordinary individual (AKBh ii.36d, in Śāstrī, 1998, p. 170). The former's constitution (*āśraya*) has been radically altered (*parāvṛtta*) by the power of the supramundane path such that there is no longer the potential (*bīja*) for certain defilements (*kleśa*)[37]—just as a seed (*bīja*) that has been burned can no longer produce rice (AKBh ii.36d, in Śāstrī, 1998, p. 170). Intention plays a key role here insofar as the intentions that constitute the mundane practice of the path create the conditions for the attainment of the supramundane path. We might even say—although Vasubandhu does not—that there are three kinds of transformation engendered by intention relevant here: the transformation that gives rise to karmic result, the transformation wrought through the cultivation of the path, and the radical transformation that brings an end to defilement (and eventually to karmic fruition).

Vasubandhu's argument against the Vaibhāṣikas touches upon all three kinds of transformation at various places in the AKBh, but the real advantage of his theory seems to be its ability to explain the psychology of intention and habituation in the cultivation of the mundane path, and specifically in the ethical discipline (*śīla*) of upholding a monastic vow. Against the Vabhāṣika claim that unmanifest matter is needed in order to explain the state of upholding the vow, Vasubandhu explains, "Owing to the intention with which the precept was previously enacted, the oath restrains the body and speech from the prohibited action" (AKBh iv.4ab, in Śāstrī, 1998, p. 464). When an interlocutor objects that a monk whose mind is no longer constituted by the intention to undertake the precepts would not be subject to discipline or restraint, Vasubandhu says, "This is not the case, because [the intention] is present as the result of remembering [it] at the time of action owing to cultivation [*bhāvanā*]" (AKBh iv.4ab, in Śāstrī, 1998, p. 464). Yaśomitra elaborates that when there arises a mind with the thought to take life a monk comes face to face with an intention that restrains his body and voice as a result of the present recollection of his pledge "I refrain from taking life, and so on,"[38] owing to the cultivation of his mental series (Śāstrī, 1998, p. 464). Sthiramati (1986, 18a) similarly explains, "As a result of the intention of restraint, there are similar minds in the mental series; the essence of cultivation is the planting of seeds in order to generate [such minds] in the future." On this view, upholding a monastic vow is not a metaphysical state divorced from the mental series but a kind of moral formation resulting from the conscious cultivation (i.e., repetition) of the intention and giving rise to its spontaneous recollection at the time of action (or restraint from action).

In response to the challenge that mere intention cannot explain the power of renunciation (*virakti*) involved in monastic discipline, which is said to be like a dike (*setu*) obstructing immorality (AKBh iv.4ab, in Śāstrī, 1998, 459),[39] Vasubandhu argues that it is *only* by defining action as an intention that one can account for such power: "Having fully remembered the promise [*pratijñā*] not to act [*akriyā*], one is shamed [*lajjita*] from engaging in immorality. This is the meaning of the undertaking of [a promise]. If, on the other hand, misconduct were prohibited as a result of unmanifest matter, then anyone bereft of memory would not transgress the training" (AKBh iv.4ab, in Śāstrī, 1998, p. 464).[40] The problem with the Vaibhāṣika theory is that unmanifest matter is not part of the monk's mental makeup. It is not something that can become an object of thought or reflection or explain the central role of memory in the psychology of moral training, particularly the way memory of a vow can trigger powerful moral emotions like shame. Although the term for "shamed" in this passage is *lajjita* (from √*laj*), Vasubandhu clearly has in mind the Abhidharma understanding of shame (*hrī*) and moral apprehension (*apatrāpya*) as the twin roots of wholesomeness.[41] In contrast to the anomalous metaphysical notion of unmanifest matter, an intention and its cultivation are mental activities that have discernible effects on a person's psychological makeup, on memory and moral emotions, and it seems it is Vasubandhu's desire to account for this bit of moral psychology that leads him to defend the definition of bodily and vocal action as intention.

13.7. Conclusion: Intention, Freedom, and Habituation

Because his interest is the natural etiology of karma and not the conditions under which a person might be deserving of karmic consequences or held responsible for his actions and because the freedom he values is not the freedom to do what one desires but liberation from suffering, Vasubandhu is not particularly concerned about whether karma might be compelled or free. Although he understands prior reflection or design to affect the gravity of karmic result, he does not define karma as intention to establish that it is always voluntary or deliberate. He defines karma as intention because he takes intention to be an ethically charged mental activity with the power to affect a genetic transformation in the mental series. This transformation promises to account for the psychological process of moral formation and soteriological cultivation as well as for the transmission of karmic results.

Despite his interest in the psychological dynamics of karma, Vasubandhu does not propose a complete psychologization of karma or a thoroughly intentionalist ethics; instead he endorses elements of moral realism such that objective factors external to the agent's mental series affect the ethical quality and results of action. He is adamant that karma cannot be understood as a kind of ethically qualified matter (contra the Jain and Vaibhāṣika views), in part because in order to distinguish action from accident, it must be a mental activity directed toward an ethically qualified object or end. Defining karma as intention also helps explain how actions influence other mental factors in the psychophysical series and how these factors influence action in return. These other mental factors include prior and subsequent intentions as well as various affections and moral sentiments, such as desire (*chanda*), faith (*śraddhā*), shame (*hrī*), and apprehension (*apatrāpya*). Importantly they also include memory (*smṛti*), and Vasubandhu is particularly sensitive to how these factors interact with intention in the processes of habituation (*abhyāsa*) and cultivation (*bhāvanā*).

While karma and even the karma that constitutes the cultivation of the Buddhist path need not always be what we would consider voluntary or deliberate, Vasubandhu does suggest that voluntary and deliberate actions have a more pronounced effect on the mental series than actions performed without much awareness or reflection. For example, the formal taking of a monastic vow and deliberate reflection on the Tathāgata have profound psychological effects and existential results, as do intentional negative actions. Thus a fair degree of reflection and purpose are essential for the effective cultivation of the path. The intentional structure of karma makes it amenable to verbal expression and explains how it can be sensitive to thought and sustained reflection regarding its ends or objects—and thus how even sustained reflection on the Buddhist worldview (such as presented in the AKBh) might influence action. In conclusion, what emerges from Vasubandhu's discussion of karma is a view of a path that involves deliberate reflection and action in the service of habituation, such that intentions come to gravitate toward wholesome ends and objects as a result of attending to them with appropriate views, desires, and moral sentiments.

Abbreviations

AN   *Aṅguttara Nikāya*, volume and page in the Pali Text Society edition. Translations are my own.

AKBh   Vasubandhu, *Abhidharmakośabhāṣya*, Śāstrī edition. Translations are my own.

KSP   Vasubandhu, *Karmasiddhiprakaraṇa*, sDe dge bsTan 'gyur series edition. Translations are my own.

SV   Yaśomitra, *Sphuṭārthavyākhyā*, Śāstrī edition. Translations are my own.

Notes

1. I use the term "karma" in its primary Buddhist sense to refer to ethically qualified (wholesome, unwholesome, or neutral) actions and "karmic result" to refer to the results (*phala*) of such actions.

2. For example: "I say, oh monks, karma is an intention [*cetanā*]. Intending, one acts with the body, speech or mind" (AN.iii, 415).

3. See de La Vallée Poussin (1927/2001, p. 127), Lamotte (1935–1936, p. 152), Gombrich (1971/1995, p. 170).

4. See Heim (2013) for an excellent discussion of this matter with respect to the concept of intention in the work of Buddhaghosa.

5. I follow here Yaśomitra's gloss of *kāyādhiṣṭhānam* as *kāyālambanam*.

6. Śāstrī has misprinted *vedanā* for *cetanā*.

7. By "unconscious" I mean states (*citta*) of sleeping or dreaming (*svapna*), states that we would typically regard as unconscious, but that (barring yogic mastery) Buddhists simply regard as having less clarity and mindfulness than waking states.

8. The *Karmasiddhiprakaraṇa* (Vasubandu, 1986a) and *Viṃśatikā* (Vasubandhu, 1925) in particular.

9. The presentation of karma in the KSP is similar to the presentation in the AKBh but addresses a broader range of Buddhist views, includes reference to Mahāyāna concepts and texts, and has a slightly more refined analysis of the three types of action.

10. This is not made explicit in the AKBh or KSP, but Yogācāra and Sarvāstivāda works commonly explain the constructive activity of intention in reference to an ethically qualified end. For example, the *Abhidharmasamuccaya* says, "[An intention] is the shaper of the mind [*cittābhisaṃskāra*], its activity [*karmika*] is impelling [*preraṇa*] the mind toward the wholesome, unwholesome or neutral" (Asaṅga, 2005, p. 4). Similarly in his *Pañcaskandhaprakaraṇa*, Vasubandhu says that an intention "is mental karma, the shaper of the mind with respect to good qualities, faults, and that which is neither" (Vasubandhu, 1986b, 48a).

11. In the Buddhist context, this is not just the fact of having an object but the dynamic mental activity of moving or being pulled toward an object (see section 13.4).

12. In the case of a material object, to say that it is "ethically qualified" does not mean that the material form itself is ethically qualified (as we saw earlier, Vasubandhu objects to this idea); it means that a mental orientation toward certain material and immaterial objects alike may be conducive to wholesome, unwholesome, or neutral actions.

13. Here "objective" means having truth independent from a subjective perspective, and "external" means existing outside of the series of psychophysical aggregates in which an action is initiated.

14. On transformation (*pariṇāma*), see section 13.5.

15. A "superior field" is a "field of merit" (*puṇyakṣetra*) or "field of virtue" (*guṇakṣetra*), typically meaning the Buddha or the *saṅgha*, but it includes other recipients whose specific qualities make an action accrue more merit or demerit than in the case of an ordinary recipient. Thus the mortal transgressions are ranked in severity according to the qualities of the field: to harm the *saṅgha* (and thereby the dharma) by creating a schism is the gravest of the mortal transgressions, patricide or matricide the lightest. See AKBh iv.105ab, in Śāstrī, 1998, pp. 578–579.

16. This is true in the case of both positive and negative actions.

17. However, a good action will never yield a bad result.

18. This is made clear in the discussion of mortal transgressions beginning at AKBh iv.96a; Śāstrī 570. For example, when a person kills someone who is not an arhat but becomes an arhat just after his death, that person only commits murder and not the mortal transgression of killing an arhat (AKBh iv.103d-104ab; Śāstrī, 578).

19. The four immeasurables are meditative absorptions in loving kindness, compassion, sympathetic joy and equanimity for all beings without preference.

20. See section 13.5.

21. In saying this is simply the "way of things" (dharmatā), Vasubandhu nods to the fact the way in which "mental series, perfumed (adhivāsita) by actions of varying quality and strengths, give rise to their specific results is only within the ken of Buddhas" (ABKh ix; Śāstrī, 955).

22. There is not space to elaborate upon it here, but there is something of an asymmetry between the way Vasubandhu calculates the results accruing to positive and negative actions, especially between positive actions that involve a field of merit and the ten unwholesome courses of action. In the case of the former, merit increases even as a result of unintended consequences of a wholesome action (e.g., when a monk enters an absorption fueled by a donor's alms). In the case of the latter, the intention to do X must correspond with actually doing X in order for the results of doing X to accrue. See Meyers (2010, pp. 225–227).

23. Although the adverb "intentionally" (sañcetanataḥ) is related to "intention" (cetanā), the gloss that follows does not apply to the mental activity of intention itself given that it is present in every mental state and also occurs without forethought and so on.

24. On preparatory and subsequent actions, see AKBh iv.68cd, in Śāstrī, 1998, pp. 534–537.

25. This might happen when a text with a mistaken view is recited from memory.

26. The ethical quality may be dependent upon mental factors other than intention as well as the object or end toward which the intention is directed.

27. Yaśomitra supplies "Tathāgatas and their disciples." SV in Śāstrī, 1998, p. 461.

28. Similarly the Loṇaphala (Salt Crystal) sutta explains that while a trifling evil deed performed by an uncultivated person leads to rebirth in hell, the results of the same deed performed by someone who has cultivated the path is experienced only momentarily in the present life, just as a salt crystal will render a cup of water undrinkable but will have a negligible effect when dropped into the Ganges (AN.i.249–253).

29. The distinction between cognitive, affective, and conative helps correct an overemphasis on the cognitive dimension of the path, but it should be noted that the mental factors discussed in Buddhist psychology often do not fall neatly into one or the other of these categories.

30. Technically it is the intention that is the resolve (saṅkalpa-cetanā) to act and precedes the intention that effects the performance of the action (kriyā-cetanā). See AKBh iv.3c, in Śāstrī, 1998, p. 455.

31. As a mental factor, vitarka does not necessarily entail explicit reflection or deliberation.

32. "Cetanā cittābhisaṃskāro manasaś ceṣṭā yasyāṃ satyām ālambanaṃ prati cetasaḥ praspanda iva bhavaty ayaskāntavaśād ayaḥpraspandavat" (Buescher, 2007, p. 58). I have translated praspanda simply as "movement" to match the Tibetan (g.yo ba) and so as not obscure the point regarding the basic function of intention, but it means something like vibration, pulsation, or quivering.

33. "Gang yod na khab long gi dbang gis lcags g.yo ba bzhin du dmigs pa la sems g.yo bar byed pa'o" (Buescher, 2007, p. 59).

34. Such as the attainment of cessation (nirodhasamāpatti). The other problems they address include (1) how merit continues to increase after the initial performance of an action; (2) what accounts for the karmic result that ensues from the completion of a course of action, especially when the action is completed by a proxy; (3) the relation between the still and silent attainment of the path of seeing and the practice of all eight branches of the path; and (4) why renunciation is said to be a dike obstructing immorality (AKBh iv.4ab, in Śāstrī, 1998, p. 456–460).

35. We can assume that this is not just any vocal utterance of assent, but assent uttered in the appropriate ritual context.

36. With respect to explaining karmic result, he admits that his theory may not be fully satisfactory either but says it is more pleasing (paritoṣa; AKBh iv.4ab, in Śāstrī, 1998, pp. 462–463), suggesting the aesthetic quality of parsimony as a criterion for good theory.

37. In the four- or five-path theory the supermundance path includes the path of seeing (darśana-mārga), the supramundane path of cultivation (bhāvanā-mārga), and the path of no more learning (aśaikṣa-mārga). Among those who attain the supermundane path, the stream-enterer, once-returner, and non-returner abandon only certain classes of defilement, while the arhat abandons all.

38. The "so on" implies the other major Prātimokṣa precepts.

39. Śāstrī has misprinted na vā bhavantī for na vā abhavantī.

40. Śāstrī is missing the negative na in the quotation.

41. Conversely lack of shame and apprehension are the defining characteristics of an unwholesome mind (AKBh ii.25-26cd, in Śāstrī, 1998, pp. 160–161) and the twin roots of unwholesome action (AKBh iv.9c, in Śāstrī, 1998, p. 471). Lack of shame is lack of veneration (agurutā) regarding good qualities in oneself or others, and lack of apprehension is not seeing the unpleasant or fearful consequences of transgressions. While the former flows from lust (lobha), the latter flows from delusion (moha; AKBh ii.32ab, in Śāstrī, 1998, pp. 158–159).

References

Asaṅga. (2005). *Abhidharmasamuccaya-bhāṣyam*. (B. K. Choudhary, Ed.). Tibetan and Sanskrit Works Series No. 17. Patna, India: Kashi Prasad Jayaswal Research Institute.

Buescher, H. (2007). *Sthiramati's Triṃśikāvijñaptibhāṣya: Critical editions of the Sanskrit text and its Tibetan translation*. Vienna: Verlag der Österreichischen Akademie der Wissenschaften.

Bronkhorst, J. (2007). *Greater Magadha: Studies in the culture of early India*. Boston: Brill.

de La Vallée Poussin, L. (1927/2001). *La morale Bouddhique*. Saint-Michel-en-l'Herm, France: Editions Dharma.

Gombrich, R. (1971/1995). *Buddhist precept and practice: Traditional Buddhism in the Highlands of Ceylon*. New York: Kegan Paul.

Heim, M. (2013). *The forerunner of all things: Buddhaghosa on mind, intention and agency*. New York: Oxford University Press.

Lamotte, É. (1935–1936). *Traité de ka Démonstration de L'Acte*. French translation of *Karmasiddhiprakaraṇa*. Leuven, Belgium: Melanges Chinois et Bouddhiques 4.

Meyers, K. (2010). Freedom and self-control: Free will in South Asian Buddhism. PhD dissertation, University of Chicago.

Śāstrī, S. D. (Ed.). (1998). *Abhidharmakośa and Bhāṣya of Acārya Vasubandhu with Sputārthā commentary of Ācārya Yaśomitra*. 2 vols. Varanasi, India: Bauddha Bharati.

Sthiramati. (1986). *Abhidharmakośabhāṣyaṭīkātattvārtha: Chos mngon pa'i mdzod kyi bshad pa'i rgya cher 'grel pa don gyi de kho na nyid*. Sna tshogs, tho 1b1-do 387a7. sDe dge bsTan 'gyur series. Delhi: Karmapae Choedhey, Gyalwae Sungrab Nyamso Partun Khang.

Vasubandhu. (1925). *Vijñaptimātratāsiddhi. Deux traités de Vasubandhu: Viṃsatikā et Trimṣikā*. (Sylvain Levi, Ed.). Paris: Librairie Ancienne Honoré Champion.

Vasubandhu. (1986a). *Karmasiddhiprakaraṇa: Las grub pa'i rab tu byed pa*. Sems tsam shi, 134b2-145a6. sDe dge bsTan 'gyur series. Delhi: Karmapae Choedhey, Gyalwae Sungrab Nyamso Partun Khang.

Vasubandhu. (1986b). *Pañcaskhandhaprakaraṇa: Phung po lnga'i rab tu byed pa*. Sems tsam, shi 11b4-17a7. sDe dge bsTan 'gyur series. Delhi: Karmapae Choedhey, Gyalwae Sungrab Nyamso Partun Khang.

Chapter 14

What Do Buddhists Think about Free Will?

Riccardo Repetti

14.1. Introduction

The Buddha and subsequent Buddhist philosophers (until very recently) apparently lacked the concept of *free will* (Garfield, 2014/2016; Flanagan, 2016; Meyers, 2014),[1] operating within an ultimately impersonal framework *orthogonal* to the free will discussion (Heim, 2014), if not diametrically opposed to it (Garfield, 2014/2016; Flanagan, 2016). However, as Western science and philosophy increasingly embrace subpersonal conceptions of mind and action (Caruso, 2013), conceptions that have informed Buddhism from its inception (Garfield, 2015), Buddhism may have much to offer the discussion of free will (Repetti, 2016c). However, because Buddhism lacks the *free will* concept, its texts underdetermine what may be said about free will from a Buddhist perspective. Consequently Buddhist exegetical attempts to extract what may be implicit about free will in Buddhism diverge. In this paper I critically review the bulk of the extant literature on Buddhist thought about free will and argue against the view that drawing Buddhism into the free will discussion is ill-advised.[2]

Until recently Buddhism has remained silent about free will (Siderits, 1987; Goodman, 2002; Harvey, 2007; Adam, 2010; Federman, 2010; Garfield, 2014/2016; Gowans, 2014, 2016; Meyers, 2014; Flanagan, 2016). One reason, among many, is that Buddhism rejects the ultimate reality of an agent or self (Siderits, 2003), and its goal is the realization of that impersonal reality.[3] Thus the question whether the agent/self is autonomous cannot arise.[4] Nonetheless the Buddha ridiculed the ideas of inevitable causation by fate, chance, gods, matter, and/or karma (Harvey, 2007; Federman, 2010; Wallace, 2011/2016), all considered *opposite* free will, and he prescribed a path promising to increase our abilities to make wise choices (Wallace, 2011/2016), completely control our own minds (Meyers, 2014), and attain the maximum of mental freedom, *nirvāṇa* (Repetti, 2010b, 2015). While "free will" talk runs orthogonally to the impersonal features of the Buddhist framework (Heim, 2014), the Buddha's rejection of inevitable causation affords Buddhism a solid warrant in the discussion.

However, because Buddhism is designed to eradicate the false sense of agency presupposed in free will discussions, some see the project of engaging Buddhism and Western philosophy in discourse on free will as misguided (Flanagan, 2016; Garfield, 2014/2016). Most Buddhists writing on the subject reject the *strong* view of free will embraced by *some* forms of libertarianism, according to which an immaterial autonomous agent/self exists outside the causal nexus, immune to material influences, able to interject phenomenal causes into the empirical realm—a kind of mini prime-mover-unmoved.[5] Clearly, in rejecting the agent/self, the Buddha implicitly rejected this idea,[6] as have others (Goodman, 2002; Adam, 2010), but this strikes me as the lowest-hanging fruit in this domain, so to speak. More subtly, others have claimed that while *ultimately* there is no self in Buddhism, *conventionally* there is agential functionality sufficient to ground a weaker, naturalistic conception of agency/self and free will (Federman, 2010; Harvey, 2007; Gier & Kjellberg, 2004; Meyers, 2014, 2016; Repetti, 2010b, 2015, 2016b, 2016c; Siderits, 1987, 2008/2016; Wallace, 2011/2016). But what might that be? Many of the answers to that question overlap, so as we proceed, my descriptions of them will decrease in detail as they refer increasingly to ideas spelled out in earlier iterations.

14.2. Friquegnon: Three Buddhist Conceptions of Freedom

Just as there are different free will conceptions in Western philosophy, Marie Friquegnon (2016) argues that there are three distinct understandings of freedom in *various* forms of Buddhism. First, all Buddhists understand agency as unconstrained by divine power or material causality. As mentioned earlier, the Buddha's rejection of inevitable causation (also by fate and chance) established a Buddhist warrant in this discussion (Harvey, 2007; Federman, 2010; Wallace, 2011/2016; see also Repetti, 2010b). While material causality and fate are not identical with determinism, they share inevitablism,[7] and chance implies indeterminism. Garfield (2014/2016) and Flanagan (2016) seem to overlook this when they argue that Buddhism should not participate in the free will discussion (see also Heim, 2014).

Second, Friquegnon (2016) adds, all Buddhists see unethical actions as the direct result of mental states governed by anger/hatred, jealousy/attachment, and ignorance/fear. For instance, the Mahāyāna philosopher Śāntideva asserts in the *Bodhicaryāvatāra* that we can no more blame someone under the impersonally caused influence of such mental states than we can blame fire for causing smoke. This suggests a causal explanation of actions as undermining an agential type of proximal control and implies a sense of unfreedom or mental bondage, the eradication of which is the goal of the Buddhist path and implies that its elimination is possible and constitutes another form of freedom. As Mark Siderits (2008/2016, citing *Bodhicaryāvatāra* 6.22–32) has emphasized, in the same passage Śāntideva suggests the aspirant, aware of this causality, can alter it. As Meyers (2014) notes, path progress cultivates this sort of self-control.

Many agree with and develop this conception (Federman, 2010; Harvey, 2007, 2016; Meyers, 2016; Wallace, 2011/2016; Repetti, 2010b, 2015, 2016c). Thus the *ārya* (advanced practitioner), in practicing self-monitoring, restraint of desires, and various forms of self-regulation, cultivates an increasingly effective will of the sort she prefers to have, that is, a dharmic will (a will in accord with the dharma).[8] This involves increasingly effective proximal control but does not imply a substantive metaphysical conception of agency—only an empirical, psychological conception. As Aaronson (2004) notes, appealing to the Buddhist "two truths" doctrine (in which *conventional* truth permits pragmatic discourse that is ultimately false or misleading, unlike *ultimate* truth),[9] *conventional* agency increases inversely with the *ārya*'s realization of the *ultimate* ontological insubstantiality of her self.

Friquegnon's (2016) third concept of freedom, unlike Śāntideva's deterministic attitude about impersonally caused behavior in unenlightened beings, involves actions flowing from enlightened beings who embody the realization of the insubstantial/empty nature of agency/self. Their ego-less behavior is free of all forms of mental conditioning but poses a puzzle for discussion of free will. For Western thinking about free will typically involves an ability possessed by persons (metaphysically substantive agents).

How this "agentless agency" (Repetti, 2010b; see also Repetti, 2016a) ought to be related to free will is a puzzle, addressed by most thinkers reviewed here only in minimalistic, metaphorical terms, if that (e.g., Aaronson, 2004; Adam, 2010; Meyers, 2014, 2016; Harvey, 2016; Wallace, 2011/2016; Repetti, 2010b, 2012a, 2012b, 2014, 2015, 2016c). Kasulis (1985), borrowing a concept from Taoism, describes it as *wu wei* (doing without doing). Wallace (2011, p. 231/

2016, p. 121) describes it similarly: "One non-conceptually rests in this time-less, pristine awareness, allowing actions to arise spontaneously and effort-lessly, aroused by the interplay of one's own intuitive wisdom and the needs of sentient beings." The paradox of agentless agency will not be resolved here, but need not be. For it involves freedom not *of* the will but *from* it—more spe-cifically, from its *adharmic elements*; compassion, generosity, and other forms of care involve volition present in enlightened beings (Repetti, 2010b).

Rather than puzzle over the metaphysics, B. Alan Wallace (2011/2016) sees the Buddhist tradition taking a pragmatic approach, exploring ways we can acquire greater freedom to make choices conducive to well-being, and describ-ing practices of Mahāyāna Buddhism that point toward mental freedom. One is the cultivation of the ability to deliberately focus attention with continuity and clarity; another is the cultivation of insight into how attitudes shape ex-perience, allowing for the possibility of altering not only the way we experi-ence but how we are influenced by memory. Wallace's pragmatism rests on a liberating form of Mahāyāna metaphysics: the Great Perfection school of Tibetan Buddhism, emphasizing the realization of the substrate dimension of consciousness—pristine awareness—transcending conceptualization and the causal nexus (and its determinism/indeterminism dichotomy). Wallace sees this as the ultimate source of freedom and the ultimate nature of human identity.

As alluring as this transcendental picture is, Wallace's interpretation of the substrate consciousness is disputed even within Tibetan Buddhism, and to my thinking this model resembles strong free will as a causality-transcendent consciousness from which free actions originate. Metaphysics aside, Wallace's pragmatic insight seems plausible: Buddhist practices *at least* support a weak (compatibilist) view of free will.

14.3. Story, Rāhula, Gómez, and Kalupahana: Wiggly Buddhist Determinism

Before we continue, let me unpack some terms. *Compatibilist* may be applied to the traditional Western sense of compatibility between free will and deter-minism but also to compatibility between Buddhist causation and impersonal agency required for moral cultivation on the path. Fischer (2006) argues that a strong conception of free will presupposes ability to do otherwise *under identical causal circumstances*, implying *indeterminism* (incompatible with *de-terminism*), but that moral responsibility is compatible with determinism, as Frankfurt (1969) argued: an agent can freely do X even if determined to, if the agent would have done X even if she could have done otherwise. Fischer adds, so long as she was able to respond to (moral) reasons for or against doing X, she is morally responsible regarding X. *Semicompatibilists* consider determinism incompatible with strong free will (which requires indeterminism) but compatible with moral responsibility or weak free will (which does not require indeterminism). I extend *semicompatible* to the broader sense of thinking Buddhist causation (and metaphysics) is incompatible with strong agency but compatible with weak agency and moral responsibility. On my analysis, most Buddhists writing on free will are semicompatibilists.

The earliest Buddhist philosophers in the contemporary period to consider Buddhist views of free will, Frances Story (1976), Walpola Rāhula (1974), Luis Gómez (1975), and David Kalupahana (1976, 1992, 1995), presented the Buddhist perspective within the narrow parameters of the traditional question whether free will is consistent with determinism (see also Griffiths, 1982). I have reviewed their contributions at length elsewhere (Repetti, 2010a), so here I will only summarize my analysis. These philosophers agree that Buddhist causation, *dependent origination* (the view that all conditioned phenomena are dependent on earlier or simultaneous conditions), is neither purely deterministic nor indeterministic: the Buddha's remarks about karma *resemble* determinism but resist a purely deterministic characterization, as does the broader doctrine of dependent origination. For these reasons, they consider Buddhist causation to involve what I have described as "wiggly determinism" (Repetti, 2010a), affording Buddhism a *middle way* between determinism and indeterminism, forming an opaque form of compatibilism between free will and causation that is probably semicompatibilist.

These thinkers are not alone among Buddhists who view dependent origination as involving the nonnecessitated *regularities* Hume described as mere "constant conjunctions," nor in thinking this circumvents the determinism/indeterminism dichotomy: if determined, they are unfree; if random, they cannot be authored (see, e.g., Garfield, 2001). However, as I have argued at length (Repetti, 2010a), if a form of causation is not purely deterministic, then by simple negation it is indeterministic. It may be misleading to try to understand Buddhism through Western frameworks (Garfield, 2015; Heim, 2014), but it is doubtful that dependent origination can escape this dichotomy via wiggly determinism, Humean regularism, or other Buddhist causal models, such as Mahāyāna interdependence.[10] Either the causation is deterministic or it is not: if the former, then the causes of decisions originate prior to the agent; if the latter, the agent cannot claim to author them. In principle, because Buddhists don't believe in the agent/self, they ought not to care, but that doesn't obliterate the problem. Let's consider more recent views.

14.4. Flanagan, Garfield, and Gowans: Buddhist Free Will Skepticism and Quietism

Owen Flanagan (2016) argues against bringing Buddhism into discourse with free will conceptions tainted by their genesis within a monotheistic theodicy Buddhism lacks. Likewise, Garfield (2014/2016) asserts Mādhyamikas (followers of Madhyamaka, Middle-Way Buddhism) lack a free will theory because they lack a monotheistic theodicy, a conception of the agent operating outside the causal nexus, and a deterministic model of causation. However, in addition to the Buddha's own rejection of inevitablism and the free will dialectical warrant generated thereby, Madhyamaka endorses the view that because there is no metaphysical foundation enabling the naive realist's worldview to be reduced or eliminated, it makes as much sense to say there are tables as to say there are table-like phenomenological appearances or that there are aggregates of atomic psychophysical tropes. Likewise it (arguably) makes as much sense to say people have free will.

Additionally both views flirt with the genetic fallacy insofar as they suggest that the notion of free will is illegitimate outside a theistic context because it has a theistic genesis. By analogy, however, if the concept of human rights had its historical genesis in Abrahamic doxography, *arguendo*, that would not necessarily invalidate the concept. Both thinkers also emphasize that Buddhism lacks a God concept, but that is neither entirely true nor entirely persuasive. It is not entirely true because there are gods in Buddhism, though they are mostly seen as caught within the karmic web like anyone else, and thus soteriologically unnecessary (exceptions involving Buddhist deities notwithstanding).[11] And it is not persuasive because free will may obtain whether or not there is a God (Fischer, 1989).

Christopher Gowans (2016) places the metaquestion, how to think about Buddhism and free will, into the context of its historical absence (see also Gowans 2014). Gowans argues that the main reason for Buddhist quietism here is that Buddhist philosophical analysis is limited by soteriological parameters: whatever promotes enlightenment. Gowans concludes that if Buddhism must pronounce on any theoretical position, it would only be justified as "skillful means" (soteriologically instrumental for certain individuals) but would nevertheless remain silent on the metaphysics.

However, the Buddha's rejection of inevitablism seems soteriologically relevant and explicitly pronouncing on metaphysics. Additionally a Buddhist meta-ethical theory would be soteriologically justified, yet Buddhism has none, historically. Also, whatever justifies extant Buddhist theories of intentionality, phenomenology, and so on conceivably justifies free will theory. I have argued that Buddhism prescribes methods for cultivating virtuoso-level abilities associated with free will (Repetti, 2010b, 2015, 2016c). This view is implicit if not explicit in the works of several Buddhist scholars (Adam, 2010, 2016; Federman, 2010; Harvey, 2007, 2016; Wallace, 2011/2016; Meyers, 2014, 2016; McRae, 2016; Friquegnon, 2016; Abelson, 2016). Intuitively, if the *ārya* has greater free will–related skills than the average person, she has greater free will, which increases, paradoxically, proportionate to the decrease in the self-sense and peaks in *nirvāṇa*, the cessation of the self-sense. I have argued that this skill undermines the most powerful free will skepticism, "hard incompatibilism" (Repetti, 2010b, 2015), the view that there is no autonomy *regardless* of whether or not we are determined, because either we are determined and not responsible for our choices, or we're not determined, and our choices are not up to us.

Derk Pereboom (2001) is a vocal advocate of hard incompatibilism, and Galen Strawson (1994) has advanced an abstract version of it with his "impossibility argument" that, irrespective of the causes of our mental states, whenever we choose, we are conditioned by the mental state we are in at the choice moment; because we cannot be the cause of our first mental state, we cannot be responsible for whatever mental state we are in at the choice moment, and thus it's *impossible* for us to be responsible for our choices. Our virtuoso, however, can escape from previous and present mental state conditioning, irrespective of its causal history. That *āryas* are able to cultivate skills that theoretically defeat the most powerful forms of free will skepticism justifies a Buddhist free will theory, if only for the explanatory purchase this exhibits on behalf of Buddhism. As Meyers (2016) put the point, Buddhism rejects the notion of autonomous agents but asserts abilities greater than those that would be possessed by them.

14.5. Meyers: Buddhist Semi-compatibilism

Like other writers in this area (Heim, 2014; Garfield, 2014/2016, 2015; Flanagan, 2016), Meyers (2016) acknowledges that the Buddhist and Western frameworks for agency are orthogonal (see also Meyers, 2014). But Meyers argues adeptly for what, on my analysis, counts as a semicompatibilist view, what may be called "agency lite," grounded in the works of the Abhidharma philosopher Vasubandhu. Paying very careful attention to the texts but informed significantly by Western analytic philosophy, Meyers critically examines Vasubandhu's (and his contemporaries') theories of karma, causation, and liberation and how they differ from modern positions on free will (and the views of other Buddhists), but also how they describe an understanding of mind, agency, and action that is compatible with causation: everything is caused (perhaps not explicitly deterministically). Meyers concludes not only that mental qualities explain what we consider free will and ground an understanding of moral responsibility but that Buddhist training increases abilities typically associated with free will in the West, to the virtuoso level, a claim I have also developed in some detail (Repetti, 2010b, 2015, 2016d).

Meyers acknowledges the importance of the two truths doctrine in Buddhist thinking about free will, however implicit. *Ultimately* there is no agent/self, but *conventionally* individuals exhibit features typically considered sufficient for holding them responsible; that is, they are able to deliberate, consider consequences, approve or disapprove their intentions, restrain or allow various intentions to form actions, and so forth. Moreover, *āryas* possess these abilities in far greater measure than the average person, and the Buddhist path requires them. Meyers's account counts as semicompatibilist: *ultimately* all behavior is impersonally caused; thus there is no genuine free will in ultimate reality, but *conventionally* individuals typically possess sufficient proximal control to qualify for moral responsibility.

14.6. Goodman: Buddhist Hard Determinism

Disagreeing, Charles Goodman (2002) argues forcefully that Buddhism is hard deterministic: dependent origination is deterministic, and determinism rules out free will; he also argues that because there is no self, there cannot be an *autonomous* self, and thus there cannot be autonomy. I think the latter inference is faulty: by analogy, just because it follows from the fact that there are no unicorns that there cannot be any *winged* unicorns, it does not follow that there cannot be any wings.

Goodman and Siderits have argued for opposing interpretations of Śāntideva's remarks in the *Bodhicaryāvatāra* at 6.22–32, where, on the one hand, Śāntideva advises the aspirant to view others' aggression as analogous to the liver's production of bile (impersonally), for purposes of self-control, but, on the other hand, when considering the objection that *because there is no self, there is nobody who can control the self*, Śāntideva suggests that the perspective of self-control is required for the path. Siderits (2008/2016) largely bases his "paleo-compatibilism" on Śāntideva's latter remark, whereas Goodman (2002, 2009) rejects that interpretation.

Goodman's argument rests on the Buddhist view that blame is a cognitive error, given that no *nonself* could be ultimately responsible for "its" behavior. However, Goodman (2016) has recently conceded a small point in the other direction. Echoing Gowans (2016), he now argues that the doctrine of skillful means might sanction belief in free will for individuals at certain stages of the Buddhist path. Goodman's concession, however, resembles a Platonic "Noble Lie" more than an acceptance of compatibilism.

Incompatibilism presupposes a strong view of free will according to which one can be free only if one's choices are *contracausal* (they could have been otherwise under identical causal conditions), something possible only in an indeterministic world. However, there are weaker, compatibilist conceptions of free will, according to which an agent is free just in case she exhibits the right sort of abilities (which may be deterministic), for example, reason-responsiveness, higher-order approval of lower-order volitions. Goodman's rejection of free will is restricted to strong free will.[12] Not all Buddhists deal only with the strong conception of free will. However, even some who do deal with the strong conception derive opposite conclusions, such as Siderits.

14.7. Siderits: Buddhist Paleo-compatibilism

Siderits's is one of the earliest, seminal, and lasting voices in the contemporary dialectic on Buddhist views of free will. Siderits calls his view "paleo-compatibilist," but I identify it as semicompatibilist, to use a term more readily recognizable within the Western philosophical literature (Repetti, 2012a). Like most Buddhists writing on free will, Siderits's view rests on the two truths doctrine. Conventionally there are persons, but ultimately (within Abhidharma reductionism) there are only deterministic atomistic psychophysical tropes. Siderits argues that ultimately, where determinism applies, there are no agents, but conventionally, where persons obtain, some exhibit strong free will.

Siderits's views on the specifics are highly complex and equally problematic (Repetti, 2012a). A better way to understand Siderits's view is to classify it as a form of semicompatibilism: ultimately there's no free will; conventionally there is. It would be more parsimonious to say we have weak free will. However, *inter*level compatibilism—between ultimate and conventional levels—is not the same as *intra*level compatibilism, but the traditional debate is intralevel. Thus this sort of approach doesn't fully resolve the problem, but rather repartitions it.[13]

14.8. Coseru and Abelson: Buddhist Ethics without Agency?

Some philosophers have posed problems for Buddhist *ethics* involving free will. Christian Coseru (2016), for example, asks whether Buddhism may consistently describe its ideal of agent-neutral negative consequentialist ethics (espoused by certain authoritative Buddhist philosophers; Goodman, 2009) and its impersonal causal model. Coseru argues that Śāntideva, by allowing moral rules to be discarded for skillful means (arguably a consequentialist principle), compromises the notion of responsibility that requires a freedom that is responsive to moral reasons.

Coseru challenges the compatibilist idea that if we dispense with strong free will, a weaker notion of responsibility, informed by cognitive science (say, "responsibility lite"), will do, suggesting our traditional notion of moral-responsibility-entailing strong free will needs revision. Responsibility-entailing conduct prescribed in the Buddhist path (and the altruistic bodhisattva ideal) demands that moral norms be endorsed independently of empirical research. If skillful means implies agent-neutral consequentialism, this implies actions can be effective outside the interdependent web of causation—but such an account jeopardizes the responsibility-entailing relation between freedom and the bodhisattva's aspirations. Thus Buddhist ethics and metaphysics seem incompatible with traditional conceptions of responsibility-entailing agency. Coseru is implicitly insisting on a strong conception of free will in the robust moral-responsibility-entailing sense that is inconsistent with the sort of consequentialism implicit especially in later Buddhism's bodhisattva ideal.

However, as I have argued (in chorus with the others mentioned earlier), Buddhism seems quite capable of accommodating revised notions of agency lite and responsibility lite. Whether or not strong free will and moral responsibility are necessary needs to be shown. Ben Abelson seems to agree, mostly. On Abelson's (2016) analysis of Buddhist reductionism, persons are impersonal psychophysical processes with only conventional existence. Buddhist reductionists, for Siderits (2003), are committed to this "Impersonal Description" (ID) thesis. Siderits defends against the charge (leveled by Strawson, 1986) that the ID thesis implies the *extreme* claim (among others) that holding people responsible cannot be rationally justified. Abelson focuses on Siderits's reply to this objection, which appeals to "shifting coalitions" of self-revision processes (in the absence of a real self) as grounds for rendering responsibility attributions rational. Abelson argues that while this idea disarms Strawson's objection, it cannot account for the robust responsibility Siderits wants, though it grounds a modest responsibility stronger than the sort Siderits (and Coseru) dismisses as too weak. Abelson applies this analysis to support a form of weak free will consistent with Buddhism.

14.9. Strawson and Blackmore: No Phenomenological Self

Galen Strawson was one of the first Western philosophers to link the Buddhist view of the unreality of the self with the unreality of free will. Strawson's (1994) free will skepticism rests on his impossibility argument, which he takes to refute strong free will. In his most recent work on the subject, Strawson (2016) focuses on only one lemma of that argument, determinism, and how even determinists find determinism hard to assimilate into their daily lives. Unlike Peter Strawson (1962), who argued that we cannot adopt the skeptical perspective because it's too alien to our interpersonal reactive attitudes (e.g., resentment), Galen Strawson ("Strawson," except when Peter Strawson is being mentioned) thinks Buddhism represents a way of life that embodies that perspective.

Strawson proposes a thought experiment whereby we are to continuously attempt to attend to the impersonal causation of each thought, desire, and so on to bring the resilience of our habitual agential thinking to light. When we see how we cannot maintain the impersonal perspective, we are advised to take up meditation, thought to reduce the gravitational pull of agential thinking. But Strawson's prescription—meditate to eliminate the self-sense—seems premature. Prognosis rightly precedes prescription. Before we prescribe free will's postmortem procedures, we must be sure free will is dead (Repetti, 2016b).

Regardless, Susan Blackmore (2016) describes how she embodies in her daily life the sort of view Strawson prescribes for the postmortem existence of the nonagent. Blackmore claims that meditation has contributed to her nonagential experience, confirming Strawson's assertion, disconfirming Peter Strawson's. This raises a metaquestion. Meditative awareness resembles phenomenological reduction, as Coseru (2012) shows, in which conceptual proliferation is bracketed. Does meditation render agency *invisible* or, worse, *disassemble* it—a kind of psychic suicide practice? It would be enough of an error to conclude something doesn't exist because one cannot, under certain circumstances, experience it, but quite another to bring about its nonexistence through such circumstances.

According to Aaronson (2004), progress along the meditative path *increases* the conventional (psychologically functional) sense of agency, say, "self lite," while diminishing the ultimate (metaphysically substantive) sense, the *ātman*. The self lite's self-regulative abilities constitute weak (compatibilist) free will. The *conventional* self becomes *more* functionally integrated along the path, not less (Harvey, 2007, 2016; Meyers, 2016; Repetti, 2010b, 2015). For Blackmore (2016), belief in strong free will diminishes with progress along the meditative path, but what Blackmore seemingly misses is that weak free will increases.

14.10. Aaronson, Harvey, and Adam: Two Senses of Self-Agency

Concurring, Peter Harvey (2010) has argued that the Buddhist path not only presupposes a conventional form of weak free will but seems to strengthen our conventional free will. More recently, Harvey (2016) claims the Buddhist version of the free will problem concerns whether its impersonal conception of the person is compatible with moral-responsibility-entailing agency, an issue we saw taken up by others (Coseru, 2016; Siderits, 2003; Strawson, 1986; Abelson, 2016; Meyers, 2014, 2016). Restricting his analysis to Theravāda Buddhism, Harvey (2007, 2016) emphasizes that the Theravāda view identifies various factors that increase conventional agency. Harvey concludes that Theravāda is compatibilist, a middle way between seeing a person as so impersonally conditioned as to lack the proximal agency ordinarily understood as required for responsibility and seeing the person as a strong agent/self with strong free will. His account resembles Aaronson's (2004) and seems semicompatibilist in both senses: He actually calls his view semicompatibilist (Harvey, 2016).

Martin T. Adam (2010, 2016) concurs with what seems clearly a semicompatibilist line of thought, based on an analysis of the *Anattālakkhaṇa Sutta* (*Discourse on the Character of Non-Self*) and an application of the views of Frankfurt (1971). Adam argues that the Buddha's views and those in the Pāli sutras are incompatible with strong free will, but not weak free will or moral responsibility. He argues that Frankfurt's distinctions, between freedom of the person, of the will, and of action, suggest that Buddhist freedom admits of degrees—as most would agree—relative to the individual's spiritual development. Frankfurt distinguishes between freedom of the will (volitional/ metavolitional harmony) and freedom of action (being able to act on one's volitions), not to define *freedom of the person* (he says nothing about this) but rather *personhood*: a person is a being with a hierarchically structured will.[14] Apart from these minor differences, Adam's view comes close to my own.

14.11. Federman, McRae, and Repetti: Approaching Agentlessness, Agency Increases

Finally, a promising turn in recent scholarship involves attention to ways in which Buddhist practices afford practitioners abilities claimed to constitute skills significantly greater than those typically associated with free will, to control all mental states—even the powerful emotions treated as exculpatory in Buddhist ethics, for example, when an *ārya* experiences rage.[15] This growing body of literature is both historically and textually grounded and empirically informed.

For example, Asaf Federman (2010), focusing on early Buddhist texts, analyzes the Buddha's rejection of inevitable causation and of the *ātman*, and he considers the importance of the many self-regulative abilities cultivated on the path, from which he concludes that Buddhism endorses a form of compatibilism. Focusing on Tibetan texts, however, Emily McRae (2016) seems to come to a similar conclusion. McRae explores how we can exercise choice regarding emotional experiences and dispositions, the sorts of things we typically experience as instinctive, deeply conditioned, if not mostly inevitable (see also McRae, 2012, 2015). McRae argues that we can choose our emotions because we can intervene in them. Drawing on mind training practices advocated by Tsongkhapa, McRae argues that Tsongkhapa's analysis shows that successful intervention in negative emotional experiences depends on four factors: intensity of the emotional experience, ability to pay attention to the workings of one's mind and body, knowledge of intervention practices, and insight into the nature of emotions.

McRae argues that this makes sense of Tsongkhapa's seemingly contradictory claims that the meditator can and should control (and eventually abandon) her anger and desire to harm others, and that harm-doers are "servants to their afflictions," a tension we saw earlier in the debate between Goodman and Siderits regarding Śāntideva's analogy about bile and aggression. McRae concludes by considering the (I think semicompatibilist) implications of Tsongkhapa's account of choice in emotional life for the place of free will in Buddhism.

I agree with these latter thinkers and conclude that analysis of Buddhist practices that engender mental freedom increase—and thereby demonstrate—a form of weak free will sufficient for responsibility lite. From a Buddhist perspective, to the extent we—particularly Westerners—exercise *certain* capacities associated with free will (i.e., acting unreflectively on desires), we tend to decrease our mental freedom because *doing as we please* strengthens ego-based habit patterns that fortify the chief culprit in our suffering, the false sense of self. Conversely, as we increase mental freedom from the ego-volitional complex, we increase self-regulative ability, strengthening will, and subsequently exercising will *less* in the service of the ego complex. Thus the closer one gets to mental freedom, the greater one's self-regulative (autonomous) abilities, but—and here's the paradoxical rub—as one attains the limit condition of mental freedom (*nirvāṇa*), one reaches maximal self-regulative ability, but there is no longer any sense of self, no *ego-based* volitional complex, in need of regulation. Thus the maximum of mental freedom (*nirvāṇa*) and of self-regulation (weak free will) coincide with the absence of any sense of self, *agentless agency*—a form of reason-responsiveness that is entirely dharmic: dharma responsiveness.

Reason-responsiveness is a central criterion in semicompatibilist accounts (Fischer, 2006); dharma-responsiveness grounds a Buddhist form of semicompatibilism. As Buddhist practitioners become increasingly dharmic (through soteriological practice), they not only increasingly approximate (or, on some views, instantiate) *nirvāṇa*; they also increasingly exhibit weak free will. But that increasingly powerful will is explicitly constructed for the sole purpose of eradicating the illusion of a metaphysically substantive agent/self, ironically, and vanishes upon its attainment of that goal.

Notes

1. Buddhist scholars have only begun to discuss free will over the past 50 years, in conversation with Western philosophers. See Repetti (2010a, 2012a, 2012b, 2014) for in-depth reviews of most of this literature; see Repetti (2016a) for a representative collection of this literature.
2. Some of my observations here are taken from Repetti (2016b).
3. See Garfield (2014/2016), Gowans (2014, 2016), Flanagan (2016), Repetti (2016c). See Strawson (2016) and Blackmore (2016) on the realization of that reality.
4. Goodman (2002) argues along similar lines.
5. Not all forms of libertarianism require supramundane conceptions. Meyers (2014, 2016) claims Buddhism is logically consistent with the more naturalistic "event-causal" libertarianism, and Wallace (2011/2016) describes enlightened action in a way that resembles libertarian descriptions (*infra*), his rejection of the strong conception of free will notwithstanding.
6. Federman (2010) compares critiques of the dualistic Cartesian model of the self with Buddhist critiques of the then-prevalent view of the *ātman* (self/soul).

7. Goodman (2002) and Wallace (2011/2016) may be interpreted as objecting to this equation, but Repetti (2012b, 2014) notes that the relevant element of resemblance—inevitability—suffices to show that the Buddha was not an inevitablist and that this is reason enough to think he was not a *hard* determinist. See also Federman (2010).

8. Frankfurt (1971) would consider this volitional/metavolitional harmony sufficient for compatibilist free will and moral responsibility. For a fusion of Frankfurt's hierarchical model and Fischer's reason-responsiveness model with features of *ārya* agency, see Repetti (2010b).

9. See Thakchoe (2007) for a comprehensive analysis and explication of the two truths doctrine.

10. See Repetti (2012a, 2012b) for critiques of these attempts.

11. See Cozort (1986) on Tibetan deity yoga.

12. For an in-depth critique of Goodman's (2002) earlier position, see Repetti (2012b).

13. For an extensive critical review of Siderits's arguments, see Repetti (2012a).

14. I have argued (Repetti, 2010b) that the sort of freedom constituted by enlightenment involves freedom from the otherwise conditioned nature of the ego-volitional complex, or freedom from the self, and that Frankfurt's metavolitional/volitional model of freedom of will may be usefully applied to identify the sort of self-regulative abilities that increase as the *ārya* cultivates dharmic intentions and deconditions from adharmic ones.

15. See Harvey (2007) for a rich discussion of a spectrum of like cases taken from the Pāli canon.

References

Aaronson, H. B. (2004). *Buddhist practice on Western ground: Reconciling Eastern ideals and Western psychology*. London: Shambhala.

Abelson, B. (2016). Shifting coalitions, free will, and the responsibility of persons. In R. Repetti (Ed.), *Buddhist perspectives on free will: Agentless agency?* (pp. 148–157). London: Routledge/Francis & Taylor.

Adam, M. (2010). No self, no free will, no problem: Implications of the *Anattalakkhana Sutta* for a perennial philosophical issue. *Journal of the International Association of Buddhist Studies, 33,* 239–265.

Adam, M. (2016). Degrees of freedom: The Buddha's views on the (im)possibility of free will. In R. Repetti (Ed.), *Buddhist perspectives on free will: Agentless agency?* (pp. 123–132). London: Routledge/Francis & Taylor.

Blackmore, S. (2016). Living without free will. In R. Repetti (Ed.), *Buddhist perspectives on free will: Agentless agency?* (pp. 84–91). London: Routledge/Francis & Taylor.

Caruso, G. (Ed.). (2013). *Exploring the illusion of free will and moral responsibility*. New York: Lexington Books.

Coseru, C. (2012). *Perceiving reality: Consciousness, intentionality, and cognition in Buddhist philosophy.* New York: Oxford University Press.

Coseru, C. (2016). Freedom from responsibility: Agent-neutral consequentialism and the bodhisattva ideal. In R. Repetti (Ed.), *Buddhist perspectives on free will: Agentless agency?* (pp. 92–105). London: Routledge/Francis & Taylor.

Cozort, D. (1986). *Highest yoga tantra: An introduction to the esoteric Buddhism of Tibet.* Boulder, CO: Snow Lion.

Federman, A. (2010). What kind of free will did the Buddha teach? *Philosophy East and West, 60*(1), 1–19.

Fischer, J. M. (Ed.). (1989). *God, freedom, and foreknowledge.* Stanford: Stanford University Press.

Fischer, J. M. (2006). *My way: Essays on moral responsibility.* New York: Oxford University Press.

Flanagan, O. (2016). Negative dialectics in comparative philosophy: The case of Buddhist free will quietism. In R. Repetti (Ed.), *Buddhist perspectives on free will: Agentless agency?* (pp. 59–71). London: Routledge/Francis & Taylor.

Frankfurt, H. (1969). Alternate possibilities and moral responsibility. *Journal of Philosophy, 66*(23), 829–839.

Frankfurt, H. (1971). Freedom of the will and the concept of the person. *Journal of Philosophy, 68,* 5–20.

Friquegnon, M. (2016). Buddhism and free will. In R. Repetti (Ed.), *Buddhist perspectives on free will: Agentless agency?* (pp. 106–112). London: Routledge/Francis & Taylor.

Garfield, J. (2001). Nagarjuna's theory of causality: Implications sacred and profane. *Philosophy East and West, 51*(4), 507–524.

Garfield, J. (2014). Just another word for nothing left to lose: Freedom of the will in Madhyamaka. In M. R. Dasti & E. F. Bryant (Eds.), *Free will, agency and selfhood in Indian philosophy* (pp. 164–185). New York: Oxford University Press. Reprinted in R. Repetti (Ed.), *Buddhist perspectives on free will: Agentless agency?* (pp. 45–58). London: Routledge/Francis & Taylor, 2016.

Garfield, J. (2015). *Engaging Buddhism: Why it matters to philosophy.* New York: Oxford University Press.

Gier, N. F., & Kjellberg, P. (2004). Buddhism and the freedom of the will: Pali and Mahayanist responses. In J. K. Campbell, M. O'Rourke, & D. Shier (Eds.), *Freedom and determinism* (pp. 277–304). Cambridge, MA: MIT Press.

Gómez, L. O. (1975, January). Some aspects of the free-will question in the Nikāyas. *Philosophy East & West, 25*(1), 81–90.

Goodman, C. (2002). Resentment and reality: Buddhism on moral responsibility. *American Philosophical Quarterly, 39*(4), 359–372.

Goodman, C. (2009). *Consequences of compassion: An interpretation and defense of Buddhist ethics.* New York: Oxford University Press.

Goodman, C. (2016). Uses of the illusion of agency: Why some Buddhists should believe in free will. In R. Repetti (Ed.), *Buddhist perspectives on free will: Agentless agency?* (pp. 34–44). London: Routledge/Francis & Taylor.

Gowans, C. (2014). *Buddhist moral philosophy: An introduction.* London: Routledge.

Gowans, C. (2016). Why the Buddha did not discuss "the problem of free will and determinism." In R. Repetti (Ed.), *Buddhist perspectives on free will: Agentless agency?* (pp. 11–21). London: Routledge/Francis & Taylor.

Griffiths, P. J. (1982). Notes toward a Buddhist critique of karmic theory. *Religious Studies, 18*, 277–291.

Harvey, P. (2000). *An introduction to Buddhist ethics: Foundations, values and issues.* Cambridge, UK: Cambridge University Press.

Harvey, P. (2007). "Freedom of the will" in the light of Theravāda Buddhist teachings. *Journal of Buddhist Ethics, 14*, 35–98.

Harvey, P. (2016). Psychological versus metaphysical agents: A Theravāda Buddhist view of free will and moral responsibility. In R. Repetti (Ed.), *Buddhist perspectives on free will: Agentless agency?* (pp. 158–169). London: Routledge/Francis & Taylor.

Heim, M. (2014). *The forerunner of all things: Buddhaghosa on mind, intention, and agency.* New York: Oxford University Press.

Kalupahana, D. J. (1976). *Buddhist philosophy: A historical analysis.* Honolulu: University of Hawaii Press.

Kalupahana, D. J. (1992). *A history of Buddhist philosophy: Continuities and discontinuities.* Honolulu: University of Hawaii Press.

Kalupahana, D. J. (1995). *Ethics in early Buddhism.* Honolulu: University of Hawaii Press.

Kasulis, T. P. (1985). *Zen action, Zen person.* Honolulu: University of Hawaii Press.

McRae, E. (2012). A passionate Buddhist life. *Journal of Religious Ethics, 40*(1), 99–121.

McRae, E. (2015). Metabolizing anger: A Tantric Buddhist solution to the problem of moral anger. *Philosophy East & West, 65*(2), 466–484.

McRae, E. (2016). Emotions and choice: Lessons from Tsongkhapa. In R. Repetti (Ed.), *Buddhist perspectives on free will: Agentless agency?* (pp. 170–181). London: Routledge/Francis & Taylor.

Meyers, K. (2014). Free persons, empty selves: Freedom and agency in light of the two truths. In M. R. Dasti & E. F. Bryant (Eds.), *Free will, agency, and selfhood in Indian philosophy* (pp. 41–67). New York: Oxford University Press.

Meyers, K. (2016). Grasping snakes: Reflections on free will, *samādhi*, and *dharmas.* In R. Repetti (Ed.), *Buddhist perspectives on free will: Agentless agency?* (pp. 182–192). London: Routledge/Francis & Taylor.

Pereboom, D. (2001). *Living without free will.* Cambridge, UK: Cambridge University Press.

Rāhula, W. (1974). *What the Buddha taught.* New York: Grove Press.

Repetti, R. (2010a). Earlier Buddhist theories of free will: Compatibilism. *Journal of Buddhist Ethics, 17*, 279–310.

Repetti, R. (2010b). Meditation and mental freedom: A Buddhist theory of free will. *Journal of Buddhist Ethics, 17*, 165–212.

Repetti, R. (2012a). Buddhist reductionism and free will: Paleo-compatibilism. *Journal of Buddhist Ethics, 19*, 33–95.

Repetti, R. (2012b). Buddhist hard determinism: No self, no free will, no responsibility. *Journal of Buddhist Ethics, 19*, 130–197.

Repetti, R. (2014). Recent Buddhist theories of free will: Compatibilism and incompatibilism. *Journal of Buddhist Ethics, 21*, 279–352.

Repetti, R. (2015, October). Buddhist meditation and the possibility of free will. *Science, Religion & Culture, 2*(2), 81–98.

Repetti, R (Ed.). (2016a). *Buddhist perspectives on free will: Agentless agency?* London: Routledge/Francis & Taylor.

Repetti, R. (2016b). Hermeneutical koan: What is the sound of one Buddhist theory of free will? In R. Repetti (Ed.), *Buddhist perspectives on free will: Agentless agency?* (pp. 1–10). London: Routledge/Francis & Taylor.

Repetti, R. (2016c). Why there ought to be a Buddhist theory of free will. In R. Repetti (Ed.), *Buddhist perspectives on free will: Agentless agency?* (pp. 22–33). London: Routledge/Francis & Taylor.

Repetti, R. (2016d). Agentless agency: The soft compatibilist argument from Buddhist meditation, mind-mastery, evitabilism, and mental freedom. In R. Repetti (Ed.), *Buddhist perspectives on free will: Agentless agency?* (pp. 193–206). London: Routledge/Francis & Taylor.

Siderits, M. (1987). Beyond compatibilism: A Buddhist approach to freedom and determinism. *American Philosophical Quarterly, 24*(2), 149–159.

Siderits, M. (2003). *Personal identity and Buddhist philosophy: Empty persons.* Aldershot, UK: Ashgate.

Siderits, M. (2008). Paleo-compatibilism and Buddhist reductionism. *Sophia, 47*(1), 29–42. Reprinted in R. Repetti (Ed.), *Buddhist perspectives on free will: Agentless agency?* (pp. 133–147). London: Routledge/Francis & Taylor, 2016.

Story, F. (1976). *Dimensions of Buddhist thought: Essays and dialogues.* Kandy, Sri Lanka: Buddhist Publication Society.

Strawson, G. (1986). *Freedom and belief.* New York: Oxford University Press.

Strawson, G. (1994). The impossibility of moral responsibility. *Philosophical Studies, 75*(1–2), 5–24.

Strawson, G. (2016). Free will and the sense of self. In R. Repetti (Ed.), *Buddhist perspectives on free will: Agentless agency?* (pp. 72–83). London: Routledge/Francis & Taylor.

Strawson, P. F. (1962). Freedom and resentment. *Proceedings of the British Academy, 48*, 1–25.

Thakchoe, S. (2007). *The two truths debate: Tsongkhapa and Gorampa on the middle way.* Boston: Wisdom.

Wallace, B. A. (2011). A Buddhist view of free will: Beyond determinism and indeterminism. *Journal of Consciousness Studies, 18*(3–4), 21–33. Reprinted in R. Repetti (Ed.), *Buddhist perspectives on free will: Agentless agency?* (pp. 113–122). London: Routledge/Francis & Taylor, 2016.

Chapter 15

Buddhist Reductionist Action Theory

Mark Siderits

15.1. Introduction

Given the growing interest in Buddhist ethics, it would be nice if there were a fully worked-out Buddhist action theory. But just as there may be nothing in the Buddhist tradition that matches what we now call ethical theory, so we might find little on this score either. The tradition has much to say about ethical matters, and likewise for actions. Abhidharma controversies concerning the machinery of karma, for instance, are a rich source of insights into Buddhist views concerning the nature of agency. But a complete action theory would begin by specifying which ontological category actions belong to and how they are related to other entities and events. It would address such questions as whether the agent's reason for performing an action can count as the cause of an action, and under what circumstances the performance of an action renders its agent justifiably subject to praise or blame. Action theory is best thought of as a branch of metaphysics, but it has important connections to ethics, meta-ethics, and philosophical psychology. Recent developments in action theory have made important contributions to work on such issues as determinism and moral responsibility, how akratic action might be possible, and what constitutes an adequate explanation of an event. Since these issues may not have been explicitly thematized within classical Indian philosophy, it would not be surprising if the Buddhist tradition lacked a full-blown action theory. Still, just as scholars have begun to develop what they take to be Buddhist ethical theory, it might prove instructive to see if a Buddhist action theory could be developed based on what one does find in the tradition.

Developing such a theory might help refine our understanding of Buddhist thought. Moreover it might show how resources from the Buddhist philosophical tradition can contribute to current debates in philosophy. This seems possible given that virtually all Indian Buddhist philosophers are committed to the reducibility, and thus the ultimate nonexistence, of an agent. As Buddhaghosa puts it, "Ultimately all things are to be known as empty [of self] due to the absence of a cognizer, an agent, one who is released and a goer," quoting in support a verse he treats as authoritative:

> *There is suffering but none who suffer,*
> *There is action but no agent,*
> *There is nirvāṇa but no one who is released,*
> *There is a Path [to release] but no goer on it.* (Vism. XVI.90)[1]

Since it seems to be a conceptual truth that an action is an event that involves an agent, how is it possible for there to be actions if there are no agents? Working out an action theory for a Buddhist Reductionist view like that of the Sautrāntikas might suggest novel approaches to some of the issues that action theory is thought to address.[2] Indeed I believe that such a theory points to a novel strategy for resolving the debate over determinism and moral responsibility. But an action theory that dispenses altogether with agents might be of some interest in its own right.

Developing such a theory from scratch would be a major undertaking, but there is reason to think that some of the work has already been done. Recently E. J. Lowe (2008) has developed an action theory that arguably comes close to what might be deemed the folk theory of action. Since this theory holds that actions are agent-involving, it would not be acceptable to Buddhist Reductionists as an account of the ultimate truth. But if it succeeded as a regimentation of the folk view of actions, it might serve as an account of what they call the conventional truth. And an investigation of the account of causation that underlies Lowe's views concerning agency might then pave the way to working out what the Buddhist should say is the ultimate truth about actions. This is the course I shall follow. I begin by discussing some passages that articulate a Buddhist Reductionist stance with respect to action and agency. I shall then describe Lowe's view and discuss how it might work as part of what Buddhists call conventional truth. This will lead to a discussion of how these two quite different views of action might form parts of a unified theory. I shall end by indicating what this might say about the dispute between compatibilists and libertarians over moral responsibility.

15.2. Actions without Agents

In "The Investigation of the Self" Vasubandhu considers various objections to the Buddhist nonself position.[3] From among these, two stand out as particularly germane here, both involving the assumption that there is karma. The first is that without a self there would be nothing to serve as agent, something action (*karman*) requires. The second is that without a self there would be nothing to serve as the subject of experiences, and karma requires that there be a reaper of the fruit—an experiencer of the pleasant and unpleasant experiences produced by earlier actions. Both objections rely on the theory of grammatical cases (*kāraka*) of the Grammarian school. According to this theory, grammaticality requires that where there is the occurrence of a verb there be a noun phrase in the nominative case. Now an action is denoted by a verb, and in the case of verbs of action the noun phrase in the nominative case refers to a sentient being. Since the nominative case expresses subjecthood, it follows that all actions require sentient beings that perform them, that is, agents. This holds equally for such paradigm instances of action as walking, and for what we might think of as "mental acts" such as cognizing.[4]

In replying to both objections Vasubandhu makes use of the point that the demands of grammar need not dictate our final ontology. This seems reasonable. We agree that the "it" of "It is raining" is a dummy subject without reference and inserted only because the grammar of English demands a subject; in Japanese, "Raining" counts as syntactically complete. But Vasubandhu goes further. Using the Buddhist distinction between the two truths, he claims that all talk of persons is a mere shorthand device for referring to a causal series of psychophysical elements. Forgetful of the fact that the series is a conceptual construction, we end up taking the device to really refer. Since the device is useful in daily life, we may say that the entity it ostensibly refers to—the person—is conventionally real. But only the causally connected psychophysical elements are ultimately real, and it is facts about these that explain the (limited) utility of the personhood concept. This is why Vasubandhu repeatedly cites the causal series as what is really denoted by some expression that seems to denote the person. He does not want to claim that the person is identical with the causal series, any more than we would say that the "it" is identical with the raining. His point is rather that once we know all the facts about the psychophysical elements and their causal connections, we will see why the conventional mode of discourse has proven so useful.

Its usefulness is illustrated elsewhere, in *Milindapañha*,[5] with the examples of the mother, the student, and the criminal. Suppose we agree with the Buddhist that in the life of a person there is no enduring self or "soul-pellet," that at any time there is just a set of impermanent, interconnected psycho-physical elements, and that each moment one set goes out of existence but causes a replacement set to arise. The claim is that by thinking of such a se-ries as a single entity, the person, we facilitate a process of "appropriation" or identification that is welfare-enhancing. Take the case of the set of elements in a causal series we would describe as a woman who has just learned of her pregnancy. Having been socialized into our convention of thinking of a causal series as one enduring person, these elements will think of their successors as "me with my baby." This will in turn foster present behavior that, by promot-ing long-term maternal and fetal health, brings about greater overall welfare. Likewise for the cases of the student and the criminal.

Of course the Buddhist insists that in all these cases the person that is believed in is no more than a useful fiction, a many masquerading as a one. Given the obvious utility of the practice of thinking of such a causal series as a person, one might wonder why the Buddhist is so insistent that there is an error involved here. The Buddhist's answer is that our personhood con-cept causes the existential suffering that inevitably poisons ordinary lives. The Buddha's discovery of a path to the cessation of such suffering consisted in finding a way to undo those cognitive and affective habits that perpetuate the intuitive sense of "I" and "mine." The goal is to learn how to reap the benefits of our personhood convention while avoiding the suffering that ordinarily results from its use.

Returning now to Vasubandhu's reply to the objections, he questions the opponent's account of agency. In response to the opponent's statement that the agent is that of which "acts" is said, he says this is a mere paraphrase and not an analysis of the meaning of "agent." The opponent replies that lexicogra-phers define the agent as one who does something autonomously, giving the examples of Devadatta's bathing, sitting, and going. Vasubandhu responds with a destructive dilemma: Either the agent is the self, an impartite enduring entity, or it is the person, understood as the enduring but partite entity con-stituted by the psychophysical elements. The first alternative is ruled out on two grounds: There is no evidence of the existence of anything like a simple soul-pellet, and a simple enduring entity could not serve as efficient cause of any event. The argument for the latter claim is likely the one developed by Śāntideva at BCA 6.29–30: Something that is permanent by virtue of being simple cannot undergo any changes, and the exercise of causal power would involve change on the part of the substance that has that power.

Concerning the alternative that the agent is partite, Vasubandhu points out that there are three kinds of action: bodily, verbal, and mental. Suppose the agent is constituted by the five *skandhas*. None of these can be autonomous in the relevant sense. Bodily action, for instance, depends on mental activity, and mental action likewise depends on bodily causes.[6] As for verbal action, since it has both bodily and mental components, it occurs dependent on both bodily and mental *skandhas*. So in none of the three cases can we locate something that acts autonomously; the action is the result of a train of causes that starts elsewhere.

Vasubandhu says as much when he describes what actually happens in the production of an action: "Desire is born of memory, deliberation is born of desire, from deliberation there is effort, from effort there is breath, from that there is action, what does a self do here?" (AKBh 477).[7] This account has it that a casual series of mental events triggers a physical event (the movement of air thought to initiate muscular movement) and thus causes the action. The springs of action can be traced back in time through a series of events that reveal nothing like an autonomous unmoved mover. What the Buddha calls *cetanā*, the choosing that is said to be distinctive of action as opposed to mere bodily movement (see Gombrich, 2009, pp. 49–50, 123–124), is one more event in a causal series of events, with nothing like an agent as its cause.

That this list begins with memory might make one wonder whether Vasubandhu has succeeded in avoiding any commitment to a substantial agent. Just this question was raised earlier in the text by another opponent (a Personalist): How can there be memory in the absence of an enduring subject of experience? (AKBh 472). The sort of episodic memory that can give rise to desire seems to require identity between something involved in the present remembering and something involved in the experience remembered. When the memory of an earlier experience of tasting a mango triggers present desire for a mango, it is because the pleasure of that experience is taken as connected to the elements presently involved in remembering in an especially intimate way. This intimate connection we think derives from the identity of the subject of the earlier pleasure and the subject of the present remembering. The thought is that since nothing else involved in the earlier experience is to be found in the present remembering, and this intimate connection is absent in the case of distinct persons, there must be some persisting entity, distinct from the impermanent *skandhas*, the diachronic identity of which grounds the intimate connection.

Vasubandhu rejects this inference. He claims that the basis of our thinking there is a subject of a mental act is the causal series the transformation of which led to the occurrence of that act. And since a series is a many, taking this as a persisting entity is taking a mere figure of speech too literally. When we say "Caitra remembers tasting a mango," what makes this true is that the present mango-remembering episode is the latest member of a causal series of psychophysical elements that includes an earlier mango-tasting episode, with the latter playing an important role in the production of the former. The opponent asks why in that case we use the genitive "Caitra's memory." Vasubandhu replies that the possession relation is also to be understood in terms of causation. We say "Caitra's cow" when Caitra is able to use the cow for transporting goods or for producing milk. Such use amounts to control, which may be analyzed in terms of causal relations between events in the "Caitra" series and the "cow" series. But it is also unclear that the possession relation could hold in the case of such basic mental events as memory. We ordinarily think of control as involving some purpose on the part of the controller: Caitra owns the cow so that he can transport his goods or produce ghee. But when Vasubandhu asks the opponent the purpose of memory, the best they can come up with is "to remember." We might think that we remember in order to be guided by our past experience, but this is not true in the case of spontaneous memory.

The opponent now proposes that the cognition is the subject of the activity of cognizing. Vasubandhu responds, "Cognition does nothing, it merely arises in conformity with its object" (AKBh 473–474). To say that a cognition cognizes its object is just to say that there arises a cognition whose form resembles that of the object involved in the immediately preceding moment of sense-object contact. At this level of description our tendency to seek an agent behind the occurrence of an event is clearly driven by our mode of description, not by what is actually observed. The opponent retorts that cognizing is a property, and every property requires a property possessor. Vasubandhu replies that while this rule might reflect our conventional linguistic practice, it violates the ontological scruples behind the principle of parsimony. The bundle-theoretic approach he subscribes to as the ultimate truth avoids all commitment to enduring substances, while at the same time explaining the commonsense conviction that enduring substances are the basic building blocks of reality.

It is well known that Vasubandhu's bundle-theoretic approach enables him to replace a substance-property ontology with a more austere trope-theoretic approach.[8] This is what stands behind his insistence that neither Caitra nor the cow ultimately exists. What has been less remarked is that the conception of causation Vasubandhu deploys is not that of common sense. The causal relation cannot be understood as a matter of a substance exercising its causal power to produce an effect. There being no substances, they cannot be what does the producing. But neither can the ultimately real tropes—at least not if production is taken as the exercise of a causal power.

Elsewhere in AKBh Vasubandhu disputes the Vaibhāṣika's claim that all three times exist (the *sarvāstivāda* doctrine). A key question is whether the efficacy of an ultimate real is distinct from its intrinsic nature. Vasubandhu denies its distinctness based on the point that a productive power must both be found in the particular to which it is attributed and also be seen to give rise to the effect (*phaladānagrahaṇa*). This, Vasubandhu points out, makes the power something that, absurdly, "exists half in the present." His point is that, given that cause precedes effect and that everything is momentary, a causal power could link cause and effect only if it had temporal parts: one part existing when the cause exists, the other when the effect exists. Given Vasubandhu's mereological nihilism, according to which anything made of spatially or analytically separable parts is not ultimately real, productive powers could only be conceptual fictions.[9] What, then, is causation, according to Vasubandhu? There being nothing like a productive power that ties together the present event and the prior aggregate of events that we call its cause, it can only be a matter of regular succession between event-types. Or as the Buddha put it, "This occurring, that comes to be; in the absence of this, that does not arise."

15.3. Lowe on Agency

So far we have seen how a Buddhist Reductionist like Vasubandhu defends the claim that there are ultimately actions but no agents. An action appears to be nothing more than the occurrence of a particular sort of mental event, one that is regularly preceded by occurrences of cognition and desire and regularly succeeded by occurrences of bodily, mental, or verbal behavior. But Vasubandhu provides no more than hints about the conventional truth concerning action and agency.[10] Here is where I think Lowe's account of action, agency, and causation can help. This may seem odd, since Lowe denies that causation is necessarily event causation; his view is that all talk of event causation is shorthand for talk of substance causation: to say that the explosion caused the collapse of the bridge is short for saying the bomb's exploding—an exercise of a power possessed by the bomb—caused the collapse of the bridge. More generally he holds that an event can count as the cause of another event only if it can be thought of as the exercise of some power of a substance. There cannot be causation in any serious sense in a pure event ontology, since events are themselves powerless: "They are mere changes in things and not the sources of those changes" (Lowe, 2008, p. 165). Yet the Sautrāntika ontology is precisely a pure event ontology: their ultimate reals are just the momentary occurrences of tropes. Vasubandhu's strictures against powers depend on just this point. Yet Vasubandhu holds nonetheless that the ultimate reals stand in causal relations. This looks like an irreconcilable difference.

However, a reconciliation is possible using the Buddhist Reductionist device of the two truths, conventional and ultimate. The strategy here is as follows: First, Lowe's views about causation can be seen as articulating a commonsense view about how things in the world work, a view with a long history of successful use. Second, despite this pedigree, the view cannot represent how things ultimately or mind-independently are, since it involves conceptual construction. Ultimately causation can only be a matter of constant conjunction of event-types. Third, Lowe's claim that all event causation reduces to substance causation is, though, conventionally true. This means we can accept his claim for this restricted sphere of application. Note, however, that for this reconciliation to succeed, the restrictions on the range of Lowe's account cannot be ad hoc but must be principled: there must be what I call semantic insulation between the two truths.

Substances are fundamental in Lowe's ontology. A substance is an independent, persisting bearer of properties, and there is no property without a bearer. Among the properties of a substance are its causal powers. For instance, every physical object has among its properties the power of gravitational attraction. When the earth exercises this power by causing a hailstone to fall, the earth is then acting on the hailstone. As this example makes clear, Lowe does not confine his use of "action" to cases in which an animate substance brings about a substance-involving event. In this he probably conforms to commonsense usage, as well as to the views of the Grammarians discussed earlier. But the concern of action theory is with events brought about by such substances as persons. Lowe shares this concern. His chief aim is to delineate just what personal agency is. His analysis is as follows: Among the person's principal powers is the will. The expression of this power is an instance of willing. And a person's actions, such as the raising of an arm, consists in the person's causing, by way of an instance of willing, what Lowe calls an "action-result," such as the rising of the person's arm. The terminology of "action-result" is meant to underline the point that persons should not be said to cause their actions, lest there result an infinite regress. Action-results correspond to the sense of an intransitive verb (e.g., "rise"), while actions are associated with transitive verbs (e.g., "raise"): The action we call a raising of the arm consists in the event of the arm's rising being caused by the owner of the arm by way of their willing to raise their arm.

An occurrence of willing is an event in the history of a person, but it should not be thought of as an action of the person. A person's actions are those events the person brings about by way of expressions of their power of the will. (The Grammarians discussed earlier would approve of the use of the instrumental "by way of" and would point out that the entity denoted by the instrumental case is never the entity denoted by the verb, namely the action.) This power is different from the powers of other substances in several important ways. First, it is not a causal power, in that its manifestation is not itself sufficient for the occurrence of the intended effect: one can will to raise one's arm only to discover that one is paralyzed. Second, it is what Lowe calls a spontaneous power in that its exercise is not caused by prior events. Here Lowe's libertarianism becomes evident. Convinced by the dating problem that the standard model of agent causation cannot be made to work,[11] Lowe adopts a form of volitionism, according to which it is volitions or willings that are causally efficacious in personal agency. While these events typically bring about distinct effects, they lack causally sufficient antecedents. In response to the standard objection to such "unmoved movings"—that this makes the exercise of personal agency utterly random and thus hardly rational—Lowe responds that in deliberate or voluntary agency the person exercises their power of willing in the light of the reasons they understand themselves to have.

Here Lowe follows Searle's (2001) approach to the issue of "reasons vs. causes." Searle claims that reasons explanations of events differ from causal explanations in that the former involve a gap between explanans and explanandum that is not present in the latter. A successful causal explanation of an event states sufficient conditions for its occurrence. But when the event is an action I have performed and I explain its occurrence by giving the reasons that led me to perform it, I do not take myself to have stated causally sufficient conditions for its taking place. Even though I may typically take the reasons I had as good and compelling reasons for doing as I did, I still take there to have been alternatives genuinely open to me—that, in some robust sense of "could," I could have done otherwise. While Searle and Lowe differ on a number of key points, they concur in their rejection of Davidson's assimilation of reasons to causes. Davidson claimed that actions are caused by the agent's reasons, in the form of their beliefs and desires. Lowe and Searle both respond that to say an agent's belief or desire caused an action is precisely to say that the action is not the agent's own, not something that was up to the agent and for which the agent can be held to account. It is just when the agent's rational control faculty has been overridden that we may look to invoke psychological states of the agent as having caused the action.

Lowe and Searle part ways over the issue of mental causation, and thus over the ways in which consideration of reasons might be said to influence the formation of volitions. But the details of their disagreement needn't concern us here. Suffice it to say that they both want to preserve the phenomenology of deliberating and choosing, with its gap between reasons and volition. This means we must take volitions to lack causally sufficient antecedent conditions.

It also requires that we posit a self with certain formal properties: it must persist through time, be conscious, be the subject of experiences, have beliefs and desires and the capacity to deliberate, and have the spontaneous, rational power of willing. For Lowe this yields a requirement that the self be a simple emergent substance, something distinct from the body and yet co-located with it. Its being emergent is said to follow from its having causal powers that "complement" and "supplement" those of the body; its powers are neither reducible to the body's powers nor independent of those powers (Lowe, 2008, p. 92). This is not Cartesian dualism in that the self also has physical properties, albeit only in virtue of its having a body with physical properties. Among the bodily properties that the self does *not* have is that of being partite (composed of parts). While all other macrophysical objects are complex, the self is simple or impartite (p. 168). Lowe supports this claim with a version of the too-many-subjects argument (see Merricks, 2001, pp. 89–114).

I said earlier that Lowe's view might work as an articulation of what the Buddhist Reductionist would call the conventional truth about human agency. Now that we have seen what Lowe's view amounts to, we should test this claim. One objection would be that if by "conventional truth" is meant what is nowadays called a folk theory, and this is understood to mean the theory subscribed to by most folk most of the time, then since most people would at best be baffled by such claims as that the self is simple or that volitions are the exercise of a spontaneous power, Lowe's view cannot count as the conventional truth concerning human agency. The question, though, is whether anything could possibly count as a folk theory, if by a theory we mean a set of highly general propositions that help explain and predict phenomena of some sort. We might agree that people think of personal agency as involving voluntary behavior, yet still wonder whether this amounts to commitment to the view that the volitions that cause behavior are spontaneous exercises of a power of the person. Similar questions led Buddhist Reductionists to distinguish the philosophers' notion of a self, or *ātman*, from the far more widespread but inchoate notion that "I" and "mine" are meaningful expressions. Their point was that refuting the former is not the same thing as dispelling the "I"-sense at work in the latter. But this dispute might be circumvented by specifying that what we seek is an articulation of commitments that may be only tacit in what people say about human agency. The claim would then be that while most people may initially be puzzled by, for instance, the statement that the self is simple, they could be brought to acknowledge that this represents a consequence of what they do say about human agency. That this is Lowe's aspiration is suggested by his likening his project to that of P. F. Strawson's *Individuals*, a work the subtitle of which is *An essay in descriptive metaphysics*.[12]

The question then is whether Lowe's view succeeds as a descriptive metaphysics of human agency. This is at least partly an empirical question, so results from the social sciences may be relevant. One recent development in cognitive science is dual-systems theory, according to which humans possess two distinct cognitive systems, called by Haidt (2001) the intuitive system and the reasoning system, but the "low-road" and "high-road" systems by others.[13] The first system runs automatically at the subpersonal level before it delivers its results to consciousness. Since it does not demand attentional resources, it is relatively fast and effortless. The second system is intentional, involving conscious access and control, and is therefore far slower and more effortful. But it is also less reliant on pattern matching and thus more analytical in nature. The working hypothesis is that the low-road system is common to at least many social mammals and may represent an adaptation for rapidly solving problems the organism frequently encountered in its environment of evolutionary adaptation. The high-road system, by contrast, may be unique to language users. Differences in the processing speeds of the two systems allow researchers to determine whether a given judgment was reached using one or the other cognitive process. And research suggests that Lowe's model conforms to the sorts of judgments that are delivered by the low-road system. There is, for instance, research suggesting that the low-road approach supports the substance-causation model of causation, while the high-road approach supports the event-causation model (Fiala, Arico, & Nichols, 2012, pp. 103–104). There is also research showing that when snap judgments of moral responsibility are preceded by unrelated discussions of the causal mechanisms involved in brain processes, subjects tend to assign a lesser degree of culpability for reprehensible behavior,[14] thereby suggesting that low-road processes would support the contention that there is a causal gap between reasons and volition. If it is plausible to hold that widely shared intuitions in such an area reflect the workings of low-road cognitive processes, this would be evidence that Lowe's view does capture something like the folk theory of human agency.

15.4. Reconciling the Two Accounts

What I have just claimed is that what Buddhist Reductionists call the conventional truth about human agency may be supported by the output of a low-road cognitive system. The next step is to claim that their ultimate truth about action is the product of a high-road system. This they would surely accept, given that the high-road system is characterized as analytical and the Buddhist

Reductionist justification of their conception of the ultimate truth is that it concerns just those entities discovered through analysis. But supposing this is right, we now have two cognitive systems with conflicting outputs. How is this conflict to be resolved? The Buddhist Reductionist will say that the algorithms, stereotypes, and other cognitive shortcuts in the system of conventional truth lead to errors avoided by the high-road system of ultimate truth. Shortcuts may work most of the time, but they cannot be relied on to work all the time. Lowe might retort that his own account was arrived at through philosophical rationality, something both sides recognize as less prone to error. The response will be that Lowe's arguments appeal to intuitions contaminated by the deliveries of the low-road system. So the conflict is to be resolved in favor of what Buddhists call ultimate truth.

Still, it is accepted by all that we would not be able to get on with ordinary life if we had to forgo all use of the theories that make up conventional truth. I indicated earlier that according to the best version of the ultimate truth, a substance is a mere conceptual fiction that is reducible without remainder to a causal series of bundles of tropes. Suppose that in order to refer to our present location we could not use the substance-term "chair" and instead had to specify each of the many tropes making up the present bundle and how they are causally related to the members of prior bundles. This would not prove easy. Not only is conventional truth more convenient to use, but it has been crowdsourced over countless generations and so is not likely to lead us far astray in most everyday matters. Of course the Buddhist claims that conventional truth's endorsement of the "I"-sense leads to disastrous error, in the form of existential suffering. Still it must be conceded that the fiction of the "I" has its uses. And this is what lies behind calling all such talk conventional *truth*: the idea is that we can escape existential suffering and yet continue to use our commonsense ways of thinking of the world provided we see its concepts for the mere useful fictions they are. This way of talking is good enough for most purposes of ordinary life.

The upshot is that we will have two different ways of talking about the world: a conventional discourse containing terms for persons and other macrophysical objects, their properties, and their powers, and an ultimate discourse containing terms for tropes and their relations. For every statement deemed true in the first discourse, there will be some (far longer) true statement in the second discourse that explains the utility of our acceptance of the first statement. Only the second statement is really true, that is, corresponds to the way things mind-independently are. But the first is acceptable in ordinary circumstances provided it is not taken too seriously.

This rapprochement is a delicate matter, however. Consider how a Buddhist Reductionist might use their distinction between conventional and ultimate truth to express reductionism about such macrophysical objects as chairs: "While it is conventionally true that there are chairs, it is ultimately true that there are tropes arranged chair-wise; the conventional truth of statements about chairs supervenes on the ultimate truth of statements about tropes arranged chair-wise." Is this ultimately true or conventionally true? It cannot be ultimately true, for it contains an expression that refers to chairs. But neither can it be conventionally true, for it contains an expression that refers to tropes. No ultimately true statement can contain expressions that refer to chairs, and no conventionally true statement can contain expressions that refer to tropes. So this claim can be neither ultimately true nor conventionally true; instead it lacks meaning.[15]

This last point requires some defense. It is based on the idea that there is semantic insulation between ultimate truth and conventional truth: that statements referring to conventionally real things lack ultimate truth-value, and statements referring to ultimately real things lack conventional truth-value. Such insulation prevents bivalence failure. Suppose we allowed that statements that are about both chairs and tropes can be true. We would then be able to ask about the tropes that are arranged chair-wise in the region where a chair is located: Is the aggregate of tropes identical with the chair, or is it distinct? The aggregate is a many, while the chair is a one, so identity seems ruled out. But their distinctness leads to systematic causal overdetermination: everything thought of as caused by the chair can be accounted for by the tropes' causal efficacy. Moreover there are *sorites* difficulties lurking when we allow statements with mixed vocabulary. For then we should want to say that the tropes compose the chair. And suppose we removed randomly chosen tropes from the aggregate: at which removal would the chair cease to exist?[16]

To understand the ultimate reals as tropes is to embrace a substance-free ontology whose particulars are nothing but property occurrences. A chair, though, is a substance, and to accept the existence of substances is to hold that properties require bearers. This is the fundamental difficulty fueling the Buddhist's "neither identical nor distinct" argument for mereological nihilism: there is no acceptable way of bringing whole and ultimate parts into relation with one another given the radically different conceptual schemes in which they figure. This is masked, though, by the fact that we use the same word "yellow" for both the property borne by the substance and for the trope. There is equivocation involved in passing from the reduction of the chair to tropes to the thought that the chair is a mereological sum of the tropes. At the conventional level a substance cannot be the mere sum of the properties it bears, since those properties require a substance to serve as their bearer. The gestalt switch involved in going from one way of talking about the world to the other is concealed by our use of the ambiguous term "yellow."

15.5. "Creeping Exculpation"

When we apply this to the case of human action, we get a two-scheme theory that provides two distinct accounts of agency separated by semantic insulation.[17] And here is where I think a Buddhist Reductionist action theory shows promise. Consider how this might affect our understanding of the problem of determinism and moral responsibility (the so-called "free will" problem). The basic idea of a two-scheme approach is to reconcile compatibilist and libertarian positions by showing that each is correct in its own way. Buddhist paleo-compatibilism says it is ultimately true that all psychological events are causally determined, while it is conventionally true that it can be up to us what we choose to do.[18] The challenge a two-scheme approach faces lies in preventing the truth of one scheme from infecting that of the other. When Kant for instance installs libertarian freedom in the noumenal self, we cannot help but see this as indicating an important gap in scientific rationality. Likewise when a Buddhist paleo-compatibilist calls libertarian freedom part of the conventional truth, we may take this to mean that freedom is merely a useful illusion. Semantic insulation is meant to serve as an impermeable membrane that prevents such infection. And understanding why such insulation might be called for may help us see just how the infection actually occurs.

Consider what happens when we attempt to mix the two discourses—to speak of the person and the psychological events making up the causal series in the same breath. Suppose I have just decided how to cast my vote for representative. And suppose we understand this decision as a volition event that came about due to the prior occurrence of certain beliefs and desires. Now when we say that this is my decision or choosing, the "my" indicates that we are operating within a framework of substance causation: the volition is an expression of a power that inheres in me; it is my self that causes the event of the pushing of this rather than that voting machine button. Voting for this candidate is, we say, up to me. But when we try to combine this way of talking with one that sees my decision as a psychological event caused by earlier psychological events, we run into difficulties. For the causation involved must be either event causation or substance causation. If we understand it in terms of event causation, it begins to look as though the "I" is no more than a series of impersonal events, and all sense of agency is lost. But if we understand it in terms of substance causation, we find ourselves confronted with a variety of competitors for the role of "me" in the up-to-me-ness we seek. Suppose we say that when my desire caused the volition, then, since my desiring is likewise a manifestation of a power of my self, it is actually me and not the desire that is the cause; this would be in line with the claim that all event causation is reducible to substance causation. But then we would be saying I am the cause of my volition, something Lowe rightly calls the start of an infinite regress. The alternative would be to say that the desire is the expression of a power of some distinct substance—call it the id—and its causing the volition is its causing a will-involving event of volition by the id's desiring as it does. If the self is identical with the will, then there are two substances involved here; if not, then there are three. But in either event it is not me who brings about the vote but something else. This is how we find ourselves saying such things as "My amygdala made me do it." When we try to apply what we think of as a scientific understanding of information processing to our decidings, we wind up outsourcing the job.

What makes this difficult to see is that we use the same words at both levels of description. At both the conventional level and the ultimate level, we speak of the *belief*, the *desire*, the *intention*. This masks the fact that these terms mean different things in their occurrences in the two schemes. At the conventional level, a believing is the manifestation of a power of the self, the power to judge, the intellect. The believing is mine by virtue of this being how I judge. And the self, it must be remembered, is simple; the intellect is not to be construed as a part of the self but rather a faculty of the self—a way that the self can behave. At the ultimate level a believing is the occurrence of a trope of a sort that figures in certain regularities. Its being "mine" is just its occurring within a particular bundle of such regularities; there is no substance in which it inheres. When I called using the two discourses in the same breath a source of infection I was suggesting that this is a mistake. The mistake manifests itself in the sort of "creeping exculpation" that attends the scientific understanding of psychological processes.[19] Now we can see that the source of the infection is just equivocation: to infer "The agent was not responsible for the action" from "The action was causally determined by prior events" is fallacious, since "action" has quite different meanings in its two occurrences.

It will be evident that a two-scheme formulation of Buddhist Reductionist action theory will not be fully adequate—that more than just two kinds of truth are necessary to make it work. The earlier appeal to high-road and low-road cognitive processes in support of the distinction between the conventional and ultimate accounts of action relied on a neuroscientific approach to mental states

that does not fit well with Sautrāntika's property dualism, which is just as difficult to reconcile with the causal closure of the physical as is substance dualism.
One way around this difficulty might be to further reduce mental tropes to
bundles of physical tropes in such a way as to show why it would prove useful
for systems of a certain sort to posit mental events. Indeed given the variety of
successful reductions one now finds in the natural sciences, it is to be expected
that this would be just one of many layers in a multischeme hierarchy. Classical
Buddhist Reductionists were not aware of these developments in scientific
practice. Still they do gesture in the direction of something like such a hierarchy
when they say that what in a certain context counts as ultimate truth might in
some distinct context count as merely conventional truth that is reducible to a
deeper ultimate truth. This gives some reason to think that their system could
be adapted to suit our situation. A Buddhist Reductionist action theory might
turn out to be an interesting alternative to what is currently on offer.[20]

Abbreviations

AKBh *Abhidharmakośabhāṣyam of Vasubandhu.* In Vasubandhu (1975).
BCA   *Bodhicāryāvatāra of Śāntideva with the Commentary Pañjika of
      Prajñākaramati.* In Śāntideva (1960). Translations are my own.
Vism *Visuddhimagga.* In Buddhaghosa (1950).

Notes

1. *paramatthena hi sabhān'eva saccāni vedaja-kāraka-nibbuta-gamakābhāvato suññānī
   ti veditabbānī. ten'etaṃ vuccati:*

   > *dukkham eva hi, na koci dukkhito
   > kārako na, kirīyā va vijjati
   > atthi nibbuti, na nibbuto pumā
   > maggam atthi, gamako na vijjatī.*

2. For the term "Buddhist Reductionism" see chapter 1 of Siderits (2015); for defense of the claim that most Buddhists espoused Reductionism, see especially
   chapters 4 and 9. I take the Sautrāntika school as my model because theirs is
   among the most philosophically sophisticated.

3. This work is usually treated as the ninth chapter of AKBh, but some consider
   it to have originally been an independent treatise. An English translation is in
   Duerlinger (2003).

4. For some schools of Indian philosophy, such as Sāṃkhya, cognition is not an
   action; for others, such as Mīmāṃsā, it is. Naiyāyikas can be found on both sides
   of the dispute.

5. Trenckner (Ed.) (1928/1962, 40); trans. in Rhys Davids (1890–1894/1965). This work by an unknown author is postcanonical but accepted by most Abhidharma schools as authoritative. Its English translation is *The Questions of King Milinda*.

6. Buddhist Reductionists are generally property dualists, but their property dualism is of a quite special sort. For details see Siderits (2015, Chapter 2).

7. *smṛtiju hi cchandaḥ cchandajo vitarko vitarkātprayatnaḥ prayatnādvāyustataḥ karmeti kimatrātmākurute?*

8. For an introduction to trope theory and the trope-theoretic formulation of bundle theory see Robb (2005).

9. For details of the argument see Siderits (2014).

10. Buddhist Reductionists generally refrain from providing a regimentation of commonsense views on a topic where these differ from what Buddhists consider the ultimate truth. This may be because their chief (soteriologically driven) concern is to show that the commonsense conviction is mistaken. At the same time they recognize that success in showing this requires them to show why a mistaken view might be widely accepted. The bundle-theoretic reduction of substances is an example of this. I shall be taking what Vasubandhu and other Buddhist Reductionists seem to take the folk theory of action and agency to be, and proposing a philosophically sophisticated account that appears to match it in important respects. I don't claim that this is what any Buddhist philosopher really had in mind. I only claim that it represents a reasonable extension of what they do say.

11. The dating problem is the difficulty that if a persisting substance is said to itself be the cause of an event's occurring at a particular time, then we don't know why this occurred at this time and not at some other time when the substance exists. For a clear statement of the problem and an attempt to solve it for the agent-causal approach see O'Connor (1995/2003, pp. 271–272).

12. Lowe makes the comparison at (2008, p. 5). I should add that Buddhist Reductionists will reject the project of descriptive metaphysics. Their project is unabashedly revisionary in nature.

13. For an overview see Table 1 of Haidt (2001, p. 818).

14. For evidence that such "snap judgments" or moral intuitions are products of low-road cognitive systems see Haidt (2001).

15. In Siderits (2009) I consider the objection that this renders Buddhist Reductionism inexpressible and reply that the Buddhist Reductionist can resort to the use of a metalanguage in order to express the relation between conventional and ultimate truth.

16. For a brief survey of other attempts at avoiding these difficulties and reasons for preferring the semantic insulation approach, see Siderits (2009) and Siderits (2015, Chapter 4).

17. I borrow the term *two-scheme* from Kent Machina.

18. Paleo-compatibilism is developed and discussed in Siderits (2008).
19. The phrase "creeping exculpation" is introduced in Dennett (1984, pp.156–158).
20. Earlier versions of this paper were presented at Illinois State University and Carleton University. Special thanks are due to Kenton Machina, Gordon Davis, Mary Renaud, and Elizabeth Shupe for helpful comments and criticisms.

References

Buddhaghosa. (1950). *The Visuddhimagga of Buddhaghosācariya*. (H. C. Warren & D. Kosambi, Eds.). Cambridge, MA: Harvard Oriental Society.

Dennett, D. C. (1984). *Elbow room*. Cambridge, MA: MIT Press.

Duerlinger, J. (2003). *Indian Buddhist theories of persons: Vasubandhu's "refutation of the theory of a self."* London: RoutledgeCurzon.

Fiala, B., Arico, A., & Nichols, S. (2012). On the psychological origins of dualism: Dual-process cognition and the explanatory gap. In M. Collard & E. Slingerland (Eds.), *Creating consilience: Integrating science and the humanities* (pp. 88–109). Oxford: Oxford University Press.

Gombrich, R. F. (2009). *What the Buddha thought*. London: Equinox.

Haidt, J. (2001). The emotional dog and its rational tail: A social intuitionist approach to moral judgment. *Psychological Review, 108*(4), 814–834.

Lowe, E. J. (2008). *Personal agency: The metaphysics of mind and action*. Oxford: Oxford University Press.

Merricks, T. (2001). *Objects and persons*. Oxford: Clarendon Press.

O'Connor, T. (2003). Agent causation. In G. Watson (Ed.), *Free will* (2nd ed.) (pp. 257–284). Oxford: Oxford University Press. (Reprinted from *Agents, causes and events: Essays on indeterminism and free will*, by T. O'Connor, Ed., 1995, Oxford: Oxford University Press).

Rhys Davids, T. W. (Trans.). (1890–1894/1965). *The questions of King Milinda*. Oxford: Oxford University Press.

Robb, D. (2005). Qualitative unity and the bundle theory. *Monist, 88*, 466–492.

Śāntideva. (1960). *Bodhicāryāvatāra of Śāntideva with the commentary Pañjika of Prajñākaramati*. (P. L. Vaidya, Ed.). Dharbanga, India: Mithila Institute.

Searle, J. R. (2001). *Rationality in action*. Cambridge, MA: MIT Press.

Siderits, M. (2008). Paleo-compatibilism and Buddhist Reductionism. *Sophia, 47*, 29–42.

Siderits, M. (2009). Is Reductionism expressible? In M. D'Amato, J. L. Garfield, & T. F. Tillemans (Eds.), *Pointing at the moon: Buddhism, logic, analytic philosophy* (pp. 57–69). New York: Oxford University Press.

Siderits, M. (2014). Causation, "Humean" causation and emptiness. *Journal of Indian Philosophy, 42*, 433–449.

Siderits, M. (2015). *Personal identity and Buddhist philosophy: Empty persons.* 2nd edition. Aldershot, UK: Ashgate.

Trenckner, V. (Ed.). (1928/1962). *The Milindapaṇho.* London: Pali Text Society.

Vasubandhu. (1975). *Abhidharmakośabhāṣyam of Vasubandhu.* (P. Pradhan, Ed.). Patna, India: Jayaswal Research Institute.

PART SIX

Politics, Anger, and Equanimity

Chapter 16

The Inherent Dignity of Empty Persons

Christopher Kelley

16.1. Introduction

The 14th Dalai Lama, Tenzin Gyatso, is a strong proponent of the Universal Declaration of Human Rights (UDHR; United Nations, 1948b). To all appearances this seems consistent with his promotion of basic human values and universal responsibility in books like *Ethics for a New Millennium* (2001) and *Beyond Religion: Ethics for a Whole World* (2011). However, upon closer scrutiny, it is unclear how his endorsement of concomitant ideas like inherent dignity and inalienable rights can be philosophically reconciled with the Tibetan Buddhist Madhyamaka ("Middle Way" or "Centrist") School's claim that all phenomena (i.e., persons, things, and ideas like dignity and alienable rights) are "empty" or "void" (*śūnyatā*) of intrinsic existence (*svabhāva*). There is, I therefore assert, a looming and unresolved metaphysical conflict between the Dalai Lama's account of Buddhist ethics and the metaphysical presuppositions inherent in the moral philosophy of the UDHR. Let us call this paradox "the inherent dignity of empty persons." In plain terms the salient question is this: Can the idea of inherent dignity and inalienable rights be made compatible with the radical anti-essentialism of the Dalai Lama's own Madhyamaka School of thought? What is more, the Madhyamaka analysis of intrinsic existence is not solely concerned with just the nature of things. It also includes an important "cognitive dimension" that concerns *how* one sees the world (Westerhoff, 2009). This more psychological side of the Madhyamaka account of intrinsic existence is, in practical terms, more important than the metaphysical because it pertains directly to the way we actually interact with the world, other people, and ideas like human rights.

In this essay I argue that a judicious assessment of the Dalai Lama's Madhyamaka School of Buddhist philosophy yields the necessary theoretical tools for making sense of this metaphysical paradox of the inherent dignity and inalienable rights of empty persons. More significant, the cognitive dimension of the Madhyamaka account of intrinsic existence also provides a new way of psychologically relating to human rights that can help thwart the proliferation of the fundamentalist mind-set that is so often associated with the violation of human rights and crimes against humanity. Hence the reconciliation of the paradox of the inherent dignity of empty persons promises a novel metaphysical account of human rights as well as a new way of thinking about the psychological mind-set that contributes to the perennial violation of human rights in the world today. In this way I hope to reunite the philosophy of human rights with its practice, two facets of human rights discourse that in recent years have become estranged.

16.2. The Nature of the Conflict

The Dalai Lama is internationally recognized as a staunch advocate of human rights. He has received numerous awards and honorary degrees and generally enjoys widespread acclaim for his ongoing efforts to peacefully safeguard the human rights of Tibetans and marginalized people everywhere. In 1989 he was awarded the prestigious Nobel Peace Prize in recognition of his nonviolent activism for Tibet and his "constructive and forward-looking proposals for the solution of international conflicts, human rights issues, and global environmental problems" (Nobel Prize, 1989). In 2007 President George W. Bush presented him with the Congressional Gold Medal—American's highest civilian honor—and declared, "They [the Chinese government] will find this good man to be a man of peace and reconciliation" (U.S. Department of State, 2007). In 2010 the U.S. National Endowment for Democracy awarded the Dalai Lama the Democracy Service Medal for his continued "commitment to advancing the principle of democracy and human dignity" (Dalai Lama Honored, 2010). And in 2011 Larry Cox, the executive director of Amnesty International, bestowed its Shine a Light Award upon the Dalai Lama and proclaimed, "There is no more powerful voice for human rights, for peace, and for non-violence than the unique voice of His Holiness the 14th Dalai Lama, Tenzin Gyatso" (Stewart, 2011, p. 6).

Before becoming a well-known champion of human rights, the Dalai Lama was (and continues to be) a proponent of the Madhyamaka School of Buddhist philosophy. According to Nāgārjuna, the recognized progenitor of the Madhyamaka (second century CE, India), the premise of intrinsic or inherent existence is a metaphysical impossibility. On the face it, this seems to give rise to a metaphysical conflict between the Dalai Lama's own Madhyamaka and his support for the Enlightenment concepts of inherent dignity and inalienable rights that constitute the philosophical foundation of the UDHR. The Madhyamaka position vis-à-vis rights is not unprecedented within contemporary human rights theory; it is consistent with the postmodern rejection of innate human rights and dignity espoused by contemporary antifoundationalist thinkers such as Richard Rorty (1993). Moreover the rejection of metaphysically inherent rights is not in and of itself unusual within the history of philosophy. As early as the 18th century, the utilitarian philosopher Jeremy Bentham (1795/2002, p. 330) derided the concept of rights as nothing less than "nonsense on stilts." Interestingly this did not prevent the contemporary utilitarian Peter Singer from adopting the language of rights in his philosophical writings. After the publication of *Animal Liberation* in 1975, the burgeoning animal rights movement adopted Singer as their intellectual public persona—despite the fact that his actual argument does not entail a rights-based theory of ethics. His defense of animal interests in fact eschews the existence of rights. Singer's (1975/2009) ethical position in *Animal Liberation* is based on a utilitarian calculation that places greater value on an animal's capacity to experience suffering than the relative usefulness of a carnivorous diet for humans. I see a similar confusion at work in the minds of most people who interpret the Dalai Lama's support for the UDHR as an espousal of human rights foundationalism and the traditional concept of human rights. The Dalai Lama, like Singer, does not subscribe to a rights-based theory of ethics, nor does he support a philosophy that recognizes the metaphysical presuppositions associated with human rights foundationalism. To overlook this fact would not only be a grave misreading of the Dalai Lama's project but would neglect the sophistication of his position as well as the potential contributions that the Madhyamaka stand to make to the field of human rights theory and practice. I believe that the Dalai Lama's adoption of the vocabulary of rights can be metaphysically reconciled if—but only if—it is framed in terms of the Buddhist doctrine of the "two truths" (*dvasatya, bden pa gnyis*).

Most theories on the nature of human rights can be plotted along a spectrum of varying degrees of philosophical foundationalism and anti- or nonfoundationalism. *Philosophical foundationalism* refers to those types of claims that appeal to an intrinsic metaphysical ground for support. For instance, one might try to defend the claim "Murder is wrong" by appealing to the command of God or the proper application of reason. In either case, a belief is considered to be "right" or universal on the grounds that it rests on a morally absolute metaphysical foundation of some sort. Most theorists consider the UDHR to be a foundationalist text because it presupposes the belief that all persons—regardless of their culture, ethnicity, gender, nationality, and so on—are endowed with and possess the capacity to discern certain core rights by virtue of their humanity or inherent dignity. In other words, certain human rights are believed to exist on account of a metaphysically inherent (or intrinsic) ground called "human dignity." Philosophical antifoundationalism is at the opposite end of the spectrum. It asserts that a belief need not, indeed should not, be grounded in any kind of assumed metaphysical foundation. Many theorists who advocate an antifoundationalist concept of human rights support the practical application of the rights described in the UDHR, but contend that traditional philosophical justifications that appeal to an intrinsic foundation are outmoded and risk being counterproductive to the realization of human rights. The problem with most of these theories is that they are usually vague in terms of how they actually square antifoundationalism with the UDHR. I contend that the Madhyamaka philosophy of the Dalai Lama presents a new and refreshing "unforced consensus" (Taylor, 2011) that can reconcile the paradox of the inherent dignity of empty persons. It also provides a robust way of explaining how the Dalai Lama can legitimately and simultaneously support both the Madhyamaka's anti-essentialist view of persons and the concepts of inherent dignity and inalienable rights in the UDHR.

The foundationalist notion of an individual's natural rights as derived from their inherent dignity is a central feature of the philosophy of Immanuel Kant. Without delving too deeply into his *Groundwork of the Metaphysics of Morals* (1785/1999), it is worth pointing out that Kant posits human dignity (*würde*)—not God—as the foundation upon which human rights can be justified. Kant's objective is to develop a purely rational justification for moral universalism. In the *Groundwork* he says the following on the subject of dignity:

> In the kingdom of ends everything has either a *price* or a *dignity*. What has a price can be replaced by something else as its *equivalent*; what on the other hand is raised above all price and therefore admits of no equivalent has a dignity.
>
> What is related to general human inclination and needs has a market price; that which, even without presupposing a need, conforms with a certain taste, that is, with a delight in the mere purposeless play of our mental powers, has a *fancy price*; but that which constitutes the condition under which alone something can be an end in itself has not merely a relative worth, that is, a price, but an inner worth, that is, *dignity*. Now, morality is the condition under which alone a rational being can be an end in itself, since only through this is it possible to

be a lawgiving member in the kingdom of ends. Hence morality, and humanity insofar as it is capable of morality, is that which alone has dignity. (Ak. 4:434–435)

Kant uses the analogy of a marketplace to convey what he deems to be the inestimable worth of the human person (as compared to everything else in the world). His claim is that human beings, by their very nature, are beyond the convention of monetary value. He envisions a "kingdom of ends," a hypothetical world in which every individual is universally entitled to be treated as an "end in itself," and not simply as a "means" for someone else's unique ends. Kant offers two axioms for attaining this kingdom of ends: what is generally referred to as his "humanity formula" and the categorical imperative (Sidorsky, 2009).

The humanity formula states, "*So act that you use humanity, whether in your own person or in the person of any other, always at the same time as an end, never merely as a means*" (Ak. 4:429). In the kingdom of ends the only thing that is not for sale is human dignity. Objects and nonhuman animals have a monetary value, but human beings do not. That is to say, humans do not have a moral obligation to inanimate things and nonhuman animals. Whatever nominal worth such entities might possess is merely ascribed to them by humans and is relative to the particular ends of a given person. Thus the value of an inanimate thing or nonhuman animal increases in proportion to the aims (i.e., ends) of the individual actor. Kant's injunction against treating humans as a means is not just an ethical one; it is a principle that he bases on what he sees as the absolute and universal law of morality. The objective value of a human being is "raised above all price" and has "not merely a relative worth, that is, a price, but an inner worth, that is, dignity." In other words, humans have an intrinsic worth (i.e., dignity) because they are rational agents with the freedom and autonomy to make their own decisions and conduct themselves according to reason (Rachels, 1986, pp. 114–117, 122–123).

Kant is a moral absolutist who believes that individuals must discover moral truth through their own exercise of the categorical imperative. The *deontology (deont-,* "being necessary") in Kant's ethics refers to the intention of the moral actor to act out of a sense of *duty* determined by the autonomous exercise of one's reason (i.e., the categorical imperative). When such rational beings act from a motivation based on this sense of obligation, they therefore become the embodiment of the moral law itself (Rachels, 1986, pp. 114–117, 122–123). Hence the only way morality can exist in the world is by means of rational beings (acting from a sense of duty) freely engaging their capacity for reason. So if you remove human beings from the world, then you also remove morality (pp. 114–117, 122–123). Human beings are not just another kind of valuable thing; rather they are the medium or locus whence all other things are ascribed a price. And their value is absolute. Kant believes that human beings should respect one another's rights and act altruistically toward each other so that they are furthering all respective ends.

Kant's claim that human beings have an inherent dignity that justifies their alienable rights is clearly echoed in the first passage of the Preamble and Article 1 of the UDHR (United Nations, 1948):

> Preamble
> *Whereas* recognition of the inherent dignity and of the equal and inalienable rights of all members of the human family is the foundation of freedom, justice and peace in the world . . .

> Article 1
> All human beings are born free and equal in dignity and rights. They are endowed with reason and conscience and should act towards one another in a spirit of brotherhood.

The philosopher Johannes Morsink (2009, pp. 17–54) describes the ontological presupposition here as a "metaphysics of inherence" or the "doctrine of inherence" and argues that it comprises a twofold thesis that roughly correlates with the two paragraphs above. The first is what he describes as the "metaphysical universality thesis" (i.e., all humans are born with inherent rights). This is expressed in the Preamble by the terms "inherent dignity" and "equal and inalienable rights" and is, I believe, consistent with the idea of natural rights put forth by Kant and other Enlightenment thinkers like John Locke. The second is his "epistemic universality thesis" (i.e., all humans have the capacity to discern this). This can be gleaned from the mention of "reason and conscience" in Article 1 and is, I think, compatible with Kant's concept of human reason. This doctrine of inherence is the major stumbling block in reconciling the Dalai Lama's Madhyamaka with the UDHR.

Morsink (2009, p. 20) argues that the members of the UDHR drafting committee were keenly aware of their debt to the Western Enlightenment, and that they choose to augment the document with the concept of natural rights originally put forth by Enlightenment thinkers like Kant, as well as others such as Thomas Paine and the American Founding Fathers: "The UDHR drafters clearly saw themselves as standing on the shoulders of these eighteenth-century predecessors as making huge improvements on the work begun earlier. They felt kinship with the American and French revolutionaries, for they felt they had just cut their own international bill of rights from the same moral and philosophical cloth." What Morsink believes attracted the drafters of the UDHR to the then archaic natural rights tradition was its uncompromising moral universalism that regards all human beings as inherently valuable and naturally worthy of inalienable rights. The restoration of the lost dignity of the common man and the installment of a comprehensive universal moral code was surely an attractive proposition in the aftermath of the Second World War. The prospect of a metaphysically intrinsic foundation to rights (i.e., inherent human dignity) must surely have been a very reassuring idea against the chaos and horrors of the Holocaust. It is, however, not just in metaphysical conflict with the Madhyamaka worldview; it is also incompatible with the most fundamental idea in Buddhism: the theory of no-self. This problem (what I have framed as the paradox of the inherent dignity of empty persons) can, I argue, be reconciled through an application of the Buddhist doctrine of the "two truths."

16.3. No-Self, Emptiness, and the Two Truths

Gautama Buddha famously asserted that the "self" cannot be found among the constituent parts of a person. According to the *Anattālakkhana Sutta*, the Buddha made the following assertion: "Bhikkhus, form [*rūpa*] is nonself ... feeling [*vedanā*] ... perception [*saññā*] ... volitional formations [*saṅkhāra*] ... consciousness [*viññāna*] is nonself" (SN.iii.66–67). These "five aggregates" or "five bundles" are considered to be an exhaustive fivefold classification of what it means to be a person. The Buddha's articulation of the five bundles is considered to be one of the earliest attempts in Indian philosophy at a theory of personal identity (King, 1999, pp. 78–80). The Indologist Richard King maintains that the metaphor of the five bundles is an allusion to the bundles of sticks required for the ritual fires used in non-Buddhist Vedic sacrifice (p. 80). It is more than likely that early Buddhists were well aware of the powerful socioreligious symbolism of Brahmanical fire sacrifice and employed the metaphor in order to subvert its influence. Previous to the emergence of Buddhism in India, sacred fire had been considered something to be nurtured in Vedic praxis. In Buddhism, however, the metaphor of fire is used to describe the cognitive and affective matrix that is responsible for all of one's pain and suffering. Throughout the Pāli *suttas* one finds numerous references to unenlightened existence as being ablaze with the flames of greed, hatred, and ignorance. These fires, and the process of combustion that is one's ordinary experience, cease when one has cut off their fuel: craving (*tṛṣṇā*) and misknowledge (*avidyā*). Quite literally, Buddhist *nibbāna/nirvāna* means the "act of blowing out, or extinguishing" the fires of delusion and destructive craving. Sue Hamilton (2001) theorizes that the Buddha of the *sut-tas/sūtras* inverted the normative symbolic role of ritual fire by redescribing it as something to be extinguished. This is the ideological basis for the more philosophically developed theory of "no-self" (*anātman*) that emerges in early mainstream Abhidharma Buddhism.

According to the philosopher Mark Siderits (2005), the no-self theory can be described as a kind of "mereological reductionism," wherein a macro-level whole (in this case the "self") is—in the final analysis—an "utterly unreal" collection of more real micro-level parts. The "self" is therefore regarded not as an intrinsic subject but as a useful fiction for referring to what is in actuality simply a system of parts in a constant state of flux. So even though the "self" cannot *ultimately* be found, it does retain a *conventional* level of existence. The Abhidharma schools (a blanket term for various "mainstream" schools of early Buddhism, represented in modern times primarily by the Theravāda tradition) are well known for their elaborate taxonomies of the many different parts that supposedly account for the "self" at various levels of analysis. They contend that the analysis of the "self" descends through an intricate schema of parts until it bottoms out at the micro level with irreducible intrinsic psychophysical "building blocks" (*dharmas*).

Proponents of the Madhyamaka School accept this schema with one very important caveat: the building blocks too are divisible. The central tenet of the Madhyamaka is the dual thesis of dependent origination and emptiness. According to Nāgārjuna (the reputed founder of this school), everything (e.g., tables, chairs, persons, and *dharmas*) lacks independent "intrinsic existence" (*svabhāva*). In other words, the way things exist is not "*in*-dependently" ("from its own side," as Tibetan Buddhists like to say) but rather "*inter*-dependently" (*pratītyasamutpāda*). Things exist relationally within a system of interdependent parts that are themselves systems of interdependent parts that exist within yet further systems of interdependent parts, and so on, ad infinitum.

The analysis never bottoms out in the Madhyamaka School, as it does in the Abhidharma School, so there is no intrinsic metaphysical foundation to anything (and that includes emptiness itself). This was a very radical premise within the extremely rich philosophical context of ancient India. The Buddhologist Robert Thurman explains some of the distinctions and the significance of Nāgārjuna's project in the context of the various other schools of Indian philosophy:

In the Buddhist thought of his day, the refined science of the Abhidharma (itself merely a systematization of the Buddha's critique of the naïve realists) had ossified into a more subtle form of realism, a kind of reductionistic pluralism that took an atomistic form with the Vaibhashikas [Buddhists], the "Analysts," and a nominalistic form with the Sautrantikas [Buddhists], the "Traditionalists." ... The problem with this system was that it was not immune to the reificatory mental habits that plague people and philosophers everywhere. ... Thus, Nagarjuna, like Kant against the rationalists of medieval theology, and like Wittgenstein against the logical atomists, had to wield the sword of analysis against the Analysts, non-Buddhists as well as Buddhist; he had to level a complete critique against their absolutisms, either spiritualistic dualism or atomistic pluralism. This he did in a series of works, whose critical thought patterns are effective for releasing us from almost any trap of dogmatism. (in Tson-kha-pa, 1984, p. 24)

As Thurman points out, Nāgārjuna targeted the psychological tendency to reify phenomena as the central flaw in both schools of the Abhidharma. What distinguishes Nāgārjuna from his Buddhist peers is his assertion that it is only *because* all things ultimately lack an intrinsic existence that they can have any real truth status at all. In other words, contrary to the common misreading of Buddhism as nihilism, Nāgārjuna argues that emptiness ensures the existences of things. Nāgārjuna lays out this thesis in his *Mūlamadhyamakakārikā*.

The *Mūlamadhyamakakārikā* is popularly considered Nāgārjuna's most influential work and is extremely important to the Tibetan tradition of Buddhism. As such it has received a tremendous amount of scholarly attention. The various types of reasoning he employs have been well documented by contemporary Buddhologists (Garfield, 1995; Tson-kha-pa, 1984; Westerhoff, 2009). Chapter 24, "Examination of the Four Noble Truths," is considered to be the central chapter for subsequent commentators such as Candrakīrti (Garfield, 1995). In it Nāgārjuna writes:

> *Whatever is dependently co-arisen*
> *That is explained to be emptiness.*
> *That, being a dependent designation*
> *Is itself the middle way.* (MMK 24.18)

The Madhyamaka position—the "middle way"—is often described in terms of avoiding the philosophical views of "extreme existence" (*yod mtha'*) and "extreme nonexistence" (*chad mtha'*), ideological poles that resemble philosophical foundationalism and antifoundationalism, respectively. By asserting that all things arise only in dependence on causes and conditions, Nāgārjuna is saying that all things are empty of intrinsic existence. Jay Garfield (1995,

p. 88) explains: "Nāgārjuna relentlessly analyzes phenomena or processes that appear to exist independently and argues that they cannot so exist, and yet, though lacking the inherent existence imputed to them either by naive common sense or by sophisticated, realistic philosophical theory, these phenomena are not nonexistent—they are, he argues, conventionally real." The distinction between *ultimate* and *conventional* truth was first developed in Buddhist commentaries on early Buddhist *sūtras*, the purpose being strictly hermeneutical, that is, to reconcile incongruent ideas in scripture (Siderits, 2005, p. 58). Later Buddhist philosophers adapted the two-truth device in order to express the nature of the self and all things. In the *Mūlamadhyamakakārikā* Nāgārjuna writes:

> *The Buddha's teaching of the Dharma*
> *Is based on two truths:*
> *A truth of worldly convention*
> *And an ultimate truth.*
> *Those who do not understand*
> *The distinction drawn between these two truths*
> *Do not understand*
> *The Buddha's profound truth.*
> *Without a foundation in the conventional truth*
> *The significance of the ultimate cannot be taught.*
> *Without understanding the significance of the ultimate,*
> *Liberation is not achieved.* (MMK 24.8–9)

What constitutes "ultimate truth" (*paramārtha satya*), according to Nāgārjuna, is emptiness. It is what is ultimately true about things: They are empty or devoid of intrinsic existence. If this were not the case, Nāgārjuna asserts, then nothing could change, be produced, or go out of existence. Proponents of the Madhyamaka use ultimate truth in two ways: first, like the Abhidharma, they believe it signifies something that is immune to analysis; second, it is what is found to be the case in the final analysis. Since the Madhyamaka School believes that primary existents cannot exist, then what is ultimately found is an absence—a vacuity of inherent existence.

"Conventional" or "deceptive truth" (*saṃvṛti satya*) is the way things exist (a kind of photo positive of the photo negative that is emptiness). Conventional truth supervenes onto a complex and interdependent system of social, psychological, biological, and chemical emergent properties. Conventional truth refers to the host of useful fictions that function as valid handles for the plurality of phenomena in the world. The distinction between the two truths should not be interpreted as referring to separate ontological realities but merely two aspects of the way things are. Nāgārjuna writes in chapter 25 of the *Mūlamadhyamakakārikā*:

> *There is not the slightest difference*
> *Between cyclic existence and nirvāṇa.*
> *There is not the slightest difference*
> *Between nirvāṇa and cyclic existence.*
> *Whatever is the limit of nirvāṇa,*
> *That is the limit of cyclic existence.*
> *There is not even the slightest difference between them,*
> *Or even the subtlest thing.* (MMK 25.19–20)

For Nāgārjuna the only difference between rebirth into cyclic existence and liberation into enlightenment is one's worldview. Hence the reified bifurcation of *samsara* and *nirvāṇa* is seen to be symptomatic of the unenlightened dichotomous mind—not ontologically independent realities. To realize the nature of things requires a cognitive shift, not a metaphysical leap. As Siderits (2005, p. 182) likes to say, "The ultimate truth is that there is no ultimate truth." In other words, the distinction is semantic and epistemological. Siderits explains, "Abhidharma claimed there are two kinds of truth, ultimate and conventional. We could accordingly say that Abhidharma has a dualist conception of truth. And then on the semantic interpretation of emptiness, Madhyamaka might be described as semantic non-dualism. For it says there is only one kind of truth" (p. 182). The Madhyamaka School rejects Platonic notions of "capital T" truth. The ultimate is not a transcendent realm of existence; it merely describes *how* the conventional exists. Ultimate and conventional are just two aspects of the same reality or self. This is a topic of great concern in Tibetan Buddhist scholarship. And it is the justification for the aforementioned qualification of the Dalai Lama's support for rights in terms of conventional truth but not ultimate.

The Tibetan monk-scholar Je Tsongkhapa (1357–1419) is credited with having been the progenitor of what is known as the "Gelug pa" order (*dge lugs pas*) of Tibetan Buddhism, with which the religious seat of the Dalai Lama is traditionally associated. Tsongkhapa is believed to have been a teacher to the first Dalai Lama. In his philosophical writings, Tsongkhapa addresses the two-truth theory with the aim of providing a strong defense of the veracity of *conventional* meaning in an *ultimately* empty world. This is vitally important to the spiritual progress of a Buddhist; should the conventional aspect of the world have no real meaning, it would invalidate the conventional efficacy of the Buddhist teachings, making liberation and enlightenment impossible. Or, in the context of human rights, it would invalidate the efficacy of the very idea of human rights. Tsongkhapa asserts that it is not acceptable to dismiss the world of conventional appearances (as several antifoundationalist and anti-essentialist philosophies often do). Broadly speaking, Buddhists subscribe to what Western philosophers refer to as the "appearance-reality distinction." In the Madhyamaka School, appearances are described as "illusion-like"—but not illusions proper. Tsongkhapa argues that conventional meaning is sub-stantiated within "frameworks of veridical worldly conventions" (Jinpa, 2002, p. 167). A framework of veridical conventions can be construed as language and conceptuality: culture. The cultural anthropologist Clifford Geertz (1973, p. 5) provides the following helpful definition of culture: "The concept of cul-ture I espouse ... is essentially a semiotic one. Believing, with Max Weber, that man is an animal suspended in webs of significance he himself has spun, I take culture to be those webs, and the analysis of it to be therefore not an experimental science in search of law but an interpretative one in search of meaning. It is explication I am after, construing social expressions on their sur-face enigmatical." What Geertz is suggesting is consonant with Tsongkhapa's teaching: human beings do not simply spin their own private webs of signif-icance in whatever way they wish; that would be subjective relativism. Rather each person is caught, "suspended" in public webs of significance that have been spun collectively. Significance or meaning exists only in relation to a host of public frameworks. In the context of human rights, the UDHR represents one such framework. Thus rights, albeit devoid of intrinsic nature, can be said to have meaning and significance within that particular veridical framework.

What is interesting and different about Tsongkhapa's account of the two truths is that he emphasizes their metaphysical equality. One might be tempted to think that ultimate truth is more real than conventional truth. Tsongkhapa, however, argues that they are not only equal, but they are also mutually sup-portive. Therefore the claim that human rights are empty of intrinsic existence is the strongest argument for their actual existence! Garfield makes this very same point using the example of a mirage : "A mirage appears to be water, but is only a mirage; the inexperienced highway traveler mistakes it for water, and for him it is deceptive, a false appearance of water; the experienced traveler sees it for what it is—a real mirage, empty of water. Just so, conventional phe-nomena appear to ordinary, deluded beings to be inherently existent, whereas in fact they are merely conventionally real, empty of that inherent existence; to the aryas [individuals who perfectly understand the nature of things] on the other hand, they appear to be merely conventionally true, hence to be empty" (Cowherds, 2010, p. 29). Garfield argues that the way conventional truth is false is that it appears to be self-existent. This, however, does not entail its actual existence. In denying the appearance of intrinsic existence one is not also denying its empirical reality. The appearance of intrinsic existence is something human beings superimpose upon the empirical world. I contend that this account of the two truths is how we can make sense of the paradox of the inherent dignity of empty persons.

As I suggested, Tsongkhapa is something of a realist; however, his is a realism that is always relative to context (i.e., the veridical framework within which the world *functions*). Function is therefore one of our best barometers of conventional truth. For example, "bus" may be a conceptual label, but it can still perform the function of running you down should you step in front of one. Thubten Jinpa (2002, p. 175) therefore describes Tsongkhapa's position as a form of "conventional realism":

> Tsongkhapa definitely accepts a high degree of objectivity in that much of the coherence that we perceive in reality is not entirely subjective. Furthermore, like all Prāsaṅgikas [Madhyamaka], Tsongkhapa does not reject the reality *out there*. What is denied is its intrinsic existence and intrinsic identity. The identity and being that the world possesses are said to be only contingent. Insofar as this is true, there is an element of relativism in Tsongkhapa's ontology. However, this is not to say that no reality exists outside our language and thought. Fire still burns, water still quenches our thirst, and sentient beings are still born under the power of their *karma*. There is nothing purely linguistic or conceptual about these facts of reality. . . . The existential status that Tsongkhapa accords to reality is nominal. It is, to use his own words, a worldly convention. . . . His ontology is also a form of realism. Thus, I have called it "conventional realism."

Jinpa goes on to explain how Tsongkhapa's ontology can also be described as a form of nominalism in that "the existential status that Tsongkhapa accords to reality is nominal." Jinpa adds, "It is, to use his [Tsongkhapa's] own words, a worldly convention" (p. 175). Hence it is perfectly consistent with Tsongkhapa's interpretation of the Madhyamaka to qualify the doctrine of inherence in the UDHR as conventionally real, while also being ultimately devoid of intrinsic existence. In other words, the concepts of inherent dignity and inalienable rights can be reconciled with the Dalai Lama's Madhyamaka by qualifying them in terms of the two truths. Human rights function and exist within a particular framework of veridical worldly conventions. And that is simply a more metaphysically coherent way of asserting that human rights really do exist.

Jinpa (2002, p. 176) offers one final label to describe Tsongkhapa's position: "anti-metaphysical." What I think he means by this is that the central aim of the Madhyamaka is not to put forth a metaphysics, but rather to "free the mind from all temptations of reification" (p. 175). The psychological tendency to seek a false sense of security in an unreal metaphysical foundation is, according to the tradition of Tsongkhapa, not just metaphysically flawed; it is a very dangerous psychological mind-set that is responsible for human suffering (e.g., crimes against humanity and human rights violations). The cessation of suffering is the result of a "cognitive shift" (Westerhoff, 2009, p. 47). Westerhoff writes, "The Mādhyamika draws a distinction between the *understanding* of arguments establishing emptiness and its *realization*. Being convinced by some Madhyamaka argument that an object does not exist with *svabhāva* does usually not entail that the object will not still appear to us as having *svabhāva*. The elimination of this appearance is achieved only by the realization of emptiness. The ultimate aim of the Mādhyamika project is therefore not just the establishment of a particular ontological or semantic theory, but the achievement of a *cognitive change*" (p. 49). Similarly I think the ultimate aim of the Dalai Lama's human rights project is not necessarily to introduce a new metaphysics of rights but rather to focus on the psychological mechanisms for affecting the way we interact with and think about the "other." Here the object of negation is not the intrinsic nature of rights but the fundamentalist mind-set that actively reifies both their real and unreal ontological status. (The reader will recall the aforementioned "two extremes" in Buddhism.) Most human rights violations are not the result of a wholesale rejection of entitlements but rather an arbitrary bias against a particular group that is deemed to be subhuman and not worthy of human rights. In other words, they have a highly selective belief in who is entitled to "human" rights. I believe this analysis of the psychology of reification—the "cognitive dimension"—is where the Dalai Lama and Tibetan Buddhism stands to make a truly meaningful contribution to contemporary human rights discourse.

16.4. Conclusion

I began this paper with a metaphysical problem: the paradox of the inherent dignity of empty persons. I argued that an unforced consensus on human rights can be achieved through an application of the Madhyamaka account of the two truths, wherein human rights can be said to have a *conventional* intrinsic existence but not an *ultimate* intrinsic existence. This kind of unforced consensus is not the same thing as finding equivalent concepts or terminology for "rights" in Buddhism (Taylor, 2011). The kind of unforced consensus I am positing is not based on equivalency but rather on the utility of the Madhyamaka account of emptiness and the two truths as a justification for human rights. The claim is that it is only because ideas like human dignity and rights are *ultimately* devoid of intrinsic existence that those ideas can have *conventional* (i.e., real) existence. According to this line of thinking, it is therefore not incoherent to say that conventional inherent dignity is a metaphysically real thing. Make no mistake—the distinction between *ultimate* and *conventional* is not simply a semantics of ontology. The emptiness thesis put forth by the Madhyamaka is a coherent theory that resonates with those of contemporary Western philosophers such as Derek Parfit, which is to say that it is coherent and sound. However, unlike the accounts put forth in Western philosophy, there is an important cognitive dimension in Nāgārjuna's account of intrinsic existence.

Proponents of the Madhyamaka, including the Dalai Lama, believe there to be a direct connection between how we think about the nature of things and the alleviation of human suffering, and that the realization of that connection requires more than just a robust metaphysical account of reality—it must also entail a cognitive shift that actually realizes the absence of intrinsic existence. This experience is a direct cognition of emptiness, or "yogic direct perception" (*rnal 'byor mngon sum, yogi pratyakṣa*) and is said to enable a Buddhist practitioner to identify his or her own learned tendency to psychologically reify the so-called self with intrinsic nature.

According to Thurman, there is an "instinctual self-habit" (*bden 'dzin lhan skyes*) and an "intellectual self-habit" (*bden 'dzin kun brtags*): "The instinctual habit of reifying intrinsic reality in persons and things [i.e., the aforementioned 'instinctual self-habit'] is so deeply engrained in our thoughts and perceptions. We *feel* intrinsic reality is 'there,' in ourselves and in things, and each time analytic investigation finds it to be absent, we automatically reify that absence into a little real disappearance, as if something solid had vanished before us" (in Tson-kha-pa, 1984, p. 158). According to Tsongkhapa, this experience of "seeing emptiness" fundamentally changes an individual's worldview by attacking his or her intellectual self-habit and manifests as a deep sensitivity to one's interdependence with others and the world. This is believed to naturally lead one to engage in the kind of moral behavior that is compatible with the protection of human rights. I believe that understanding emptiness counteracts the natural reification of human rights as being either intrinsically existent or intrinsically nonexistent—both of which can potentially lead to a fundamentalist mind-set that is counterproductive to the project of human rights.

Understanding the metaphysical argument that all things lack intrinsic existence is critical to the destruction of the intellectual tendency to reify phenomena. When incorporated into a comprehensive contemplative practice it can transform not only the way one understands the nature of things but also how one actually interacts with the world on a psycho-emotional level. As I have argued elsewhere, this is precisely why the Dalai Lama's approach to human rights and ethics so strongly emphasizes the role of a new kind of education that aims to develop both the mind and the heart (Kelley, 2015). I believe this kind of contemplative "heart" education is compatible with Article 26 in the UDHR (United Nations, 1948), stating, "Education shall be directed to the full development of the human personality and ... promote understanding, tolerance and friendship among all nations, racial or religious groups." I conclude with the Dalai Lama's (2001, p. 64) comments on visiting the Auschwitz-Birkenau State Memorial and Museum: "Events such as those which occurred at Auschwitz are violent reminders of what can happen when individuals—and by extension, whole societies—lose touch with basic human feeling. But although it is necessary to have legislation and international conventions in place as safeguards against future disasters of this kind, we have all seen that atrocities continue in spite of them. *Much more effective and important than such legislation is our regard for one another's feelings at a simple human level*" (emphasis added).

Abbreviations

Ak.   Prussian Academy edition of Kant's complete works. Translations
         from M. Gregor in Kant (1785/1998).

MMK   Nagarjuna, *Mulamadhyamakakarika*. Translations from Garfield
         (1995).

SN   *Saṃyutta Nikāya*, volume and page in the Pali Text Society edition.
         Translations from Bodhi (2000).

References

Bentham, J. (2002). Rights, representation, and reform: Nonsense upon stilts and other writings on the French Revolution. In. P. Schofield, C. Pease-Watkin, & C. Blamires (Eds.), *The collected works of Jeremy Betham*. Oxford: Oxford University Press. (Original text 1795).

Bodhi, B. (Trans.). (2000). *The connected discourses of the Buddha: A new translation of the Saṃyutta Nikāya*. Somerville, MA: Wisdom Publications.

The Cowherds. (2010). *Moonshadows: Conventional truth in Buddhist philosophy*. Oxford: Oxford University Press.

Dalai Lama XIV Bstan-ʾdzin-rgya-mtsho. (2001). *Ethics for the new millennium*. New York: Penguin.

Dalai Lama XIV Bstan-ʾdzin-rgya-mtsho. (2011). *Beyond religion: Ethics for a whole world*. New York: Houghton Mifflin Harcourt.

Dalai Lama honored with NED Democracy Service Medal at Library of Congress. (2010, June 21). Accessed January 3, 2017. Retrieved from National Endowment for Democracy: http://www.ned.org/dalai-lama-honored-with-ned-democracy-service-medal-at-library-of-congress/.

Garfield, J. L. (Trans.) (1995). *The fundamental wisdom of the middle way: Nagarjuna's Mulamadhyamakakarika*. Oxford: Oxford University Press.

Geertz, G. (1973). *The interpretation of cultures: Selected essays*. New York: Basic Books.

Hamilton, S. (2001). *Indian philosophy: A very short introduction*. Oxford: Oxford University Press.

Jinpa, T. (2002). *Self, reality and reason in Tibetan philosophy: Tsongkhapa's quest for the middle way*. New York: Routledge.

Kant, I. (1998). *Groundwork of the metaphysics of morals*. (Trans. M. Gregor). Cambridge: Cambridge University Press. (Original text 1785).

Kelley, C. D. (2015). Toward a Buddhist philosophy of human rights. PhD dissertation, Columbia University.

King, R. (1999). *Indian philosophy: An introduction to Hindu and Buddhist thought*. Edinburgh: Edinburgh University Press.

Morsink, J. (2009). *Inherent human rights: Philosophical roots of the Universal Declaration*. Philadelphia: University of Pennsylvania Press.

Rachels, J. (1986). *The elements of moral philosophy*. New York: Random House.

Rorty, R. (1993). Human rights, rationality, and sentimentality. In S. Shute & S. L. Hurley (Eds.), *On human rights* (pp. 111–134). New York: Basic Books.

Siderits, M. (2005). *Buddhism as philosophy*. Indianapolis: Hackett.

Sidorsky, D. (2009). Moral philosophy syllabus V3701. Columbia University. Retrieved from http://philosophy.columbia.edu/files/philosophy/content/PHILV3701MoralPhilosophySIDORSKYFall2009.pdf.

Singer, P. (1975/2009). *Animal liberation: The definitive classic of the animal movement*. New York: HarperCollins.

Stewart, T. (2011). 50 years: Amnesty International. *Amnesty International* (AIUSA Newsletter), *38*(1), 6.

Taylor, C. (2011). *Dilemmas and connections : Selected essays*. Cambridge, MA: Belknap Press of Harvard University Press.

United Nations. (1948). The Universal Declaration of Human Rights. Retrieved from http://www.un.org/en/documents/udhr/.

U.S. Department of State, Office of Electronic Information, Bureau of Public Affairs. (2007). President Bush attends Congressional Gold Medal ceremony honoring the Dalai Lama. Accessed October 17. Retrieved from http://2001-2009.state. gov/p/eap/rls/rm/2007/93648.htm.

Tson-kha-pa, B. (1984). *Tsong Khapa's speech of gold in The essence of true elo-quence. Reason and enlightenment in the central philosophy of Tibet.* (R. Thurman, Trans.). Princeton Library of Asian Translations. Princeton, NJ: Princeton University Press.

Westerhoff, J. (2009). *Nagarjuna's Madhyamaka: A philosophical introduction.* Oxford: Oxford University Press.

Chapter 17

Ethics without Justice

ELIMINATING THE ROOTS OF RESENTMENT

*Amber Carpenter**

17.1. Some Intuition Pumping

The Earthquake and the Arsonist

> SCENARIO A: You are an averagely decent person, no more outstanding
> than the rest but with no significant wrongs, crimes, or harms to your
> name. One day there is a tremendous earthquake nearby; you and your
> family are lucky enough to find safe shelter, but your house is shaken
> to its foundations and all your worldly possessions are irrecoverably
> destroyed.
>
> SCENARIO B: You are an averagely decent person, no more outstanding than
> the rest but with no significant wrongs, crimes, or harms to your name.
> Persons motivated by racist hatred—by an impersonal and implacable
> malice—delight one day in burning down your house, while your family
> are all safely elsewhere. Your house is burned to its foundations and all
> your worldly possessions are irrecoverably destroyed.

Let us reflect.

In both cases, the outcome as it affects you is the same. You and your
family are homeless and bereft of whatever material possessions constituted
your life, including not just practical necessities (e.g., clothes, pots and pans)

*My thanks to Thomas Doctor, Malcolm Keating, Sandra Field, and Matthew Walker for
discussion of these ideas as they were developing, and to Sherice Ngaserin for invaluable
research assistance.

but also those material objects of intangible value (e.g., legal documents, pho-
tographs, keepsakes). If one took a wholly pragmatic, results-oriented perspective, these two scenarios look indistinguishable.[1]

And yet there seems to many, at least, a vast gulf between the two cases.
Indeed, it is the crucial difference between whether we are within or outside of the domain of morality. The first scenario presents a natural evil—
unfortunate, regrettable, and requiring fairly ordinary and pedestrian steps
toward recovery. The second, by contrast, presents a moral evil, to which the
appropriate responses are not just dismay surveying the wreckage, but outrage
and indignation.[2] Only such reactive attitudes, and the interpersonal activities
of blame and demanding restitution, retribution or punishment, adequately
acknowledge (or show acknowledgment of) the fact that *origins matter*—that it
makes a difference that I have lost my house due to *someone's willfully destroying it,* rather than because of an unfortunate shifting of tectonic plates.[3] Only
recognizing this difference will respect the way the family in Scenario B has
been *wronged* (thus avoiding a further injustice against them), and only this
will do justice to the humanity of the offender.[4]

Our humanity, on this view, is distinctively marked by the fact that things
can be "up to us," and this feature becomes coextensive with the domain of the
moral. For only what we choose to do is liable to praise and blame—or at least
to *moral* praise and blame; indeed, the marker "moral" here simply indicates
that it is the sort of praise and blame reserved for the kind of being capable of
action in the proper sense of it, and so of responsibility (in the sense of *morally*
responsible, as this might be distinguished from causally responsible[5]). As "up
to us" indicates, the point was first put sharply by Aristotle (*Nicomachean Ethics*
III.5);[6] it became especially associated with rational choice and "will" (*prohaire-
sis*) by the Stoics, and then in the Christian era became the "free will" with
which we are familiar, and by we which might absolve an almighty Creator god
of our sins.[7] The possibility for autonomy, for being determined through and
by oneself and not by another, is *definitive* of the domain of the moral.[8]

Thinking the domain of the moral in this way gives justice a special place
and has corresponding difficulty in accommodating responsive values.[9] We
might say that in the European tradition, since Plato at least, the domain
of the moral has typically been *centered on* justice. This is coextensive with
the domain of the moral, or constitutive of it.[10] As Kant puts it, justice or
right (*Recht*) "is a concept of the understanding, and represents a property
(the moral property) of actions, which belongs to them in themselves" (*KrV*
A44/B61, trans. Kemp Smith in Kant, 1871/1963). Justice is the paradigmatic
moral virtue, emblematic of whatever is distinctive when we (now, in English)
feel compelled to attach the word "moral" to act, intention, motivation, virtue,

quality, concern, and so on.[11] Injustice, conversely, captures what is wrong, over and above material and emotional harms, when an autonomous individual—someone *capable* of autonomy and responsibility—violates another individual of the same sort. Views vary, but they are variants on whatever it is that makes us say that the victims in Scenario B have suffered twofold: misfortune, as in Scenario A, and in *being wronged*.

The Buddhist emphasis on care (*karuṇā*, compassion) seems intent on minimizing this difference. In fact, it is worse than that: deploying care as the superordinate or governing virtue positively debars us from differentiating the very thing justice requires us to differentiate—namely, the offender from his victim—for both are *equally* entitled to our compassion. This is not an inadvertent implication of Buddhist ethics; it is a core feature, reiterated in several contexts. The central practice of loving-kindness meditation explicitly enjoins loving-kindness for those who "are my enemies" or who have harmed me.[12] Compassion is to be extended to all beings *without distinction*. Nowhere is this more apparent, and more disturbing, than in the Buddhist insistence that we eliminate all anger, and in Śāntideva's treatment of the anger question in particular.

In what follows, I will try to show there is something deep and important at stake here, and that this extreme position on anger shows us nothing less than a fundamental difference in ways of conceiving of morality.

Justice and its cluster of related concerns—such as impartiality, autonomy, blame, and punishment—are not front and center of the Buddhist outlook, and indeed may have no place at all.[13] With suffering as the first Noble Truth, care—the active concern to eliminate suffering—is central in defining the moral as such. Opportunities for care mark out the domain of the moral, and wise care is the mark of moral goodness, in action and in attitude and in motivation. I will set out the connection between the first, metaphysical and existential claim (suffering) and the second, moral and practical claim (care). If there is this fundamental distinction in ways of conceiving of and defining the domain of the moral, then classifying Buddhist moral thought as a variant of any of the traditional European theories will be not just futile, but disfiguring—obscuring precisely that in Buddhist moral thought that is most interesting.

17.2. The Charge

Disregarding the principal cause, such as a stick and the like, if I become angry with the one who impels it, then it is better if I hate hatred, because that person is also impelled by hatred. (BCA 6.41, trans. V.A. Wallace, & B. A. Wallace in Śāntideva, 1997, p. 66)

Don't blame the assailant, Śāntideva says here; his hatred made him do it.

Now the context for these remarks is Śāntideva's philosophico-meditational treatment of the perfection of patience, or forbearance, in the *Bodhicaryāvatāra*. So one might want to play down this verse taken out of context. The *Bodhicaryāvatāra*, we might argue, is a meditational exercise, and a Madhyamaka one at that. Its purpose is to get us to try out various alternative ways of looking at situations, without taking any of these as a definitive declaration of How Things Really Are, because the changing of perspective itself will have an edifying effect on our own motivational set.[14] (Śāntideva isn't *really* saying there is no difference between the assailant's responsibility and that of the weapon he uses; and he doesn't *really* mean we should regard victims of child abuse as having brought it on themselves.)

And it is certainly true that the *Bodhicaryāvatāra* is a protreptic text; its aim is to affect the reader, turning her toward a better way of life and way of seeing.[15] But there is only so far this fact can go in mitigation, for the text, and the Buddhist eliminativist view of anger, certainly intends to challenge and transform our ordinary notions. An interpretation that leaves everything in our ordinary thinking in place will have missed the point.

In any case, this is far from the only verse in chapter 6 of Śāntideva's *Bodhicaryāvatāra* that is likely to set alarm bells ringing in those of a contemporary, and especially of an Anglophone sensibility. Consider the following verse, which actively erases the difference between personal and impersonal causes, and disallows even the small window apparently left open in 6.41 for justified anger at the real cause: "I am not angered at bile and the like even though they cause great suffering. Why be angry at sentient beings, who are also provoked by conditions?" (BCA 6.22).

As anti-anger positions go, the Buddhist position articulated here is extreme.[16] Śāntideva is advising the victim of wanton physical abuse to consider the abuser as culpable *in just the same way* that, in indigestion, excess bile is "culpable"—that is, not at all, in the sense that that term properly has of demarcating a domain of the moral from the nonmoral. Even Seneca does not go that far. It gets worse: "Those who hurt me are impelled by my actions, as a result of which they will go to the infernal realms. Surely it is I alone who have ruined them" (BCA 6.47).

The explicit willingness to blame the victim is breathtaking. A sober survey of the daily crimes committed against vulnerable persons makes it difficult to take such advice quite seriously. Indeed, one might begin to worry for one's own moral character if one did.

Forget whether the wholesale elimination of anger is a plausible, achievable, or even appealing ideal—it is a *moral* catastrophe. To achieve such an ideal would make us worse persons, incapable of correctly identifying injustice, incapable of caring enough to want to do something about it, incapable of apportioning blame fairly.[17] The charge reveals the special connection there is thought to be between anger and injustice in the Aristotelian-Christian tradition.[18] Everyone can agree that *excessive* and *unwarranted* anger is bad, but this just shows that there is proportionate and justified anger—namely, as a response to injustice.[19]

The Buddhist anger-eliminativist can reject the claim; there is no special connection between injustice and anger. But they cannot thereby avoid conceding the substance of the main point: the Buddhist no-self view does not just take an ironic stance toward personal boundaries;[20] it eschews altogether any categorical difference between personal and nonpersonal causes. With that goes suffering injustice as a distinct sort of harm. Candrakīrti's rhetorical question "If you respond in anger when another harms you, does your wrath remove the harm inflicted?' (MA 3.4) has force only if there is not some distinct harm in being treated unjustly—a damage to status, or standing, or dignity, say—which could indeed be healed or recovered by resentment, or righteous indignation, anger or blame. If, conversely, Śāntideva is not *really* saying there is no difference between the assailant's responsibility and that of the weapon he uses, then he is not giving us any reason or means to abandon afflictive emotions associated with perceiving oneself as having been *wronged*. Examining closely just *how* the sixth chapter of the *Bodhicaryāvatāra* functions as a meditational exercise will reveal how inhabiting an impersonal metaphysical outlook decenters justice from the moral point of view, or indeed makes its concerns vanish. The absence of justice is not an oversight nor an accident, but the inevitable implication of adopting the outlook of dependent arising that underwrites care (*karuṇā*).

17.3. What Is Wrong with Anger?

Śāntideva is not in any way remarkable among Buddhists in so emphatically eschewing all forms of anger, even supposedly legitimate anger at injustice.[21] Take this vivid piece of advice from the *Middle-Length Discourses* of the Pāli canon: "Bhikkhus, even if bandits were to sever you savagely limb by limb with a two-handled saw, he who gave rise to a mind of hate towards them would not be carrying out my teaching" (MN.i.129). The *Milindapañha* is not so graphic, but reiterates that anger "is a thing that is weakening to the mind" (Miln. 289), and that "on approaching the world which is abounding in anger and malice and is overset by quarrels, strife, contention and enmity, [one should] anoint his mind with the medicament of loving-kindness" (394). Vasubandhu is content to list anger among the unequivocal impediments alongside "enmity, dissimulation, jealousy, stubbornness, hypocrisy, greed, the spirit of deception, pride-intoxication, the spirit of violence, etc." (AKBh. 2.27). Buddhaghosa reminds us at *Visuddhimagga* IX.1 2, "No higher rule, the Buddhas say, than patience, and no *nibbana* higher than forbearance" (referring us to DN.ii.49 and *Dhammapada* 184), and "No greater thing than patience exists" (quoting SN.i.222). Candrakīrti returns us to the intensity of the *Kakacūpama Sutta*: "All anger felt towards a Bodhisattva destroys within an instant all merits that arise through discipline and giving of a hundred *kalpas*. No other evil is there similar to wrath" (MA 3.6).

Strong words, and unequivocal from all sides, cutting across the Mahāyāna/Theravāda divide. But what is actually *wrong* in anger?

However much cultural variation there may be in its forms, anger is associated with a phenomenology of agitation and aggression, a physiognomy inflamed and distorted, a physiological intensity and impetuosity toward destructive and counter-productive action. Indeed, these common markers are the indicators that we have sufficiently "the same" phenomenon in view across cultural contexts. Thus, for instance, both Buddhaghosa (Vism. IX.15) and Seneca (*de Ira* I.1) point to the physical agitation and physiognomic changes characteristic of anger. "Wrath disfigures the face and form and leads to evil states," says Candrakīrti (MA 3.7). There are characteristic occasions, feelings, physiological reactions, and types of action associated with anger. Śāntideva opens his discussion of anger with the observation that "anger destroys all good conduct" (BCA 6.1a), and Buddhoghosa observes that anger makes one "misconduct himself in body, speech and mind," (Vism. IX.15) so that he experiences bad results (bad rebirth). Anger's intense affective qualities are unpleasant in themselves, and they cause one not to think clearly, and therefore to act badly—whether that "badly" is prudential or moral. In preferred Buddhist terms, just as craving causes the confused thinking that informs unconstructive actions, so too does its inverse, aversion.

But for the Buddhist, anger is bad not just because it feels bad and leads to bad results. It *does* feel bad, and it *does* lead to bad results, on the whole. Buddhaghosa specifically advises against it on these grounds, as does a verse from the *Dhammapadā*:

Suppose an enemy has hurt you now in what is his domain, why try to hurt your mind yourself as well? That is not his domain. (Vism. IX.22)[22]

Do not speak harshly to anyone. Those who are harshly spoken to might retaliate against you. Angry words hurt other's feelings, even blows may overtake you in return. (Dhp. 133)

Śāntideva too picks up on this, articulating the negative consequences of anger for the angry person, whether the direct effect of anger on her own mind, or the effect of expressing anger on one's relations with others:

The mind does not find peace, nor does it enjoy pleasure and joy, nor does it find sleep or fortitude when the thorn of hatred dwells in the heart. Even dependents whom one rewards with wealth and honours wish to harm the master who is repugnant due to his anger. Even friends fear him. He gives, but is not honoured. In brief, there is nothing that can make the angry person happy. (BCA 6.3–5)

But recognizing this much gives us reason only to moderate our anger and its expression—to not *show* our anger, not get carried away with anger, not let anger eat us up inside. None of that sound advice would tell against the judicious feeling and expression of anger at the right time, in the right way, under the right circumstances. One might even go further and claim that however distorting anger *might* be, it can also be a cognitively correct response. Let anger be, as Śāntideva says, "finding its fuel in discontent originating from an undesired event and from an impediment to desired events" (BCA 6.3–5). Surely some events *ought* to be undesired, or are genuine impediments to what ought to be desired. If anger can be an appreciation of what is *rightly undesired*—say, injustice—then anger is as apt to be insightful as it is to be distorting.[23] Eliminating anger requires an altogether different sort of view of its badness, as the Stoics (those other infamous anger-eliminativists) also recognized.

What is fundamentally and most illuminatingly wrong with anger, on the Buddhist view, is not that it confuses our thinking, but that it manifests confused thinking. That is, anger is cognitively rich, but it is never apt. Anger is the particular form that misapprehension of reality takes under certain circumstances. As an embodiment of confusion, experiencing anger tends to reinforce the confused ways of thinking that enable it to arise in the first place—and this will be quite apart from the question of the tendency of anger to cause me to make prudentially bad judgments about what to do. So on the Buddhist view, anger is bad simply because it *is* suffering and it *causes* suffering. But these are both rooted in a prior cognitive fault, for anger cannot arise without a false way of seeing the world; and insofar as it has cognitive content at all, it embodies and reinforces that confused cognition.

It will be no surprise that the fundamental misapprehension of reality underwriting anger (as so many things) is a false belief in self. Candrakīrti is explicit: "For Bodhisattvas, those who see the absence of self, Agent, object, time, and manner of the wounds—All things are like the image in a glass. By understanding thus, all torments are endured" (MA 3.3). And we see this claim already in the *suttas*, where a false sense of self gives rise not just to unhappiness generally (*Alagaddūpama Sutta*, MN.i.130ff.), but specifically to divisiveness and hostility between people (*Tittha Sutta*, Ud. 70ff.).[24]

Both Buddhaghosa and Śāntideva introduce impersonal metaphysics into their respective anti-anger homilies, with the idea that correctly seeing the selflessness of reality removes the necessary preconditions for anger to arise: "Since states last but a moment's time, those aggregates, by which was done the odious act, have ceased, so now what is it you are angry with? Whom shall he hurt, who seeks to hurt another, in the other's absence?" (Vism. IX.22).

We will consider Śāntideva's treatment more closely.

17.4. The Course of *Bodhicaryāvatāra* VI

Śāntideva begins with the easy cases: gadflies and mosquitoes, thirst and cold (BCA 6.15–16). He frames this with the practical attitude he aims to instill in place of the counter-productive anger we may be prone to: "If there is a remedy, then what is the use of frustration? If there is no remedy, then what is the use of frustration?" (6.10).

He then turns to the truly difficult cases—those wherein we feel our anger is *justified*. We can easily recognize the silliness and futility of getting angry at falling branches or failed harvests. But anger is more difficult to dislodge when we mistakenly judge (1) ourselves (or those we care about) to be harmed; (2) to have been harmed by some responsible agent; and (3) not to be ourselves responsible for the harm. Śāntideva does not argue, Stoic-wise, that there is no harm done, really—at least he does not try to sweep away all cases with that particular broom.[25] Rather the mistake that we must actively identify and undo if we are to dislodge our attachment to anger is the judgment that *I* am being made to suffer *by* someone else, who, as responsible, should be held to account (is a fitting target of revenge). In effect, Śāntideva draws on what is already established regarding the easy cases and explicitly recommends that we see all possible cases in a similar light. And this is where the bile comes in: "I am not angered at bile and the like even though they cause great suffering. Why be angry at sentient beings, who are also provoked to anger by conditions?" (6.22). Śāntideva is explicitly refusing to distinguish personal from impersonal causes, placing all occasions for anger into a common, mutually conditioning field.

The Metaphysical Turn

Then Śāntideva emphasizes this very fact—*and so starts doing metaphysics*: "All offences and vices of various kinds arise under the influence of conditions, and they do not arise independently" (6.25). There is nothing—not any supposed Self, autonomous and free, nor some other primordial principle, nor any particular part of reality—that wishes itself into being. Nothing can be responsible for its own arising, nor therefore for its particular quality or character when it does arise. Of course some evils arise due to wicked intentions, and others do not; but that wicked intention did not *choose* to be, any more than a flower chooses to grow. In both cases, there are causes and enabling conditions and innumerable factors which are responsible for the item picked out. The direct implication of the sheer generality of the claim is that, if we are going to go in for the business of determining responsibility or fault, we will inevitably become mired down in an interminable exercise in futility. Better not to start down that road at all.

The critique of the substantiality of persons in particular (vv. 26–31) should show us a way of looking at the world, others, and our own experiences such that "Whose fault is it?" is not the decisive and pressing question that arises.

And so Śāntideva recommends in light of this, "Therefore, upon seeing a friend or an enemy committing a wrong deed, one should reflect, 'Such are his conditions,' and be at ease" (6.33).

Why should we "be at ease" here? And does this mean that we should not, when it is in our power, prevent people from doing wrong? This may look like another *reductio* of the anger-eliminativist position (or the same again in new words). For if someone is about to do wrong, "at ease" is precisely what I *ought not* feel, particularly if I have any sense of justice.

In fact, it is precisely one's sense of justice—with its fault-finding and blaming, its righteous indignation and its insistence on the splendid isolation of the individual will for forensic purposes—that this little exercise in impersonalism is *meant* to erode. This is where, as above, the Buddhist can only concede the point. Yet consider precisely what this "eroding of our sense of justice" amounts to when achieved by this route. By insisting on the embeddedness of all causes, and by refusing to distinguish one kind as special, Śāntideva removes any warrant for that special moral emotion, blame. I can, without difficulty, recognize that it is *this* stick, held by *this* hand, impelled by *that* malicious impulse, provoked by *this or that* perception in conjunction with *this or that* memory and cognition, each of which, by regarding them in this way, I acknowledge to have their own causes, which I can only guess at and which may—well, why not?—include indigestion. This is not a problem, and indeed is the very activity toward which our attention has been redirected. Seeing the stick-wielder as impelled by malice, say, does not *absolve* him of responsibility (*moral* responsibility—the only sort needing absolution), because I am not even asking the question of responsibility. The lack of control he has over the malice is not exonerating, but it is pitiable; to lack control, and be riven with afflictive emotions, is suffering. Notice the emphasis on concern for suffering in the immediately following verses (6.34–38). Addressing myself to the situation in this way, I do indeed see the aggressor in the same way I see reality as a whole, and myself within it—namely, under the aspect of suffering (*sub specie doloris*). But precisely because there is no further fact to find here, no further cause of agitation and distress, I can focus entirely on the pragmatic question of what is to be done.

Doing and Being Done To

But is Śāntideva entitled to this practical conclusion? Isn't the perspective on reality that enables me to stop asking "Whose fault is it?" necessarily enervating? For if the aggressor is not culpable, because there is no one there to *be* culpable, then neither can I be responsible for my own action or inaction, resentment or forbearance—there is no "I" to act, and "my own" here can be used only in distancing scare quotes to indicate its falsifying attribution of ownership.[26] Śāntideva entertains precisely this objection at 6.32: "Averting anger is inappropriate; for who averts what?"

Śāntideva's initial reply to the qualm is not especially illuminating—6.32 finishes with "It *is* appropriate, because it is a state of dependent origination and is considered to be the cessation of suffering." The verses that follow should help us to understand how this thought meets the Enervating Objection. But it is just here that Śāntideva entertains the case of one's being a witness to someone else's evil-doing and recommends, "One should reflect, 'Such are his conditions,' and be at ease" (6.33). The very fact that this is meant to be an *answer* to the concern about the impossibility of our own agency in averting anger should make us read this verse rather differently. "Be at ease" is not, I suggest, the recommendation that we just accommodate ourselves to someone else's evil actions ("It's their business, and in any case, nothing I can do anything about since I'm not any more of a person than they are."). It is rather the recommendation that we not *become angry*—agitated, blaming, hostile—ourselves, *so that* we might contribute to deflecting and diffusing the anger that is there, rather than adding to it. Only understood in this way would it in any way address the Enervating Objection. This reading is supported by the fact that Śāntideva goes on at 6.39 to observe, "If inflicting harm on others is the nature of the foolish, then my anger toward them is as inappropriate as it would be toward the fire, which has the nature of burning."

It is, admittedly, still difficult to make out how this answers the worry. If I dissolve hostile, harmful people into impersonal aggregations of natural events; and if this is meant to be a perspective on reality as a whole—and after all, why should only I be exempted from this impersonalization?—then it is still not clear how I can coherently be exhorted to do *anything*, whether it is giving up anger or preventing injustice.

This worry arises, I suggest, from overlooking a seldom appreciated feature of Buddhist no-self: dissolving the self-other distinction likewise dissolves the distinction between agent and patient. More precisely, Buddhist no-self *replaces* a metaphysics of beings (distinct, well-defined, autonomous individuals) with becoming (dependent arising). This is particularly clear in Candrakīrti (e.g., MA 6.113–116), but some version of the claim will be endorsed by non-Mādhyamikas as well. Individuation is an activity of mind, not a perception of reality. It is liable, therefore, to criteria of efficacy; individuation is correctly done not when it maps reality but when it facilitates achievement of our ends. Our ultimate end ought to be the elimination of suffering, and so the correct ways to individuate will be as and when this helps to remove suffering. So far, so familiar. The less familiar implication is that *classifying* as "agent" or "patient" is just one form of individuation. That which is thus individuated is no more *really* a cause or *really* an effect than one group of psychophysical elements is *really* a person. Attributions of agency and patiency are something we do, and they are correctly done when they contribute to removing suffering.

In order to remove the conceptual preconditions of anger, Śāntideva has just engaged us in an exercise of dissolving persons into the conditions giving rise to the various aspects of the person. If individuals are heaps of conditions arising from other conditions, themselves contributing to causing innumerable further effects in various ways, then identifying agency is impossible; and taking away the effective attribution of agency undermines the ability to generate anger, for anger presupposes some agent at whom we can direct our hostility. Now if at this point we recall the first Noble Truth, we may suppose that Buddhist no-self simply removes all agency from reality—there is only suffering, "being done to." From here, we are likely to describe the Buddhist view as a species of determinism, and so worry (or not) that all the hortatory is in vain, and the supposition that there is any indeterminacy, and so scope for freedom, is incoherent.[27]

What this line of thought overlooks is that if a distinct, individual *agent* is removed from the picture, so therewith is a distinct, individual *patient*. What we have lost is not *agency*, but the supposition that there is a clear and stable distinction in reality between agent and patient. This is what it means for "dependent origination" to replace claims of "existence," and this is why Śāntideva invokes dependent origination precisely here. Having eliminated individuals capable of being conceived as distinct agents *or patients*, we have *replaced* that with a view of everything as dependently arising—everything as equally agent *and* patient. And just as individuating is something *we do*—not a way the world is—and something we could *do differently* or *leave off doing*, if it suited us, so likewise and *for that reason* identifying agents and patients is something *we do*, not something we read off of reality. It is a way of organizing our thoughts and experiences. And since this organizing is not beholden to some ultimate truth for its correctness—there is no way these things are *really*—they are either beholden to no standard of correctness ("Call whatever you want *this* or *that*; call whomever you like 'agent' and 'patient'"), or else they are beholden to quite a different standard of correctness.[28] Having been relieved of the supposition that I get it right in my ways of organizing reality when my conceptual divisions match the structure of reality, the possibility opens up of measuring correctness according to efficacy: agency and passivity are rightly assigned when thus assigning those categories contributes to the elimination of suffering.

It is in this way that, although there are conditions for everything, this is not a recommendation to universal apathy. Instead, it is an invitation to do just what Śāntideva goes on to do here: to recognize that I too am embedded within this complex of conditions. This is why Śāntideva addresses the Enervating Objection by first calling our attention to the several sorts of situations in which someone is *both agent and patient*: "People hurt themselves with thorns and the like out of negligence, with fasting and so on out of anger, and by desiring to obtain inaccessible women and so forth. Some kill themselves by hanging, by jumping from cliffs, by eating poison or unwholesome substances, and by non-virtuous conduct. When under the influence of mental afflictions, they kill even their own dear selves in this way; then how could they have restraint towards the bodies of others?" (BCA 6.35–37). These rather odd, and oddly lengthy, considerations seem out of place, unless we suppose that the first move Śāntideva aims to make in addressing the Enervating Objection is to call our attention to the complexity of agency attributions, and in particular to the fact that impersonalism does not turn everyone into mere patients (as determinism would have it), but rather reveals all aspects of persons to be involved both as condition and as conditioned. Our first task is to recognize the suffering (both felt and metaphysical) of those toward whom we might naturally become angry were we to instead regard them as autonomous agents—because this is the way of organizing the complex interconnections of conditioning that will be effective in eliminating suffering. It is here that Śāntideva encourages us to regard the cause of our assault as not different in kind from the sort of cause that bile or phlegm might be in causing the discomfort of indigestion (6.39–41). Our further task, however, and the next consideration in addressing the Enervating Objection, is to recognize that one of the implications of this is that we are ourselves embedded within this co-conditioning network of phenomena. This is why Śāntideva goes on with his lengthy passage about how I got myself a body through my being "blinded by craving" (6.44):

> In the past, I too have inflicted such pain on sentient beings; therefore, it is fitting that I who have caused harm to sentient beings should suffer in return. . . .
>
> Those who hurt me are impelled by my actions, as a result of which they will go to the infernal realms. Surely it is I alone who have ruined them. (6.42, 47)

This is only the orgy of victim-blaming it appears to be if one has not taken the point of the impersonalism in the previous verses. Buddhist no-self is nonaccidentally related to dependent origination. In this particular context demonstrating the flexibility and nonabsoluteness of "agent" and "patient" invites us to take those assignments as liable not to truth conditions but to efficacy conditions. What is needed is a sober look at which assignments *are in fact* helpful. As it turns out, it is not the ones we typically make. Recognizing that someone else's wickedness does not come from some originary malevolent will, and acknowledging my own involvement in constructing situations, are strategically more effective in eliminating suffering. The latter allows me to avoid becoming consumed with debilitating resentment—a phenomenon captured well by Buddhaghosa's recognition of the way anger ties us to the one who has harmed us, and in Śāntideva's reference to "the thorn of hatred [that] dwells in the heart" (BCA 6.3).[29] And reconceiving myself as co-creator of prevailing circumstances opens up appreciation of my potential for affecting situations. Śāntideva uses the flexible individuation of dependent arising to recommend attributions of responsibility that engage one with the project of eliminating suffering—inasmuch as that is in one's power, for another lesson of this impersonalism is that it is always only partly in anyone's power to affect situations.

17.5. Conclusion

This study in the Buddhist claim that we *ought* to eliminate anger, and the distinctively Buddhist mode of doing so, has shown that the link between injustice and anger presumes a metaphysics. The moral perspective that picks out injustice as a special and additional *kind* of harm requires a metaphysics of discrete individuals, doing and "being done to" in turn, with a clear distinction between the two. But such a metaphysics and its moral categories engender in turn certain typical modes of thought—in particular, obsessing about Who is to Blame. Particularly in our victim-status-claiming age, we should wonder whether this is especially fruitful—or apt.

The Buddhist cannot show that their view will confirm or conform to all our intuitions about injustice because their basic metaphysical presumptions do not support the centrality of autonomous agency as a distinctive sort of cause, nor the violation of that by such free agents as a distinctive sort of harm. This is not, however, just an oversight or a morally horrifying omission. The proposal of an alternative metaphysics *is* the proposal of an alternative way of conceiving the moral. For every exercise in appreciating what no-self means, and what its implications are, is simultaneously an exercise in detachment, in recognizing the impulse to blame and resent as harmful assertions of oneself over and against others. Removing the conceptual structures for righteous indignation strips our evaluations of situations and persons of its self-assertiveness. Rather than being enervating, or blinding us to what moral responsiveness demands, this outlook is resolutely practical. None of this denies the no-self anger-eliminativist the resources necessary for forensics: we can see that some sets of conditions have intentions among them, and we can recognize that under some circumstances, these are more effectively engaged with in modes that differ from how we would engage with a forest fire.[30] To regard someone's raging violence as a forest fire does not mean that we turn the fire hose on it; it means that we consider the enabling conditions and defeating conditions and seek to eliminate the one and enhance the other.[31]

At the same time, as no-self introduces fluidity into our practices of individuation, it presents us with the entangled mutual causation of all factors and the simultaneous suffering. To see no-self, Buddhist-wise, just is to see that everything is conditioned and conditioning. Released from the demands of indignation, we are left with the only attitude that is appropriate in the face of suffering—a practically oriented *care* to relieve that suffering. *Karuṇā* is not an additional feature of a Buddhist outlook or the next thing on the list of dogmata. Care just is the affective and practical recognition of no-self metaphysics. Without discrete individuals to appeal to in any situation—*these* the perpetrators, *these* the victims—we have only efficacy in removing suffering as the standard preventing us from nihilism. Where before there were culprits to blame, and myself to exonerate or assert in retaliation, there is now only suffering, for which care to alleviate it is simply what is left when I am no longer distracted by righteous indignation.

Abbreviations

AKBh.   Vasubandhu, *Abhidharmakośabhāṣya*. Translations from L. de La Vallée Poussin & L. M. Pruden in Vasubandhu (1991).

BCA   Śāntideva, *Bodhicaryāvatāra*. Translations from V. A. Wallace, & B. A. Wallace in Śāntideva (1997).

DN   *Dīgha Nikāya,* volume and page the Pali Text Society edition.

KrV   *Kritik der reinen Vernunft.* Translations from N. Kemp Smith in Kant (1781/1963).

MA   Candrakīrti, *Madhyamakāvatāra*. Translations from Padmakara Translation Group in Candrakīrti (2002).

Miln.   *Milindapañha,* page in in the Pali Text Society edition. Translations from I.B. Horner (1963/1964).

MN   *Majjhima Nikāya,* volume and page in the Pali Text Society edition. Translations from B. Ñāṇamoli & B. Bodhi (1995).

SN   *Saṃyutta Nikāya,* volume and page in the Pali Text Society edition.

Ud.   *Udāna,* page in the Pali Text Society edition.

Vism.   Buddhaghosa, *Visuddhimagga*. Translations from B. Ñāṇamoli in Buddhaghosa (1956).

Notes

1. One might argue that there *is* a difference in the results alone in the two scenarios: in the second case, there are also persons abroad animated by impersonal malice who might strike again at any moment. This, however, will not do; for it is equally true that, in the first scenario, there are natural disasters lurking about, floods and fires and famines that might strike at any moment.

2. Or resentment, as the Anglophone philosophical literature since Strawson (1962) will have it. As Wolf (2011, 336) writes, echoing Seneca and Aristotle,

"It seems perfectly appropriate to get angry or resentful when one is insulted, disrespected, or unjustifiably harmed."

3. Note, however, our tendency to moralize natural evils: supposing either that victims must be guilty of some unknown crime or, more commonly, that if misfortune is suffered, there must be someone to blame building codes not instituted or enforced, warning systems not in place, and so on. This positivist attitude is distinguished from a pragmatic consideration of the same broad range of factors, including human actions as well as social institutions and circumstances, by the appropriateness or otherwise of reactive attitudes (resentment, indignation, blame).

4. While this outlook is theorized by philosophers (e.g., Wolf, 2011), it is given especially powerful voice by Jan Philip Reemtsma (1998) in his account of being kidnapped and held for ransom, *Im Keller*. Practices of holding morally accountable are moves in a shared conversation that bring the victim back into the social fold: "..., die Strafe die Solidarität des Sozialverbandes mit dem Opfer demonstriert. Die Strafe grenzt den Täter aus und nimmt damit das Opfer herein. Die Strafe für den Täter ist im Grunde nichts anderes, als es viele freundliche Briefe von Menschen sind, die sagen: 'Welcome back.' Diese Begrüßung ist von entscheidender Bedeutung für das seelische Weiterleben" (Reemtsma, 1998, p. 215).

5. This latter, one is tempted to say, is not *real* responsibility at all. True responsibility requires one be a "*causa sui*, at least in certain crucial mental respects" (Strawson, 1994, 5), and blame is criterial of "true" responsibility attributions (Strawson, 2010, p. 1).

6. Vernezze (2008, 2) aptly characterizes "most of us" as "Aristotelians when it comes to anger."

7. Frede (2012) traces this trajectory.

8. Scanlon (2008) retains blame without "could have done otherwise" by reconceiving blame as an attitude adjustment based on a judgment of relationship impairment. This revisionary account meets with strong resistance, for the connection between (real) responsibility and blame is built deeply into the cultural history of these two concepts. "We cannot," writes Wolf (2011, p. 343), "so much as understand that (very large) part of the free will problem that is concerned with moral responsibility and blame if we do not recognize that a kind of blame different from Scanlonian blame was thought to be at stake."

9. Carpenter (2014) surveys the ways a metaphysics of autonomous individuals might accommodate responsive values, arguing that attempts to bolt them onto justice-autonomy views are inherently unstable.

10. Indeed it goes back further than Plato. Hesiod in *Works and Days* (pp. 274–281) distinguishes human and nonhuman according to the possession of a sense of justice (*dikē*), where this sense of justice opens up a new dimension of right and wrong in action.

11. There are dissenters, of course, both historically and in the 20th-century Anglophone tradition; prominent among the latter are Gilligan (1982), Noddings (1982), and more recently Robinson (1999) and Held (2006). But these contemporary dissenters are responding to a real hegemony of justice-centered morality. One implication of this paper is just how much must be rethought in order to challenge the centrality of justice, and put care in its place.

12. We could consider as representative Buddhaghosa's treatment of cultivation of loving-kindness at Vism. IX.1–39, especially X.20.

13. Carpenter (in press) discusses the sidelining of blame and questions of desert in Buddhist ethics.

14. In this vein, we might point to the active perspective-changing enjoined in Śāntideva's discussion of the perfection of meditation (e.g., BCA 8.140) and the meditational exercises of "exchanging self for other" (e.g., BCA 8.120). Bommaritto (2011) finds the assimilation of personal and impersonal causes so rebarbative that he prefers to convict Śāntideva of irrationality in the service of practical exhortation than take him at his word.

15. Garfield (2010–2011) draws attention to this feature of the *Bodhicaryāvatāra*.

16. Naturally there are those who have tried to make it less extreme, and not just among contemporary interpreters. McRae (2015) discusses Dharmarakṣita's argument that Buddhism need not entail the elimination of all anger, but rather its transformation into an uncompelled tantric anger. Obviously that would require some acrobatic interpretations of the texts at hand.

17. The extent of the moral catastrophe may be even greater. Consider this reflection from Reemtsma (1998, p. 187) "[Dieses] Gefühl der Sympathie mit den Verbrechern [ist] nicht das Geringste ... was sie mir angetan haben. Es ist wie eine Schändung, und der Verlust der Fähigkeit, in eigener Sache hassen zu können, läuft auf eine psychische Deformation hinaus. (Ich sage: der Fähigkeit. Was den individuellen Willen angeht, den Hass zu überwinden, so folge jeder den Werten, die er für sich anerkennt. Sich für einen Verzicht auf den Hass zu entscheiden setzt aber voraus, sich auch anders entscheiden zu *können*.)"

18. As Seneca puts it, "Anger is the impression of apparent injury," acted upon as true, "being an exciting of the mind to revenge" (*de Ira* II.i.3). Aristotle's more status-conscious original linked anger to insult, but Stoic and Christian equalizing of persons as moral agents makes being treated unjustly the true insult or injury worthy of indignation. The medieval Christian anti-anger strand turned not on challenging this connection between injustice and indignation, but rather on the humility required of humans in making judgments of injustice— anger is God's prerogative (or possibly the king's). Rosenwein (1998) has many excellent discussions of the topic. The Stoics and Spinoza are among the historical dissenters from this mainstream view, advocating the genuine elimination of anger—the sage, or free man, will not ever feel it. However, in the Stoic case at least this may have more to do with the sage's proper appreciation of the

fundamental good order of the universe, so that (when rightly seen) there *is no cause* for indignation, rather than with any dissociation of anger from injustice.

19. For a contemporary articulation of the position, and the associated charge against the anti-anger position, see for instance Frye (1983), Narayan (1988), and Jaggar (1989), all of whom argue that anger can be epistemically productive. An unpublished paper by Amia Srinivasan argues vigorously that anger elimination would eliminate moral cognition and responsiveness.

20. Siderits (2003, pp. 99–111) argues that a self may be "worn" by bodhisattvas in the mode of "ironic engagement"; whether or not sufficient agency can be thus recovered within the no-self view, any such "ironic engagement" is against the background of an entirely earnest dissolution of any categorial distinction between the personal and the impersonal.

21. He is not even anomalous in the Indian tradition generally, where anger is evaluated very negatively, not necessarily as morally bad but as disastrously imprudent. In the *Rāmāyana* (*Bālakaṇḍa, sarga* 47–48, in Goldman, 1984), Indra deliberately provokes the ascetic Gautama's wrath, for this anger dissipates the deity-threatening spiritual powers Gautama had accumulated by his ascetic practices. Dundas (1992, p. 15) recounts the Jaina story of Yaśodhara, who went to hell for violent thoughts despite making an offering of a mere image of a chicken, made of dough.

22. Śāntideva echoes this thought that, anger being so bad for the angry person, to be angry is to give one's enemies what they want—namely, one's own misfortune—arguing that it is the anger itself that is one's real enemy (BCA 6.6–12).

23. Srinivasan (n.d., p. 24) suggests, for instance, that "by reflecting on our anger, and the reactions of the powerful to our anger, we can come to know something about the existence and structure of previously unrecognised injustice. So while anger might have ill effects on our rationality, it can also have positive epistemic effects, and the ill must be weighed against the good. Moreover, if apt anger is itself a cognitive good, like true belief or knowledge—not a mere feeling, but (when apt) an appreciation of the facts—then, whatever its negative effects on rationality, its own intrinsic value must be totted up against them."

24. See also the quarrelling contemplatives of *Majjhima Nikāya* 48, and right view as removing disputatiousness in *Majjhima Nikāya* 18 and *Sutta Nipāta* 4.11. My thanks to Sherice Ngaserin for chasing down these passages.

25. He *does* use it, interestingly enough, when it comes to desecration: "My hatred toward those who revile and violate images, *stūpas*, and the sublime Dharma is wrong, because the Buddhas and the like are free from distress" (BCA 6.64). This is useful advice for our times.

26. As McGarrity (2015, p. 1083) observes in a specifically Madhyamaka context, we cannot "take the pedagogical *strategy* of advocating a self seriously if we only ever consider it as *just* a strategy, lest the stance of 'ironic engagement' adopted

by the bodhisattva be confused with the 'ironic disengagement' of the skeptic or cynical nihilist."

27. Thus Goodman (2002) supposes the Buddhist must be a hard determinist. Siderits (2008) offers instead semi-determinism, setting the mere conventionality of freedom and responsibility alongside an ultimate reality that is deterministic. Both take the lesson to be that ultimately all is determined. Repetti (2012) extensively reviews the literature on Buddhism and determinism or free will. I join Garfield (2014) in thinking that if we are posing the question in this way, something has already gone wrong.

28. Although "there is no way these things are *really*" tends to be associated in the contemporary discourse with Madhyamaka, there is a perfectly acceptable Abhidharma version of this thought, fully adequate to the point at hand. If (what we call) persons are streams of interconnected, impersonal *dharmas*, mutually giving rise to each other, then our attributions of agency are just that: *attributions*, and not discoveries or perceptions of how things really are.

29. "In tears you left your family. They had been kind and helpful too. So why not leave your enemy, the anger that brings harm to you?" (Vism. IX.22).

30. Carpenter (2017) discusses the possibilities for Buddhist forensics in more detail.

31. It is instructive to compare here Plato's revisionary account of punishment without blame as strictly educative, which has similar difficulty accommodating our ordinary conceptions of justice and desert (see Mackenzie, 1981, Chapters 11–13).

References

Bommaritto, N. (2011). Bile and bodhisattvas: Śāntideva on justified anger. *Journal of Buddhist Ethics, 18*, 356–381.

Buddhaghosa. (1956). *The path of purification.* (Bhikku Ñāṇamoli, Trans.). Colombo, Ceylon: R. Semage.

Candrakīrti. (2002). *Introduction to the Middle Way: Chandrakirti's Madhyamakavatara with Commentary by Ju Mipham.* (Trans. Padmakara Translation Group). Boston: Shambala Publications.

Carpenter, A. D. (2014). Ethics of substance. *Aristotelian Society Supplemental Volume, 18*(1), 145–167.

Carpenter, A. D. (2017). The Saṁmitīyas and the case of the disappearing *who*? A Buddhist whodunit. In A. Haag (ed.), *The return of consciousness—A new science on ancient questions* (pp. 211–236). Stockholm: Axson Johnson Foundation.

Carpenter, A. D. (in press). "... and none of us deserving the cruelty or the grace"— Buddhism and the problem of evil. In S. Emmanuel (ed.), *Philosophy's perennial questions.* New York: Columbia University Press.

Dundas, P. (1992). *The Jains*. London: Routledge.

Garfield, J. (2010–2011). What is it like to be a bodhisattva? *Journal of the International Association of Buddhist Studies, 33*(1–2), 333–357.

Garfield, J. (2014). Just another word for nothing left to lose. In M. Dasti & E. Bryant (Eds.), *Freedom of the will in a cross-cultural perspective* (pp. 164–185) New York. Oxford University Press.

Gilligan, C. (1982). *In a different voice: Psychological theory and women's development*. Cambridge, MA: Harvard University Press.

Goldman, R. P. (Trans.). (1984). *The Rāmāyana of Vālmīki*. Vol. 1. Princeton, NJ: Princeton University Press.

Goodman, C. (2002). Resentment and reality. *American Philosophical Quarterly, 39*(4), 359–372.

Frede, M. (2012). *A free will: The origins of the notion in ancient thought*. (A. A. Long, Ed.). Berkeley: University of California Press.

Frye, M. (1983). Note on anger. In *Politics of reality: Essays in feminist theory* (pp. 84–94). Freedom, CA: Crossing Press.

Held, V. (2006). *The ethics of care: Personal, political, and global*. Oxford: Oxford University Press.

Horner, I. B. (Trans.). (1963/1964). *Milinda's Questions*. London: Luzac & Company. (Original text *Milindapañha*).

Jaggar, A. (1989). Love and knowledge: Emotion in feminist epistemology. *Inquiry, 32*(2), 151–176.

Kant, I. (1963). *Immanuel Kant's critique of pure reason*. (N. Kemp Smith, Trans.). New York: St. Martin's Press. (Original text published as *Kritik der reinen Vernunft*, 1781/1787).

Mackenzie, M. M. (1981). *Plato on punishment*. Berkeley: University of California Press.

McRae, E. (2015). Metabolizing anger: A Tantric Buddhist solution to the problem of moral anger. *Philosophy East and West, 65*(2), 466–484.

McGarrity, L. (2015). Mādhyamikas on the moral benefits of a self: Buddhist ethics and personhood. *Philosophy East and West, 65*(4), 1082–1083.

Ñāṇamoli, B. & Bodhi, B. (Trans.). (1995). *The middle length discourses of the Buddha: A new translation of the Majjhima Nikāya*. Boston: Wisdom.

Narayan, U. (1988). Working together across difference: Some considerations on emotions and political practice. *Hypatia: A Journal of Feminist Philosophy, 3*, 31–47.

Noddings, N. (1982). *Caring: A feminine approach to ethics and moral education*. Berkeley: University of California Press.

Reemtsma, J. P. (1998). *Im Keller* (6th ed.). Hamburg: Rowohlt Taschenbuch Verlag.

Repetti, R. (2012). Recent Buddhist theories of free will. *Journal of Buddhist Ethics, 21*, 279–352.

Robinson, F. (1999). *Globalizing care: Ethics, feminist theory, and international relations*. Boulder, CO: Westview Press.

Rosenwein, B. H. (Ed.). (1988). *Anger's past: The social uses of an emotion in the Middle Ages*. Ithaca, NY: Cornell University Press.

Śāntideva. (1997). *A Guide to the Bodhisattva way of life*. (V.A. Wallace & B.A. Wallace, Trans.). Ithaca, NY: Snow Lion Publications.

Scanlon, T. M. (2008). *Moral dimensions: Permissibility, meaning, blame*. Cambridge, MA: Harvard University Press.

Siderits, M. (2003). *Personal identity and Buddhist philosophy: Empty persons*. Hampshire, England & Burlington, VT: Ashgate.

Siderits, M. (2008). Paleo-compatibilism and Buddhist reductionism. *Sophia*, 47(1), 29–42.

Srinivasan, A. (N.d.). The aptness of anger. Accessed March 16, 2016. Retrieved from UCL Faculty of Laws: http://www.laws.ucl.ac.uk/wp-content/uploads/2014/12/Aptness-of-Anger.pdf.

Strawson, G. (1994). The impossibility of moral responsibility. *Philosophical Studies*, 75, 5–24.

Strawson, G. (2010). *Freedom and belief* (2nd ed.). Oxford: Oxford University Press.

Strawson, P. F. (1962). Freedom and resentment. *Proceedings of the British Academy*, 48, 1–25.

Vasubandhu. (1991). *Abhidharmakośabhāṣyam of Vasubandhu*. (L. de La Vallée Poussin, French trans. from Sanskrit; L. M. Pruden, English trans.). Berkeley, CA: Asian Humanities Press.

Vernezze, P. (2008). Moderation or the middle way: Two approaches to anger. *Philosophy East and West*, 58(1), 2–15.

Wolf, S. (2011). Blame, Italian style. In *Reasons and recognition* (pp. 332–347). New York: Oxford University Press.

Chapter 18

Equanimity in Relationship

RESPONDING TO MORAL UGLINESS

Emily McRae

18.1. Introduction

In Buddhist ethical traditions, equanimity along with love, compassion, and sympathetic joy form what are called the four boundless qualities, which are affective states one cultivates for moral and spiritual development. But there is a sense in which equanimity seems very unlike the three others: love, compassion, and sympathetic joy all imply an emotional investment in others, whereas equanimity seems to imply an absence of such investment. This observation has provoked debate as to how to properly understand the relationship between equanimity and the other three boundless qualities (see section 18.3). In this paper, I propose that equanimity—like love, compassion, and sympathetic joy—is itself a virtue of good intimate relationships and not in conflict with such virtues.

To show this, I focus on an important activity of intimate, loving relationships, which, I argue, requires equanimity: dealing with ugliness. By "ugliness" I mean personal faults or failings that may count as minor immoralities or minor imprudence, such as a desire to control others that borders on disrespect or a kind of laziness that borders on moral irresponsibility. No matter how loveable our beloved, the intimacy of love ensures that we will eventually witness some of her ugliness. And, of course, no matter how committed we may be to self-improvement, it is nearly impossible for our loved ones to escape having to deal with our own ugliness. One important activity of love, then, is learning how to deal with both the beloved's ugliness and the exposure of one's own. I argue that an investigation of this activity of interpersonal relationships reveals an aspect of relating to others that cannot be captured by the concepts that are usually invoked to explain such relationships, such as love, care, emotional investment, and compassion. Rather this activity of good relationships is best understood in terms of the affective attitude of equanimity.

I begin by explaining the concept of equanimity by drawing on several Buddhist sources (in section 18.2) and explore the supposed tension between equanimity and other laudable affective states in the Buddhist traditions, particularly love, compassion, and sympathetic joy (in section 18.3). In section 18.4 I present the "challenge of ugliness" and delineate the set of harms caused by ugliness in the context of interpersonal relationships. I argue that equanimity is uniquely situated to respond to these harms (in section 18.5). I conclude by responding to two objections to the view that equanimity is a virtue of interpersonal relationships (in section 18.6).

18.2. Equanimity

In Buddhist philosophical contexts, equanimity is usually contextualized within the framework of the four boundless qualities, a set of admirable moral emotions that one cultivates as a central part of one's moral and spiritual development. Along with equanimity (Pāli: *upekkhā*, Tibetan: *btang snyoms*), the other boundless qualities are love (*metta, byampa*), compassion (*karuna, snying rje*), and sympathetic joy (*mudita, dga' ba*). These four are called "boundless" or "immeasurable" (*appamāṇa, tsad med*) because they are considered to be states that, with proper training, one could feel without limit. Someone who has perfected these four qualities feels them for all sentient beings and with boundless depth and sincerity.[1]

The fifth-century Indian Buddhist scholar Buddhaghosa describes equanimity as a "neutral" attitude toward all beings and claims that the function of equanimity is "to see equality in all beings," which "is manifested by quieting resentment and approval" (Vism. IX.96). The philosopher Vasubandhu's fourth-century commentary to the *Mahāyānasūtrālaṅkāra* (*The Universal Vehicle Discourse Literature*) defines equanimity as being "free from addictions in the midst of (pleasant and unpleasant) experiences" (Maitreyanatha & Aryasanga, 2004, p. 228). The ninth-century Indian scholar Kamalasila (2001, p. 48), whose work was very influential in Tibet, describes equanimity as simply "eliminating attachment and hatred." Tsongkhapa (2000, p. 36), a 14th-century Buddhist scholar and the founder of the Gelug school of Tibetan Buddhism, offers a similar definition in *The Great Treatise on the Stages of the Path to Enlightenment* (*Lamrim chenmo*), in which he calls equanimity "an even-minded attitude, eliminating the bias which comes from attachment to some living beings and hostility to others." The 19th-century Tibetan Buddhist master Patrul Rinpoche (1994, p. 196) equates equanimity with "giving up our hatred for enemies and infatuation with friends, and having an even-minded attitude towards all beings, free of attachment for those close to us and aversion for those who are distant."

This brief tour of Buddhist philosophical definitions of equanimity sets the groundwork for formulating a working definition of equanimity:

> *Equanimity* is the freedom from two main kinds of vicious habits of mind, namely craving habits (infatuation, neediness, clinginess) and aversion habits (resentment, hostility, hatred), which is characterized by feelings of tranquility and spaciousness that allows one to engage with others (and oneself) in novel—and more virtuous—ways.

This definition highlights some of the features of equanimity that set the stage for thinking of equanimity as a virtue of relationship. First, equanimity involves giving up craving and aversion, *especially* in the context of intimate relationships with others (giving up "hatred for enemies and infatuation with friends"). In this basic way, equanimity does not differ from the more obviously relational affects and attitudes of love (defined as the earnest commitment to another's happiness), compassion (the perception of another's suffering as bad and the desire to alleviate it), and sympathetic joy (taking sincere joy in another's accomplishments and happiness).

It would, however, be misleading to define equanimity just as the absence of craving (and its ilk) and aversion (and its ilk). This marks the second main theme in Buddhist conceptions of equanimity: equanimity is an affective state (and not the absence of affect) that is characterized by feelings of calmness, tranquility, freedom, and spaciousness.[2] Just as we can distinguish between negative freedom (freedom *from*) and positive freedom (freedom *to*) in the context of action, we can also distinguish negative and positive senses of freedom in the context of affect. Although equanimity entails a freedom *from* compulsive and destructive habits of thinking and feeling, it also includes as freedom *to* engage with others in more virtuous ways.

Finally, one common and, for our purposes, important feature of Buddhist discussions of equanimity is that they tend to see the four boundless qualities as mutually supportive states. That is, the achievement of equanimity depends on the achievement of love, compassion, and sympathetic joy, and the achievement of these three qualities likewise depends on the achievement of equanimity.[3] Equanimity is not, then, just one virtue of relationship among three others; rather it supports love, compassion, and joy, and these three dispositions support equanimity.

18.3. Coherence between Equanimity and the Other Boundless Qualities

It is not immediately obvious, however, why the boundless qualities would be mutually supportive, since it seems that the investment and intensity of love and compassion would be at odds with the freedom from craving and aversion that is constitutive of equanimity.[4] Sometimes attempts in Buddhist philosophy to integrate equanimity with love, compassion, and sympathetic joy seem strange or forced. Consider Buddhaghosa's analogy between the four boundless qualities and the attitudes of good parenting (or, at least, mothering): "And one abiding in the measureless states should practice lovingkindness and the rest like a mother with four sons, namely, a child, an invalid, one in the flush of youth, and one busy with his own affairs; for she wants the child to grow up, wants the invalid to get well, wants the one in the flush of youth to enjoy for long the benefits of youth, and is not at all bothered about the one who is busy with his own affairs" (Vism. IX.108, trans. by B. Ñāṇamoli in Buddhaghosa, 1956). That is, a mother's attitude toward the child is love, toward the invalid is compassion, toward the adolescent is sympathetic joy, and toward the functional adult son is equanimity.

There are several interesting aspects of this passage that deserve attention, including the implicit conception of motherhood and the patriarchal structure (we may wonder, for example, how daughters fit into this example; Ohnuka, 2012, pp. 18–22). I will bracket these concerns to focus on the relational aspect of equanimity. Buddhaghosa does not differentiate equanimity from the other boundless qualities as one might expect but rather sees them all as applicable in the context of relationships (even the very emotionally invested relationship between a parent and a child). The mother who does not concern herself with or intervene in the minutiae of her adult child's affairs is a model of equanimity because she is not in fact bothered by something (her adult child's affairs) that need not bother her.[5] And, presumably, she does this without becoming emotionally indifferent or disrespectful to her child.

In her excellent analysis of the use of "mother-love" in Buddhist texts, Reiko Ohnuka (2012, p. 20) notes the awkwardness of this analogy: "We can see this tension clearly within Buddhaghosa's comparison: On the one hand, mother-love is a natural and easy metaphor for positive emotions such as lovingkindness and compassion, but on the other hand, the only way to extend this metaphor to the most highly valued state of detached equanimity is to cite the example of a mother who has no anxiety about an adult son managing his own affairs. In other words, only the weakest and most attenuated version of mother-love can stand for equanimity—and not very effectively, I might add." The tension that Ohnuka sees in this passage is not limited to the context of mother-love, although it is especially obvious in this context. There seems to be a more basic tension between affective attitudes of love, compassion, and sympathetic joy, which demand an emotional investment with other beings, and equanimity, which seems to require a certain kind of divestment.

There are several ways to resolve this tension. One way is to argue that equanimity and the other boundless qualities are mutually supportive because it is equanimity that introduces the necessary impartiality in one's feelings of love, compassion, and joy. Patrul Rinpoche (1994, p. 195), for example, argues that, without developing equanimity (and developing it first), our cultivation of love, compassion, and joy is bound to be partial and biased.[6] A student of Patrul Rinpoche, Khenpo Ngawang Pelzang (2004, pp. 140–145), focuses on the need to infuse equanimity with love, compassion, and joy in order for it to be effective. If equanimity makes one cold, indifferent or distant, it ceases to be proper equanimity and becomes "mindless equanimity" (p. 139). In fact Buddhaghosa himself similarly warns against cultivating the "near enemy" of equanimity, which is an unknowing indifference (Vism. IX.101).

But these ways to integrate equanimity with the other boundless qualities may not be able to adequately address the tension between equanimity and, say, love when both of these attitudes are applied to a single person. Both Patrul Rinpoche and Khenpo Ngawang Pelzang point to the role of equanimity in preventing the other boundless qualities from becoming biased, for example, loving some and hating others. When we develop equanimity we challenge these biases, which allows our love, compassion, and joy to be felt toward more beings and in a deeper way. But in Buddhaghosa's example it seems that the equanimity, like the other boundless qualities, is directed at a person (the functional son) and is not (or not only) cultivated in an effort to make the mother's love more unbiased (say, between her children). We could imagine, for example, Buddhaghosa claiming that love is like the mother's attitude toward her child, compassion is like her attitude toward her sick child, sympathetic joy is like her attitude toward her healthy adolescent child, and equanimity is what allows her to care for all her children equally without favoring one over another. That he does not say this suggests that either, as Ohnuka claims, he is glossing over a deep and unresolved tension, or there is a sense in which equanimity is a virtue of personal relationships beyond its function as a way to impartially apply one's love, compassion, and joy among sentient beings.

In a previous paper I argued that equanimity is primarily a self-regarding emotion, in that it targets the biases (created by aversion and craving) in one's own mind (McRae, 2013). While equanimity certainly fulfills that function in Buddhist ethics, I argue that it is also the case, as Buddhaghosa's analogy illustrates, that equanimity plays a more direct role in interpersonal relationships that is not reducible to eliminating biases in order to extend one's love, compassion, and joy. There is a sense in which the mother in Buddhaghosa's example who is not engaging in the day-to-day minutiae of her son's activities is relating to her son in a way that is itself supportive of their intimate relationship.

This suggests another way to defend the claim that the boundless qualities are mutually supportive that does not focus on equanimity's role in developing impartiality: equanimity and the other three qualities are mutually supportive because they are all necessary foundational components of good relationships. Relationships with both intimates and strangers cannot thrive unless all four qualities are present, including equanimity. But what direct role does equanimity play in relating to others, especially intimate others? In what follows I argue that equanimity is uniquely situated to respond to a characteristic challenge that arises in interpersonal relationships: the challenge of ugliness.

18.4. The Challenge of Ugliness in Personal Relationships

There are some uncontroversial cases in which equanimity is necessary for good relationships: there are some relationships from which it is very difficult or undesirable to extricate oneself, and cultivating equanimity may be the only admirable response in such cases. Living with a child with mental illness, for example, requires equanimity, and the parent who can embody that ideal is admirable. But in this kind of case, equanimity is good only in a very qualified sense, that is, as a disposition that is admirable only in bad or challenging circumstances. I want to argue that equanimity is good for love relationships in a broader sense, that is, even for love relationships between good people in favorable conditions. Like patience, which, although mainly a response to hardship, is nevertheless a broadly applicable virtue, equanimity is a broadly admirable disposition even though it is especially relevant with respect to challenges in relationships. In the context of good relationships, equanimity is most relevant as a response to what I call the "challenge of ugliness."

In Western ethics, we are used to thinking about personal failings in terms of either immorality or imprudence. When one's actions violate a moral law or principle or when one's character fails to exhibit moral virtue, this constitutes an immorality; failing to advance one's nonmoral interests even though doing so would not constitute an immorality indicates an imprudent action (or disposition to be imprudent).[7] The category of ugliness straddles both immorality and imprudence. To be ugly in this sense is to have minor faults that do not constitute serious immoralities and do not have dire enough consequences to personal happiness to be characterized as serious imprudence. Nevertheless these vaguely moral (and often vaguely imprudent) faults and flaws can present major challenges to intimate, interpersonal relationships. To get a sense of this category consider the following three examples:

> *Controlling behavior.* Consider the person who has the tendency to try to control others. He understands that to really control another through manipulation or force is to disregard the other's autonomy as a rational agent who sets her own ends, and so he restrains himself from committing that kind of moral violation. Instead he nags others when he sees them pursuing ends, however minor, of which he does not approve. When people he loves are, for example, spending more money than he thinks is appropriate, eating foods he thinks are unhealthy, or making friends with people he does not care for, he nags them or argues with them in an attempt to change them. Although he does not actually prevent them from pursuing their ends, his nagging and judging makes the people he loves feel, at times, controlled and harassed.
>
> *Laziness.* Consider the person who has the tendency to do as little as possible for herself or others while still maintaining a standard level of moral decency. She keeps her promises, occasionally helps others without being asked, and develops her talents enough to be a functional member of society (she holds down a job, votes, returns her library books, etc.). But out of laziness, she does not push herself further and takes little active interest in helping others in a way that goes above and beyond minimal moral decency. She rarely surprises her loved ones with any great effort to help or please them. This makes those she loves feel that she does not care for them as much as they care for her and that they cannot count on her to the degree they would like.
>
> *Failure to set boundaries.* Consider the case of someone who, perhaps from habit or perhaps from admirable aspirations, cannot set appropriate boundaries around what he is willing to do. Because he does not have a

clear sense of his own limitations, he takes on too many projects, exposes himself to too much negativity, and pushes his physical, emotional, and mental stamina to unsustainable levels. As a consequence, he lacks the time and the physical and emotional energy to nurture relationships with his loved ones. At times he becomes irritable with or withdrawn from loved ones. His loved ones do not doubt his genuine love and affection for them, nor do they believe his projects are unworthy of his effort, but they feel neglected by him and, at times, feel that they have a heavy burden to cheer him up and soothe his exhausted mind.

What these three examples have in common is the exposure of faults that (1) do not constitute a serious immorality or imprudence and (2) arise mainly in the context of intimate personal relationships. The more subtle ways that someone is controlling, lazy, or unrealistic about her limitations is not something to which strangers or even acquaintances or colleagues usually have access. To see such characteristics requires long periods of time spent together sharing thoughts, feelings, and activities. Assuming that indeed "nobody's perfect," exposure to at least some ugliness is unavoidable even in what are otherwise good relationships.

These three examples were given from the point of view of being exposed to a loved one's ugliness. But similarly challenging is exposing one's own ugliness to a loved one, which, again, is unavoidable in the context of long-term intimate relationships. One's own tendencies to try to control others, to be lazy, or to exhaust oneself at the expense of our loved ones (to stick with the above examples) are also exposed in the context of relationship. This exposure itself can be difficult to bear, as it makes one vulnerable to the negative judgments and disappointment of one's beloved.

These three examples also illustrate what I take to be the characteristic harms of exposure to ugliness (or exposing one's own ugliness), harms that make ugliness a "challenge" rather than simply a neutral, common experience of life in relationship. The harms associated with the exposure of ugliness in the context of an intimate relationship are frustration, anger, hurt feelings, resentment, and disappointment for the one who is exposed to the ugliness and the fear of these reactions to the one whose ugliness is exposed. Both parties, it seems, stand to be hurt in the exposure of ugliness. Sometimes these harms are negligible, especially when compared to harms associated with egregious immorality or imprudence, but they are sometimes substantial harms. Perhaps more important, they are harms that nearly everyone who is in a close relationship experiences.

18.5. Equanimity and the Challenge of Moral Ugliness

Recall our earlier definition of equanimity:

> Equanimity is the freedom from two main kinds of vicious habits of mind, namely craving habits (infatuation, neediness, clinginess) and aversion habits (resentment, hostility, hatred), which is characterized by feelings of tranquility and spaciousness that allows one to engage with others (and self) in novel and more virtuous ways.

My claim is that the harms of exposure to (and of) ugliness are best responded to by equanimity, for which I will offer two main arguments.

The first focuses on the specific harms of ugliness and argues that these are kinds of harms that equanimity, by definition, can ameliorate. I call this the *Harms of Ugliness Argument*. I refer to the second argument as the *De-identification Argument* because it draws on the idea that equanimity requires one to de-identify with certain aspects of self and others in a way that does not corrode intimacy but actually enhances it. Such de-identification is necessary in relationships, especially in the face of the challenge of ugliness.

The Harms of Ugliness Argument

(1) The harms of the exposure to and of ugliness are anger (and frustration), disappointment, hurt feelings, resentment, and the fear of these. (2) These harms are best understood in terms of habits of craving and aversion. (3) Equanimity, as a response to the habits of craving and aversion, is especially well suited to respond to these harms. Therefore equanimity can respond to the challenge of ugliness. I argued for premise (1) in section 18.4, and premise (3) follows from the definition of equanimity given in section 18.2. The remaining premise (2), namely that the harms of the exposure to and of ugliness are best understood in terms of the habits of craving and aversion, still requires explanation.

The two main problematic habits of mind—aversion habits and craving habits—are what is primarily activated when reacting to our beloved's ugliness or exposing our own. When reacting to another's ugliness, we usually experience aversion to his acting or feeling in ways that we do not approve or would not prefer. We may also fixate on his ugly habits and crave for him to change them. When we expose our own ugliness to our beloved we also feel not only aversion to the ugliness itself (if we see it as ugliness) but also the disappointment or frustration of the beloved. In general, the harms of ugliness—hurt, anger, frustration, disappointment, resentment, the fear of these and their subsequent consequences—can be explained in terms of habits of craving and aversion. Dealing with such harms requires dealing with these habits of craving and aversion, which is what equanimity, by definition, does.

The De-Identification Argument

The second argument for the claim that equanimity is the best response to the challenge of ugliness focuses on the way equanimity requires a certain kind of de-identification and that de-identification is necessary to adequately address this challenge. (1) Equanimity involves de-identifying with certain aspects of self and refraining from identifying with certain aspects of others, even intimate others. (2) The exposure to ugliness and the exposure of one's own ugliness are circumstances in which such de-identification is necessary. (3) This de-identification (of equanimity) does not diminish love, compassion, or sympathetic joy but in fact enhances them. (4) Other attitudes that are foundational for good relationships, such as compassion, love, and joy, do not result in the kind of de-identification necessary to respond to the challenge of ugliness. (5) So equanimity, again, seems uniquely situated to respond to the challenge of ugliness. I will defend each premise in order.

As a process of giving up craving and aversion, the cultivation of equanimity can be seen as a process of intentionally de-identifying with some aspect of self or some aspect of the beloved with which one might otherwise identify. There is a sense in which craving and aversion are "all about me"–type experiences. Craving involves a sense of "I must have this"; aversion involves the judgment "I can't possibly handle that." These reactions naturally elicit a strong sense of identification; when we feel craving and aversion regarding our own and others' ugliness, we—intentionally or unintentionally—end up identifying with that ugliness in some way. But when dealing with ugliness, it can be helpful to *not* identify with it or make too much meaning from it. In this context, de-identification does not mean repressing or ignoring what one does not want to acknowledge. Rather the ugliness is acknowledged but not identified with. That is, it is not automatically interpreted as a meaningful thread in one's own or one's beloved's sense of self. Applying equanimity in such circumstances gives the time and space to effectively address the ugliness because it becomes less urgently meaningful for one's conception of self. The de-identification of equanimity, then, does not imply a decrease in intimacy or love. Sometimes we have to de-identify *in order* to love and be intimate.

Consider the example of the person who exhibits controlling behavior. This behavior is not so severe (in contrast to outright manipulation or violence) that it would imply that his beloved should end the relationship or radically redefine it. It is more everyday, mundane, and less morally objectionable. As an example, consider the tendency to say things such as "Maybe you should do it this way (that is, my way)," In the context of a long-term, intimate relationship this habit could cause harm to both parties, the harms of ugliness (frustration, hurt feelings, anger, resentment, etc.).

When the beloved feels strong aversion to her loved one there is a sense in which she is reaffirming this aspect of his character: "I can't stand the way he always tries to get me to do everything his way!" When she becomes habituated to reactions like this, especially over long periods of time in the context of one intimate relationship, she sets herself up for thinking of her loved one's controlling tendencies as central to his character, which they may or may not be. Her loved one's controlling habits may be more or less integral to his personality or character; they may be more or less pervasive; and they may be more or less compatible with his own aspirations for how he wants to be. Aversion responses tend to obscure these distinctions by moving too quickly from "I don't like what you are doing" (or, in this example, "I don't like the way you are trying to control me right now") to "You're a person who does bad (controlling) things" to "You're a bad (controlling) person." But this is a significant move, and one that Buddhist ethicists warn is rife with problems. At the very least, it should not be made unconsciously, as it often is when we experience strong feelings of aversion.

Her aversion also has an effect on her loved one's self-narrative about his controlling habits. He may feel defensive and feel the need to convince himself and others that he is not actually controlling after all (it is just that others are too sensitive to constructive criticism). This reaction will make it more difficult for him to accurately recognize the ways that he is controlling and to change his habits in this regard. Or, in the face of his loved one's aversion, he may feel resigned to being a controlling person, which further solidifies this ugly habit. Her aversion to his attempts to control her activities, then, has the effect of solidifying her understanding of him as "a controlling person" and his understanding of himself as either a controlling person or, out of defensiveness, as absolutely not a controlling person. But either way, these reactions create identifications that may not be at all accurate or helpful.

It seems that what is required in this kind of case is for the beloved to de-identify with her loved one's controlling tendencies. That is, she would do well to recognize the behavior as controlling and objectionable in certain ways without immediately perceiving the person who exhibits it as a "controlling person." De-identifying with the loved one's ugliness would have the additional benefit of decreasing the likelihood that the loved one would become resigned to his ugly tendencies or become defensive about them. If neither partner is strongly identifying with the ugly tendencies, then it becomes easier to change those tendencies since they are not perceived as integral to one's character.

Although the concept of de-identification is not explicitly mentioned in traditional Buddhist accounts of equanimity, it is an implication of the concept of "equality of beings" that nearly every definition of equanimity in historical Buddhist texts includes or implies. Recall, for example, Buddhaghosa's comment that equanimity "sees the equality of beings"; the Tibetan word for "equanimity" (*btang snyoms*) includes the verb "to make equal" (*snyoms*). The overidentification with others, including loved ones, reveals a subtle, often indirect, but nevertheless significant clinging to narratives about the self, often in relation to the other (e.g., "If my child has this fault, then that means that I'm a bad parent, and that does not fit into my conception of myself"). But being attached to such narratives about oneself, however subtle or indirect, is in fact a failure of equanimity, since it implies an unjustified clinging to the self and thus fails to see the equality between self and others. It is also a failure of love, compassion, and joy, since one's interest in the other is mediated through interest in the self, albeit a subtle one. To love well and to feel sincere compassion or sympathetic joy for others, even loved ones, requires the de-identification that equanimity practices isolate and cultivate.

By challenging the craving and aversion responses that help solidify perceptions of identity, equanimity promises to be a successful response to the problem of ugliness. When one decreases the strength or frequency of aversion and craving through equanimity practices, what remains are the feelings associated with equanimity, namely calmness, tranquility, spaciousness, and freedom. These feelings are empowering, especially in the context of personal relationships, because they allow one to address interpersonal problems without the emotional pressure that causes one to see every conflict as failure and every flaw as evidence of a corroded moral character.

It may be helpful to make a few remarks about what the de-identification of equanimity is not. It is not ignoring problems or resigning oneself to problems. Rather it is the feeling of calm spaciousness (and the absence of the more desperate feelings of craving and aversion) that allows one to address an interpersonal problem in an appropriate way, that is, without exaggerating it or downplaying it.[8] It is also not apathy about relationships. In fact, as I argued earlier, sometimes not identifying so completely with a loved one's ugly habits can reflect a profound sense of caring about his moral and spiritual development and his own sense of what kind of character he wants to achieve.

18.6. Conclusion: Some Objections

If my arguments have been correct so far, equanimity serves a foundational role in good interpersonal relationships because it is uniquely situated to respond to an important and pervasive challenge in relationship, namely the challenge of ugliness. This gives us reason to think that equanimity, like love, compassion, and sympathetic joy, is a fundamental excellence of relationship.

To conclude, I will consider two objections to my argument. First, we may wonder what is so special about the category of ugliness that makes it uniquely responsive to the antidote of equanimity. If equanimity is, most basically, about eliminating craving and aversion, then surely it is applicable in a much broader way. Craving and aversion arise in the response to more serious immoralities, such as violent coercion, and serious imprudence, such as drug addiction. Furthermore everyday incompatibilities between people that are not indicative of the presence of ugliness can also elicit craving and aversion responses. The tension, for example, between an introvert and her extroverted beloved can cause aversion even though neither trait could be fairly classified as ugly.

Buddhist texts do not, as far as I know, differentiate between equanimity with regard to injustice, imprudence, ugliness, or incompatibilities that are non-ugly, non-imprudent, and amoral. It is also true that in Buddhist ethics equanimity is considered to be a broadly applicable response, since craving and aversion (what equanimity subdues or eliminates) are felt in a wide range of circumstances. Although equanimity can apply to more serious immorality or imprudence, these more serious faults are likely to end or radically redefine the relationship in question, thus making it difficult to address the question of equanimity *within* an interpersonal relationship. With regard to non-ugly, amoral incompatibilities, such as the introversion/extroversion incompatibility, the value of equanimity as a response is fairly obvious. Since such traits are morally neutral, moral censure is obviously inappropriate. I focus on the category of ugliness, then, for two reasons. First, compared to the other categories of situations that produce craving and aversion, it stands out as being more serious than incompatibility and more common than serious immorality or imprudence. Second, because ugliness is not so serious as to doom the relationship to end or be radically redefined it is most clearly an *interpersonal* (as opposed to a personal or social) challenge.

In the case of Buddhaghosa's example of the mother, we have no reason to think that the son for whom she feels equanimity is displaying any ugliness or even traits that are incompatible with the mother's. All we know about the son is that he is successfully going about his business and is not an immediate cause of concern for his mother. But he and his mother are, of course, two different people with different aims, styles, personality traits, and ways of going about their business. For the mother to try, for example, to manage her functional adult son's affairs would be a mistake that would threaten rather than strengthen their relationship. I do not mean to suggest that this is what Buddhaghosa must have had in mind when using this analogy. I am making a conceptual rather than interpretative point: If we think about equanimity as a virtue of relationship in the way I have described, then examples such as Buddhaghosa's are not as forced as they may at first seem. The disengagement of equanimity itself strengthens the loving relationship.

The second objection to my claim that equanimity is relational excellence is that, even if equanimity is adequate to address the harms of ugliness, all that really amounts to is the decrease (or, at best, elimination) of certain kinds of suffering (namely disappointment, frustration, resentment, and fear) in certain interpersonal contexts (ugliness). The ability to do this hardly seems to be an excellence; it may be better described as damage control.

Since I do not have the space in this paper to investigate what is required for a trait to be characterized as an excellence or virtue, a few suggestive comments for thinking that equanimity is not just about damage control will have to suffice. Equanimity is clearly concerned with the alleviation of suffering (since, according to Buddhist ethical systems, craving and aversion are foundational sources of suffering), but it also plays a more positive role in interpersonal relationships. Because we are not distracted by or caught up in our craving and aversion and its attendant suffering, when we have equanimity we are able to address interpersonal challenges with more freedom, clarity, and creativity. It is not just that the person with equanimity suffers less than the person without it; *because* she suffers less she can relate to others in more virtuous ways.

Abbreviation

Vism.   *Visuddhimagga*. Translations from B. Ñāṇamoli in Buddhaghosa (1956).

Notes

1. See McRae (2013) for a discussion of the distinction between inner and outer boundlessness. See also Heim (2008), Wallace (2010).
2. Buddhaghosa describes equanimity as "peaceful" (Vism. IX.88). Khenpo Ngawang Pelzang (2004, p. 144) claims that equanimity is "restful." In his commentary on Buddhaghosa, B. Allan Wallace (2010, p. 151) characterizes equanimity as an "utterly calm ocean."
3. Patrul Rinpoche(1994, p. 194); Khenpo Ngawang Pelzang (2004, pp. 140–145).
4. This is especially true if we think about equanimity as a form of "dispassion." See Marks (1995), McRae (2012).
5. See Rita Gross's discussion of the mother as model versus object of the compassion (p. 234).
6. See also McRae (2013).
7. Of course these concepts collapse in certain normative theories, such as normative egoism, that command acting so as to advance one's own interests.
8. Of course sometimes it is appropriate to downplay or even ignore bad behavior, for example, when it is anomalous and the offending party immediately regrets it. Censuring such a wrong may be overkill.

References

Buddhaghosa. (1956). *The path of purification.* (Bhikku Ñāṇamoli, Trans.). Colombo, Ceylon: R. Semage.

Gross, R. (1993). *Buddhism after patriarchy: A feminist history, analysis, and reconstruction of Buddhism.* Albany: SUNY Press.

Heim, M. (2008). Buddhism on the emotions. In J. Corrigan (Ed.), *Oxford handbook of religion and emotion* (pp. 190–210). New York: Oxford University Pres.

Kamalasila. (2001). *Stages of meditation* (Ven. G. L. Jordhen, L. C. Ganchenpa, & J. Russell, Trans.). Ithaca, NY: Snow Lion Press.

Khenpo Ngawang Pelzang. (2004). *A guide to the words of my teacher.* (Padmakara Translation Group, Trans.). Boston: Shambala.

Maitreyanatha & Aryasanga. (2004). *The universal vehicle discourse literature (Mahayanasutralamkara).* (R. Thurman, Trans.). New York: Columbia University Press.

Marks, J. (1995). Dispassion as an ethical ideal. In J. Marks, R. Ames, & R. Solomon (Eds.), *Emotions in Asian thought* (pp. 139–159). Albany: State University of New York Press.

McRae, E. (2012). A passionate Buddhist life. *Journal of Religious Ethics*, 40(1), 99–121.

McRae, E. (2013). Equanimity and intimacy: A Buddhist-feminist approach to the elimination of bias. *Sophia*, 52(3), 447–462.

Ohnuka, R. (2012). *Ties that bind: Maternal imagery and discourse in Indian Buddhism.* New York: Oxford University Press.

Patrul Rinpoche. (1994). *The words of my perfect teacher.* (Padmakara Translation Group, Trans.). San Francisco: Harper Collins.

Tsongkhapa. (2000). *The great treatise of the stages of the path to enlightenment.* (Lamrim Chenmo Translation Committee, Trans.). Ithaca, NY: Snow Lion.

Wallace, B. A. (2010). *The four immeasurables: Practices to open the heart.* Ithaca, NY: Snow Lion.

Index